总主编 胡壮麟

英语综合教程

第 2 册

（学生用书）

主　编　刘世铸
编　者　刘世铸　马　文　姜晓梅
　　　　靳　锁　张　丽　程洪梅
　　　　徐荣娟

图书在版编目(CIP)数据

英语综合教程.第 2 册(学生用书)/ 刘世铸主编.—北京：北京大学出版社，2007.9

(21 世纪英语专业系列教材)

ISBN 987-7-301-12965-4

Ⅰ.英… Ⅱ.刘… Ⅲ.英语-高等学校-教材 Ⅳ.H31

中国版本图书馆 CIP 数据核字(2007)第 169854 号

书　　　名：	英语综合教程.第 2 册(学生用书)
总　策　划：	张　冰
著作责任者：	刘世铸　主编
责 任 编 辑：	姜　军
标 准 书 号：	ISBN 978-7-301-12965-4/H·1876
出 版 发 行：	北京大学出版社
地　　　址：	北京市海淀区成府路 205 号　100871
网　　　址：	http://www.pup.cn
电　　　话：	邮购部 62752015　发行部 62750672　编辑部 62767315　出版部 62754962
电 子 邮 箱：	zbing@pup.pku.edu.cn
印　刷　者：	北京大学印刷厂
经　销　者：	新华书店

　　　　　　　787 毫米×1092 毫米　16 开本　20.25 印张　460 千字
　　　　　　　2007 年 9 月第 1 版　2009 年 12 月第 2 次印刷

定　　　价：33.00 元(配有光盘)

未经许可，不得以任何方式复制或抄袭本书之部分或全部内容。
版权所有，侵权必究　举报电话：010-62752024
　　　　　　　　　　　电子邮箱：fd@pup.pku.edu.cn

21世纪英语专业系列教材编写委员会

(以姓氏笔画排序)

王守仁　王克非　申　丹
刘意青　李　力　胡壮麟
桂诗春　梅德明　程朝翔

总 序

  北京大学出版社自2005年以来已出版"语言与应用语言学知识系列读本"多种,为了配合第十一个五年计划,现又策划陆续出版"21世纪英语专业系列教材"。这个重大举措势必受到英语专业广大教师和学生的欢迎。

  作为英语教师,最让人揪心的莫过于听人说英语不是一个专业,只是一个工具。说这些话的领导和教师的用心是好的,为英语专业的毕业生将来找工作着想,因此要为英语专业的学生多多开设诸如新闻、法律、国际、经济、旅游等其他专业的课程。但事与愿违,英语专业的教师们很快发现,学生投入英语学习的时间少了,掌握英语专业课程知识甚微,即使对四个技能的掌握并不比大学英语学生高明多少,而那个所谓的第二专业在有关专家的眼中只是学到些皮毛而已。

  英语专业的路在何方?有没有其他路可走?这是需要我们英语专业教师思索的问题。中央领导关于创新是一个民族的灵魂和要培养创新人才等的指示精神,让我们在层层迷雾中找到了航向。显然,培养学生具有自主学习能力和能进行创造性思维是我们更为重要的战略目标,使英语专业的人才更能适应21世纪的需要,迎接21世纪的挑战。

  如今,北京大学出版社外语部的领导和编辑同志们,也从教材出版的视角探索英语专业的教材问题,从而为贯彻英语专业教学大纲做些有益的工作,为教师们开设大纲中所规定的必修、选修课程提供各种教材。他们把英语专业教材的出版看作是第十一个五年计划期间组织出版国家"十一五"重点出版规划项目——《面向新世纪的立体化网络化英语学科丛书》的重要组成部分。这套系列教材要体现新世纪英语教学的自主化、协作化、模块化和超文本化,结合外语教材的具体情况,既要解决语言、教学内容、教学方法和教育技术的时代化,也要坚持弘扬以爱国主义为核心的民族精神。因此,今天北京大学出版社在大力提倡专业英语教学改革的基础上,编辑出版各种语言、文学、文化课程的教材,以培养具有创新性思维的和具有实际工作能力的学生,充分体现了时代精神。

  北京大学出版社的远见卓识,也反映了英语专业广大师生盼望已久的心愿。由北京大学等全国几十所院校具体组织力量,积极编写相关教材。这就是说，这套教材是由一些高等院校有水平有经验的第一线教师们制定编写大纲，反复讨论，特别是考虑到在不同层次、不同背景学校之间取得平衡，避免了先前的教材或偏难或偏易的弊病。与此同时，一批知名专家教授参与策划和教材审定工作，保证了教材质量。

  当然，这套系列教材出版只是初步实现了出版社和编者们的预期目标。为了获得更大效果，希望使用本系列教材的教师和同学不吝指教，及时将意见反馈给我们，使教材更加完善。

  航道已经开通，我们有决心乘风破浪，奋勇前进！

胡壮麟

北京大学蓝旗营

2007年2月

前　言

《英语综合教程》是根据《高等学校英语专业英语教学大纲》编写,致力于培养学生具有扎实的语言基本功、宽广的知识面、一定的相关专业知识、较强的能力和较高的人文素质。本套教材为基础英语课程教材,共四册,可供高等院校英语专业一、二年级学生使用。本册为第二册,适用于一年级第二学期。本册基本遵循第一册的编写原则,主要有以下特点:

- 重视学生自主学习能力的培养。要求学生通过自己查词典、参考书和网络资源解决大部分语言问题和掌握课文相关的背景知识。
- 启发学生独立思考问题,发展批评性思维。通过比较、对照、提示和归纳等方法启发学生思考问题。
- 通过构词扩大词汇量。简要介绍构词知识,通过构词法扩大词汇量。
- 阅读理解和语言练习强调综合运用语言知识,使学生的语言能力得到全面发展。
- 培养学生的探究性学习能力。

本册共15个单元,选材以扩大学生知识面、培养学生的综合素质为主要原则,内容涉及童话、爱情、友谊、幸福、教育、社会问题、网络、名人传记、理想、科技、经济、体育等15个主题。每单元包括八个主要部分。

- **Unit Goals**:明确本单元的学习目标,使学生对所学知识做到心中有数。
- **Before Reading**:要求学生在阅读课文前通过查阅与本单元主题相关的背景知识,自己动手,独立思考,培养自主学习的能力。本部分有三项内容:
  ◇ **Hands-on Activities**:提供可供查阅的参考资料和网站,旨在培养学生的自主学习能力。
  ◇ **Brainstorming**:提出与单元主题相关的问题,旨在培养学生独立思考和批判性思维能力。通过寻求问题的答案,了解本单元的文化背景知识。
  ◇ **A Glimpse at Words and Expressions**:通过上下文和查字典熟悉本单元Text A中出现的部分重点词汇和表达方式。
- **Text A**:课文按主题编排,长度在1000字左右,所有课文均选自原文。

每篇课文后有两项内容：

◇ **Better Know More**：对课文中出现的文化背景知识提供必要的解释。

◇ **Check Your Understanding**：课文后提供了数量不等的问答题或多项选择题，旨在帮助学生更好地理解课文。

☞ **A Sip of Word Formation**：介绍部分构词规则，本册主要介绍前缀和后缀，并配有针对性的词汇练习，通过练习扩大学生的认知词汇量。

☞ **You'd Like to Be**：该部分是针对 Text A 的练习，练习形式不拘一格，这部分练习较适合于课堂由教师掌握使用，更多的自主性练习将另册出版。课后练习分五项内容：

◇ **A Skilled Text Weaver**：强化主课文中出现的词汇、短语和主要语言难点。

◇ **A Sharp Interpreter**：检验学生对课文中的重点句子的理解和活用。

◇ **A Careful Writer**：对课文中出现的常用词汇进行同义词辨析，进一步理解词汇意义和用法的细微差异。

◇ **A Solid Sentence Constructor**：训练学生对课文中重点句型和新词语的运用能力，理解句子和语篇的结构机制。

◇ **A Superb Bilingualist**：对课文中的常用词汇和短语通过汉译英进一步强化，了解两种语言表达的异同。

☞ **Text B**：与主课文的主题一致，通过阅读使学生对同一主题作更深入的了解。课文后有必要的注释和阅读理解问答题。

☞ **Writing Practice**：要求学生围绕本单元主题书面表达自己的阅读心得，写作形式不拘一格。

☞ **Further Study**：向学生提供进一步探究本单元主题的资源，要求学生通过查阅相关资料，更深入理解主题，逐步培养学生独立进行研究的能力以及通过研究获取知识的能力。

本册由山东大学主持编写，刘世铸负责教材的总体设计和编写，参加编写的有马文、姜晓梅、靳锁、张丽、程洪梅、徐荣娟等。在本书的编写过程中，总主编胡壮麟教授在总体思路上给予了精心的指导，责任编辑姜军和北京大学出版社外语编辑部的编辑们为本书的编辑出版付出了艰辛的劳动，在此向他们表示诚挚的感谢。

由于编者水平有限，书中难免有疏漏和不当，诚望使用本书的教师和学生提出批评。

编者
2007 年 5 月

Contents

Unit 1	Fairy Tale	1

Text A   Beauty and the Beast / 3
Text B   Beauty and the Beast / 15

Unit 2	Love	21

Text A   The Power of Love / 22
Text B   The Love I'll Never Forget / 32

Unit 3	Money and Happiness	39

Text A   The Real Truth about Money / 41
Text B   Happiness / 52

Unit 4	Education	58

Text A   National Wealth Tax to Fund Education? / 60
Text B   Are Single-Sex Classrooms Legal? / 71

Unit 5	Social Issues	77

Text A   The Scope of the Teen Pregnancy Problem / 79
Text B   Is Abortion Murder? / 91

Unit 6	Cyberspace	97

Text A   Vulnerability of the Internet and World Wide Web / 99
Text B   Internet Evolution: Cyber Youth Culture in China / 109

Unit 7	Biography	119

Text A   Earnest Hemingway / 120
Text B   Joseph Heller / 132

Unit 8　Reflections on Life 140

　　Text A　Think Inside the Square to Keep Those Love Fires Burning　/　142
　　Text B　Learn How to Face Difficulty　/　150

Unit 9　Ambition 154

　　Text A　Ambition: Why Some People Are Most Likely to Succeed　/　156
　　Text B　The Roots of My Ambition　/　168

Unit 10　China Today 176

　　Text A　China: Past and Prensent　/　177
　　Text B　Cultural Healing　/　187

Unit 11　Friendship 196

　　Text A　The Value of Friendship　/　197
　　Text B　All Un-Alone in the City　/　208

Unit 12　Honesty 214

　　Text A　Honesty Is the Best Policy　/　216
　　Text B　To Lie or Not to Lie?　/　229

Unit 13　Sports 235

　　Text A　A Change Will Do Them Good　/　237
　　Text B　Cheerleading　/　247

Unit 14　Science 258

　　Text A　Can We Know the Universe-Reflections on a Grain of Salt　/　260
　　Text B　Future Tech　/　273

Unit 15　Economy 279

　　Text A　Terry Semel's Long Pause; Yahoo　/　281
　　Text B　Feeling Fitter? The Euro Area's Economy　/　291

生词总表 296

Unit 1

Fairy Tale

Unit Goals

After completing the lessons in this unit, students will be able to:
- identify some typical characteristics of a fairy tale using literary terms such as character, setting, and plot;
- develop the ability to read narratives critically;
- extend vocabulary through recognition of negative prefixes.

Before Reading

Hands-on Activities

1. Look in your university library's fairy tale section and browse through Dr. D. L. Ashliman's Folklore and Mythology Electronic Texts website http://www.pitt.edu/~dash/type0510a.html. Plan to include stories that exemplify a variety of tale types, such as "*Cinderella,*" "*The Fisherman and His Wife,*" and so on, to gain an understanding of the special characteristics of folk and fairy tales.

   The following questions may help you get a better understanding of the nature of fairy tales:

   (1) What is a fairy tale?
   (2) What are some special characteristics of fairy tales?
   (3) What kinds of plots, characters, and settings do we expect to find in these stories?
   (4) What makes each fairy tale unique?
   (5) Why are fairy tales so prevalent as a form of storytelling throughout the world?

2. Write down a list of emotions and try to share memories of experiences you have had with these feelings.

Brainstorming

Brainstorm the following questions. Work in pairs or groups to discuss these questions.

1. How are standards of beauty established in a particular society, in a particular time period?
2. How are those standards articulated to the culture at large?
3. What are the standards of beauty that females and males are held to today? How are those standards different based on gender, age, race?
4. To what extent is intelligence a component of "beauty"? How have certain stereotypes reinforced or challenged the notion that someone who is beautiful is not necessarily intelligent? What puts intelligence at odds with being beautiful?

A Glimpse at Words and Expressions

Please read the following sentences. Pay attention to the underlined part in each sentence and see how these expressions are used in the context, and then write down their meanings in the blanks provided.

1. They gave themselves ridiculous airs, and would not <u>keep company with</u> any but persons of quality. (   )
2. This news had liked to have <u>turned the heads of</u> the two eldest daughters, who immediately flattered themselves with the hopes of returning to town. (   )
3. ...they <u>went to law with</u> him about the merchandise. (   )
4. If your daughter refuse to die <u>in your stead</u>, you will return within three months. (   )
5. Will you <u>give me leave</u> to see you sup? (   )
6. ...her newly found happiness and material <u>comfort with</u> the Beast. (   )

Text A

Beauty and the Beast

By Jeanne-Marie LePrince de Beaumont
(Abridged and Edited)

There was once a very rich merchant, who had six children, three sons, and three daughters. His daughters were extremely handsome, especially the youngest. When she was little everybody admired her, and called her "The little Beauty."

5　　The two eldest had a great deal of pride, because they were rich. They gave themselves ridiculous airs, and would not keep company with any but persons of quality. They went out every day to parties of pleasure, plays, concerts, and so forth, and they laughed at their youngest sister,
10 because she spent the greatest part of her time in reading good books.

All at once the merchant lost his whole fortune, excepting a small country house at a great distance from town, and told his children with tears in his eyes, they must
15 go there and work for their living.

The family had lived about a year in retirement, when the merchant received a letter with an account that a vessel, on board of which he had effects, was safely arrived. This news had liked to have turned the heads of the two eldest daughters, who immediately flattered themselves with the hopes of returning to town, for they were quite weary of a country life;
20 and when they saw their father ready to set out, they begged of him to buy them new gowns, headdresses, ribbons, and all manner of trifles; but Beauty asked for nothing but a rose. The good man went on his journey, but when he came there, they went to law with him about the merchandise, and after a great deal of trouble and pains to no purpose, he came back as poor
25 as before.

He was within thirty miles of his own house, thinking on the pleasure he should have in seeing his children again, when going through a large forest he lost himself. He began
30 to apprehend being either starved to death

---

air /eə/ *n.* appearance or manner
flatter /ˈflætə/ *v.* to praise (somebody) too much or insincerely in order to gain flavor for oneself
gown /gaʊn/ *n.* woman's dress, especially a long one for special occasions
trifle /ˈtraɪfəl/ *n.* thing that has little value or importance
merchandise /ˈmɜːtʃəndaɪz/ *n.* goods for sale

with cold and hunger, or else devoured by the wolves. All of a sudden, he saw a light at some distance. The merchant returned God thanks for this happy discovery, and hastened to the place, but was greatly surprised at not meeting with any one in the outer courts of a castle.

35   He waited a considerable time, until it struck eleven, and still nobody came. At last he was so hungry that he could stay no longer, but took a chicken, and ate it in two mouthfuls. As he was very much fatigued, and it was past midnight, he concluded it was best to shut the door, and go to bed.

It was ten the next morning before the merchant waked, and as he was going to rise he
40 was astonished to see a good suit of clothes in the room of his own. He looked through a window, but instead of snow saw the most delightful arbors, interwoven with the most beautiful flowers that were ever beheld.

The good man drank his chocolate, and then went to look for his horse, but passing through an arbor of roses he remembered Beauty's request to him, and gathered a branch on
45 which were several; immediately he heard a great noise, and saw such a frightful Beast coming towards him, that he was ready to faint away.

"You are very ungrateful," said the Beast to him, in a terrible voice; "I have saved your life by receiving you into my castle, and, in return, you steal my roses, which I value beyond any thing in the universe, but you shall die for it; I give you but a quarter of an hour to prepare
50 yourself, and say your prayers."

The merchant fell on his knees, and lifted up both his hands, "My lord," said he, "I beseech you to forgive me, indeed I had no intention to offend in gathering a rose for one of my daughters, who desired me to bring her one."

"My name is not My Lord," replied the monster, "but Beast; I don't love compliments.
55 But you say you have got daughters. I will forgive you, on condition that one of them come willingly, and suffer for you. If your daughter refuse to die in your stead, you will return within three months."

60   The merchant had no mind to sacrifice his daughters to the ugly monster, but he thought, in obtaining this respite, he should have the satisfaction of seeing them once more, so he promised he would return, and the Beast told
65 him he might set out when he pleased, "but," added he, "you shall not depart empty handed; go back to the room where you lay, and you will see a great empty chest; fill it with

devour /dɪˈvaʊə/ v. to eat sth. hungrily or greedily
hasten /ˈheɪsən/ v. to hurry
fatigue /fəˈtiːg/ n. great tiredness
interweave (interwove, interwoven) /ˌɪntəˈwiːv/ v. to join together; to combine
frightful /ˈfraɪtfəl/ adj. very unpleasant; dreadful
ungrateful /ʌnˈɡreɪtfəl/ adj. not recognizing a kindness, service, etc.
beseech /bɪˈsiːtʃ/ v. to ask sb. earnestly; to implore sb.
compliment /ˈkɒmplɪmənt/ n. expression of praise, admiration
sacrifice /ˈsækrɪfaɪs/ v. to offer sth. valuable to a god
respite /ˈrespɪt/ n. interval of rest or relief
depart /dɪˈpɑːt/ v. to go away, leave

whatever you like best, and I will send it to your home."

70 "Well," said the good man to himself, "if I must die, I shall have the comfort, at least, of leaving something to my poor children." He returned to the bedchamber, and finding a great quantity of broad pieces of gold, he filled the great chest, and in a few hours the good man was at home.

His children came round him, but instead of receiving their embraces with pleasure, he
75 looked on them, and holding up the branch he had in his hands, he burst into tears.

On giving Beauty the rose, her father cannot help but tell her what happened. The brothers offer to slay the Beast but the father knows that they would die in the process. Beauty insists on taking her father's place, and so she returns with him
80 to the Beast's palace where he reluctantly leaves her.

As soon as her father was gone, Beauty sat down in the great hall, and fell a crying likewise; but as she was mistress of a great deal of resolution, she recommended herself to God, and resolved not to be
85 uneasy the little time she had to live; for she firmly believed Beast would eat her up that night.

But at night, as she was going to sit down to supper, she heard the noise Beast made, and could not help being sadly terrified. "Beauty," said the monster, "will you give me leave to see you sup?"

"That is as you please," answered Beauty trembling.

90 "No," replied the Beast, "you alone are mistress here; you need only bid me gone, if my presence is troublesome, and I will immediately withdraw. But, tell me, do not you think me very ugly?"

"That is true," said Beauty, "for I cannot tell a lie, but I believe you are very good natured."

95 "Yes, yes," said the Beast, "my heart is good, but still I am a monster."

"Among mankind," says Beauty, "there are many that deserve that name more than you, and I prefer you, just as you are, to those, who, under a human form, hide a treacherous, corrupt, and ungrateful heart."

Beauty spent three months very
100 contentedly in the palace. Every evening Beast paid her a visit, and talked to her, during supper, very rationally, with plain good common sense, but never with what the world calls wit; and Beauty daily discovered some
105 valuable qualifications in the monster, and seeing him often had so accustomed her to his

slay /sleɪ/ v. to kill in a violent way
reluctantly /rɪˈlʌktəntli/ adv. unwillingly
resolution /ˌrezəˈluːʃən/ n. quality of being resolute or firm; determination
bid /bɪd/ v. to order; to tell
withdraw /wɪðˈdrɔː/ v. to go away
treacherous /ˈtretʃərəs/ adj. betraying
rationally /ˈræʃənəli/ adv. reasonably

deformity, that, far from dreading the time of his visit, she would often look on her watch to see when it would be nine, for the Beast never missed coming at that hour. There was but one thing that gave Beauty any concern, which was, that every night, before she went to bed, the monster always asked her, if she would be his wife. One day she said to him, "Beast, you make me very uneasy, I wish I could consent to marry you, but I am too sincere to make you believe that will ever happen; I shall always esteem you as a friend, endeavor to be satisfied with this."

> deformity /dɪˈfɔːmɪti/ n. being deformed
> dread /dred/ v. to fear greatly
> esteem /ɪˈstiːm/ v. to have a high opinion of, respect greatly
> endeavor /ɪnˈdevə/ v. to attempt; to try
> pine /paɪn/ v. to be very unhappy
> fret /fret/ v. (cause sb. to) to become unhappy, bad tempered, or anxious about sth.
> assent /əˈsent/ v. to express agreement

"I must," said the Beast, "for, alas! I know too well my own misfortune, but then I love you with the tenderest affection. However, I ought to think myself happy, that you will stay here; promise me never to leave me."

Beauty blushed at these words; she had seen in her glass, that her father had pined himself sick for the loss of her, and she longed to see him again. "I could," answered she, "indeed, promise never to leave you entirely, but I have so great a desire to see my father, that I shall fret to death, if you refuse me that satisfaction."

"I had rather die myself," said the monster, "than give you the least uneasiness. I will send you to your father, you shall remain with him, and poor Beast will die with grief."

"No," said Beauty, weeping, "I love you too well to be the cause of your death. I give you my promise to return in a week. You have shown me that my sisters are married, and my brothers gone to the army; only let me stay a week with my father, as he is alone." The Beast assents on the condition that she return in seven days, lest he die.

The next morning she is at home. Her father is overjoyed to see her, but the sisters are jealous of Beauty, her newly found happiness and material comfort with the Beast. They persuade Beauty to stay longer, which she does, but on the tenth night she dreams of the Beast who is dying. She threw herself upon him without any dread, and finding his heart beat still, she fetched some water from the canal, and poured it on his head. Beast opened his eyes, and said to Beauty, "You forgot your promise, and I was so afflicted for having lost you, that I resolved to starve myself, but since I have the happiness of seeing you once more, I die satisfied."

"No, dear Beast," said Beauty, "you must not die. Live to be my husband; from this moment I give you my hand, and swear to be none but yours. Alas! I thought I had only a friendship for you, but the grief I now feel convinces me, that I cannot live without you." Beauty scarce had pronounced these words, when she saw the palace sparkle with light; and fireworks, instruments of music, everything seemed to give notice of some great event. But nothing could fix her attention; she turned to her dear Beast, for whom she trembled with fear; but how great was her surprise! Beast was disappeared, and she saw, at her feet, one of the

145 loveliest princes that eye ever beheld; who returned her thanks for having put an end to the charm, under which he had so long resembled a Beast.

> behold /bɪˈhəʊld/ *v.* to see
> resemble /rɪˈzembəl/ *v.* to be like or similar to
> condemn /kənˈdem/ *v.* to say what sb.'s punishment is to be; to sentence sb.

A wicked fairy had condemned him to
150 remain under that shape until a beautiful virgin should consent to marry him. Beauty, agreeably surprised, gave the charming prince her hand to rise; they went together into the castle, and Beauty was overjoyed to find, in the great hall, her father and his whole family.

Better Know More

Jeanne-Marie Leprince de Beaumont (1711—1780)

Jeanne-Marie LePrince de Beaumont was born in Rouen, France in 1711. She was born into a large family that could not provide her with a dowry sizeable enough to enter into an advantageous marriage. She turned to teaching, which was a radical move for an unmarried woman of her station. She entered into a brief and unhappy marriage thereafter, producing one child. The marriage lasted for two years and was annulled in 1745.

In 1748 Madame de Beaumont moved to England. There she worked as a governess to the children of the Prince of Wales and published educational magazines for young girls. She herself wrote many of the not-so-subtle stories published in the magazines, the most famous of which is "Beauty and the Beast," first published in 1757. Beaumont's version of the fairy tale was by no means the first, but has proven to be the most popular source for adaptations.

In 1762, Beaumont married a man named Thomas Pichon and moved to Savoy, a small dukedom in the Rhone-Alps region, which is today part of France. She died in 1780.

Check Your Understanding

Answer the following questions based on the text you have just learned.

1. What is the difference between Beauty and her sisters?
2. What was the reaction of the two eldest daughters when they heard that the ship had safely

arrived?

3. Why did the old merchant move his family to the countryside?
4. Why was Beast happy with the return of the old merchant?
5. Why did Beauty finally agree to marry Beast?
6. Why is this story so popular, in your opinion?
7. What connotations does the word "beauty" have?
8. What connotations does the word "beast" have?
9. What lesson(s) is the story trying to teach?

A Sip of Word Formation

A great part of English words are formed through affixation. Affixation is generally defined as the formation of words by adding word forming or derivational affixes to stems. This process is also known as derivation, for new words created in this way are derived from old forms. The words formed in this way are called derivatives. According to the positions, which affixes occupy in words, affixation falls into two subclasses: prefixation and suffixation.

Prefixation is a way of forming new words by adding prefixes to stems. Usually, prefixes do not change the part of speech of a word. Their chief function is to modify its meaning, although there are exceptions. Prefixes can be divided, based on their meanings, into: negative prefixes, reversative prefixes, pejorative prefixes, prefixes of degree or size, locative prefixes, prefixes of time and order, number prefixes and miscellaneous prefixes.

Negative Prefixes

Dis-, in-, un-, non- are negative prefixes.

1. *Dis-* is usually added to verbs. It means "opposite feeling" or "opposite action":
   Example: You like him but I *dislike* him.
2. *Un-* is used to negate simple and derived adjectives: *uncomplicated, unhappy, unsuccessful, unreadable.* Adjectival *un-* derivatives usually express contraries, especially with simple bases.
   Pay attention to the different prefixes used in the following nouns and adjectives:
   unsatisfactory (adjective)　　　　dissatisfaction (noun)
   uncomfortable (adjective)　　　　discomfort (noun)
3. *In-* negative meaning used for many adjectives of Latin origin, also those ending in *-ible*. Different forms of *in-*

in- + l = ill	illogical
in- + m = imm	immodest
in- + p = imp	impossible
in- + r = irr	irregular

4. *Non-* can be attached to adjectives and has the general meaning of 'not X': *non-biological, non-commercial, non-returnable*. In contrast to *un-* and *in-*, negation with *non-* does not carry evaluative force, as can be seen from the pairs *unscientific* vs. *non-scientific, irrational* vs. *non-rational*. Furthermore, *non-* primarily forms contradictory and complementary opposites.

Nouns prefixed with *non-* can either mean "absence of X" or "not having the character of X": *non-delivery, non-member, non-profit, non-stop*.

Build Your Vocabulary

A. Decide which form of the negative prefix to use to make each word. Add the prefix and write the whole word.

active		adequate	
agree		approve	
believe		please	
complete		sufficient	
conclusive		dependent	
equal		even	
frequent		distinct	
kind		friendly	
legible		proper	
organic		legal	
personal		reversible	
probable		mobile	
prove		continue	
responsible		measurable	
satisfied		moral	
success		formal	
usual		satisfactory	
existent		stop	

B. *The word at the end of each of the following sentences can be used to form a word that fits suitably in the blank space. Fill each blank this way.*

Example: He said "Good morning" in a most <u>friendly</u> way. (friend)

1. There is no doubt that cannabis will remain an _____ drug for the foreseeable future. (legal)
2. It was quite _____ for us to drive all the way from Paris to Madrid in one day. (possible)
3. He made a(n) _____ attempt to climb the highest mountain in the range. (successful)
4. To take the boat out with four children under the age of ten and with no life jackets on board was quite _____ of him. (responsible)
5. The dress she was wearing was quite _____ for the occasion. (appropriate)
6. It was very _____ of him to insult his mother in front of his aunt. (polite)
7. They were a completely _____ family and I never thought that one day I would marry one of the daughters. (religious)
8. As a politician he was _____ and it was not long before nobody trusted him. (honest)
9. The goods were _____ and had to be returned to the store we bought them from. (perfect)
10. She was _____ with her life and decided that things had to change. (contented)

You'd Like to Be

A Skilled Text Weaver

Fill in each blank with an appropriate word from the text.

1. Education in Chinese institutions should fill young students with national _____ and self-esteem so that they feel proud of their rich and varied cultural heritage.
2. To _____ a person is to try to please by complementary speech or attention, to complement insincerely, to praise effusively or excessively, to play upon the vanity or sceptibilities of a person.
3. It was difficult for him to stay focused on decisions made months earlier as he became _____, weak, and sad as he realized what was happening to his physical being.

4. As I _____ that this position better suits my professional goals, I decided to submit my resignation.
5. He was _____ to his benefactors and treacherous to his friends.
6. Blessed is he who has learned to _____ but not envy, to follow but not imitate, to praise but not flatter, and to lead but not manipulate. (William A. Ward)
7. The very first law in advertising is to avoid the concrete _____ and cultivate the delightfully vague.
8. In the early 1970s, IBM discovered that large customers were _____ to trust unreliable communications networks to properly automate important transactions.
9. If we spoke a different language, we would _____ a somewhat different world.
10. The start of the New Year is a perfect time to start a stop doing list and to make this the cornerstone of your New Year _____.
11. Bush has said that he will _____ the troops from Iraq if the government asks him to do so.

A Sharp Interpreter

Paraphrase the following sentences, referring to the contexts in which the sentences are located.

1. They gave themselves ridiculous airs, and would not keep company with any but persons of quality.
2. This news had liked to have turned the heads of the two eldest daughters.
3. ...after a great deal of trouble and pains to no purpose, he came back as poor as before.
4. He began to apprehend being either starved to death with cold and hunger, or else devoured by the wolves.
5. As he was very much fatigued, and it was past midnight, he concluded it was best to shut the door, and go to bed.
6. I had no intention to offend in gathering a rose for one of my daughters.
7. The merchant had no mind to sacrifice his daughters to the ugly monster.
8. The merchant was so afflicted at the thoughts of losing his daughter.
9. ...as she was mistress of a great deal of resolution, she recommended herself to God.

A Solid Sentence Constructor

A. Complete each sentence with one of the expressions listed below. Make changes where necessary.

keep company with	set out	insist on	endeavour to
in return	die for	fell on one's knees	have no intention to
to one's amazement	weary of		

1. Mary Shelley, due to the popularity and early success of her father, _____ some of the most important literary figures of her day, including Percy Bysshe Shelley (her eventual lover and husband), William Wordsworth, Samuel Taylor Coleridge, and Lord Byron amongst others.
2. I watched that Senate hearing for a while today and got _____ listening to those men and women drone on and on.
3. One night he took out all the cleaning tools, but when he brought out the pieces of wire, _____ he saw that all the wire was finally clean!
4. If you benefit from what we're doing and want to give something _____, you can make a donation!
5. In spite of a Chinese's suggestion, the captain _____ getting across around the rock. Consequently, the boat crashed on the rocks with no survivors.
6. As the United States grew throughout the nineteenth century, an ever-increasing number of tourists _____ to discover the beauty and splendor of their country.
7. One day when she was feeling particularly hopeless, she _____ and asked God to forgive her.
8. Since 1975 the Government has _____ strengthen the stability of society and has instituted national development policies on a "step by step" basis.
9. Patriotism must be drilled into young minds if children are to grow up willing to _____ the motherland.
10. In 2000, China further declared that it _____ assist any country in any way in the development of ballistic missiles that can be used to deliver nuclear weapons.

B. Finish each of the following sentences in such a way that it means the same as the sentence printed before it.

Example: I haven't enjoyed myself so much for years.
Answer: It's years since I enjoyed myself so much.

1. At last he was so hungry that he could stay no longer.

At last he was too _____.
2. "You are very ungrateful," said the Beast to him.
   The Beast blamed _____.
3. Beauty gave the charming prince her hand to rise.
   The charming prince _____.
4. If your daughter refuse to die in your stead, you will return within three months.
   Unless _____.
5. When they had supped they heard a great noise.
   A great noise _____.
6. All at once the merchant lost his whole fortune, excepting a small country house at a great distance from town.
   The only thing _____.
7. It was ten the next morning before the merchant waked.
   When _____.
8. No sooner had he shut his chamber door, than, to his great astonishment, he found it by his bedside.
   As soon as _____.
9. As soon as her father was gone, Beauty sat down in the great hall, and fell a crying likewise.
   The moment _____.
10. The Beast assents on the condition that she return in seven days, lest he die.
    He _____.

A Careful Writer

Study the following synonyms and complete the sentences.

astonish   surprise   amaze

1. He was _____ to see how his home town had changed in the past twenty years.
2. Much to my _____ I received a Christmas tree and ornaments in the mail today.
3. When the archaeologists reconstructed the fragments, they were _____ to find that the goddess turned out to be a very modern-looking woman.

terrible   frightful   dreadful   horrid   terrified

4. However, though it was _____ to be alone in this frozen vault, with no other society than that of the dead, I could not but feel that for the moment I was safe.

5. I was awakened by a _____ dream of some giant shape stalking down the slope of ice to seize and devour me, and sat up trembling with _____ that was not a little increased by my inability to recollect myself, and by my therefore conceiving the canvas that covered me to be the groping of the ogre's hand over my face.

6. Anger was a rare thing with him, but it was _____ when it did burst forth.

7. All that night the sound of _____ bells was ringing in Di's ears, and for several days she lay sick at her grandmother's shanty. ... when all of a sudden, at noon, she was _____ by the sound of horses' feet in the distance...

8. Well, for the moment I was _____ with the impotent _____ of nightmare, and I stopped my ears and just ran from the place and got back to the house panting, trembling, literally in a panic.

9. He had each night a _____ dream. He dreamed he was—or was really—suddenly awakened by some person entering his room, and in looking around saw the room brilliantly lighted, while at the window stood a lady elegantly attired, in the act of throwing something out. This accomplished, she turned her face toward the only spectator showing a countenance so distorted by evil passions that he was thrilled with _____. Soon the light and the figure with the _____ face disappeared, leaving the artist suffering from a _____ nightmare.

> agree   consent   assent

10. Yet he was no sooner firm in his power than he _____ to one of the worst Acts of Parliament ever passed. Under this law, every minister who should not give his solemn _____ to the Prayer-Book by a certain day, was declared to be a minister no longer.

11. He referred to his _____ to a mutually _____ termination under Regulation 9.1(c).

> satisfactory   content   satisfied

12. All in all, I was very _____ with this hotel. The price was less expensive than most places. We stayed here for the conference; it was _____.

13. I was _____ with having obtained some applause without seeking it by means which would have ensured it without any merit.

14. Saxon was _____ with a hut of branches and skins, and then let him reflect that this once wealthy and thriving town... This was _____ to King Abagha.

15. That was _____ to everyone, but then Vila halted. "What about Orac?" he asked.... _____ with the explanation, he went off to look for the others. A young man he met in the passage directed him to the mess hall.

14

A Superb Bilingualist

Please translate the following sentences into English with the prompts provided in the brackets.

1. 千万不要与不诚实的人交往。(keep company with)
2. 如果一个人没有找到他愿意为之牺牲的事业，他就不适合活在这个世界上。(die for)
3. 我们坚持让她不要去日本。(insist)
4. 30 年前他被迫离开了家乡。(be obliged to)
5. 爱通常只不过是人与人之间的一种融洽的互动，得到他们所期望的。(nothing but)
6. 我儿子喜欢讲笑话，虽然他没有意图想当一个相声演员。(have no intention to)
7. 成功之后，她对世界感到失望和厌倦了。(be weary of)
8. 爱是不求回报的。(in return)
9. 听到那消息后，他放声大哭。(burst into tears)
10. 让我们携手并肩，为实现中非发展，为推动建设持久和平、共同繁荣的和谐世界而共同努力！(endeavour)

Text B

Beauty and the Beast

By A. J. Jacobs
(Abridged and Edited)

Once upon a time there was a magnificent golden castle on a silver cloud high up in the sky, which has nothing to do with anything because our story is about an old woodchopper who lived in a shack, but that's a good way to start a fairy tale. The old man was very happy, but he had a daughter, who was very unhappy because... well, she was rather plain. Actually, she was really plain. In fact, she had a face like five miles of bad road.

Anyway, it was time for her to marry, but because she was so fat and ugly, none of the young men of the kingdom ever came to ask for her hand, or any other part of her body, for that matter. Then one day, the old man decided to cheer her up.

"Child, it is your birthday and I've brought you something to keep you from being so lonely."

"A man?" she asked, wide-eyed.

"Nope. A mule."

woodchopper /ˈwʊdˌtʃɒpə/ *n.* person who cuts down trees as an occupation
shack /ʃæk/ *n.* roughly built shed, hut or house
plain /pleɪn/ *adj.* not beautiful; ordinary

He pointed to a brown, furry, four-legged, grunting beast. Well, a mule wasn't exactly the kind of
15 companion she had in mind, but at least it was somebody to talk to.

"Hi there, silly beast," said the girl to the mule. "I wonder if you were once a handsome prince changed into a mule by a wicked witch. If so, I could break
20 the spell with a kiss." She smacked the mule right on it's lips. It was no use. The mule was a mule and had always been a mule.

The next day the old man instructed his daughter to take a bundle of sticks to the village.

"A bundle of sticks?" she asked him. "What for?"

25 "How should I know," said the old man. "But somebody is always carrying a bundle of sticks around in fairy tales. You know that."

So the young girl took the bundle of sticks and decided to ride her trusty mule into the village. But something very strange happened. Unknown to her, the moment she climbed onto the mule's back, she turned into a beautiful maiden. You know the type: blond hair, blue eyes,
30 a figure like she spends days doing Jazzercise.

Anyway, when she reached the village, she could hardly believe her eyes, for all the young men, instead of laughing and throwing mud at her, bowed, tipped their hats and made catcalls. She was still trying to figure it out when a handsome young prince rode up to her on a snow-white horse.

35 "Ah, fair lady!" he exclaimed. "You are truly the most lovely beauty in the land."

"Why, my young prince," she replied, batting her eyes. "Are you nuts or sumpthin?"

"With your permission," said the prince,
40 "I should like to call upon you tonight. How about when the clock strikes the hour of eightish?"

Flushed with excitement, the girl raced home, but when she arrived and stepped off
45 her mule—she immediately returned to her fat, little ugly self. That night, promptly at eightish o'clock, the prince, sitting astride his white charger, knocked on the door.

The girl opened the door and smiled her
50 crooked—toothed smile—one that made

furry /ˈfɜːri/ *adj.*	of furs; covered with fur
grunt /grʌnt/ *v.*	(of animals, esp. pigs) to make a low rough sound from deep in the throat
spell /spel/ *n.*	words which when spoken are thought to have magic power; charm
smack /smæk/ *n.*	loud kiss
trusty /ˈtrʌsti/ *adj.*	trustworthy
tip /tɪp/ *v.*	(cause sth. to) to rise, lean or tilt on one side or at one end
catcall /ˈkætkɔːl/ *n.*	shrill whistle
bat /bæt/ *v.*	to blink, wink
nut /nʌt/ *n.*	foolish, eccentic or mad person
flush /flʌʃ/ *v.*	(of a person's face) to become red because of a rush of blood to the skin
promptly /ˈprɒmptli/ *adv.*	punctually
astride /əˈstraɪd/ *adv.*	with one leg on each side
charger /ˈtʃɑːdʒə/ *n.*	horse ridden by a soldier
crooked /ˈkrʊkɪd/ *adj.*	not straight or level; twisted

chopped yak liver seem appealing—and chirped, "Helloooo."

"Um," said the prince, who at that moment was desiring a bit of Pepto-Bismol, or the medieval equivalent, "Is your sister at home?"

"I don't have a sister," the girl said.

55 "Your aunt then," the prince said.

"I don't have an aunt."

"Your cousin? Your best friend? Your babysitter?"

"What are you talking about?" 60 asked the girl. "I live here alone with my father."

The prince, figuring he had found the wrong house, galloped quickly off on his white stead. The poor girl was left 65 standing at the door, broken-hearted and trying to understand what had gone wrong. The following day, her father again asked her to go into the village. This time to pick up a bundle of sticks.

"It'll take your mind off your ugliness," the old man said patting her kindly on her head.

No sooner had the girl climbed on the mule's back than—once again she changed into a 70 beautiful maiden. On the way to the village she chanced to pass a clear, still pool of water. Looking into it, she saw her reflection and was shocked to see she was now very beautiful. She hopped off her mule for a close look and instantly she changed back into her former ugly self. And then, she suddenly realized what had happened.

"I get it now," she said out loud to no one in particular, as people in fairy tales sometimes 75 do. "This is a magic mule. As long as I sit on this beast, I'm a beauty!"

The girl climbed back onto the mule, and beautiful again. And the beauty and the beast dashed to find the prince. When he saw her coming, he rode up to her on his gallant steed.

80 "Ah, lovely beauty," he said. "I have found you again. Please say you will be mine so that we may be married."

"Yes, but on one condition," she said. "That I remain on my mule at all times."

85 Of course, this seemed like a strange request, but the prince agreed.

"So be it, my love," he said. "And so that we start off on the right foot—or on the right

chop /tʃɒp/ v. to cut
yak /jæk/ n. wild or domesticated ox of Central Asia, with long horn or hair
chirp /tʃɜːp/ v. to short sharp sound made by a small bird or a cricket
medieval /ˌmediˈiːvəl/ adj. of the Middle Ages
gallop /ˈɡæləp/ v. (of a horse) to go at a gallop
stead /sted/ n. horse
chance /tʃɑːns/ v. to happen by chance
reflection /rɪˈflekʃən/ n. thing reflected, especially an image in a mirror, still water
hop /hɒp/ v. (of a person) to move by jumping on one foot
gallant /ˈɡælənt/ adj. brave

hoof—I shall stay on my horse as long as you stay on your mule."

And thus they were married by a priest, who delivered the sermon on a donkey. As the years went by, the young girl was very happy, although the poor mule did get a bit of a backache. And true to his word, the prince also stayed on his horse.

And as any good husband would, he took her dancing every Saturday night at the palace, where they were the most striking couple on the dance floor. Or actually, the most striking quadruple on the dance floor.

hoof /huːf/ *n.*	horny part of the foot of a horse
sermon /ˈsɜːmən/ *n.*	talk on a moral or religious subject
quadruple /ˈkwɒdrʊpəl/ *n.*	consisting of four
bonnet /ˈbɒnɪt/ *n.*	hat tied with strings under the chin by babies and formerly by women
hag /hæg/ *n.*	ugly old woman; witch
scramble /ˈskræmbəl/ *v.*	to climb or crawl quickly, usu over rough ground or with difficulty
saddle /ˈsædl/ *n.*	seat for a rider on a horse
gulp /gʌlp/ *v.*	to make a swallowing motion
blasted /ˈblɑːstɪd/ *adj.*	very annoying
wart /wɔːt/ *n.*	small hard dry growth on the skin
glee /gliː/ *n.*	feeling of great delight
sore /sɔː/ *n.*	painful place on the body

One day, as the girl rode in the garden—the wind blew off her bonnet. Not stopping to think, she hopped off her mule to get the hat and—she immediately turned into an ugly, disgusting hag again. Realizing her mistake, she scrambled to get back in the saddle again. But it was too late, for just then the prince rode up.

"Pardon me, old hag," said the prince. "Have you seen my wife? Wait a minute, this is her mule?"

"Yes," blushed the hag, gulping. "And I am your wife."

She began to sadly confess the whole story to her husband, but instead of being angry, he did an amazing thing. He clapped his hands and laughed for joy.

This is what he said: "Ha, ha, ha, ha. Yahoo! Yipee!"

"I don't get it," said the girl. "Are you happy to find out that I'm really ugly?"

"No!" said the prince. "I'm happy to know that I can finally get off this blasted horse. You see, I'm only a handsome prince when I stay on him."

And with that, the prince hopped off his horse and he changed into one of the ugliest men ever to walk the earth. He was fat and short and bald and full of warts. His face looked like ten miles of bad road.

"Ugh! You're uglier than me!" said the girl, with glee.

"We were meant for each other!" said the man, as they embraced.

"Just think—no more saddle sores!"

And so, the ugly man and the ugly girl were able to live happily ever after. Which only goes to prove that "A mule and his honey are soon parted."

Notes

1. A. J. Jacobs
The editor of *What It Feels Like* and the author of *The Two Kings, Jesus and Elvis, America Off-Line*, and *Fractured Fairy Tales*. He is the senior editor of *Esquire* and has written for The *New York Times, Entertainment Weekly, Glamour, New York Magazine, The New York Observer*, and many other publications.

2. Nope
Slang for "no".

3. Jazzercise
A fitness program that combines elements of jazz dance into aerobic exercise. The name also refers to the company that develops and markets the program. The Jazzercise program was first created in 1969 by Judi Sheppard Missett, who is now the CEO of Jazzercise, Inc. Missett first thought of the program while teaching traditional jazz dance classes in Evanston, Illinois. Missett moved to Carlsbad, California to start Jazzercise, Inc. and began training instructors.

4. Pepto-Bismol
A strictly controlled medicine used as a remedy to relieve the symptoms of an upset stomach.

5. Yahoo! Yipee
Happy.

Comprehension Questions

1. How does the writer start the story? Why does the writer mention "a magnificent golden castle on a silver cloud high up in the sky?"
2. Why was the old man's daughter unhappy?
3. What does the writer mean by "five miles of bad road?"
4. What did the father give her as a birthday present?
5. Why did the old man ask her daughter to take a bundle of sticks to the village?

6. Who is the beauty? Who is the beast?
7. What does the sentence "A mule and his honey are soon parted" mean?
8. What is the moral of this tale?

Writing Practice

Sometimes the most attractive person can also be the meanest and "ugliest." Someone may be pleasant to look at, but nevertheless cruel and hurtful. Have you ever experienced this? Has a "beautiful" person tried to make you feel ugly? If yes, jot down the details of your experience. If no, use your imagination to make up a fictional experience in which you meet someone beautiful who is in the end ugly nonetheless. Then, consider whether you would prefer to meet someone who is beautiful on the outside, or someone who is beautiful on the inside. Explain your reasoning in a paragraph.

Further Study

Here, in its entirety, is a tale from The Wolf and His Stones (1986) by Chris Schauff:

Once upon a time there was a dwarf who got into the fairy tale by mistake. For there were already seven other dwarfs who did their work. He himself was only the eighth, and nothing was actually prepared for him. So the eighth dwarf trotted about the pages in a bad mood and did not know what to do with himself. He came to that spot where the giant was killed, and he found it completely senseless as he always had each time he had come across it. He peevishly sauntered further on until he came to the spot where the handsome prince, who was usually on his knees before the princess, was missing. The dwarf felt so embarrassed that his hair stood on its end, and he rushed away from there. When he did not encounter any of the other dwarfs along the way, he finally ran to the end of the fairy tale. There, however, the dwarf saw that they lived happily ever after. So he really became furious and trampled on the terrible words with his feet.

Is this a fairy tale? Why or why not? You'll need to explain the generic criteria on which you base your argument, drawing on at least one of the theoretical approaches we've considered. In what ways does the tale conform to the criteria you present? In what ways does it not? Comment on the usefulness and limitations of generic categorization.

For more details on the elements of a fairy tale, please visit: http://www.readwritethink.org/lesson_images/lesson42/RWT027-4.pdf

Unit 2

Love

Unit Goals

After completing the lessons in this unit, students will be able to:
- ☞ understand the essence of love;
- ☞ develop the ability to read between the lines;
- ☞ extend vocabulary through recognition of reversative prefixes.

Before Reading

Hands-on Activities

Look up the dictionary or try the website http://encyclopedia.thefreedictionary.com to get the concept and different views about love. Report your findings to your classmates in class.

Brainstorming

Brainstorm the following questions. Work in pairs or groups to discuss these questions.

1. What do you think Text A will tell us at the first sight of the title?
2. There are many sources of power in nature. Make a list of what you know.
3. Describe what true love should be like in your expectation? Work in pairs and express your viewpoints to each other.
4. Are there any love songs or movies you like very much? List your favorite ones. Try to hum the songs or share the main ideas of the movies with your partner(s).

A Glimpse at Words and Expressions

Please read the following sentences. Pay attention to the underlined part in each sentence and see how these expressions are used in the context, and then write down their meanings in the blanks provided.

1. Almost every major movement in the history of human progress was brought about by the unlocking of some mighty source of power in nature. ( )
2. They have no faith in it. ( )
3. Most people usually identify love with sex. ( )
4. They lose contact with its higher dimensions and superior possibilities. ( )
5. It is trite to say that the scarcity of happiness among many people is due to the corresponding scarcity of love among them. ( )
6. When Romeo saw Juliet on the balcony, he was so taken by her beauty he exclaimed... ( )
7. It is true that goodness cannot be imposed from without. ( )

Text A

The Power of Love

By Benito F. Reyes
(Abridged and Edited)

The story of civilization may sometimes be conveniently summarized as the story of man's search for more and more sources of power. Almost every major movement in the history of human progress was brought about by the unlocking of some mighty source of power in nature.

5 The power of the wind, the power of water in motion, the power locked up in coal and in oil, steam power, magnetic power, electric power, and now, atomic power—man has tapped them all and harnessed them to the service of his needs and his desires. He has learned, in

> unlock /ʌnˈlɒk/ v. to provide a key to; to disclose or reveal
> tap /tæp/ v. to make use of a source of energy, knowledge, etc., that already exists
> harness /ˈhɑːnɪs/ v. to control and use the force or strength of sth. to produce power or to achieve sth.

10 fact, to use even the mysterious power of thought, as shown by its increasing employment in war and peace.

There is one power, however, which people, in general, have not learned to use at all, or have refused, somehow, to use, in solving their individual as well as
15 collective problems. This is the power of love. Either they have no faith in it, or they do not know how to use it effectively. One reason, probably, is that most people usually identify love with sex. As a consequence of this wrong attitude, they lose contact with its higher
20 dimensions and superior possibilities, and thus find themselves unable to release its hidden and inexhaustible stores of energy. These people do not know that sex is but one of the many possible expressions of love, and that love has powers more abundant, more profound, and more significant than the power of the propagation of the species.

Many people think that love is just a sentiment good for poetry or for novels. How easy it is
25 to forget that love is a law as inescapable in the world of human relations as gravitation is in the world of physical objects. But it is precisely just that—an inexorable law of thought and emotion the violation of which can bring about broken hearts and broken lives just as the violation of the law of gravitation can bring about broken arms and broken legs. Being a law, its operation involves energy transformation. The energy of love is the most unique kind of energy in the
30 universe. It is creative, it is intelligent, and it is wise. It fills the entire universe, but its mightiest seat of operation is in the heart of man. Every object in nature manifests, but man and man alone can manipulate it by the use of his mind.

All the great teachers of humanity from the earliest times taught it and demonstrated it in
35 their lives. Buddha, Lao Tzu, Confucius, Mohammed, St. Paul—to mention only a few— all declared in varying ways that love is the law as well as the fulfilling of the law and that without it no peace, no happiness, no perfection is possible.

40 Love has the power to create happiness. This fact is so common an experience to most people that it is not even necessary to mention it. And if the happiness it creates is sometimes short-lived, the reason probably is that the
45 love that creates it is still imperfect.

It is trite to say that the scarcity of happiness among many people is due to the

---

inexhaustible /ˌɪnɪɡˈzɔːstəbəl/ *adj.* that can not be finished; very great
propagation /ˌprɒpəˈɡeɪʃən/ *n.* reproduction
sentiment /ˈsentɪmənt/ *n.* (formal) a feeling or an opinion, especially one based on emotions
inescapable /ˌɪnɪsˈkeɪpəbəl/ *adj.* (of a fact or situation) that can not be removed or changed
inexorable /ɪnˈeksərəbəl/ *adj.* (formal) (of a process) that cannot be stopped or changed
manifest /ˈmænɪfest/ *v.* to show sth. clearly, especially a feeling, an attitude or a quality
manipulate /məˈnɪpjʊleɪt/ *v.* (disapproving) to control or influence sb./sth., often in a dishonest way so that they do not realize it
trite /traɪt/ *adj.* (of a remark, an opinion, etc.) dull and boring because it has been expressed so many times before; not original
scarcity /ˈskeəsɪti/ *n.* there is not enough of it and it is difficult to obtain it

corresponding scarcity of love among them. It is also commonplace to say that the unhappy man is almost *invariably* also an unloving man.

Yes, these ideas are so elementary that we probably tire of hearing them. But the fact is that we seem to have such a *facility* to ignore them, or to forget them.

We forget that selfishness is almost always at the root of all unhappiness and that love, unselfish love, is the basis of all happiness. The man who says, "I am unhappy," actually proclaims to the world what he would be ashamed to admit openly, namely, that he is selfish.

To be happy it is necessary to love, and to love truly it is necessary to be completely unselfish. Only the unselfish heart is capable of love and only the loving heart is capable of happiness.

There is a great law of happiness which should rank in importance with any other great discovery in science. It is the law which says: No man is capable of happiness who is incapable of loving one other person than himself.

One power of love which makes it most unique is its power to create goodness, or at least to awaken it. Love is the basic goodness, and if it be true that love alone can awaken love, then it follows that love alone can awaken goodness. It is a fact in psychology that a child raised in an atmosphere of hate generally becomes cruel. A cruel man is very often an unloved man who, almost surely, was once an unloved child.

It is true that goodness cannot be *imposed* from without, that it must be a growth from within. Nevertheless, this inward growth cannot even start without the *stimulating* touch of love. Theoretically, a child raised among wolves would probably grow to howl like a wolf. Love is the power which makes a child grow into a human being. It is the humanizing force in the human family.

Goodness may awaken love, but it may also awaken envy or resentment or even positive hate. We may love a man because he is good, but we may also learn to dislike him because he presents a contrast to our badness. Love, however, can never fail to awaken goodness, sooner or later. The reason is that love is more basic than goodness. Even a hardened criminal may become good, if he should fall in love.

When Romeo saw Juliet on the balcony, he was so taken by her beauty he exclaimed, "That is the dawn and Juliet is the sun." How beautiful Juliet was to Romeo, even if she

---

invariably /ɪnˈveəriəbli/ *adv.* always
facility /fəˈsɪlɪti/ *n.* a natural ability to learn or do sth. easily
impose /ɪmˈpəʊz/ *v.* to force sb./sth. to have to deal with sth. that is difficult or unpleasant
stimulating /ˈstɪmjʊleɪt/ *adj.* full of interesting or exciting ideas; making people feel enthusiastic

might have looked unlovely to his family. How handsome Romeo was to Juliet, even if he might have seemed unattractive to her family.

George Santayana once said that beauty is
90 simply pleasure or happiness objectified. If this be true, then beauty is a creation of love, because happiness is created by love. But whether true or false, one thing love can do: it can irradiate the face of a lover with beauty and
95 attractiveness.

Perhaps, it is just some kind of magic. But the fact is that the magic is there, the magic of love. And if this magic can be lasting, then beauty can be everlasting. Never, never will
100 beauty pass away, as long as there is love.

Perhaps, when in love, one sees not the body but the soul. Perhaps love is clairvoyant and can penetrate the veil of flesh and see the radiant spirit within. Perhaps old age and ugliness are the illusion, and youth and beauty are the reality which, however, we cannot see, as long as we are not in love, or have ceased to
105 love.

If we could only be in love every minute of our lives. If we could only be completely without hate, without anger, without malice, without vengeance, without fear, without worry, without envy, without lie, without delusion, without cruelty, without greed, without selfishness, without any negative thought or emotion whatever; then, we would have a
110 peaceful and harmonious world.

---

irradiate (literary) /ɪˈreɪdieɪt/ v. to make sth. look brighter and happier
clairvoyant /kleəˈvɔɪənt/ adj. the power that some people are believed to have to be able to see future events or to communicate with people who are dead or far away
penetrate /ˈpenɪtreɪt/ v. to go into or through
radiant /ˈreɪdiənt/ adj. showing great happiness, love or health
illusion /ɪˈluːʒən/ n. something that seems to exist but in fact does not, or seems ot be sth. that it is not
malice /ˈmælɪs/ n. a feeling of hatred for sb. that causes a desire to harm them
vengeance /ˈvendʒəns/ n. (formal) the act of punishing or harming sb. in return for what they have done to you, your family or friends
delusion /dɪˈluːʒən/ n. the act of believing or making yourself believe sth. that is not true

Better Know More

1. Benito F. Reyes

An educator; philosophy professor of Harvard University and founder of World University in Ojai, California.

2. Buddha

Indian mystic and founder of Buddhism. He began preaching after achieving supreme enlightenment at the age of 35.

3. **Lao Tzu**

A Chinese philosopher who is traditionally regarded as the founder of Taoism.

4. **Confucius**

A Chinese thinker and philosopher, the founder of Confucianism, whose teachings and philosophy have deeply influenced East Asian life and thought.

5. **Mohammed**

An Arab religious, political, and military leader who established Islam and the Muslim community.

6. **St. Paul**

Paul of Tarsus, the most notable of early Christian missionaries, together with Simon Peter. Paul was the second most prolific contributor to the New Testament, after Luke the Evangelist.

7. **Remeo and Juliet**

Remeo and Juliet are two young star-crossed lovers in The Most Excellent and Lamentable Tragedy of Romeo and Juliet, commonly referred to as Romeo and Juliet, a tragedy by William Shakespeare concerning the fate of two young lovers. This tragedy is one of the most famous plays of Shakespeare, one of his earliest theatrical triumphs, and is thought to be the most archetypal love story in Renaissance time period.

8. **George Santayana**

A spanish philosopher, essayist, poet, and novelist.

Check Your Understanding

Answer the following questions based on the text you have just learned.

1. How many sources of power are there in nature?
2. Why hasn't the power of love been well used by people to solve their problems?
3. What is the relation between sex and love?
4. Why does the author compare love with gravitation?
5. What did the great teachers of humanity think about love?
6. The author holds that "goodness cannot be imposed from without, that it must be a growth

from within." Do you agree or disagree?
7. Why does the author hold that love can awaken goodness?
8. What is the connection between love and beauty?
9. What does the author tell us about the magic of love?
10. Why does the author believe that if we could only be in love without any negative thought or emotion, we would have no sickness, no old age, no death?

A Sip of Word Formation

Reversative or Privative Prefixes

Reversative prefixes are prefixes that take the meanings of reversing the action. Commonly found reversative or privative prefixes are *un-*, *de-* and *dis-*.

1. un-
    Unlike the negative prefix *un-*, this prefix is used with verbs and indicates "opposite action."
    Example: We covered the hole, but later *uncovered* it.
2. de-
    de- combines with verbs to form new verbs; it indicates actions which have the opposite effect of the process described by the original verb.
    Example: Word processors are likely to *depersonalize* working relationships.
    It also combines with nouns to form verbs which indicate that the thing referred to by the noun is removed.
    Example: You should *defrost* your fridge once in a fortnight.
3. dis-
    Closely related semantically to *un-* and *de-*, the prefix *dis-* forms reversative verbal bases.
    Examples: He connected the wire, but you *disconnected* it.

Build Your Vocabulary

A. Decide which form of the reversative prefix to use to make each word. Add the prefix and write the whole word.

activate		mount	
articulate		continue	
assemble		associate	
bind		cork	
caffeinate		flea	
charge		connect	
courage		locate	

do		code	
dress		settle	
leash		saddle	
mantle		join	
coil		button	
pollute		throne	
proof		qualify	
select		colonize	
tie		buckle	
wind		wrap	

B. *The word at the end of each of the following sentences can be used to form a word that fits suitably in the blank space. Fill in each blank this way.*

Example: He said "Good morning" in a most *unfriendly* way. (friend)

1. In the end, he was _____ of that responsibility. (burden)
2. A man explained to a CHP officer that his seat belt was _____ because he wanted to smell his feet. (fast)
3. When he _____ the basement batteries, the system continued to operate powered by ground current alone. (connect)
4. Like Fiona Jones, she also fell out with her local party and was _____ before the 2005 election. (select)
5. The boy was _____ at not having found any game and he sat beside the stream to quench his thirst with the cool water. (courage)
6. The doctor _____ my wound, squished out lots and lots of puss, and repacked me. (pack)
7. Africa was _____ four decades ago but still remains underdeveloped. (colony)
8. He _____ my hands and allows me to go to wash myself and prepare for the evening meal. (bind)
9. He reported to the examiner that he _____ both hips in a helicopter crash. (locate)
10. The president made it clear that he would not hesitate to _____ the currency if it became necessary. (value)

You'd Like to Be

A Skilled Text Weaver

Fill in the gaps with words or phrases chosen from the box. Change the form where necessary.

trite	propagate	illusion	facility	clairvoyant
harness	irradiate	inexhaustible	inescapable	radiant
scarcity	impose	vengeance	sentiment	stimulate

1. He labored under the _____ that he could never make a mistake.
2. In the graduation ceremony, Jane's face _____ with joy.
3. Most house plants can be _____ from stem cuttings.
4. It is an _____ part of any state apparatus.
5. His _____ for languages is astonishing.
6. He gave a _____ smile when he heard her news.
7. There is a great deal of interest in _____ wind and waves as new sources of power.
8. Very high taxes have recently been _____ on cigarettes.
9. There seemed to be an _____ supply of champagne at the wedding.
10. That was true no matter how _____ it sounded.
11. These antiques are valued for their _____.
12. On the day after the terrorist attack, the overall mood in the town was one of _____.
13. There's no place for _____ in business.
14. The government plans to cut taxes in order to _____ the economy.
15. She went to see a _____ person who said he could communicate with her dead husband.

A Sharp Interpreter

Paraphrase the following sentences. Change the sentence structure if necessary.

1. Almost every major movement in the history of human progress was brought about by the unlocking of some mighty source of power in nature.
2. Love has powers more abundant, more profound, and more significant than the power of the propagation of the species.

3. It fills the entire universe, but its mightiest seat of operation is in the heart of man.
4. It is trite to say that the scarcity of happiness among many people is due to the corresponding scarcity of love among them.
5. If we could only be in love every minute of our lives.

A Solid Sentence Constructor

Make sentences with the following words and expressions. You may refer to the original sentence in Text A.

1. search for
2. bring about
3. have faith in
4. identify... with...
5. lose contact with
6. due to
7. sooner or later
8. as long as

A Careful Writer

Study the following synonyms and complete the sentences.

sentiment   emotion   passion   feeling

1. "The mystic reverences, the religious allegiance, which are essential to a true monarchy, are imaginative _____ that no legislature can manufacture in any people." (Walter Bagehot)
2. "I have said that poetry is the spontaneous overflow of powerful _____: it takes its origin from emotion recollected in tranquility." (William Wordsworth)
3. When our grandmother died, we remembered her life with strong _____.
4. He has difficulty controlling his _____.
5. His rapid promotion caused much bad _____ among his colleagues.
6. "They seemed like ungoverned children inflamed with the fiercest _____ of men." (Francis Parkman)
7. "Poetry is not a turning loose of _____, but an escape from emotion." (T.S.Eliot)

illusion   delusion   fantasy

8. The disappointment of manhood succeeds to the _____ of youth; let us hope that the heritage of old age is not despairing. (Benjamin Franklin)
9. A dream is a psychosis, with all the absurdities, _____ and _____ of a psychosis. (Sigmund Freud)
10. It is sheer _____ to imagine that the cause of socialism is all plain sailing.
11. A sequence of photographs were projected noto a screen with sufficient rapidity as to create the _____ of motion and continuity.
12. He is in that rare and blissful state wherein a man sees his dreams stalk out from the crannies of _____ and become fact.

reveal   disclose   unlock

13. Companies generally need not _____ loss contingencies if the risk of a material loss is considered remote.
14. All his attempts to _____ the door were futile, because he was using the wrong key.
15. These writings _____ an immensely sophisticated idealism that is the principal musical legacy of ancient China.
16. The relevant authorities shall not _____ the business proprietary information provided by the dealers.
17. She failed to _____ the safe in spite of all her exertions.
18. A group of scientists demanded that the federal government _____ all the studies it has funded on cloning and related field of cell biology.

A Superb Bilingualist

Translate the following sentences into English.

1. 人已经懂得如何利用大自然中的能源以满足自己的需求。(harness)
2. 就像在物质的世界里地心引力是一个无法逃避的规律一样，在人类关系的世界里，爱情是一个必然法则。(inescapable)
3. 很多人缺乏幸福正是因为他们缺少爱，这种说法已不新鲜。(trite)
4. 伟大的幸福之道，其重要性应等同于科学上的其他任何伟大发现。(rank)
5. 他对家庭从来都是尽职尽责。(fail)
6. 爱情使她的面容愈加发出美丽、迷人的光彩。(irradiate)
7. 爱能够透视一切，能够穿透肉体的遮蔽一睹内在闪耀的灵魂。(clairvoyant)
8. 凯丽对她明天能够见到那个著名的电影明星仍然抱有幻想。(illusion)

Text B

The Love I'll Never Forget

By Tim Madigan
(Abridged and Edited)

Crookston, Minn, my hometown, is a farming community of 8,000 people, tucked into the northwest corner of the state. Not a lot extraordinary passes through. Gretchen was an exception.

For one thing, she was an Eickof, one of Crookston's wealthiest families. They lived in a
5 sprawling brick place on the banks of the Red Lake River and spent summers at their vacation home on Union Lake, 30 miles away.

Despite her numerous blessings, which included great physical beauty, there was nothing snooty about Gretchen. She was among the first to befriend new kids at school and tutored students less able than herself—she moved through the various elements of
10 high-school society—farm kids, jokes and geeks—dispensing bonhomie to all. Gretchen, the Central High Homecoming Queen of 1975, clearly was going places.

I knew Gretchen only enough to exchange greeting when we passed in the halls. I was a good athlete and, in the
15 parlance of the time, kind of cute. But I was insecure, especially around females-creatures I found mysterious and more intimidating than fastballs hurled high and tight.

All of which may explain my
20 bewilderment one midsummer night in 1977 when Gretchen and I bumped into each other at a local hangout. I had just finished my freshman year at the University of North Dakota in nearby Grand Forks. Gretchen,
25 whose horizons were much broader, was home from California after her first year at Stanford.

Gretchen greeted me happily. I remember the feel of her hand, rough as
30 leather from hours in the waters of Union

---

tuck /tʌk/ *v.* to be situated in a quiet place, where not many people go
exception /ɪk'sepʃən/ *n.* a person or a thing that is not included in a general statement
sprawling /'sprɔːlɪŋ/ *adj.* (only before noun) spreading in an untidy way
snooty /'snuːti/ *adj.* treating people as if they are not as good or as important as you
dispense /dɪ'spens/ *v.* to give out sth. to people
bonhomie /'bɒnəmi/ *n.* a feeling of cheerful friendship
parlance /'pɑːləns/ *n.* a particular way of using words or expressing yourself, for example one used by a particular group
intimidating /ɪn'tɪmɪdeɪtɪŋ/ *adj.* frightening in a way which makes a person feel less confident
hurl /hɜːl/ *v.* to throw sth./sb. violently in a particular direction
bewilderment /bɪ'wɪldəmənt/ *n.* a feeling being completely confused
hangout /'hæŋaʊt/ *n.* a place where sb. lives or likes to go often

Lake, as she pulled me toward the dance floor. She was nearly as tall as I, with perfect almond skin. Soft features and fluorescent white teeth. Honey-blond hair hung in strands past her
35 shoulders. Her sleeveless white shirt glowed in the strobe lights, setting off arms that were brown and strong from swimming, horseback riding and canoeing.

Gretchen was a poor dancer, I noticed that
40 night. But she moved to the music enthusiastically, smiling dreamily. After a few dances we stood and talked, yelling to each other over the music. By the time I walked her to her car. Main Street was deserted. Traffic lights blinked yellow. We held hands as we walked. And when we arrived at her car, she
45 invited me to kiss her. I was glad to oblige.

Summer fun: I never had much purchase on Gretchen's heart. She was fond of me, no doubt. Two years earlier, she eventually revealed, she had been my "Guardian Angel"—the anonymous benefactor who left cookies and inspirational notes at my locker before my hockey games.
50 But where Crookston boys were concerned, Gretchen could be as elusive as mercury. As passionately as she would return some of my kisses that summer and the next, for her I was part of the interlude between childhood and the more serious endeavors of adulthood to come.

Thus, Gretchen and I rarely ventured beyond the surface of life. She never mentioned the future in any respect, or any nagging worry or
55 sorrow. She never told me of the time in sixth grade when she broke both legs skiing and for months had to be carried around by her father. Gretchen had to teach herself to walk again after that, and years later her family pointed to
60 the injury as the root of both her compassion and her independence.

I was dizzy for her, of course, and had a bad habit of saying so. Each time I did, she pulled away from me. These were college summers, not
65 the time for moony eyes and vows of undying devotion.

One night in 1978 when Gretchen and I were together, out of nowhere she spoke the

---

> fluorescent /fluəˈresənt/ *adj.* (of substance) producing bright light by using some forms of radiation
> strand /strænd/ *n.* a single thin piece of thread, wire, hair, etc.
> strobe /ˈstrəʊb/ *n.* a bright light that flashes rapidly on and off, used especially at disco
> deserted /dɪˈzɜːtɪd/ *adj.* (of a noun) with no people in it
> oblige /əˈblaɪdʒ/ *v.* to help sb. by doing what they ask or what you know they want
> anonymous /əˈnɒnɪməs/ *adj.* written, given, made, etc. by sb. who does not want their name to be known or made public

> benefactor /ˈbenɪˌfæktə/ *n.* a person who gives money or other help to a person or an organization such as a school or charity
> inspirational /ˌɪnspɪˈreɪʃənəl/ *adj.* providing inspiration
> elusive /ɪˈluːsɪv/ *adj.* difficult to find, define, or achieve
> mercury /ˈmɜːkjʊri/ *n.* a chemical element. Mercury is a poisonous silver-white liquid metal, used in thermomerers.
> endeavor /ɪnˈdevə/ *n.* an attempt to do sth., especially sth. new or difficult
> venture /ˈventʃə/ *v.* to go somewhere even though you know that it might be dangerous or unpleasant
> nag /næɡ/ *adj.* complaining
> dizzy /ˈdɪzi/ *adj.* silly or stupid
> vow /vaʊ/ *n.* a formal and serious promise, especially a religious one, to do sth.

words that guys in my situation dread above all.

70 　　"Tim," she said, "I think we should just be friends."

I told her I was tired of her games and was not as much of a fool as she thought. And I stormed away. By morning I cooled off. I sent Gretchen some roses that day, and a note offering an apology and my friendship.

75 　　Gretchen and I started dating again about a month later. But this time I had learned my lesson. No more moony eyes. I could be as detached and aloof as the next guy.

It worked beautifully for a few weeks. Finally Gretchen asked, "What's wrong with you?"

80 　　"What do you mean, what's wrong?"

"You're not yourself," she said. "You haven't been for a long time." "No," I said. I let her in on my ruse, the feigned standoffishness designed to keep her near. For the only time I remember, she became angry. Then she proposed a deal.

"You be who you are," she said, "and I won't go anywhere, at least for the rest of the 85 summer."

It was a bargain I quickly accepted. She was as good as her word.

Not long before Gretchen left again for Stanford, she and her sister hosted a large party at the lake. With all the duties as hostess, Gretchen would have little time for me, I surmised.

But midway through the raucous event, 90 she gestured for me to follow as she sprinted the length of the dock, dove into the cold water and set off swimming toward a distant floating platform. I watched her brown arms slice the water with power and grace. I nearly drowned 95 before getting to the platform myself, and she helped pull me up.

The two of us lingered there for a long while, toeing the small waves and watching the throng on shore. I thought it a very nice way 100 for her to acknowledge our friendship in front of the crowd.

Those weeks seemed golden, a bit unreal. One times as we said goodnight, I discarded the final wisp of my caution and told Gretchen 105 that I loved her. She only smiled.

In early September I left for college in

---

dread /dred/ *v.* to be very afraid of sth.; to fear that sth. bad is going to happen

detached /dɪˈtætʃt/ *adj.* showing a lack of feeling

aloof /əˈluːf/ *adj.* not friendly or interested in other people

ruse /ruːz/ *n.* a way of doing sth. or of getting sth. by deceiving sb.

feign /feɪn/ *v.* to pretend that you have a particular feeling or that you are ill, tired, etc.

standoffishness /ˌstændˈɒfɪʃnəs/ *n.* not friendly towards other people

bargain /ˈbɑːɡɪn/ *n.* an agreement between two or more people or groups, to do sth. for each other

surmise /səˈmaɪz/ *v.* to guess or suppose sth. using the evidence you have, without definitely knowing

raucous /ˈrɔːkəs/ *adj.* sounding loud and harsh

sprint /sprɪnt/ *v.* to run a short distance very fast

linger /ˈlɪŋɡə/ *v.* to stay somewhere for longer because you do not want to leave; to spend a long time doing sth.

throng /θrɒŋ/ *n.* a crowd of people

wisp /wɪsp/ *n.* a small, thin pieces

Grand Forks. Gretchen and her friend Julie Janecky drove over from Crookston and surprised me in my dorm room, hauling me out dancing.

I came back to Crookston to see her off to Stanford in mid-September. While Gretchen packed, I absently shot pool at her father's table. When she finished, we took a last walk around her family's horse pasture in the gathering September chill. I thought of how dramatically our lives were about to diverge and was saddened. But more than anything I felt gratitude for the fine, fun times we had spent over the last two summers.

Gretchen planned to find work in California the next summer. For her, the serious part of life beckoned, and I knew what that meant.

"Good-bye," I said as we stood at her front door.

"Don't say good-bye," she replied. "Say 'see you later.'"

Back at school, emboldened by my experience with Gretchen, I began dating a student in the journalism department. Gretchen fell in love with a ruggedly handsome center on the Stanford football team.

The evening of October 9, 1978, I called her in California to wish her a happy 21st birthday. She thanked me for calling, but sounded distracted. A loud party was obviously in progress. I quickly ran off.

The last of the autumn leaves were falling on October 13, but sky was a cloudless blue, the air crisp and invigorating. Classes were done for the day. It is rare when happiness and contentment consciously register with a person, but they did that morning.

The telephone rang the school I stepped inside my dorm room. I recognized Julie Janecky's voice on the other end of the line, and my heart soared. Julie was to be married the following month, and maybe Gretchen would be returning to Crookston for the wedding after all.

But hearing the uncharacteristically quiet scratch of Julie's voice, I knew Gretchen was dead.

The previous morning, Julie told me, Gretchen had collected one of her birthday presents from a college friend: a ride in a small plane. Shortly after takeoff, the craft lurched out of control and pitched into a marsh. Gretchen and her friend were killed instantly.

---

haul /hɔːl/ v. to pull sth./sb. with a lot of effort
pasture /ˈpɑːstʃə/ n. land covered with grass that is suitable for feeding animals on
diverge /daɪˈvɜːdʒ/ adj. very different from each other and of various kinds
gratitude /ˈɡrætɪtjuːd/ n. the feeling of being grateful and wanting to express your thanks
beckon /ˈbekən/ v. to be sth. that is likely to happen or will possibly happen to sb. in the future
embolden /ɪmˈbəʊldən/ v. to male sb. feel braver or more confident
ruggedly /ˈrʌɡɪdli/ adv. (of a person) determined to succeed in a difficult situation, even if this means using force or upsetting other people
distracted /dɪˈstræktɪd/ adj. unable to pay attention to sb./sth., because you are worried or thinking about sth. else
crisp /krɪsp/ adj. (of the air or the weather) pleasantly dry and cold
invigorating /ɪnˈvɪɡəreɪtɪŋ/ adj. to make sb. feel healthy and full of energy
contentment /kənˈtentmənt/ n. a feeling of happiness or satisfaction
scratch /skrætʃ/ n. the unpleasant sound of sth. sharp or rough being rubbed against a surface

"Gretchen's parents wondered if you would be a pallbearer," Julie said.

"I'd be honored," I replied.

The word sounded strange even as it left my mouth. Honored? Is that what you felt when you helped bury a friend—a smart, sunny beauty queen who was going places? I left my dormitory and walked aimlessly, I am told I sought out a campus priest, but 18 years later I have no memory of that.

Back home in Crookston that afternoon, I knocked on the door of my high-school hockey coach, he took me out for a drive. As we talked, I thought it strange that people should be concerned with such trivial matters as buying groceries and putting gas in their cars when Gretchen Eickhof was dead.

marsh /mɑːʃ/ *n.* an area of low land that is always soft and wet because there is nowhere for the water to flow away to

pallbearer /ˈpɔːlˌbeərə/ *n.* a person who walks beside or helps to carry the coffin at a funeral

squint /skwɪnt/ *v.* to look at sth. with your eyes partly shut in order to keep out bright light or to see better

congregate /ˈkɒŋɡrɪɡeɪt/ *v.* to come together in a group

consolation /ˌkɒnsəˈleɪʃən/ *n.* alleviation of sorrow or mental distress

torrent /ˈtɒrənt/ *n.* a large amount of sth. that comes suddenly and violently

unleash /ʌnˈliːʃ/ *v.* to suddenly let a strong force emotion, etc. be felt or have an effect

procession /prəˈseʃən/ *n.* a number of people who come one after another

urn /ɜːn/ *n.* a tall decorated container, especially one used for holding the ashes of a dead person

How does a person grieve? I wondered, puzzled by my lack of tears.

Saturday night, I drove out to the Eickhof place, past the horse pasture where Gretchen and I had walked together. The grieving family took me in as one of them. At one point Gretchen's mother left the room and returned with a photograph of her daughter and me, taken a few weeks before. I was squinting, my arm lightly around Gretchen's shoulder. She was smiling broadly, her teeth so white against her almond skin.

"Gretchen was very fond of you, Tim," her mother said.

The night after the funeral, Joel Rood and I sat in his Chevy Vega outside the restaurant where Gretchen's mourning friends planned to congregate. During high school Joel and I had been teammates and best buddies, spending countless Saturday nights cruising the country roads, talking about sports or school, or love, or what the years after Crookston might bring. Seeing him now was the beginning of both my pain and my consolation.

In the yellow Vega, as Joel spoke of Gretchen, his voice briefly failed. That tiny catch in my old friend's voice dissolved whatever stood between and my sorrow. My torrents of grief were unleashed.

Then next morning Joel joined a procession from the Erickhof's lakeside summer house into the nearby woods, Gretchen's sister took turns carrying a small urn that contained her ashes. It was cool and sunny, and the fallen leaves cracked underfoot.

185　　We came to a lone birch tree, its magnificent white bark standing out among the surrounding brown maples. Many years before, Gretchen, her father and younger sister had discovered the tree and carved the date and their
190　names in the bark.

　　Someone said a prayer. Gretchen's father placed the urn in the ground below the birch. Above us, wind rustled through newly barren branches.

195　　I was among the last to leave. I emerged from the woods that day into a different world, an adult world, where memories of first love linger, but summers always end.

> **crack** /kræk/ *v.* to break without dividing into separate parts; to break sth. in a way
> **birch** /bɜːtʃ/ a tree with smooth bark and thin branches, that grows in northern countries
> **maple** /'meɪpəl/ *n.* a tall tree with leaves that have five points and turn bright red or yellow in the autumn
> **rustle** /'rʌsəl/ *v.* if sth. dry and light rustles or you rustle it, it makes a sound like paper, leaves, etc. moving or rubbing together
> **emerge** /ɪ'mɜːdʒ/ *v.* to come out of a dark, enclosed or hidden place

Notes

1. Minn.
An abbreviation of Minnesota, USA.

2. Guardian Angel
A guardian angel is a spirit who is believed to protect and to guide a particular person. The concept of tutelary angels and their hierarchy was extensively developed in Christianity in the 5th century by Pseudo-Dionysius the Areopagite. The theology of angels, and tutelary spirits, has undergone many refinements since the 400's, and contemporary orthodox belief in both the eastern and western churches is that guardian angels protect the body and present prayers to God, protecting whichever person God assigns them to. The Roman Catholic Church calendar of saints includes a memorial for guardian angels on October 2.

3. Chevy Vega
The name of a type of car. (The Chevrolet Vega was a subcompact car sold from 1971 through 1977. Introduced during the second wave of the American auto industry's attempt to vanquish imported cars, the Chevrolet Vega is one of the vehicles Chevrolet designated as their first line of attack and defense against the imports of that time. It was a replacement for the Chevrolet Corvair.)

Comprehension Questions

1. According to the author, what kind of person is Gretchen like? Is she a self-important girl?
2. What did the author feel about females?
3. Why did the author consider Gretchen to be his "Guardian Angel?"
4. How to understand the sentence "For her, the serious part of life beckoned" in Lines 122—123? And what does that mean to the author?
5. After receiving Julie Janecky's phone, the author's mood seemed to have experienced a tremendous change. What does it like? When did they two meet for the last time before Gretchen's death?
6. For what reason Gretchen's parents expected the author to be a pallbearer in Gretchen's funeral?
7. After getting the news about Gretchen's death, the author sought out a campus priest. What do you think of the reasons?
8. Why does the author hold that seeing Joel Rood was the beginning of both his pain and his consolation?
9. What does the author mean by the last sentence in the last paragraph?

Writing Practice

Search in your memory for an impressive love story that you know from a book, a movie or some other sources, and share it with your partner. Tell him/her what really moves you in the story. Then write an essay entitled *My Favorite Love Story*.

Further Study

You must have read some English poems about love. A good poem can paint a thousand images in your mind's eye. Try the website http://www.love-poems.me.uk/a_love_poems_index.htm, you will find a list of some famous English love poems and the biographies and pictures of their poets. Though the list is clearly not comprehensive, the poems are regarded as some of the most popular ones with the theme, which can help you to achieve a better understanding of the power and magic of love.

Unit 3

Money and Happiness

Unit Goals

After completing the lessons in this unit, students will be able to:
- ☞ understand the nature of happiness, the relevant factors (money, psychological condition, etc.) connected with happiness and the ways in which one can achieve and maintain happiness;
- ☞ develop the ability to distinguish between major details and minor details;
- ☞ extend vocabulary through recognition of pejorative prefixes.

Before Reading

Hands-on Activities

1. Look up an encyclopedia or try the website http://encyclopedia.the freedictionary.com/happiness to get a review of different theories of happiness.
2. List as many factors as possible that are said to make people happy. Which one do you think is the most important for maintaining happiness?
3. Make a list of words and expressions associated with happiness, and another list of contrasting feelings.

Brainstorming

Brainstorm the following questions. Work in pairs or groups to discuss these questions.

1. The dictionary defines happiness as "a state of well-being characterized by emotions ranging from contentment to intense joy." Like many dictionary definitions, this may be accurate, but needs to be more specific to be of practical use. How do you experience this

"state of well-being?"

2. Nowadays, such an opinion as "the wealthier a person is, the happier he would be." Do you agree with it? Give your reasons.

A Glimpse at Words and Expressions

Please read the following sentences. Pay attention to the underlined part in each sentence and see how these expressions are used in the context, and then write down their meanings in the blanks provided.

1. A depression so debilitating that it's hard to get out of bed. (　　　　　)
2. Too many Americans view expensive purchases as "shortcuts to well-being." (　　　　　)
3. The poor are rendered unhappy by the relentless frustration and stress of poverty. (　　　　　)
4. The study, which has been replicated in the U.S., shows that Grandma had a point. (　　　　　)
5. That seems true because of a phenomenon that sociologists call reference anxiety—or, more popularly, keeping up with the Joneses. (　　　　　)
6. Most people knew relatively little about those who were living higher on the hog. (　　　　　)
7. Income growth has almost come to a halt for the middle class. (　　　　　)
8. But because we are all conditioned to think there's something wrong if we don't make more money each year. (　　　　　)

Text A

The Real Truth about Money

By Gregg Easterbrook
(Abridged and Edited)

If you made a graph of American life since the end of World War II, every line concerning money and the things that money can buy would soar upward, a statistical monument to materialism. Inflation-adjusted income per American has almost tripled. The size of the typical new house has more than doubled. A two-car garage was once a goal; now we're nearly a three-car nation. Designer everything, personal electronics and other items that didn't even exist a half-century ago are now affordable. No matter how you chart the trends in earning and spending, everything is up, up, up. But if you made a chart of American happiness since the end of World War II, the lines would be as flat as a marble tabletop. In polls taken by the National Opinion Research Center in the 1950s, about one-third of Americans described themselves as "very happy." The center has conducted essentially the same poll periodically since then, and the percentage remains almost exactly the same today.

Yet if you charted the incidence of depression since 1950, the lines suggested a growing epidemic. Depending on what assumptions are used, clinical depression is 3 to 10 times as common today as two generations ago. A recent study by Ronald Kessler of Harvard Medical School estimated that each year, one in fifteen Americans experience an episode of major depression—meaning not just a bad day but a depression so debilitating that it's hard to get out of bed. Money jangles in our

---

statistical /stəˈtɪstɪkəl/ *adj.* relating to, or employing statistics or the principles of statistics

inflation /ɪnˈfleɪʃən/ *n.* a general rise in the prices of services and goods in a particular country, resulting in a fall in the value of money; the rate at which this happens.

affordable /əˈfɔːdəbəl/ *adj.* able to be afforded

chart /tʃɑːt/ *v.* to record or follow the progress or development of sb./sth.

poll /pəʊl/ *n.* the process of questioning people who are representative of a larger group in order to get information about the general opinion

incidence /ˈɪnsɪdəns/ *n.* ~ of sth. (written) the extent to which sth. happens or has an effect

depression /dɪˈpreʃən/ *n.* a medical condition in which a person feels very sad and anxious and often has physical symptoms such as being unable to sleep, etc.

debilitate /dɪˈbɪlɪteɪt/ *v.* to make sb.'s body or mind weaker

jangle /ˈdʒæŋɡl/ *v.* to make a harsh sound, like two pieces of metal hitting each other

wallets and purses as never before, but we are basically no happier for it, and for many, more money leads to depression. How can that be?

Of course, our grandmothers, many of whom lived through the Depression and the war, told us that money can't buy happiness. We don't act as though we listened. Millions of us spend more time and energy pursuing the things money can buy than engaging in activities that create real fulfillment in life, like cultivating friendships, helping others and developing a spiritual sense.

We say we know that money can't buy happiness. In the *TIME* poll, when people were asked about their major source of happiness, money ranked 14th. Still, we behave as though happiness is one wave of a credit card away. Too many Americans view expensive purchases as "shortcuts to well-being," says Martin Seligman, a psychologist at the University of Pennsylvania. But people are poor predictors of where those shortcuts will take them.

To be sure, there is ample evidence that being poor causes unhappiness. Studies by Ruut Veenhoven, a sociologist at Erasmus University in Rotterdam, show that the poor—those in Europe earning less than about $10,000 a year—are rendered unhappy by the relentless frustration and stress of poverty. But you knew that.

The surprise is that after a person's annual income exceeds $10,000 or so, Veenhoven found, money and happiness decouple and cease to have much to do with each other. The study, which has been replicated in the U.S., shows that Grandma had a point. Over the past two decades, in fact, an increasing body of social-science and psychological research has shown that there is no significant relationship between how much money a person earns and whether he or she feels good about life. *TIME*'s poll found that happiness tended to increase as income rose to $50,000 a year. (The median annual U.S. household income is around $43,000.) After that, more income did not have a dramatic effect. Edward Diener, a psychologist at the University of Illinois, interviewed members of the Forbes 400, the richest Americans. He found the Forbes 400 were only a tiny bit happier than the public as a whole. Because those with wealth often continue to feel jealousy about the possessions

purse /pɜːs/ *n.* a small bag made of leather, plastic, etc. for carrying coins and often also paper money, cards, etc used especially by women

cultivate /ˈkʌltɪveɪt/ *v.* (sometimes disapproving) to try to get sb.'s friendship or support

predictor /prɪˈdɪktə/ *n.* (formal) something that can show what will happen in the future

render /ˈrendə/ *v.* to cause sb./sth. to be in a particular state or condition

relentless /rɪˈlentləs/ *adj.* not stopping or getting less strong

frustration /frʌˈstreɪʃən/ *n.* the feeling of being frustrated

decouple /diːˈkʌpəl/ *v.* to end the connection or relationship between two things

replicate /ˈreplɪkeɪt/ *v.* to copy sth. exactly

significant /sɪgˈnɪfɪkənt/ *adj.* large or important enough to have an effect or to be noticed

median /ˈmiːdiən/ (only being noun) (technical) having a value in the middle of a series of values

or prestige of other wealthy people, even large sums of money may fail to confer well-being.

That seems true because of a phenomenon that sociologists call reference anxiety—or, more popularly, keeping up with the Joneses. According to that thinking, most people judge their possessions in comparison with others'. People tend not to ask themselves, does my house meet my needs? Instead they ask, is my house nicer than my neighbor's? If you own a two-bedroom house and everyone around you owns a two-bedroom house, your reference anxiety will be low, and your two-bedroom house may seem fine. But if your two-bedroom house is surrounded by three- and four-bedroom houses, with someone around the corner doing a tear-down to build a McMansion, your reference anxiety may rise. Suddenly that two-bedroom house—one that your grandparents might have considered quite nice, even luxurious—doesn't seem enough. And so the money you spent on it stops providing you with a sense of well-being.

Our soaring reference anxiety is a product of the widening gap in income distribution. In other words, the rich are getting richer and faster, and the rest of us are none too happy about it. During much of U.S. history, the majority lived in small towns or urban areas where conditions for most people were approximately the same—hence low reference anxiety. Also, most people knew relatively little about those who were living higher on the hog.

But in the past few decades, new economic forces have changed all that. Rapid growth in income for the top 5% of households has brought about a substantial cohort of people who live notably better than the middle class does, amplifying our reference anxiety. That wealthier minority is occupying ever larger homes and spending more on each change of clothes than others spend on a month's rent. It all feeds middle-class anxiety, even when the middle is doing O.K. In nations with high levels of income equality like the Scandinavian countries, well-being tends to be higher than in nations with unequal wealth distribution such as the U.S. Meanwhile, television and the Web make it easier to know how the very well off live. (Never mind whether they're happy.) Want a peek inside Donald Tramp's gold-plated world? Just click on the TV, and he'll show you. Wonder what Bill Gates' 66,000-sq.-ft. mega mansion is like? Just download the floor plan from the Internet!

Paradoxically, it is the very increase in money—which creates the wealth so visible in today's society—that triggers dissatisfaction. As material expectations keep rising, more money may engender only more desires.

---

prestige /pre'stiːʒ/ n.   the respect or admiration that sb./sth. has because of their special position, or what they have done

confer /kən'fɜː/ v.   to give sb. an award, a university degree or particular honor or right

phenomenon /fɪ'nɒmɪnən/ n.   a fact or an event in nature or society, especially one that is not fully understood

surround /sə'raʊnd/ v.   to be all around sth./sb.

soar /sɔː/ v.   to rise very quickly

substantial /səb'stænʃəl/ adj.   large in amount or value; important

cohort /'kəʊhɔːt/ n.   a group of people who share the common feature or aspect of behavior

amplify /'æmplɪfaɪ/ v.   to increase sth. in strength, especially sound

peek /piːk/ n.   a look at sth.

mega /'megə/ adj.   very large or impressive

"What people want in terms of material things and life experiences has increased almost exactly in lockstep with the postwar earnings
110 curve," Diener notes. As men and women move up the economic ladder, most almost immediately stop feeling grateful for their elevated circumstances and focus on what they still don't have. Suppose you lived in a
115 two-bedroom house for years and dreamed of three bedrooms. You finally get that three-bedroom house. Will it bring you happiness? Not necessarily. Three bedrooms will become your new norm, and you'll begin
120 to long for a four-bedroom abode.

> **lockstep** /ˈlɒkstep/ *n.* a situation where things happen at the same time or change at the same rate
> **elevated** /ˈelɪveɪtɪd/ *adj.* high in rank
> **brim** /brɪm/ *v.* to be full of sth., to fill sth.
> **abode** /əˈbəʊd/ *n.* the place where sb. lives
> **condition** /kənˈdɪʃən/ *v.* to train sb./sth. behave in a particular way or to become used to a particular situation
> **lot** /lɒt/ *n.* a person's luck or situation in life
> **anticipate** /ænˈtɪsɪpeɪt/ *v.* to think with pleasure and excitement about sth. that is going to happen
> **foresee** /fɔːˈsiː/ *v.* to think sth. is going to happen in the future; to know about sth. before it happens
> **decent** /ˈdiːsnt/ *adj.* (especially spoken) of a good enough standard or quality
> **licensed** /ˈlaɪsənst/ *adj.* having official permission to do sth.
> **stability** /stəˈbɪlɪti/ *n.* the quality or state of being steady and not changing or being disturbed in any way (= the quality of being stable)

That money never satisfies is suggested by this telling fact: polls show that Americans believe that, whatever their income level, they need more to live well. Even those making large sums said still larger sums were required. We
125 seem conditioned to think we do not have enough, even if objectively our lives are comfortable.

Then again, if we think our lot is improving, happiness follows. Carol Graham, an economist at the Brookings Institution in Washington, found that people's expectations about the future may have more influence on their sense of well-being than their current state does.
130 People living modestly but anticipating better days to come, Graham thinks, are likely to be happier than people living well but not looking forward to improvements in their living standards. Consider two people: one earns $50,000 a year and foresees a 10% raise, and the other makes $150,000 but does not expect any salary increase. The second person is much better off in financial terms, but the first is more likely to feel good about life.

135 And guess what? The U.S. hasn't had a decent raise in two decades. Income growth has almost come to a halt for the middle class. In real terms, although median household income is higher than ever, median household income has increased only around 15% since 1984. That means most people have never had it better but do not expect any improvement in the near future. People tend to focus on the negative part and ignore the positive.

140 Living standards, education levels and other basic measures of U.S. social well-being have improved so much so quickly in the postwar era that another big leap seems improbable. If the typical new house is more than 2,300 sq. ft., if more than half of high school graduates advance to college, if there are more cars and trucks in the U.S. than there are licensed drivers — all current statistics—then the country may need stability and equality more than it needs

more money. But because we are all conditioned to think there's something wrong if we don't make more money each year, high standards of living in the U.S. may, paradoxically, have become an impediment to happiness. Fixated on always getting more, we fail to how much we have. Of course, in the grand scheme it's better that there are large numbers of Americans who are materially comfortable, if a bit whiny about it, than who are destitute. And never forget: one in eight Americans are poor. Poverty remains a stark reality amid American affluence.

> paradoxically /ˌpærəˈdɒksɪkli/ *adv.* inconsistently
> impediment /ɪmˈpedɪmənt/ *n.* something that delays or stops the progress of sth.
> scheme /skiːm/ *n.* a plan or system for doing or organizing sth.
> destitute /ˈdestɪtjuːt/ *adj.* without money, food and the other things necessary for life
> stark /stɑːk/ *adj.* unpleasant, real, and impossible to avoid
> affluence /ˈæfluəns/ *n.* abundance

Psychology and sociology aside, there is a final reason money can't buy happiness: the things that really matter in life are not sold in stores. Love, friendship, family, respect, a place in the community, the belief that your life has purpose—those are the essential of human fulfillment, and they cannot be purchased with cash. Everyone needs a certain amount of money, but chasing money rather than meaning is a formula for discontent. Too many Americans have made materialism and the cycle of work and spent their principal goals. Then they wonder why they don't feel happy.

Better Know More

1. Gregg Easterbrook

Gregg Easterbrook is an American writer who is a senior editor of The *New Republic*. He also writes a weekly column during the National Football League season called *Tuesday Morning Quarterback*, currently on ESPN.com. Easterbrook also often writes for *Slate*, *The Atlantic Monthly*, *The New York Times*, *The Los Angeles Times*, and *Wired*. He is a fellow at the Brookings Institution, a Washington, D.C. think tank.

2. National Opinion Research Center

The National Opinion Research Center (NORC), established in 1941, is one of the largest and most highly respected social research organizations in the United States. Its headquarters are located on the University of Chicago campus, at 1155 E. 60th Street, Chicago. It also has offices in Chicago's downtown Loop, and in Washington DC, and San Francisco. NORC conducts social research for government agencies, non-profit agencies and corporations.

3. Ruut Veenhowen

Ruut Veenhoven (1942) is a sociologist. He is also accredited in social psychology and social-sexuology. Veenhoven is a professor of "social conditions for human happiness" at Erasmus University Rotterdam in the Netherlands.

4. sq.

An abbreviation of "square."

5. ft.

An abbreviation of "feet or foot."

Check Your Understanding

Answer the following questions based on the text you have just learned.

1. Could you describe the general conditions in U.S. after the World War II according to the text?
2. How do you understand the sentence "more money leads to depression?"
3. What is the function of the example given by the text about Grandma?
4. Why are the wealthier less happier than common ones?
5. How does wealth affect people's choices and attitudes towards life?
6. What is the meaning of "reference anxiety" referred to by sociologists?
7. On the basis of the text, what is the best therapy for unhappiness?
8. From the whole text, can you summarize the relationship between money and happiness?
9. What lessons can you learn from the Text?

A Sip of Word Formation

Pejorative Prefixes

Mis-, *mal-*, *pseudo-* **are the pejorative prefixes.**

1. The prefix *mis-* can be traced back to Old English. The basic meaning of the prefix *mis-* is "bad, badly; wrong, wrongly." *Mis-* forms compounds primarily by attaching to verbs;
   For example: misfortune means "bad fortune"
   misbehave means "to behave badly"
   Besides, *mis-* also frequently forms compounds by attaching to nouns that come from verbs:
   for example: miscalculation, mismanagement, mispronunciation.

2. The prefix *mal-* denotes total opposite to the stem, which means "not correct or correctly; bad or badly."
   For example: maltreat means "treat badly"
   malpractice means "do something incorrectly"

3. *Pseudo-* means "fake, false, not genuine or pretended."
   For example: pseudoscience means "false science"
   pseudointellectual means "pretended intellectual"

Build Your Vocabulary

A. *Add a prefix to each word to make it match the meaning given. Write the new word you have made.*

_____	nym	false name
_____	function	work wrongly
_____	understand	understand wrongly
_____	direct	get somebody in the wrong direction
_____	judge	judge something wrongly
_____	manage	manage something badly
_____	content	a person who is discontented or disgusted
_____	classic	not genuine classic

B. *The word at the end of each of the following sentences can be used to form a word that fits suitably in the blank space.*

1. The cat sat in front of the bird cage in an agony of _____ at being so near and yet so far. (frustrate)
2. Having such a close similarity or resemblance as to be _____ equal or interchangeable. (essential)
3. Some people care more about the _____ life than the spiritual life. (substantially)
4. _____ prose into other languages is difficult. (render)
5. Our house needs whitewashing again, but we can't afford one in the _____ future. (foresee)
6. The _____ of unemployment has increased over the last year. (incident)
7. His unwillingness to give five minutes of his time proves that he is disinterested in finding a solution to the problem, a proportion that is not _____ different from the 93 percent who disapproved of the same usage in an earlier survey. (significant)
8. In the feudal society, the landlord exploited the farmers _____. (relentless)
9. _____ she may be, but she is not sure what to tip the doorman. (affluence)
10. A part or surface, such as a wing, propeller blade, or rudder, whose shape and orientation control _____, direction, lift, thrust, or propulsion. (stable)

You'd Like to Be

A Skilled Text Weaver

Choose the correct words and then fill in the blank board with their appropriate forms.

| trigger | line | amplify | fail | incidence |
| cultivate | exceed | condition | adjust | render |

1. He's _____ up a live band for the party.
2. The riots were _____ (off) by a series of police arrests.
3. Any of several devices that convert incident electromagnetic radiation of mixed frequencies to one or more discrete frequencies of highly _____ and coherent ultraviolet, visible, or infrared radiation.
4. I _____ to see why you find it so amusing.

5. This area has a high _____ of crime, disease, unemployment, etc.
6. His fatness _____ him unable to bend down.
7. We must _____ our own garden and find the joy of doing it in our own heart.
8. Animals can be _____ to expect food at certain times.
9. Over the years, we all learned to _____, to become more comfortable with each other, and to adapt to our new family arrangement.
10. If your liabilities _____ your assets, you may go bankrupt.
11. He's in excellent _____ for a man of his age.
12. He can't _____ himself to the whirl of modern life in this big city.
13. The artist had _____ her gentle smile perfectly.
14. The brakes on my car _____ half way down the hill.
15. A figure of a head worn by actors in Greek and Roman drama to identify a character or trait and to _____ the voice.
16. Their research proceeded along sound _____.
17. A pulse to gate the output of a core memory sense amplifier into a _____ in a register.

A Sharp Interpreter

Paraphrase the following sentences. Change the sentence structure if necessary.

1. The study, which has been replicated in the U.S., shows that Grandma had a point.
2. That seems true because of a phenomenon that sociologists call reference anxiety—or, more popularly, keeping up with the Joneses.
3. The second person is much better off in financial terms, but the first is more likely to feel good about life.
4. But because we are all conditioned to think there's something wrong if we don't make more money each year, high standards of living in the U.S. may, paradoxically, have become an impediment to happiness.
5. Paradoxically, it is the very increase in money—which creates the wealth so visible in today's society—that triggers dissatisfaction.
6. Our soaring reference anxiety is a product of the widening gap in income distribution.
7. We seem conditioned to think we do not have enough, even if objectively our lives are comfortable.

A Solid Sentence Constructor

Choose an appropriate word into the blank sheet.

| beings | raise | variations | however | prevail | after |
| therefore | in | for | means | that | |

It is an agreed fact that all the creatures want happiness and are afraid of pain and grief. The question, _____, is "what is real happiness?" What really is called happiness? The desire _____ happiness has no meaning without understanding the real nature of happiness.

Generally, ordinary _____ consider sensual pleasures as happiness and their attempts are also directed towards these. According to them search for happiness _____ search for pleasures of the senses. The question "what is happiness" does not _____ in their hearts, because in their hearts they treat life full of sensory joys as a happy life.

It is on account of this _____ whenever we think of happiness and welfare, it is considered desirable to lead a life of attachments, work hard, grow more food and develop industries and science. The country will prosper by all these and all will be happy. Ideals are talked of and it is said that a day will come when everyone will have nutritious food to eat, clothes to put on according to _____ of seasons and modern residence with all scientific facilities and then all will be happy.

We do not want to discuss whether such conditions will _____ or not. Our question is, if _____ having all these comforts, life will be happy. If yes, people having all these comforts, should be happy even now. The countries touching the limitations of all these comforts must, then, have all happy and quiet people. We, however, find that all on this earth are disturbed, impatient, unhappy, afraid and worried. It is, _____ necessary to consider seriously what happiness really is. We cannot make true efforts _____ this direction and achieve happiness without once for all deciding what real happiness is.

A Careful Writer

Study the following synonyms and complete the sentences.

| economical | frugal | sparing | thrifty |

1. My father is excessively _____ because he remembers the poverty of his childhood.

2. The new kind of machine is not only very powerful but also _____ .
3. This is a poor family where the father should go to towns to earn money and the other members have _____ meals.
4. Everyone should be _____ with his time and money.
5. They lived a very _____ existence, avoiding all luxuries.

| discern | figure | perceive | recognize |

1. The students _____ the teacher's steps of coming upstairs and hurriedly sat still.
2. In the gloom I could only just _____ the outline of his slim body.
3. I didn't _____ him, for he had his hair cut.
4. John isn't here today. That _____, he looked very unwell yesterday.
5. We perceive two persons afar off without being able to _____ whether they are men or women.

| meddle | interfere | interrupt |

1. The parents should stop _____ and let the children make their own decisions.
2. Study to be quiet, and to _____ with your own business.
3. These new flats will _____ our view of the sea.

A Superb Bilingualist

Translate the following sentences into English.

1. 据描述这个女孩身材苗条,深色皮肤,年龄在 15 岁左右。(describe... as)
2. 这个地区的犯罪率、发病率、失业率都很高。(the incidence of)
3. 该艺术家把她那温柔的笑容表现得惟妙惟肖。(render)
4. 帽子的帽檐完全遮住了她的脸。(the brim of)
5. 国王授予几位杰出人士爵士头衔。(confer... on)
6. 这些动物已经训练过了,想出笼子时就会按铃。(condition)
7. 懒惰是影响他学习进步的障碍之一。(impediment)
8. 他特意设法同同学建立良好的关系。(cultivate)
9. 当代,每个行业都大量地引进先进技术。(line)
10. 他是活着离开战俘集中营的很少几个人中的一个。(live through)

Text B

Happiness

By Jenny McPhee
(Abridged and Edited)

For centuries, scientists and academics have studied what is wrong with us, paying scant attention to exploring what already works. The new happiness movement, which involves psychologists, neurologists, sociologists, and even economists, investigates
5 not what is wrong but what is right, and seeks to discover how we can use our positive emotions to improve our quality of life.

A harbinger of this growing field is Martin E.P. Seligman, Ph.D., former head of the American
10 Psychological Association and author of the best-selling book *Learned Optimism*. He calls his brand of happiness "positive psychology" and promotes it as a healthy alternative to either years of exploring an unhappy childhood with a psychotherapist or drugs such as Prozac, Zoloft, and Paxil. "This relentless focus on the negative," Seligman claims,
15 "has left psychology blind to the many instances of ... drive and insight that develop out of undesirable, painful life events."

Basically, Seligman's idea is that you can train yourself to spin the events in your life from an optimistic point of view. For example, if you're fired from your job, see it as an
20 opportunity for a new beginning. Your relationship breaks up, so you decide to find someone who plays to your strengths, not your weaknesses. And you learn to fully appreciate the good things that happen to you—no
25 thinking you pulled the wool over their eyes when you get a promotion. Seligman is convinced that "the positive social science of the 21st century will have as a useful side effect the possibility of prevention of the serious
30 mental illnesses; for there are a set of human

---

scant /skænt/ *adj.* hardly any, not very much and not as much as there should be
neurologist /njʊˈrɒlədʒɪst/ *n.* a doctor who studies and treats diseases of the nerves
harbinger /ˈhɑːbɪndʒə/ *n.* a sign that shows that sth. is going to happen soon, often sth. bad
psychotherapist /ˌsaɪkəʊˈθerəpɪst/ *n.* a person who studies the psychotherapy
spin /spɪn/ *v.* to present information or a situation in a particular way, especially one that makes you or your ideas seem good
appreciate /əˈpriːʃieɪt/ *v.* (not used in the progressive tenses) to recognize the good qualities of sb./sth.

strengths that most likely buffer against mental illness: courage, optimism, interpersonal skill, work ethic, hope.... But it will have as its direct effect a scientific understanding of the practice
35 of civic virtue and of the pursuit of the best things in life."

Recent studies linking happiness—in particular laughter—and health would appear to back Seligman's theory: People who smile more
40 frequently tend to have lower blood pressure and stronger immune systems. A current UCLA study is attempting to find clear biological evidence for laughter's therapeutic effects on cancer patients. And filmmaker Mira Nair
45 recently made a documentary on India's laughing clubs, a widespread phenomenon in which people laugh together for about 20 minutes a day with beneficial results. Employers have found that since initiating the laughing
50 clubs in factories, there is less absenteeism and better performance among the workers.

buffer /'bʌfə/ v.	to protect sb. from sth.
ethic /'eθɪk/ n.	a system of moral principles or rules of behaviour
civic /'sɪvɪk/ adj.	connected with the people who live in a town or city
immune /ɪ'mjuːn/ adj.	that can not be catched or be affected by a particular disease or illness
therapeutic /ˌθerə'pjuːtɪk/ adj.	designed to help treat an illness
initiate /ɪ'nɪʃieɪt/ v.	(formal) to make sth. begin
absenteeism /ˌæbsən'tiːɪzəm/ n.	the fact of being frequently away from work or school, especially without good reasons
adage /'ædɪdʒ/ n.	a well-known phrase expressing a general truth about people or the world
reinforce /ˌriːɪn'fɔːs/ v.	to make a feeling, an idea, etc. stronger
preliminary /prɪ'lɪmɪnəri/ adj.	happening before a more important action or event
intriguing /ɪn'triːgɪŋ/ adj.	very interesting because of being unusual or not having an obvious answer
neurobiology /ˌnjʊərəʊbaɪ'ɒlədʒi/ n.	the study of cells of the nervous system and the organization of these cells into functional circuits
perceive /pə'siːv/ v.	to understand or think of sth. in a particular way

But doesn't "the pursuit of the best things in life" cost money? How many times have we said to ourselves, If only I were rich, I would be so much happier? Economists are increasingly interested in just how money does contribute to our happiness levels. In fact, in 2000, the
55 Woodrow Wilson School of Public and International Affairs at Princeton University opened its Center for Health and Well-being, staffed by a significant number of economists. For some time now, psychologists have been declaring that the old adage is true: Money can't buy happiness.

There is, in fact, a wide body of evidence showing
60 that people who aspire to have money, fame, and beauty are less happy than those who engage in daily activities they find fulfilling and pleasurable.

Pursuing the small pleasures of life as a formula for happiness is reinforced by the preliminary findings
65 of perhaps the most intriguing, indeed revolutionary, area in the new happiness studies: the neurobiology of happiness. Emotions—happiness, sadness, fear, anger, love, desire—have traditionally been perceived as

spiritual, *ephemeral* things that were not of the
70 body, belonging instead to the realm of the soul.
Now, however, researchers are making connections between brain activity and emotions. As
neurologist Antonio Damasio, Ph.D., M.D.,
best-selling author of *The Feeling of What*
75 *Happens*, describes, "We are not thinking machines. We are feeling machines that think."

    Some studies suggest that about 50 percent
of a person's capacity for happiness is *inherited*.
But others are wary of putting a fixed numerical
80 value on the possibility for happiness, especially
since one amazing neurological discovery of the
past 15 years is the brain's *plasticity*. At one
time, scientists thought that after the first years of life the brain was *hardwired* never to be altered. Neuroscientists are now finding that our environment not only can cause enduring
85 changes to our DNA, it can affect the very shape of the brain, even into old age.

    This discovery has led experts to prescribe brain exercises for a wide range of conditions from massive *strokes* to mild memory loss. "The brain is like a muscle," says behavioral neuroscientist Edward Taub, Ph.D. "And the more that you exercise it, the better it gets." Taub and others in the field *recommend* daily mind exercises for everyone, things like brushing your
90 teeth with your left hand if you are right-handed, *alternating* the wrist on which you wear your watch, or making a mental list of all the objects you see when you walk into a room. Above all, they are recommending what Buddhists and New Agers have long been telling us: Avoid or *minimize* stress. Studies by Stanford University neuroscientist and biologist Robert Sapolsky, Ph.D., suggest that stress takes a
95 large *toll* not only on memory but on the overall well-being of your brain.

    Which brings us back to the science of happiness and how we might go about reshaping our brains and lives in order to
100 maintain lower levels of stress and higher levels of *contentment*. Drugs are one way, but if a *psychopharmacological* solution is not for you (there is still the side-effects problem), there may be a more organic solution.
105 Exercises devised to help improve your overall sense of well-being could involve

---

ephemeral /ɪˈfemərəl/ *adj.* lasting or used for only a short period of time

inherit /ɪnˈherɪt/ *v.* to have qualities, physical features, etc. that are similar to those of your parents, grandparents, etc.

plasticity /plæˈstɪsɪti/ *n.* the quality of being easily made into different shapes

hardwired /ˌhɑːdˈwaɪəd/ *adj.* (technical) (of computer functions) built into the permanent system and not provided by software

stroke /strəʊk/ *n.* A sudden serious illness when a blood vessel in the brain bursts or is blocked, which can cause death or the loss of the ability to move or to speak clearly

recommend /ˌrekəˈmend/ *v.* to tell sb. that sth. is good or useful, or that sb. would be suitable for a particular job, etc.

alternate /ɔːlˈtɜːnɪt/ *v.* (of things or people) to follow one after the other in a repeated pattern

minimize /ˈmɪnɪmaɪz/ *v.* to reduce sth., especially sth. bad, to the lowest possible level

toll /təʊl/ *n.* the amount of damage or the number of deaths and injuries that are caused in a particular war, disaster, etc.

contentment /kənˈtentmənt/ *n.* a feeling of happiness or satisfaction

psychopharmacological /ˌsaɪkəʊˌfɑːməˈkɒlədʒɪkəl/ *adj.* of or relating to psychopharmacology (the branch of pharmacology that deals with the study of the actions, effects, and development of psychoactive drugs) determining the specific environmental cues in your life that activate neural systems that cause you to feel happy—eating a perfectly ripe persimmon, perhaps. Then, make sure you frequently do the things that fill you with a sense of joy, fun, and satisfaction. In *The New York Times*, behavioral geneticist David Lykken, Ph.D., gave this advice: "Be an experiential epicure... Find the small things that you know give you a little high... and sprinkle your life with them."

Forty-two years ago, Rodgers and Hammerstein, in their musical The Sound of Music, gave us the prescription in song: "I simply remember my favorite things. And then I don't feel so bad." And, as Aristotle indicated over two millennia ago, being happy is "an activity in accordance with excellence," and excellence is something one must continuously work toward, not unlike engaging in regular exercise for a healthy body. Soon, it will be perfectly normal to go to your personal neurotrainer to work out the mind in order to have a happier and healthier life. In the meantime, just what is it that makes you happy?

> cue /kjuː/ *n.* an action or event that is a signal for sb. to do sth.
> neural /ˈnjʊərəl/ *adj.* (technical) connected with a nerve or the nervous system
> persimmon /pəˈsɪmən/ *n.* a sweet tropical fruit that looks like a large orange tomato
> geneticist /dʒɪˈnetɪsɪst/ *n.* a scientist who studies genetics
> epicure /ˈepɪkjʊə/ *n.* a person who enjoys food and drink of high quality and knows a lot about it
> millennium /mɪˈleniəm/ (pl. millennia) a period of 1000 years, especially as calculated before or after the birth of Christ

Notes

1. Martin E. P. Seligman

Martin E. P. Seligman, Ph.D., currently the Fox Leadership Professor of Psychology in the Department of Psychology at the University of Pennsylvania, works on learned helplessness, depression, and as well as optimism and pessimism. His bibliography includes fifteen books and 150 articles on motivation and personality.

2. Antonio R. Damasio

Antonio R. Damasio is the M.W. Van Allen distinguished professor and Head of the Department of Neurology at the University of Iowa College of Medicine and Adjunct Professor at the Salk Institute for Biological Studies in La Jolla, California. He is a member of the American Academy of Arts and Sciences and the National Academy of Sciences, Institute of Medicine.

3. Edward Taub

Edward Taub is a behavioral neuroscientist who developed a new family of techniques, termed Constraint—Induced Movement therapy or CI therapy, which has been shown to be effective in improving the rehabilitation of movement after stroke and other neurological injuries.

4. David Lykken

David Lykken is a behavioral geneticist and Emeritus Professor at the University of Minnesota. He is the proponent of a set-point theory of happiness, the idea that one's sense of well-being is half determined by genetics and half determined by circumstances. He is the author of *Happiness: What Studies on Twins Show Us about Nature, Nurture, and the Happiness Set Point*.

5. Psychopharmacology

The Study of Psychiatric Drugs. This is the discipline of relating to the study, prescription and appropriate use of drugs for psychiatric illness and for neuropsychiatric conditions. It is sometimes used synonymously with neuropharmacology although technically not so. Psychopharmacology is not an official medical specialty in that there is no current specialist board.

Comprehension Questions

1. What is the meaning of the sentence "seeks to discover how we can use our positive emotions to improve our quality of life?"
2. Do you think the "positive psychology" is a much more effective way to promote one's happiness than the medical therapy?
3. Do you believe Seligman's theory that "People who smile more frequently tend to have lower blood pressure and strong immune system?" Can you give an example?
4. In your opinion "the more you have got, the more you will want" is right or not?
5. Do you believe one's capacity for happiness is inherited? Why?
6. Could you give some advice to improve and maintain people's happiness?
7. What is the main idea of the text?

Writing Practice

For happiness, there are many different opinions, such as: **A.** The best remedy for those who are afraid, lonely or unhappy is to go outside, somewhere where they can be quiet, alone with the heavens, nature and God. Because only then does one feel that all is as it should be and that God wishes to see people happy, amidst the simple beauty of nature. **B.** Happiness belongs to the self-sufficient. **C.** Action may not always bring happiness, but there is no happiness without action. **D.** The happiness that is genuinely satisfying is accompanied by the fullest exercise of our faculties and the fullest realization of the world in which we live. **E.** Happiness comes when your work and words are of benefit to yourself and others. As for this, combining with what has mentioned above, what do you think happiness really is?

Further Study

Factors which influence one's happiness are innumerable, such as family, career, health etc. So are the ways to achieve happiness. Apart from what is mentioned, one's spiritual condition has an intimate relation with happiness. This unit only puts forward a fraction of it. You can go to your libraries to browse through books and newspapers or search on Internet to find out why modern people's life is filled with anxiety and for the wealthier, why it is harder to find happiness than man in the street?

Unit 4

Education

Unit Goals

After completing the lessons in this unit, students will be able to:
- ☞ understand the controversy over single-sex education; the main crux of public education and its temporary condition in America;
- ☞ develop the ability of critical thinking;
- ☞ extend vocabulary through recognition of prefixes of degree or size.

Before Reading

Hands-on Activities

1. Browse the website, http://www.usastudyguide.com/usaeducationsystem.htm, and try to get familiar with the development of American Education System.
2. Look through relevant books or newspapers to list advantages and disadvantages of American Education System.

Brainstorming

Brainstorm the following questions. Work in pairs or groups to discuss these questions.

1. Which kind of education, the education for all-round development or the exam-oriented education, do you approve of? Give your reasons.
2. What orientation, do you think, should Chinese education system direct at?
3. In some countries, single-gender education is popular, is it good or not? If good, put forward its advantages, and vice versa.

A Glimpse at words and Expressions

Please read the following sentences. Pay attention to the underlined part in each sentence and see how these expressions are used in the context, and then write down their meanings in the blanks provided.

1. Academic standards have sunk out of sight.   (   )
2. When those poor results are recognized, the system and its defenders can be counted on to say that the problem is insufficient spending.   (   )
3. Reich argues that while public school systems in affluent areas are turning out students who are college or work-ready because they have learned "to identify and solve new problems, recognize patterns, and think critically," schools in poorer areas aren't able to do that.   (   )
4. Therefore, we have to do something to equalize spending so that all students will have an equal shot at a good education.   (   )
5. We know that because there are many nongovernmental schools in poor urban areas that produce remarkably skilled graduates, despite the fact that they operate on shoestring budgets.   (   )
6. He wants to do away with local property taxes to fund public education and institute a national wealth tax instead.   (   )
7. People are entitled to do what they want with their own income or wealth.   (   )
8. Education establishment's appetite for money is unending, and once the camel had its nose inside the wealth-tax tent, it would continue pushing in.   (   )
9. The late Peter Bauer used to point out that foreign aid did far more to prop up tyrannical regimes than to help hungry people.   (   )

Text A

National Wealth Tax to Fund Education?

By George C. Leef
(Abridged and Edited)

"Public education" in the United States is very high in cost and very low in positive results. While some students graduate from public schools with sharp intellectual skills (often owing more to their home environment than to their
5 school instruction), many others drift aimlessly through 12 years of classes where little is  expected of them, academic standards have sunk out of sight, and discipline is a joke. The teachers are protected by union
10 contracts with piranha-like teeth and they have little incentive to do their best.

And what their best might be is highly questionable. Thanks to strict state licensing laws, it is almost obligatory for
15 anyone who wants to teach in public schools to go through a lengthy course of study in a college or university "school of education," where the emphasis is on dubious pedagogical theories such as cooperative
20 learning and multicultural sensitivity rather than on the mastery of subject matter and how best to impart that knowledge to students. School administrators seldom have the freedom to hire teachers who
25 haven't been through the school swamp,

---

intellectual /ˌɪntɪˈlektjuəl/ *adj.* connected with or using a person's ability to think in a logical way and understand things

drift /drɪft/ *v.* to happen or change or to do sth. without a particular plan or purpose

discipline /ˈdɪsɪplɪn/ *n.* the practice of training people to obey rules and orders and punishing them if they do not; the controlled behavior or situation that results from this training

piranha-like *adj.* having the feature of piranha which is a small American fresh water fish that attacks and eats live animals

incentive /ɪnˈsentɪv/ *n.* ~(for/to sb./sth.) (to do sth.) something that encourages you to do sth.

obligatory /əˈblɪɡətəri/ *adj.* ~(for sb.) to do sth.(formal) that you must do because of the law, rules, etc.

lengthy /ˈleŋθi/ *adj.* very long, and often too long, in time or size

dubious /ˈdjuːbiəs/ *adj.* that you can not be sure about; that is probably not good

pedagogical /pedəˈɡɒdʒɪkəl/ *adj.* concerning teaching methods

sensitivity /ˌsensɪˈtɪvɪti/ *n.* the ability to experience and understand deep feelings, especially in art and literature

impart /ɪmˈpɑːt/ *v.* (formal) to pass information, knowledge, etc. to other people

swamp /swɒmp/ *n.* an area that is very wet or covered with water and in which plants, trees, etc. are growing

> **competent** /ˈkɒmpɪtənt/ *adj.* having enough skill or knowledge to do sth. well or to the necessary standard
> **uncertify** /ˌʌnˈsɜːtɪfaɪ/ *v.* not to give sb. an official document proving that they are qualified to work in particular profession
> **innumerable** /ɪˈnjuːmərəbəl/ *adj.* too many to be counted; very many
> **impede** /ɪmˈpiːd/ *v.* [often passive](formal) to delay or stop the progress of sth.
> **overarching** /ˌəʊvərˈɑːtʃɪŋ/ *adj.* [usually before nouns] very important because it includes or influences many things
> **penalty** /ˈpenlti/ *n.* (~ for sth.) a punishment for breaking a law, rule, or contract
> **recipe** /ˈresɪpi/ *n.* (~ for sth.) a method or an idea that seems likely to have a particular result
> **equivalent** /ɪˈkwɪvələnt/ *n.* (of/to sth) a thing, amount, word etc that is equivalent to sth else

no matter how much more competent uncertified people who happen to really know their math, chemistry, history, English, etc., may be.

30　　From its innumerable regulations that impede efficiency to the overarching fact that there is no penalty for failure, public education follows a socialist recipe and we get 35 educational results that are the equivalent of Soviet-built cars.

　　When those poor results are recognized, the system and its defenders can be counted on to say that the 40 problem is insufficient spending. Never mind that real spending on public education has been rising steadily for decades or that non-government schools produce better educational results with far lower per-pupil spending. The problem is always that we aren't "investing" enough in public education. In a recent National Public Radio commentary, Robert Reich (who served as Bill Clinton's secretary of labor and now teaches at Brandeis University) took ex-45 actly that approach.

　　Reich argues that while public school systems in affluent areas are turning out students who are college or work-ready because they have learned "to identify and solve new problems, recognize patterns, and think critically," schools in poorer areas aren't able to do that. The reason, of course, is money. Poorer school districts can't afford to hire really well-trained 50 teachers and have small classes, Reich says. Therefore, we have to do something to equalize spending so that all students will have an equal shot at a good education.

　　Before we get to Reich's solution, let's stop and ask whether a shortage of money is really the problem. In many states, public schools in poorer areas receive state assistance that boosts their spending to levels that rival that of the most prosperous areas. In Michigan, for example, 55 per-pupil spending in Detroit in 2002 was $9,532, compared to the state average of $7,733. "Poor" Detroit was not far behind ritzy neighboring Birmingham, where per-pupil spending was $11,456. True, there is some 60 difference, but it's not Appalachia versus Beverly Hills. Furthermore, we have already experimented with huge increases in educational spending in poor areas. In

> **equalize** /ˈiːkwəlaɪz/ *v.* to make things equal in size, quantity, value, etc. in the whole of a place or group
> **assistance** /əˈsɪstəns/ *n.* (formal) help or support
> **boost** /buːst/ *v.* to make sth. increase, or became better or successful
> **prosperous** /ˈprɒspərəs/ *adj.* rich and successful
> **ritzy** /ˈrɪtsi/ *adj.* expensive and fashionable
> **furthermore** /ˌfɜːðəˈmɔː/ *adv.* in addition to what has just been stated. Furthermore is used especially to add a point to an argument

Kansas City, because of an edict from a federal judge in 1985, spending was vastly increased to build state-of-the-art schools that have been called Taj Mahals. After nearly 20 years of that policy, however, student test scores were as low as ever. High per-pupil spending is not a sufficient condition for good educational results.

Nor is it a necessary condition. We know that because there are many nongovernmental schools in poor urban areas that produce remarkably skilled graduates, despite the fact that they operate on shoestring budgets. Often, those schools use makeshift buildings, hire uncertified teachers, and have relatively large classes (something that is common in Japan, where high teacher quality is regarded as far more beneficial than low class size). There is a great deal of information on the success of non-government urban schools; one good source is Sol Stern's book Breaking Free. It is therefore true that high spending is not a necessary condition for educational success.

The problems that beset public education are deep and inherent, rooted in the very nature of any enterprise that obtains its revenue not from willing payers, but from taxes. Throwing more money at public education can not solve the problems.

Still, Professor Reich wants to throw more money into public education. He wants to do away with local property taxes to fund public education and institute a national wealth tax instead, which he recommends setting at "one tenth of one percent of everyone's total assets each year, to be distributed to school districts around the country on the basis of the number of kids they have to educate." Reich contends that his national wealth tax would be "simple and fair," a means of giving "every school a fighting chance."

How could there be any objections to that?

First it wouldn't be simple. We would need a new federal agency to determine the value of everyone's assets. The Internal Revenue Code goes on for thousands of pages in the attempt to define "income" and the effort to place a value on everyone's wealth would be hardly less difficult. A new federal bureaucracy demands reports on the value of everything from houses to stamp collections, golf clubs to fishing boats. Maybe Reich isn't bothered by that prospect, but I

---

edict /ˈiːdɪkt/ *n.* an official order or statement given by sb. in authority
federal /ˈfedərəl/ *adj.* (within the federal system, especially the US) connected with national government rather than the local government of an individual state
shoestring /ˈʃuːstrɪŋ/ *adj.* that uses very little money
beset /bɪˈset/ *v.* to affect sb./sth. in an unpleasant or harmful way
inherent /ɪnˈhɪərənt/ *adj.* that is a basic or permanent part of sth. and that cannot be removed
enterprise /ˈentəpraɪz/ *n.* a company or business
revenue /ˈrevmjuː/ *n.* (also revenues) the money that a government receives from taxes or that an organization, etc. receives from its business
distribute /dɪˈstrɪbjuːt/ *v.* ~ sth. (to/among sb./sth.) to give things to a large number of people; to share sth. between a number of people
contend /kənˈtend/ *v.* to say that sth. is true, especially in an argument
agency /ˈeɪdʒənsi/ *n.* (especially AmE) a government department that provides a particular service
asset /ˈæset/ *n.* [usually pl.] a thing of value, especially property, that a person or company owns, which can be used or sold to pay debts

find it most unappealing.

Second, it wouldn't be fair. There is nothing fair about confiscating any amount of wealth from people who don't want to support schools in Detroit, New York, Washington, D.C., or even their hometown. People are entitled to do what they want with their own income or wealth. Professor Reich is free to give as much money as he wants to help poor schools from his own pocket, and he's free to implore us to do likewise, but he has no moral right to compel the rest of us to do the same.

Third, it would never stop. Reich may think that his initial .001 wealth tax would be enough money, but as sure as the sun will rise tomorrow, it wouldn't be. The education establishment's appetite for money is unending, and once the camel had its nose inside the wealth-tax tent, it would continue pushing in. Just as the income tax started out small but rapidly grew, so would the wealth tax for education.

And fourth, it wouldn't do any good. The reason inner-city schools do so poorly is not that they don't have enough money to spend, but that the funds they receive are sent into a bureaucratic black hole. In New York, for example, schools remain in pathetic condition, despite an enormous budget, because of such monstrosities as the School Construction Authority. The late Peter Bauer used to point out that foreign aid did far more to prop up tyrannical regimes than to help hungry people and that is exactly what would happen with increased government spending on public education. Dumping more money into public education would fatten the wallets of those who feed at the public education trough, but it wouldn't lead to better student learning.

Poor people can buy high-quality food, clothing, and other necessities because they get the benefit of a free market in those things. For good education, what they need is a free market in schools. If you really care about the education of children—and not just poor ones—you should forget about new taxes or "reforms" and advocate the separation of school and state.

---

unappealing /ˌʌnəˈpiːlɪŋ/ *adj.* not attractive or pleasant

confiscate /ˈkɒnfɪskeɪt/ *v.* to officially take sth. away from sb., especially as a punishment

entitle /ɪnˈtaɪtl/ *v.* [often passive] ~ sb. to do sth.; to give sb. the right to have or to do sth.

implore /ɪmˈplɔː/ *v.* to ask sb. to do sth. in an anxious way because you want or need it very much

appetite /ˈæpɪtaɪt/ *n.* (~ for sth.) a strong desire for sth.

bureaucratic /ˌbjʊərəˈkrætɪk/ *adj.* (often disapproving) connected with a bureaucracy or bureaucrats and involving complicated official rules which may seem unnecessary

pathetic /pəˈθetɪk/ *adj.* making you feel pity or sadness

monstrosity /mɒnˈstrɒsɪti/ *n.* something that is very large and very ugly, especially a building

prop /prɒp/ *v.* (often disapproving) to help sth. that is having difficulties

tyrannical /tɪˈrænɪkəl/ *adj.* using power or authority over people in an unfair and cruel way

regime /reɪˈʒiːm/ *n.* a method or system of government, especially one that has not been elected in a fair way

fatten /ˈfætn/ *v.* to make sb./sth. fatter, especially an animal before killing it for food; to become fatter

trough /trɒf/ *n.* a long narrow open container for animals to eat or drink from

advocate /ˈædvəkɪt/ *v.* to support sth. publicly

Better Know More

1. George C. Leef

Dr. George C. Leef—born in Feb. 4, 1951 in Milwaukee, Wisconsin. B.A. from Carroll College, Waukesha, Wisconsin in 1973. J.D. from Duke University Law School in 1977. He worked for Milliken & Co. 1977—1979 and taught economics, law, logic and philosophy at Northwood University 1980—1989 with rank of assistant professor.

2. Public education

Public education is schooling provided by the government, and paid for by taxes. It emerged in the early 19th century as a tool of industrialisation and still uses mass production techniques to achieve its ends. Proponents of public education assert it to be necessary because of the need in modern society for people who are capable of reading, writing, and doing basic mathematics. However, some libertarians argue that education is best left to the private sector; in addition, advocates of alternative forms of education such as unschooling argue that these same skills can be achieved without subjecting children to state-run compulsory schooling. In most industrialized countries, these views are distinctly in the minority.

3. Robert B. Reich

Robert B. Reich is Professor of Public Policy at the Goldman School of Public Policy at the University of California at Berkeley. He has served in three national administrations, most recently as secretary of labor under President Bill Clinton. He has written ten books, the best-sellers of which are *The Future of Success* and *Locked in the Cabinet*, and his most recent book, *Reason*.

Check Your Understanding

Answer the following questions based on the text you have just learned.

1. According to the description of the first paragraph, what can we conclude?
2. What, according to text A, do teachers in public school lack?
3. Compared with public schools, what are advantageous factors to private schools?
4. Is "money problem" the key factor that determines the quality of education? Why?
5. According to the author, what is the final solution to the problems of public education?
6. In Text A, metaphor is employed. Could you find them out?
7. In order to improve the quality of education, what measures should be taken?

A Sip of Word Formation

Prefixes of Degree or Size

Arch-, super-, out-, sur-, sub-, over-, under-, hyper-, ultra-, mini- are prefixes of degree or size.

1. **Arch-**   it is usually added to nouns, which means most important, most extreme or main.
   For example: *arch*-enemy   *arch*-fascist
2. **Super-**   it can attach to the noun, adjective, verb and adverb. When it forms the noun, adjective and adverb, it means extremely; more or better than normal.
   For example: He is a *superman*.
         He is a *superrich* man.
   Sometimes, when it forms the noun and verb, it can be explained as "above; over."
   For example: The economic foundation of one country determines its *superstructure*.
         He was appointed to *superintend* the toy department.
3. **Out-**   it can be added to verb, noun and adjective. When attached to verb, it means "greater, better, further, longer, etc."
   For example: Two prisoners *outwitted* their guards and got away.
   When attached to nouns and adjectives, it means "outside; away from."
   For example: She's very *outgoing*.
         Person with the infectious disease are often treated as social *outcasts*.
4. **Over-**   it forms noun, verb, adjective and adverb, it means (1) more than usual; too much; (2) completely; (3) upper; outer; extra; (4) over; above.
   For example: *overcurious*   *overeat*   *overcrowding*
5. **Under-**   it can be added to nouns, verbs, and adjectives, which has three kinds of meaning. (1) being under or below the thing mentioned. For example: undercover; underneath; (2) below another rank or status. For example: undersecretary; (3) something done to an insufficient amount or degree. For example: *underfed*
   Sometimes can also be added to participles such as *underspending* and *underexercised*.
6. **Hyper-**   it comes from the Greek prefix huper-, which comes from the preposition huper-, with the meaning of "over, beyond." The basic meaning of the prefix hyper- is "excessive or excessively."
   For example: *hyperactive* means "highly or excessively active."
7. **Ultra-**   it can be added to adjective and noun, with the meaning of "extremely; beyond a particular limit." For example: *ultraconservative*
8. **Mini-**   it can be attached to nouns, meaning " small."
   For example: *miniskirt*: the skirt is very short. *Miniature* means a very small version of sth.

9. **Sub-**   The prefix *sub-* can be traced back to the Latin preposition *sub*, meaning "under." Some words beginning with *sub-* that came into English from Latin include *submerge*, *suburb*, and *subvert*.

Sub- can form compounds by combining with verbs as well as with adjectives and nouns. When *sub-* is used to form words in English, it can mean

1) "under"

   For example: *submarine, subsoil*

2) "subordinate"

   For example: *subcommittee, subplot*

3) "less than completely"

   For example: *subhuman, substandard*

10. **Sur-**   The prefix sur- means "over; above" or "around."

   For example: *surround, surpass, surrealism*

📖 Build Your Vocabulary

A. The word at the end of each of the following sentences can be used to form a word that fits suitably in the blank space. Fill in each blank this way.

Example: He said "Good morning" in a most *friendly* way. (friend)

1. Such a _____ assertion is sure to provoke criticism. (question)
2. Any of _____ small bodies thought to have orbited the sun during the formation of the planets. (numerable)
3. It is _____ that he didn't pass the exam. (disappoint)
4. She is an _____ person but her husband is a real nothing. (interest)
5. The soldiers were seen _____ in the hall. (assemble)
6. I shall be _____ to meet you here. (delight)
7. She endowed with a _____ voice. (please)
8. I am only too _____ to do business with you. (please)
9. Snobs are usually _____ of people they feel to be beneath them. (contempt)
10. She is a _____ teacher, for she is very kind and knowledgeable. (respect)

B. Add a prefix to each word to make it match the meaning given. Write the new word you have made.

1. bishop	_____	a bishop of the highest rank, responsible for all the church in large area
2. class	_____	a class that is very poor and has no status
3. bid	_____	to make a lower BID than sb. else

4. balance	_____	to lose your balance and fall	
5. human	_____	having much great power, knowledge	
6. grass	_____	a criminal who informs the police about the activities of a large number of other criminals, usually in order to get a less severe punishment	
7. cover	_____	conducted with or marked by hidden aims or methods	
8. critical	_____	inclined to judge too severely	
9. sound	_____	very high frequency sound; used in ultrasonography	
10. computer	_____	a digital computer of medium size	
11. tax	_____	tax excessively	
12. pure	_____	extremely pure	

You'd Like to Be

A Skilled Text Weaver

A. Fill in the blanks with the words and phrases (change the forms where necessary).

impede	graduate	afford	shortage	recommend
compel	dump	pathetic	prop up	happen to

1. You can ill _____ to criticize others when you behave so badly yourself.
2. The development of the project was seriously _____ by a reduction in funds.
3. These trees _____ a pleasant shade.
4. The lack of rain aggravated the already serious _____ of food.
5. The college _____ 50 students from the science department last year.
6. She dances well, but as a singer, she is _____.
7. I'm not the person to _____ how the job should be done.
8. Sealed containers of nuclear waste have been _____ in the sea.
9. I was _____ to acknowledge the force of his argument.
10. It is not the government's policy to _____ declining industries.
11. It's ok that can _____ the best of us.
12. There is no _____ reason to believe him.

B. Match the words with the corresponding meanings.

1. questionable   a) the quality of doing sth. well with no waste of time and money

2. sensitivity
3. obligatory
4. innumerable
5. efficiency
6. identify
7. rival
8. makeshift
9. inherent
10. institute
11. prospect
12. appetite
13. late
14. necessity
15. beneficial
16. overarching

b) an idea of what might or will happen in the future
c) a strong desire for sth.
d) to introduce a system, policy, etc., or start a process
e) used temporarily for a particular purpose because the real thing is not available
f) that you have doubts about because you think it is not accurate or correct
g) that you must do because of law, rules, etc.
h) no longer alive
i) a thing that you must have and can't manage without
j) improving a situation; having a helpful or useful effect
k) that is a basic or permanent part of sb./sth. and that can't be removed
l) to be as good, impressive etc. as sb./sth. else
m) to many to be counted; very many
n) the ability to experience and understand deep feelings, esp. in art and literature
o) very important because it includes or influences many things
p) to recognize sth./sb. and be able to say who and what they are

A Sharp Interpreter

Paraphrase the following sentences. Change the sentence structure if necessary.

1. While some students graduate from public schools with sharp intellectual skills (often owing more to their home environment than to their school instruction), many others drift aimlessly through 12 years of classes where little is expected of them, academic standards have sunk out of sight, and discipline is a joke.
2. School administrators seldom have the freedom to hire teachers who haven't been through the school swamp, no matter how much more competent uncertified people who happen to really know their math, chemistry, history, English, etc., may be.
3. Therefore, we have to do something to equalize spending so that all students will have an equal shot at a good education.
4. The problems that beset public education are deep and inherent, rooted in the very nature of any enterprise that obtains its revenue not from willing payers, but from taxes.
5. Reich contends that his national wealth tax would be "simple and fair," a means of giving "every school a fighting chance."
6. The reason inner-city schools do so poorly is not that they don't have enough money to spend, but that the funds they receive are sent into a bureaucratic black hole.

7. Dumping more money into public education would fatten the wallets of those who feed at the public education trough, but it wouldn't lead to better student learning.

A Solid Sentence Constructor

Fill in the blanks with the appropriate form of structures listed below.

> not...but...   not that...but that...   more...than...   rather than   while

1. The present crisis is much _____ an economic _____ a political crisis.
2. It is _____ the government _____ the enterprise that should be to blame.
3. The reason why he falls behind is _____ he is slow-witted, _____ he always wanders away when studying.
4. _____ have the radio repaired, he'd like to buy a new one.
5. Jim is _____ daring _____ quick-witted.
6. We should help him _____ he should help us.
7. In delivering his lecture, Jason makes sure not to include _____ things _____ the students can understand.
8. He is _____ good at maths, _____ he is good at English.
9. _____ I want to go aboard to study, I do not have much money available.
10. _____ risk breaking up his marriage he told his wife everything.

A Careful Writer

Study the following synonyms and complete the sentences.

> incentive   motive   impulse

1. All spontaneous animal motion is performed by mechanical _____.
2. There were still other things in her head which she felt a strong _____ instantly checked, to say to pansy about her father.
3. The police have excluded robbery as a _____ for the murder.
4. A patent is a governmental grant of an exclusive monopoly as an _____ and a reward for a new invention.
5. By _____, I mean the whole of that which moves, excites, or invites the mind to volition, whether that be one thing singly, or many things conjunctively.

> obligatory   compulsory

1. As long as the law is _____ , so long our obedience is due.
2. This contribution threatening to fall infinitely short of their hopes, they soon made it _____ _____.
3. It is _____ upon us to protect the world from nuclear war.
4. Prior to the shipment of the said products at the port of departure should be in accordance with the _____ requirements of the technical norms of the state.

> competent   capable   qualified

1. I admit that Li Hua is not so _____. But she is the salt of the earth.
2. He's a _____ novelist, but none of his novels is good enough to set the world on fire.
3. For your safety, being aware this water heater is _____ of producing hot water at a temperature sufficient enough to cause scalding injury.
4. But when peace came, he proved to be even more _____ as a lawgiver and administrator than as a soldier.
5. For this reason, she was regarded as a _____ person to link up Chinese and Western dance culture.
6. The _____ authorities shall also have authority to give the importer an equivalent opportunity to have any such goods inspected.

A Superb Bilingualist

Translate the following sentences into English.

1. 由于她的努力，我们获得了比预期更大的成功。(thanks to)
2. 与其说她买的这件便宜不如说它漂亮。(rather than)
3. 按一般人在这些问题上的看法，选民常常着眼于国内问题来选择候选人。(on the basis of)
4. 早年对军用火箭进行的实验为发展航天技术奠定了基础。(experiment with)
5. 政府废除了学校免费提供膳食的做法。(do away with)
6. 在吉姆担任公司总裁期间，无论何时，任何人都不允许同他顶嘴。(on no account)
7. 没有什么比独立自由更宝贵的了。(more... than)
8. 我不缅怀过去的历史，而致力于未来的梦想。(better than)
9. 光勤劳是不够的，蚂蚁也是勤劳的。要看你为什么而勤劳。(so)
10. 列宁恢复了马克思和恩格斯关于国家的看法。(in regard to)

Text B

Are Single-Sex Classrooms Legal?

By Elizabeth Green
(Abridged and Edited)

Two years ago, after reading a book called *Why Gender Matters*, Jo Lynne DeMary, who was then superintendent of Virginia public schools, became convinced
5 that separating boys and girls into single-sex classrooms and schools could help both genders learn better. So she started developing a plan to help Virginia schools split up the groups, even recruiting an expert
10 who could do training and making an instructional video. Then, in a phone call, Leonard Sax— the book's author—told her that her plan might violate federal rules.

At the time, rule books suggested that Title IX, the 1972 law against sex discrimination in education, effectively prohibited single-sex classrooms except in a few special cases. Upon learning this, DeMary canceled the whole project. "Right there, just in the state of Virginia, we
15 could have had hundreds of schools doing this," says Sax, an advocate of single-sex classrooms.

But on October 24, the Department of Education announced new Title IX regulations based on the guidelines of a *No Child Left Be-*
20 *hind* amendment. Old regulations allowed for same-gender classes only in rare cases like physical education and human sexuality classes. But lawmakers in 2001 wanted to make those rules more flexible, and so the new ones
25 expand that option to any class or school that can prove gender separation leads to improved student achievement. The change could lead to a wave of single-sex classrooms and even schools in public systems across the country.
30 But it will also likely lead to legal challenges.

---

superintendent /ˌsuːpərɪnˈtendənt/ *n.* a person who has a lot of authority and manages and controls an activity, a place, a group of workers, etc.
violate /ˈvaɪəleɪt/ *v.* to go against or refuse to obey a law, an agreement etc.
discrimination /dɪsˌkrɪmɪˈneɪʃən/ *n.* the practice of treating sb. or a particular group in society less fairly than others
advocate /ˈædvəkɪt/ *n.* a person who supports or s speaks in favor of sb. or of a public plan or action
guideline /ˈgaɪdlaɪn/ *n.* rules or instructions that are given by an official organization telling you how to do sth., especially sth. difficult
amendment /əˈmendmənt/ *n.* a small change or improvement that is made to law or document; the process of changing law and a document
gender /ˈdʒendə/ *n.* the fact of being male or female

While advocates such as Sax see the new regulations as a welcome and long-overdue change, opponents like Marcia Greenberger, co-president of the National Women's Law Center, call it "an invitation to discriminate." The new regulations, they say, actually violate the original Title IX law. Therefore, schools that separate boys and girls will do so "at their peril," says Jocelyn Samuels, NWLC's vice president for education and employment. Potential legal battles will focus on how Title IX should be interpreted, but at the heart of the debate is one question: How would we rather our children learn, apart or together?

In the past 10 years, more public schools have been answering "apart." One of the first of the new groups to promote gender separation was the Young Women's Leadership School, founded in 1996 by Ann Rubenstein Tisch, then a journalist at NBC. "Single-sex schools existed for affluent girls and parochial girls and Yeshiva girls," Tisch says, "but not for inner-city girls." So in 1996, with the blessing of then-Mayor Rudolph Giuliani and a team of lawyers who assured her a single-sex school would not violate Title IX, she went to East Harlem and opened a public school for girls. The results, Tisch says, have been stunning: In its six graduating classes, the Harlem school has produced a 100 percent graduation rate, a 100 percent rate of enrollment in four-year colleges, and an 82 percent retention rate once the girls enter college.

Even in 2001, the Harlem program had already impressed Hilary Rodham Clinton, who talked about the school on the floor of the Senate. "We could use more schools such as this," Clinton declared, joining Sen. Kay Bailey Hutchison in proposing an amendment to the No Child Left Behind education reform act that would make this possible. That amendment is responsible for last week's changes.

The increased flexibility of these revised Title IX regulations ordered in No Child Left Behind did not become official federal policy until last week, but the original NCLB laws already had initiated some changes anyway. As of this past September, 241 public schools were offering single-sex classes, and 51 of them were fully sex-segregated, according to the National Association for Single Sex Public Education, which Sax runs.

Some of these attempts have come under fire. This August, a school district in Louisiana dropped plans to offer single-sex classes in two junior high schools after the American Civil Liberties Union brought a case against it. Years before, the ACLU's New York affiliate group joined with the National Organization for Women to file a Title IX complaint against Tisch's Harlem school, but the Department of Education "never issued a ruling one way or another," says Emily Martin, deputy director

---

promote /prəˈməʊt/ *v.* to help sth. to happen or develop

affluent /ˈæfluənt/ *adj.* having a lot of money and a good standard of living

parochial /pəˈrəʊkiəl/ *adj.* [usually before noun] (formal) connected with a church parish

retention /rɪˈtenʃən/ *n.* the action of keeping sth. rather than losing it or stopping it

flexibility /ˌfleksəˈbɪlɪti/ *n.* ability to change to suit new conditions or situation

affiliate /əˈfɪlieɪt/ *n.* a company, an organization, etc. that is connected with or controlled by another one

of the ACLU Women's Rights Project.

Both NOW and the ACLU are members of the National Coalition for Women and Girls on Education, whose members have been circulating E-mails about how to respond to the new regulations. "There are actually more differences within the sexes than there are between them," says Lisa Maatz, director of public policy and government relations at the American Association of University Women, another coalition member.

Separation may not only be unnecessary, they say, but it could have adverse effects such as increasing gender inequality over the long term or perpetuating stereotypes. A culture of equality, NOW President Kim Gandy says, requires that males and females learn to work together early on. "How can you expect a boy who's never been beaten by a girl on an Algebra test to think that it's OK for a girl to be his boss?" she asks. "Our experience has been, when it comes to separating girls and boys and men and women, separation has not been equal. At every turn, women and girls are the ones who are shortchanged."

A review by the Department of Education concluded research is too limited to be definitive in favor of either argument. But advocates of the gender separation options say the anecdotal evidence already is compelling enough. DeMary of Virginia, who retired from the Virginia schools last December and now directs the Center for School Improvement at Virginia Commonwealth University, describes a young girl—only middle school classroom in Virginia who spoke to the state Department of Education. "She said, 'I don't have to worry about the boys... I can focus on the content.'"

Single-sex education is not a "silver bullet," DeMary says, but if it could help, why remove it from the tool kit of educational options? After all, she says, with state testing laws and federal No Child Left Behind policy, "we have enough accountability on student achievement that if it's not working—we're not going to keep doing it."

> coalition /ˌkəʊəˈlɪʃən/ n. a group formed by people from several different groups, especially political ones, agreeing to work together for a particular purpose
> adverse /ˈædvɜːs/ adj. negative and unpleasant; not likely to produce a good result
> perpetuate /pəˈpetʃueɪt/ v. to make sth. such as a bad situation, a belief continue for a long time
> stereotype /ˈstɪəriəʊtaɪp/ n. a fixed idea or image that many people have a particular person or thing, but which is not true in reality
> anecdotal /ˌænɪkˈdəʊtl/ adj. based on anecdotes or possibly not true or accurate
> Algebra /ˈældʒɪbrə/ n. a type of mathematics in which letters and symbols are used to represent quantities
> compelling /kəmˈpelɪŋ/ adj. that makes you think it is true
> kit /kɪt/ n. a set of tools or equipment that you use for a particular purpose

Notes

1. Title IX

Title IX was the first comprehensive federal law to prohibit sex discrimination against students and employees of educational institutions. Title IX benefits both males and females, and is at the heart of efforts to create gender equitable schools. The law requires educational institutions to maintain policies, practices and programs that do not discriminate against anyone based on sex.

2. No Child Left Behind Amendment

Flanked by jubilant members of Congress and standing in front of a cheering crowd, President George W. Bush declared the start of a "new era" in American public education with the signing of the No Child Left Behind Act. The new law represented a sweeping reauthorization of the Elementary and Secondary Education Act, which was originally enacted in 1965 as part of Lyndon Johnson's War on Poverty—and has since been reauthorized every four to six years, usually under a catchy new banner. Its signature program, Title I, funnels nearly $12 billion annually to schools to support the education of disadvantaged children. "As of this hour," said the president, "America's schools will be on a new path of reform, and a new path of results."

3. NWLC: National Women's Law Center

The National Women's Law Center was founded in 1972 as a non-profit advocacy organization working to advance the progress of women, girls, and families with emphasis on employment, education, reproductive rights and health, and family issues.

4. ACLU

The American Civil Liberties Union is a major American non-profit organization with headquarters in New York City, whose stated mission is "to defend and preserve the individual rights and liberties guaranteed to every person in this country by the Constitution and laws of the United States". It works through litigation, legislation, and community education. According to its annual report, the ACLU had over 500,000 members at the end of 2005.

5. Hilary Rodham Clinton

Hillary Diane Rodham, born on October 26, 1947 is the junior United States Senator from New York, serving her freshman term since January 3, 2001. She is married to Bill Clinton, the 42nd President of the United States, and was First Lady of the United States during his two terms from 1993 to 2001. Before that, she was a lawyer and the First Lady of Arkansas.

6. Kim Gandy

Kim Gandy (b. 1954) is an American feminist, and currently the President of the National Organization for Women (NOW). Gandy was born in Louisiana in 1954, and graduated from Louisiana Tech University with a Bachelor's of Science in mathematics.

Comprehension Questions

Decide which of the following Statements are True (T) or False (F) according to Text B.

1. (　) According to Text B, it is better to separate boys and girls into a single-sex classroom.
2. (　) DeMary canceled his project because it disobeyed the Law.
3. (　) As for single-sex education, co-president of NWLC can't agree more.
4. (　) YWLS is one of the first groups to advocate gender separation.
5. (　) Hilary Rodham Clinton claimed that single-sex education is a feasible form.
6. (　) NOW and ACLU disapprove of gender education for they think it increases sexual inequality.
7. (　) The Organizations (NOW and ACLU) adopt such an opinion that relation between sexes is more important.
8. (　) From Text B, we can infer that the Department of Education's attitude towards single-sex education is neutral.

Writing Practice

Nowadays, all countries in the world place their premium on education, for it plays a key role in boosting the competitiveness of countries in such environment with never-ending changes and improvement. Nowadays, coupled with the development of Skill Intensive Industry, talents become more and more important, to a certain extent, as a determinative factor. Therefore, in order to bring up specialists, every country makes their every effort to... perfect their educational system such as: to enact new laws; to implement education reform and so on. As a student, can you give your own viewpoints on education reform, and list some feasible measures and expound them in details?

Further Study

Review what we have learned in Text A and Text B, and then on the basis of your stored knowledge, go to further study:
1. Why so many questions underlie the educational system; why public education is on the ebb?
2. Search the following websites to understand general conditions of edcation around the world.
   http://www.fff.org/freedom/fdo606e.asp (Public School Have Flunked Out)
   http://www.fff.org./comment/com0309m.asp (To Homeschool or Not to Homeschool: How Both Sides Got it Wrong)
   http://www.fff.org/freedom/fd0601b.asp (Who Made the State the State Ultimate Parent?)
   http://www.fff.org/freedom/fd0412d.asp (The Great Voucher Fraud)

Unit 5

Social Issues

Unit Goals

After completing the lessons in this unit, students will be able to:
- learn about problems that teen pregnancy brings to the teens themselves and society;
- develop abilities to solve problems on their own;
- extend vocabulary by practicing prefixes of attitude.

Before Reading

Hands-on Activities

Search the library or surf the internet, and find materials about problems that children come across when growing, such as video games, puppy love, alcoholism, stealing and psychological problems and analyze how they become a problem child.

Brainstorming

Brainstorm the following questions. Work in pairs or groups to disuss these questions.

1. Who do you think should take the major responsibility for teen pregnancy problem, why?
2. Do you think abortion should be legal or illegal? Why?
3. Do you have prejudice against the college students who ever had an abortion? If not, why?

A Glimpse at Words and Expressions

Please read the following sentences. Pay attention to the underlined part in each sentence and see how these expressions are used in the context, and then write down their meanings in the blanks provided.

1. The children born to teens <u>bear the brunt of</u> their mother's young age. (   )
2. Several important trends <u>underlie</u> the problem of teen pregnancy, setting the context within which prevention programs must operate. (   )
3. There is also <u>considerable</u> cost to the taxpayers and society generally. (   )
4. Teen pregnancy is not <u>a random event</u>; it is linked to a known set of factors that increase its likelihood. (   )
5. The average age of sexual maturity for males and females has decreased while the average age of marriage has <u>substantially</u> increased, creating a larger window between when teens become physically mature and fertile and when they marry. (   )
6. ... and are more likely either to want to have a child or to <u>feel ambivalent about</u> having a child during adolescence. (   )
7. <u>Out-of-wedlock</u> childbearing (as opposed to divorce) is currently the driving force behind the growth in the number of single parents, and half of first out-of-wedlock births are to teens. (   )
8. Children with adolescent parents often <u>fall victim to</u> abuse and neglect. (   )
9. <u>Simply put</u>, if more children in this country were born to parents who are ready and able to care for them, we would see a significant reduction in a host of social problems afflicting children in the United States, from school failure and crime to child abuse and neglect. (   )
10. Continuing to reduce teen pregnancy will <u>sustain</u> the recent decreases in welfare dependency and poverty, especially persistent child poverty. (   )

Text A

The Scope of the Teen Pregnancy Problem

By Douglas Kirby

High rates of teen pregnancy burden us all: teenagers, their children, and society at large. When adolescent girls give birth, their future prospects decline. Compared to young women who delay their first birth until ages 20 or older, teen mothers complete less school, are more likely to have large families, and are more likely to be single parents. The children born to teens bear the brunt of their mother's young age: when compared to children born to women aged 20 and older, babies born to mothers aged 15-17 have less supportive and stimulating home environments, poorer health, lower cognitive development, worse educational outcomes, higher rates of behavior problems, and higher rates of teen childbearing themselves. There is also considerable cost to the taxpayers and society more generally. After adjusting for other factors related to teen parenthood, the estimated annual cost to taxpayers of births to young women aged 15-17 years is at least $6.9 billion in lost tax revenues and increased spending on public assistance, health care for the children, foster care, and the criminal justice system.

Several important trends underlie the problem of teen pregnancy, setting the context within which prevention programs must operate. The average age of sexual maturity for males and females has decreased while the average age of marriage has substantially increased, creating a larger window between when teens become physically mature and fertile and when they marry. Consequently, over time, an increasing percentage of teens have initiated sex by any given age, have sex more frequently prior to marriage, and have sex with a greater number of partners prior to marriage. For example, in 1995, 66 percent of high school students reported having sex prior to graduation. Contraceptive use among sexually experienced youths has

---

pregnancy /'pregnənsi/ *n.* the state of being pregnant

adolescent /ˌædə'lesənt/ *adj.* of a young person who is developing from a child into an adult

decline /dɪ'klaɪn/ *v.* to become smaller, fewer, weaker, etc.

brunt /brʌnt/ *n.* blow, attack

cognitive /'kɒgnɪtɪv/ *adj.* [usually before noun] connected with mental processes of understanding

estimated /'estɪmɪtɪd/ *adj.* of forming an idea of the cost, size, value, etc. of sth., but without calculating it exactly

revenue /'revnjuː/ *n.* (also revenues [pl.]) the money that a government receives from taxes or that an organization, etc. receives from its business

foster /'fɒstə/ *adj.* used with some nouns in connection with the fostering of a child

underlie /ˌʌndə'laɪ/ *v.* [no passive] (formal) to be the basis or cause of sth.

substantially /səb'stænʃəlɪ/ *adv.* very much; a lot

fertile /'fɜːtaɪl/ *adj.* (of people, animals or plants) that can produce babies, young animals, fruit or new plants

contraceptive /ˌkɒntrə'septɪv/ *adj.* capable of preventing conception or impregnation

improved during the last few decades, and a large majority of sexually experienced youths do use some method
35 of contraception. However, a minority of sexually experienced youths use condoms or other effective methods of contraception properly every time they have sex. As a result, about three million
40 teens (about one in four sexually experienced teens) contract a sexually transmitted disease (STD) each year, and about one million teens become pregnant.

> **contraception** /ˌkɒntrəˈsepʃən/ *n.* the practice of preventing a woman from becoming pregnant; the methods of doing this
> **condom** /ˈkɒndəm/ *n.* a thin rubber covering that a man wears over his penis during sex to stop a woman from becoming pregnant or to protect against disease
> **contract** /ˈkɒntrækt/ *v.* (written) to get an illness
> **random** /ˈrændəm/ *adj.* done, chosen, etc. without sb. thinking or deciding in advance what is going to happen
> **residential** /ˌrezɪˈdenʃəl/ *adj.* (of an area of a town) suitable for living in; consisting of houses rather than factories or offices
> **turnover** /ˈtɜːnˌəʊvə/ *n.* the total amount of goods or services sold by a company during a particular period of time

45 Teen pregnancy is not a random event; it is linked to a known set of factors that increase its likelihood. Research shows that youths at greatest risk are more likely to live in areas with high poverty rates, low levels of education, high residential turnover, and high divorce rates. Their parents are more likely to have low levels of education, to be poor, and to have experienced a divorce or separation or to never have married, and their mothers and older
50 sisters are more likely to have given birth as adolescents. In addition, their parents' childrearing practices are likely to be poorer, and these parents provide less support or supervision to their children. The youths themselves are likely to invest less effort in school, do more poorly in school, and have low expectations for their futures. Even in elementary

> **divorce** /dɪˈvɔːs/ *n.* the legal ending of a marriage
> **supervision** /ˌsuːpəˈvɪʒən/ *n.* being in charge of sb. / sth. and making sure that everything is done correctly, safely, etc.
> **invest** /ɪnˈvest/ *v.* to spend time, energy, effort, etc. on sth. that you think is good or useful
> **aggressive** /əˈɡresɪv/ *adj.* angry, and behaving in a threatening way; ready to attack
> **testosterone** /teˈstɒstərəʊn/ *n.* a hormone produced in men's testicles that causes them to develop the physical and sexual features that are characteristic of the male body
> **puberty** /ˈpjuːbəti/ *n.* the period of a person's life during which their sexual organs develop and they become capable of having children
> **permissive** /pəˈmɪsɪv/ *adj.* allowing or showing a freedom of behavior that many people do not approve of, especially in sexual matters
> **premarital** /ˌpriːˈmærɪtəl/ *adj.* happening before marriage

school, they are more aggressive and
55 less well-liked by their peers. They are more likely to use alcohol and drugs and engage in other unconventional and unhealthful behaviors. Males have higher levels of
60 testosterone, and both males and females experience puberty at earlier ages. They are more likely to experience sexual pressure. They begin dating when they are younger
65 and, if female are more likely to have a relationship with an older male. They hold more permissive attitudes toward premarital sex. If they are

having sex, they have sex with more partners, have more negative attitudes toward
70 condoms and other forms of contraception, have less confidence about getting and
using contraception correctly, and are more likely either to want to have a child or to feel

ambivalent about having a child during adolescence. Clearly, not all youths who engage in unprotected sex and become pregnant (or impregnate others) share all of these
75 characteristics, but all of these risk factors do increase the odds of unprotected sex and pregnancy.

Teen pregnancy is bad for the mother. First, future prospects for teenagers decline significantly if they have a baby. Teen mothers are less likely to
80 complete school and more likely to be single parents. There are serious health risks for adolescents who have babies. Common medical problems among adolescent mothers include poor weight gain, anemia and sexually transmitted diseases. Later in life, adolescent mothers tend to be at greater risk for obesity and
85 hypertension than women who were not teenagers when they had their first child.

Teen pregnancy is closely linked to poverty and single parenthood. A 1990 study showed that almost one-half of all teenage mothers and over three-quarters of unmarried teen mothers began receiving welfare within five years of the birth of their first child. The growth in single-parent families remains the single most important reason for increased poverty among
90 children over the last twenty years. Out-of-wedlock childbearing (as opposed to divorce) is currently the driving force behind the growth in the number of single parents, and half of first out-of-wedlock births are to teens.

Teen pregnancy is bad for the child, too. Children born to teen mothers suffer from higher rates of low birth weight and related health problems. Despite having more health
95 problems than the children of older mothers, the children of teen mothers receive less medical care and treatment. Children born to teen mothers are at higher risk of poor parenting because their
100 mothers—and often their fathers as well— are typically too young to master the demanding job of being a parent. Still growing and developing themselves, teen mothers are often unable to provide the kind
105 of environment that infants and very young children require for optimal development.

ambivalent /æmˈbɪvələnt/ adj. (written) having or showing both good and bad feelings about sb./ sth.
impregnate /ˈɪmpregneɪt/ v. (formal) to make a woman or female animal pregnant
anemia /əˈniːmiə/ n. a medical condition in which sb. has too few red cells in their blood, making them look pale and feel weak
obesity /əʊˈbɪsɪti/ n. people who is very fat, in a way that is not healthy
hypertension /ˌhaɪpəˈtenʃən/ n. (medical) blood pressure than is higher that is normal
out-of-wedlock adj. born of parents not married to each other; illegitimate
optimal /ˈɒptɪməl/ adj. the best possible; producing the best possible results

Children with adolescent parents often fall victim to abuse and neglect. Children of teenagers often suffer from poor school
110 performance. Children of teens are 50 percent more likely to repeat a grade; they perform much worse on standardized tests; and ultimately they are less likely to complete high school than if their mothers
115 had delayed childbearing.

Teen pregnancy is closely linked to a host of other critical social issues—welfare dependency and overall child well-being, out-of-wedlock births, responsible father-
120 hood, and workforce development in partic- ular. The National Campaign to Prevent Teen Pregnancy believes that preventing teen pregnancy should be viewed not only as a reproductive health issue, but as one that
125 works to improve all of these measures.

performance /pəˈfɔːməns/ n.	how well or badly you do sth.
ultimately /ˈʌltɪmətli/ adv.	in the end; finally
dependency /dɪˈpendənsi/ n.	the state of needing the help and support of sb./sth. in order to survive or to be successful
afflict /əˈflɪkt/ v.	[often passive] (formal) to affect sb./sth. in an unpleasant or harmful way
consequence /ˈkɒnsɪkwəns/ n.	[C, oftern pl.] a result of sth. that has happened
premature /ˌpreməˈtʃʊə/ adj.	happening before the normal or expected time
sustain /səsˈteɪn/ v.	to make sth. continue for some time without becoming less
persistent /pəˈsɪstənt/ adj.	continuing for a long period of time without interruption, or repeated frequently, especially in a way that is annoying and cannot be stopped
impoverished /ɪmˈpɒvərɪʃt/ adj.	very poor; without money
disadvantaged /ˌdɪsədˈvɑːntɪdʒd/ adj.	not having the things, such as education, and enough money, that people need in order to succeed in life

Simply put, if more children in this country were born to parents who are ready and able to care for them, we would see a significant reduction in a host of social problems afflicting chil- dren in the United States, from school failure and crime to child abuse and neglect.

Not only does teen childbearing have serious consequences for teen parents, their
130 children, and society; it also has important economic consequences. Helping young women avoid too-early pregnancy and childbearing—and young men avoid premature fatherhood—is easier and much more cost effective than dealing with all of the problems that occur after the babies are born.

Continuing to reduce teen pregnancy will sustain the recent decreases in welfare depen-

135 dency and poverty, especially persistent child poverty. Poverty is a cause as well as a consequence of early childbearing, and some impoverished young mothers may end up faring poorly no matter when
140 their children are born. Nevertheless, most experts agree that although disad- vantaged backgrounds account for many of the burdens that young women shoul- der, having a baby during adolescence

only makes matters worse.

Reducing teen pregnancy will enhance child well-being. The children of teen mothers bear the greatest burden of teen pregnancy and childbearing, and are at significantly increased risk for a number of economic, social, and health problems.

> enhance /ɪnˈhɑːns/ v.   to increase or further improve the good quality, value or status of sb./sth.
>
> sobering /ˈsəʊbərɪŋ/ adj.   making you feel serious and think carefully

A key conclusion that emerges from all these sobering facts is this: Preventing teen pregnancy is critical to improving not only the lives of young women and men but also the future prospects of their children. Indeed, one of the surest ways to improve overall child well-being is to reduce the proportion of children born to teen mothers.

Better Know More

1. Douglas Kirby

Douglas. Kirby is a Senior Research Scientist at ETR Associates in Scotts Valley, California. For almost 25 years, he has directed state-wide or nation-wide studies of adolescent sexual behavior, abstinence-only programs, sexuality and HIV education programs, school-based clinics, school condom-availability programs and youth development programs. He co-authored research on the *Reducing the Risk* and *Safer Choices curricula*, both of which significantly reduced unprotected sex, either by delaying sex, increasing condom use, or increasing contraceptive use. He has painted a more comprehensive and detailed picture of the risk and protective factors associated with adolescent sexual behavior, contraceptive use, and pregnancy, and has identified important common characteristics of effective sexuality education and HIV education programs. Over the years, he has also authored or co-authored more than 100 volumes, articles and chapters on adolescent sexual behavior and programs designed to change that behavior.

2. The National Campaign to Prevent Teen Pregnancy

US non-profit organization provides statistics on adolescent pregnancy, poll results and analyses of factors affecting teenage sexual behavior, sex education materials, advice on what prevention measures work, and other resources. The goal of it is to reduce the rate of teen pregnancy by one-third between 2006 and 2015.

Check Your Understanding

Choose the best answer to each of the following questions based on the text you have just learned.

1. In paragraph two, the author speaks of several important trends underlying the problem of teen pregnancy, which of the following is one of the trends?
    A. The average age of sexual maturity for males and females has decreased while the average age of marriage has substantially increased.
    B. An increasing percentage of teens have sex more frequently but with less number of partners prior to marriage.
    C. A majority of sexually experienced youths use condoms or other effective methods of contraception properly every time they have sex.
    D. Neither of the above is true.
2. Which of the following factors that increase the likelihood of teen pregnancy is **wrong** according to the text?
    A. Youths are more likely to live in areas with high poverty rates, low levels of education, high residential turnover, and high divorce rates.
    B. Their parents are more likely to have low levels of education, to be poor, and to have experienced a divorce or separation or to never have married.
    C. Their parents' childbearing practices are likely to be poorer, and these parents provide less support or supervision to their children.
    D. Their parents try to provide a supportive and stimulating home environment to them, but they are rebellious.
3. What bad results can teen pregnancy produce according to the text?
    A. It is bad for the teen mothers, who are less likely to complete school and be single parents, also they have serious health risks.
    B. It is bad for children born to teen mothers, they suffer from higher rates of low birth weight and related health problems, and also at higher risk of poor parenting.
    C. Teen pregnancy is closely linked to a host of critical social issues—welfare dependency and overall child well-being; out-of-wedlock births, responsible fatherhood, and workforce development.
    D. All of the above are included.
4. In paragraph six, still growing and developing themselves, teen mothers are often unable to provide the kind of environment that infants and very young children require for optimal development. Here "optimal" can be best explained as
    A. optional.　　　B. further.　　　C. ideal.　　　D. the best possible.

5. Which of the following statements is **wrong** according to the text?
   A. In 1995, 66 percent of high school students reported having sex prior to graduation.
   B. Youths are more likely either to want to have a child or to feel guilty about having a child during adolescence.
   C. Poverty is a cause as well as a consequence of early childbearing.
   D. Teen childbearing has not only serious consequences for teen parents, their parents, society but also important economic consequences.
6. How many ways does the author provide to improve overall child well-being?
   A. One.   B. Two.
   C. Three.   D. They aren't mentioned in the text.

A Sip of Word Formation

Prefixes of Attitude

Co-, pro-, counter-, anti- are prefixes of attitude.
1. *Co-* is usually added to nouns, verbs and adjectives with the meaning of *together with:*
   For example: co-operate, co-author
2. *Pro-* is usually added to adjectives, nouns with the meaning of *in favor of, supporting.*
   Fox example: pro-government, pro-democracy
3. *Counter-* is usually added to nouns, verbs, adjectives and adverbs with the meaning of (1) *against; opposite.* (2) *corresponding.*
   For example: counter-culture, counter-revolution
4. *Anti-* is usually added to nouns, adjectives with the meaning of (1) *opposed to; against.* (2) *the opposite of.* (3) *preventing.*
   For example: anti-hero, anti-social

Build Your Vocabulary

A. Complete each of the following sentences with proper form of the word given in brackets.

1. However, if the wrong moment was chosen, or a _____ is poorly executed, a military disaster could result for the defending side. (attack)
2. _____ Brits produce a video campaign: "A World Without America", to combat anti-Americanism in the U.K. (American)
3. To be _____ means to be opposed to the use of nuclear energy. (nuclear)

4. Li Jia is the _____ of Li Junyi, champion of Shanghai Rally this year. (driver)
5. The foreign minister held talks with his American _____. (part)
6. The _____ really is a usable down jacket for extreme cold and damp winter conditions. (freeze)
7. _____ is a subjective term applied to a person who supports the European Union (EU) and generally further 'deepening' of European. (European)
8. Last June, the Chinese People's Institute of Foreign Affairs sponsored the International Seminar on the Five Principles of Peaceful _____. (existence)
9. The United Nations Summit last week turned out to be an _____, although it gathered heads of government and state of 149 countries to its headquarters in New York. (climax)
10. The _____ movement started by a woman whose son was killed in the war. (war)
11. We are seeking for the _____ partner in the following fields to bring benefit from the scientific and technical achievements to society as early as possible. (operative)
12. The leaders of government decided to firmly suppress _____ activities. (revolutionary)

B. Study the meaning of the words given below and then complete the following sentences with the proper forms of these words.

co-author   co-produce   co-edit   pro-government   anti-social
anti-hero   anti-body   counter-culture   counter-measure
counter-terrorism/anti-terrorism

1. _____ behavior is an activity that impacts on other people in a negative way.
2. Professor Zhao has been the author or _____ of 10 books including *New Development of International Trade*.
3. As the day went on, serious street clashes developed between Christian youth connected to opposition and _____ forces, and between Shiite and Sunnis.
4. Though deeply influenced by the American _____ movement in the 1960s, the New-Human Literature has its special context and distinctive historical backgrounds.
5. HIV _____ testing is used to determine whether or not a person is infected with HIV.
6. The product takes coal or oil as the heat source, which _____ many kinds of environment pollutants such as CO and SO_2.
7. They discuss real difficulty brought by new policies and the _____, and communicate with such departments as the territory, tax, bank, etc.
8. China's armed police hold several _____ exercises in Beijing in Aug., 2003.
9. Professor Cohen tells me that he will continue to _____ the stimulating *Boston Re-*

view, which will also continue to be a Boston-based publication.
10. An _____ is the main character in a story, but one who doesn't have the qualities of a typical hero.

You'd Like to Be

A Skilled Text Weaver

Fill in the blanks in the following sentences with the words given below. Change the form where necessary.

| sobering | revenue | impoverished | cognitive | stimulating | contract |
| substantially | fertile | residential | turnover | hypertension | |

1. _____ science is the interdisciplinary study of mind and intelligence embracing philosophy, psychology, artificial intelligence, etc.
2. This year, the region is _____ by drought.
3. Researchers find that diet, exercise, _____ environment helps old dogs learn.
4. The hero's death has had a _____ effect on people in that country.
5. The exercise consists of stretching and _____ the leg muscles.
6. Advertising _____ finances the commercial television channels.
7. Allocation for various railway projects in Tamil Nadu is _____ higher for the next financial year compared to the current year.
8. A large area of desert was reformed to turn to _____ soil in the northwest region.
9. This company offers services including local _____ phone service, long distance, cellular phone plans, etc.
10. Obesity can increase the risk of _____.
11. A survey conducted by the Hong Kong Institute of Human Resource Management (HKIHRM) has found that the _____ rate for Hong Kong employees last year was 12%, with the average job vacancy rate being 2.6%.

A Sharp Interpreter

Paraphrase the following sentences. Change the sentence structure if necessary.

1. High rates of teen pregnancy burden us all: teenagers, their children, and society at large.

2. The children born to teens bear the brunt of their mother's young age.
3. Several important trends underlie the problem of teen pregnancy, setting the context within which prevention programs must operate.
4. Even in elementary school, they are more aggressive and less well-liked by their peers. They are more likely to use alcohol and drugs and engage in other unconventional and unhealthful behaviors.
5. Simply put, if more children in this country were born to parents who are ready and able to care for them, we would see a significant reduction in a host of social problems afflicting children in the United States, from school failure and crime to child abuse and neglect.
6. Nevertheless, most experts agree that although disadvantaged backgrounds account for many of the burdens that young women shoulder, having a baby during adolescence only makes matters worse.
7. A key conclusion that emerges from all these sobering facts is this: Preventing teen pregnancy is critical to improving not only the lives of young women and men but also the future prospects of their children.

A Solid Sentence Constructor

A. Fill in each of the blanks in the following sentences with a suitable preposition.

1. Here is the opinion of the public _____ large.
2. I have had some difficulties, but they are nothing compared _____ yours.
3. They made full preparations during the week prior _____ the meeting.
4. _____ addition, the survey found that air pollution was at the top of Europeans' list of environment concerns, with traffic being blamed as the number one culprit.
5. The terrorists fired the crowd _____ random.
6. She was engaged _____ protecting wild birds.
7. The child was born _____ wedlock.
8. Cigarette smoking is responsible _____ 90% of deaths from lung cancer.

B. Fill in the blanks in the following sentences with the phrases or expressions given below. Change the form where necessary.

bear the brunt of	put at risk	fall victim to	bear the burden of
account for	under supervision	simply put	end up

1. If the countries go to war, innocent lives will _____.
2. In this harsh winter, many plants _____ the sudden frost.

3. The Chinese market _____ 36% of the company's revenue.
4. The children of teen mothers _____ teen pregnancy and childbearing.
5. According to the directions, the drug should only be used _____ medical _____.
6. _____, the game is fun, and nothing more really needs to be said.
7. At first they hated each other, but they _____ getting married.
8. Their aim was to highlight the problems faced by the border residents of the country, especially the women folk who had to _____ keeping and running the household.

C. *Combine the following sentences with not only... but also.*

Model: Teen childbearing has serious consequences for teen parents, their children, and society.
It has important economic consequences.
→ Not only does teen children have serious consequences for teen parents, their children, and society; it also has important economic consequences.

1. He refused the gift. He severely criticized the sender too.
2. The garage overcharged me. They hadn't done a very good repair job either.
3. Proletarians should emancipate themselves. They should emancipate the whole mankind too.
4. Television appeals to those who can read. It appeals to those who can't read too.
5. Everything Albert Einstein had was taken away. His citizenship was deprived of too.
6. This is a handy portable phone, but it's also a calculator.

A Careful Writer

Study the following synonyms and complete the sentences. Change the form where necessary.

outcome   consequence   result

1. He has deliberately chosen to lead the life he leads and is fully aware of the _____.
2. But it would be premature to forecast the _____ of the war.
3. The book embodies the _____ of his ten years of original research.
4. The _____ of the Revolution was largely determined by American Indian women.
5. The financial _____ of the company for the last half year were very satisfactory.
6. Before taking actions, you must consider the _____.

> decrease   reduce   lessen

7. They were _____ to begging in the streets.
8. There has been a _____ in our imports this year.
9. The number of illiberal people is _____.
10. She _____ her picture so it would fit in her passport.
11. These measures can't help to _____ the existing tension.
12. The heat will _____ during the evening.

> improve   enhance   increase   advance

13. He put forward a plan for _____ the rate of production.
14. The sauce will _____ the flavor of the meat.
15. Can you _____ me two dollars on my salary?
16. I hope the weather will _____ before Friday.
17. Beautiful colored illustrations _____ the book.
18. She _____ her leisure by learning foreign languages.
19. He who does not _____ falls backwards.
20. An _____ number of people are beginning to realize that education is not complete with education.
21. They talked over at great length the matter of how to _____ the sale of your products.

A Superb Bilingualist

Translate the following sentences into English with the phrases or expressions given below. Change the form where necessary.

1. 我的决定以众多因素为基础。(underlie)
2. 有很多人要来参加这次会议。(a host of)
3. 对国家的安全和经济命脉来说,至关重要的部分是什么?(be critical to)
4. 通过英语考试会增加你获得这个职位的机会。(enhance)
5. 改革是我军现代化建设的动力和出路。(the driving force)
6. 人们对于民工的心情是复杂的。(ambivalent)
7. 有进取心的青年人在本公司能大展宏图。(aggressive)

Text B

Is Abortion Murder?

Anonymous
(Abridged and Edited)

Not all killing is murder, of course. Murder is actually a small subset of all killing, which includes accidental homicide, killing in self-defense, suicide, euthanasia, etc. When pro-life activists call abortion "murder," they are suggesting that abortion fits the definition of murder, namely, "illegal killing with malice aforethought." However, abortion fails this definition for two reasons. First, abortion is not illegal, and second, mothers hardly feel malice towards their own unborn children.

Some might object the first point is overly legalistic. Just because killing is legal doesn't make it right. Exterminating Jews in Nazi Germany was certainly legal, but few doubt that it was murder.

But why do we still consider the Holocaust murder? The answer is that we hold the Nazis to a higher law. When the Nazis were tried in Nuremberg for their war crimes, they were not accused of "crimes against Germans" or even "crimes against Jews." Instead, they were charged with "crimes against humanity." The reason is because there was no legal basis to charge them otherwise. The massacre of Jews was legal under German law. So in order to punish the German leaders for clearly wrong behavior, the Allies had to evoke a higher law, a law of humanity. The Holocaust was condemned as illegal, and therefore murder, because it violated this law.

Many pro-life advocates claim that the same reasoning applies to abortion. Although abortion is legal under current U.S.

---

subset /ˈsʌbset/ *n.* a smaller group of people or things formed from the members of larger group

homicide /ˈhɒmɪsaɪd/ *n.* the crime of killing sb. deliberately

euthanasia /ˌjuːθəˈneɪzɪə/ *n.* the practice (illegal in most countries) of killing without pain a person who is suffering from a disease that can not be cured

abortion /əˈbɔːʃən/ *n.* the deliberate ending of a pregnancy at an early stage

malice /ˈmælɪs/ *n.* a feeling of hatred for sb. that causes a desire to harm them

aforethought /əˈfɔːθɔːt/ *n.* premeditation; in the mind beforehand

legalistic /ˌliːgəˈlɪstɪk/ *adj.* (disapproving) obeying the law very strictly

exterminate /ɪksˈtɜːmɪneɪt/ *v.* to kill all the members of a group of people or animals

holocaust /ˈhɒləkɔːst/ *n.* a situation in which many things are destroyed and many people killed, especially because of a war or a fire

charge /tʃɑːdʒ/ *v.* to accuse sb. formally of a crime so that there can be a trial in a court of law

humanity /hjuːˈmænɪti/ *n.* people in general

massacre /ˈmæsəkə/ *n.* the killing of a large number of people especially in a cruel way

evoke /ɪˈvəʊk/ *v.* to bring a feeling, a memory or an image into your mind

condemn /kənˈdem/ *v.* to express very strong disapproval of sb./sth., usually for moral reasons

violate /ˈvaɪəleɪt/ *v.* (formal) to go against or refuse to obey a law, an agreement, etc.

law, it is not legal when it is held up to a higher law, namely, the law of God.

Let's assume, for argument's sake, that the Bible is indeed the law of God. Unfortunately, this doesn't help the pro-life movement, because there is no Biblical law against abortion. (Abortion is as old as childbirth.) The Hebrew word for "kill" in the commandment "Thou shalt not kill" is *rasach*, which is more accurately interpreted as "murder," or illegal killing judged harmful by the community. It is itself a relative, legalistic term!

Many forms of killing were considered legal in ancient Israel, and levitical law listed many of the exceptions. Generally, levitical law permitted killing in times of war, the commission of justice and in self-defense. Sometimes, God even gave Israel permission to kill infant children. In I Samuel 15:3, God ordered Saul to massacre the Amalekites: "Do not spare them; put to death men and women, children and infants? quot."

Unfortunately, the levitical law we find in the Bible today is incomplete, and comes to us in large gaps. That is because the ancient Jews passed down their laws orally, and only wrote down the more complicated laws to jog their memory. As a result, levitical law is filled with tremendous omissions; for example, we know little of their laws on libel, business, lending, alimony, lease, rental agreements and civil rights. But perhaps the most unfortunate gap in ancient Jewish law is abortion. If a law *did* exist on abortion, then we simply do not know what it was. Fortunately, we have an excellent idea of what the law might have been. The Jews are legendary for their fanatical preservation of the law, and they have *never* considered abortion to be a sin. That alone should make many pro-life advocates stop and reconsider

commandment /kəˈmɑːndmənt/ *n.* a law given by God, especially any of the Ten Commandments given to the Jews in the Bible

permit /pəˈmɪt/ *v.* (formal) to allow sb. to do sth. or allow sth. to happen

commission /kəˈmɪʃən/ *n.* an official group of people who have been given responsibility to control sth., or to find out about sth., usually for the government

jog /dʒɒg/ *v.* to say or do sth. that makes sb. remember sth.

tremendous /trɪˈmendəs/ *adj.* very great

libel /ˈlaɪbəl/ *n.* the act of printing a statement about sth. that is not true and that gives people a bad opinion of them; a printed statement about sb. that is not true

alimony /ˈælɪməni/ *n.* (especially AmE) the money that a court of law orders sb. to pay regularly to their former wife or husband when the marriage is ended

lease /liːs/ *n.* a legal agreement that allows you to use a building, a piece of equipment or some land for a period of time, usually in return for rent

rental /ˈrentl/ *n.* the act of renting sth. or an arrangement to rent sth.

legendary /ˈledʒəndəri/ *adj.* very famous and talked about a lot by people, especially in a way that shows admiration

fanatical /fəˈnætɪkəl/ *adj.* of a person, action, etc., characterized by or filled with excessive and mistaken enthusiasm, especially in religion

preservation /ˌprezəˈveɪʃən/ *n.* the act of making sure that sth. is kept

the legal basis, holy or otherwise, for their opposition to abortion.

Some pro-life Christians claim that just because there is no commandment prohibiting abortion does not give us the right to perform it. Since human life is so precious, we should err on the side of caution, they argue. But according to this logic, we should not drive cars! Each year in America, there are about 40,000 deaths due to automobile accidents. These deaths are accidental, to be sure, but our decision to participate in a mode of transportation that we already know will kill 40,000 people is not accidental. We also know there were virtually no deaths in horse-and-buggy days. We have decided to accept those 40,000 deaths a year simply because we value the convenience—a notion surely not found anywhere in the Bible. But should we stop all automobile travel just because of Biblical silence on the issue?

One could equally argue that if God thought the issue were important, he would have made sure to include such a law in the Bible. The omission of such a law suggests that God allows humans to exercise their best judgment in the matter.

The second part of the definition of murder involves malice. Is it really reasonable to assume that mothers feel malice towards their own unborn children? Why would they even feel that? What has the fetus done to inspire the mother's hatred, anger, hostility and revenge? This is not the way women react to news of their pregnancy, even an unwanted one, as any woman who has gone through an abortion will tell you. It is a reaction that only men in the pro-life movement find plausible.

Some abortion opponents may then try to claim that the murder is cold-blooded, that the malice involved is really a callous, unfeeling disregard for human life. But again, any woman

---

prohibit /prəˈhɪbɪt/ *v.* (formal) to stop sth. from being done or used especially by law
perform /pəˈfɔːm/ *v.* to do sth., such as a piece of work, task or duty
precious /ˈpreʃəs/ *adj.* valuable or important and not to be wasted
err /ɜː/ *v.* (old fashioned, formal) to make a mistake
participate /pɑːˈtɪsɪpeɪt/ *v.* to take part in or become involved in activity
virtually /ˈvɜːtjuəli/ *adv.* almost, or very nearly, so that any slight difference is not important
buggy /ˈbʌgi/ *n.* a light carriage for one or two people, pulled by one horse
notion /ˈnəʊʃən/ *n.* an idea, a belief or an understanding of sth.
omission /əʊˈmɪʃən/ *n.* a thing that has not been included or done

assume /əˈsjuːm/ *v.* to think or accept that sth. is true but without having proof of it
fetus /ˈfiːtəs/ *n.* a young human or animal before it is born, especially a human more than eight weeks after fertilization
inspire /ɪnˈspaɪə/ *v.* to make sb. have a particular feeling or emotion
hostility /hɒˈstɪlɪti/ *n.* unfriendly or aggressive feelings or behavior
revenge /rɪˈvendʒ/ *n.* something that you do in order to make sb. suffer because they have made you suffer
plausible /ˈplɔːzəbəl/ *adj.* (of an excuse or explanation) reasonable and likely to be true
callous /ˈkæləs/ *adj.* not caring about other people's feelings or suffering
unfeeling /ʌnˈfiːlɪŋ/ *adj.* not showing care or sympathy for other people
disregard /ˌdɪsrɪˈɡɑːd/ *n.* the act of treating sb./sth. as unimportant and not caring about them/it

who has gone through an abortion will tell you that it just isn't so. They are fully aware of what they are doing and the moral impli-
110 cations of it. All would prefer not to go through the abortion, and feel sorrow and regret for having to do so. But they ultimately decide that the abortion is for the best, that they are not ready for the even greater moral responsibility of bringing a child into the world.
115 Christian conservatives may question the wisdom of such a choice, but they can hardly question the emotions behind it.

The accusation that abortion is murder, in fact, places the burden of proof on the accuser. If women do indeed feel malice towards their own flesh and blood, then the accuser needs to supply the requisite proof, studies, or surveys to make his case. But such evidence will probably
120 never be forthcoming.

> **implication** /ˌɪmplɪˈkeɪʃən/ n. a possible effect or result of an action or a decision
> **conservative** /kənˈsɜːvətɪv/ n. a conservative person
> **requisite** /ˈrekwɪzɪt/ adj. (formal) necessary for a particular purpose
> **forthcoming** /fɔːθˈkʌmɪŋ/ adj. ready or made available when needed

Notes

1. Levitical Law

The Law of Leviticus. The book of Hebrew scripture named Leviticus contains a plethora of laws and regulations, the purpose of which is to maintain the purity of the Jewish nation. Some of these laws are concerned with ritual issues and some of them are concerned with ethical issues, while many of the laws on face value appear to be concerned with issues incomprehensible to the modern reader.

2. Commandment

10 Commandments—God's Holy Standards revealed in the Old Testament. Exodus 20.

3. Amalekites

An ancient tribe, or collection of tribes, in the south and south-east of Palestine, often mentioned in the Old Testament. Shortly after the Israelites left Egypt and were wondering the desert, the Amalekites attacked the weary nation, God punished the Amalekites by ordering Saul to destroy them (1 Sam 15:2-3).

4. Saul

He was chosen the first king of Israel after the sons, and potential successors, of the high priest Samuel were rejected by the people as corrupt (1 Samuel 8:1-9).

Comprehension Questions

Decide which of the following statements are true (T) or false (F) according to Text B.

(   ) 1. Abortion fails the definition of murder for two reasons, abortion is legal and mothers never feel malice towards their own unborn babies.
(   ) 2. The massacre of Jews was legal under German law.
(   ) 3. Many pro-life advocates think that abortion is illegal under the law of God although abortion is legal under current U. S. law.
(   ) 4. The author elaborates his first argument from only one aspect.
(   ) 5. Women ultimately decide that abortion is for the best, that they are not ready for the even greater moral responsibility of bringing a child into the world.
(   ) 6. The writer's attitude towards abortion is that of support.
(   ) 7. Throughout the passage, the writer's tone towards the abortion opponents is bitter.
(   ) 8. In the writer's opinion, the accuser needs to supply the evidence to prove that abortion is murder if they think so.

Writing Practice

Write a short passage on **Parents and Their Children's Education.**
Your composition should be based on the outline below:
a. Present situation;
b. Possible reasons;
c. My suggestions.

Further Study

1. Study the two reports and write a summary of your point of view.
   (1) The report shows that Chinese youth are physically maturing faster and showing signs of sexual development earlier. So they are looking for mates at younger ages, and at the same time, spending more money on their love affairs.
       A recent survey shows that the average expense of a couple in college is about 2000

RMB each month, while the average cost of living for the typical college student is 500 to 600 RMB. Spending money while in love is driving some young couples into debt.

—Adapted from *China Youth* online: Fall in Love Earlier at Higher Cost

(2) Last month, a Peking University student was offering 1,000 yuan ($125) to potential "girlfriends" if they would rent themselves to him for 10 days during Spring Festival to impress his parents.

—Adapted from *Women of China English Monthly*

2. Revised National Regulations for Students of Colleges and Universities no longer had specified articles prohibiting college students from getting married while in school. The policy had ever provoked a wide range of response. What's your attitude towards the college students' marriage? Have you ever learned some cases of college students' marriage?

Unit

Cyberspace

*U*nit *G*oals

After completing the lessons in this unit, students will be able to:
- ☞ understand vulnerability of the Internet and World Wide Web;
- ☞ develop the ability to make judgement on their own;
- ☞ extend vocabulary through recognition of locative prefixes.

*B*efore *R*eading

Hands-on Activities

1. Compare the security of information policies on the Web sites of several large corporations in different areas, such as retail, financial institutions, government institutions. Create a poster rating the sites in order from most to least secure.
2. Create an illustrated timeline of Internet viruses, such as Melissa, Y2k, ILOVEYOU, Panda Burning Joss Sticks and Code Red. Explain how the virus works, how it affects the Internet, and what happens to the creators of the viruses. Create a "Guide to Safe and Secure Internet Usage" for consumers. Provide information about the different types of information security offered by Web sites, tips on how to keep one's information from being vulnerable, and resources for more information or help.

Brainstorming

Brainstorm the following questions. Work in pairs or groups to discuss these questions.

1. Brainstorm technology controversies regarding security, privacy, and intellectual property on the Internet.

2. Respond to the following prompt: You are visiting an Internet shopping site. Before you are allowed to check out, a page is displayed that asks for personal information, such as age, gender, income, and marital status. A note reads: "This site is secure. Your information will not be provided to any other institutions and individuals." Do you give your information? Why or why not?

3. What is a "hacker?" Do you think the act of "hacking" is always negative, or is it possible to be an "ethical hacker?" Explain.

4. Do you often chat with people on the internet and do you believe cyber love?

5. If a familiar stranger who has been chatting with you in the chat room for quite a period of time tells you that he or she wants to meet you, what will you respond?

A Glimpse at Words and Expressions

Please read the following sentences. Pay attention to the underlined part in each sentence and see how these expressions are used in the context, and then write down their meanings in the blanks provided.

1. Furthermore, security issues are not well understood and <u>are rarely given high priority</u> by software developers, vendors, network managers, or consumers.   (   )

2. One can <u>draw parallels with</u> open system development: there are many developers and a large, reusable code base.   (   )

3. The difficulty of criminal investigation of cyber crime, <u>coupled with</u> the complexity of international law, means that successful apprehension and prosecution of computer criminals is unlikely, and thus little deterrent value is realized.   (   )

4. Because of the factors described above, organizations and individuals using the Internet <u>are vulnerable to</u> many kinds of cyber attacks.   (   )

5. There are indications that the processes for discovering vulnerable sites, compromising them, installing daemons (programs used in the attack), and concealing the intrusion are largely automated, with each step being performed in <u>"batch" mode</u> against many machines in one "session."   (   )

6. The bottom line is that an organization's systems may <u>be subject at any time to</u> distributed attacks that are extremely difficult to trace or defend against.   (   )

7. Although an organization may be able to "harden" its own systems to help prevent having its systems used as part of a distributed attack, there is essentially nothing a site can do with currently available technology to prevent becoming a victim of, for example, a coordinated network flood. (   )
8. Many network service providers are well positioned to offer security services to their clients. (   )

Text A

Vulnerability of the Internet and World Wide Web

By Richard D. Pethia
(Abridged and Edited)

Vulnerabilities associated with the Internet put government, business, and individual users at risk. Security measures that were appropriate for mainframe computers and small, well-defined networks inside an organization, are not effective for the Internet, a complex, dynamic world of interconnected networks with no clear boundaries and no central control.
5 Because the Internet was not originally designed with security in mind, it is difficult to ensure the integrity, availability, and privacy of information. The Internet was designed to be "open," with distributed control and mutual trust among users. As a result, control is in the hands of users, not in the hands of the provider; and use cannot be administered by a central authority. Furthermore, security issues are not well understood and are rarely
10 given high priority by software developers, vendors, network managers, or consumers.

In addition, because the Internet is digital, not physical, it has no geographic location and no well-defined boundaries. Traditional physical "rules" are difficult or
15 impossible to apply. Instead, new knowledge and a new point of view are required to understand the workings and the vulnerabilities of the Internet. Another factor is the approach typically taken by intruders.
20 There is (loosely) organized development in the intruder community, with only a few months elapsing between "beta" software and

> vulnerability /ˌvʌlnərəˈbɪlətɪ/ n. susceptibility to injury or attack
> administer /ədˈmɪnɪstə/ v. to manage and organize the affairs of a company, an organization, a country, etc.
> vendor /ˈvendə/ n. a person who sells things, for example food and newspapers, usually outside on the street
> intruder /ɪnˈtruːdə/ n. a person who enters a building or an area illegally
> elapse /ɪˈlæps/ v. to pass
> beta /ˈbiːtə/ n. software that has not yet been released but has received an alpha test and still has more bugs than a regular release

active use in attacks. Moreover, intruders take an open-source approach to development. One can draw parallels with open system development: there are many developers and a large, reusable code base.

Intruder tools are becoming increasingly sophisticated and also becoming increasingly user friendly and widely available. For the first time, intruders are developing techniques to harness the power of hundreds of thousands of vulnerable systems on the Internet. Using what are called distributed-system attack tools, intruders can involve a large number of sites simultaneously, focusing all of them to attack one or more victim hosts or networks. The sophisticated developers of intruder programs package their tools into user-friendly forms and make them widely available. As a result, even unsophisticated intruders can use them.

> sophisticated /sə'fɪstɪkeɪtɪd/ *adj.* clever and complicated in the way that it works or is presented
> harness /'hɑːnɪs/ *v.* to control and use the force or strength of sth. to produce power or to achieve sth.
> apprehension /ˌæprɪ'henʃən/ *n.* the act of capturing or arresting sb., usually by the police
> prosecution /ˌprɒsɪ'kjuːʃən/ *n.* the process of trying to prove in a court of law that sb. is guilty of a crime; the process of being officially charged with a crime in a court of law
> deterrent /dɪ'tɜːrənt/ *adj.* making sb. less likely to do sth.; that is meant to deter
> misconfigure /ˌmɪskən'fɪɡə/ *v.* to configure sth. incorrectly or suboptimally

The current state of Internet security is the result of many additional factors. A change in any one of these can change the level of Internet security and survivability.

Because of the dramatically lower cost of communication on the Internet, use of the Internet is replacing other forms of electronic communication. The Internet itself is growing at an amazing rate. An additional 16 million computers connected to the Internet between July 1999 and January 2000, bringing the estimated total to 72.4 million.

Internet sites have become so interconnected and intruder tools so effective that the security of any site depends, in part, on the security of all other sites on the Internet.

The difficulty of criminal investigation of cyber crime, coupled with the complexity of international law, means that successful apprehension and prosecution of computer criminals is unlikely, and thus little deterrent value is realized.

The Internet is becoming increasingly complex and dynamic, but among those connected to the Internet there is a lack of adequate knowledge about the network and about security. The rush to the Internet, coupled with a lack of understanding, is leading to the exposure of sensitive data and risk to safety-critical systems. Misconfigured or outdated operating systems, mail programs, and

Web sites result in vulnerabilities that intruders can exploit. Just one naive user with an easy-to-guess password increases an organization's risk.

Because of the factors described above, organizations and individuals using the Internet are vulnerable to many kinds of cyber attacks, including the denial of service attacks that were widely publicized. Distributed attack tools based on the client/server model have become increasingly common. In recent months, there has been an increase in the development and use of distributed network sniffers, scanners, and denial-of-service tools. Attacks using these tools can involve a large number of sites simultaneously and be focused to attack one or more victim hosts or networks.

Damaged systems include those used in the attack as well as the targeted victim. For the victim, the impact can be extensive. For example, in a denial-of-service attack using distributed technology, the attacked system observes simultaneous attacks from all the nodes at once—flooding the network normally used to communicate and trace the attacks and preventing any legitimate traffic from traversing the network.

There are indications that the processes for discovering vulnerable sites, compromising them, installing daemons (programs used in the attack), and concealing the intrusion are largely automated, with each step being performed in "batch" mode against many machines in one "session". Attack daemons have been discovered on a variety of operating systems with varying levels of security and system management.

It is critical to plan and coordinate before an attack to ensure an adequate response when an attack actually happens. Since the attack methodology is complex and there is no single-point solution or "silver bullet," resolution and restoration of systems may be time-consuming. The bottom line is that an organization's systems may be subject at any time to distributed attacks that are extremely difficult to trace or defend against. Only partial solutions are available.

Although an organization may be able to "harden" its own systems to help-prevent having its systems used as part of a

publicize /'pʌblɪsaɪz/ v. to make sth. known to the public; to advertise sth.
sniffer /'snɪfə/ n. a software or hardware that monitors all network traffic
node /nəʊd/ n. a point at which two lines or systems meet or cross
legitimate /lɪ'dʒɪtɪmɪt/ adj. allowed and acceptable according to the law
traverse /'trævɜːs/ v. to cross an area of land or water
compromise /'kɒmprəmaɪz/ v. to come to terms by mutual concession
daemon /'diːmən/ n. a creature in stories from ancient Greece that is half man and half god
batch /bætʃ/ n. a way of running a group of programs at the same time, usually automatically

distributed attack, there is essentially nothing a site can do with currently available technology to prevent becoming a victim of, for example, a coordinated network flood. The impact upon the site and its operations is dictated by the (in)security of other sites and the ability of a remote attacker to implant the tools and, subsequently, to control and direct multiple systems worldwide to launch an attack. The result may be reduced or unavailable network connectivity for extended periods of time, possibly days or even weeks depending upon the number of sites attacking and the number of possible attack networks that could be activated in parallel or sequentially.

The problem is serious and complex, and a combination of approaches must be used to reduce the risks associated with the ever-increasing dependence on the Internet and the possibility of a sustained attack on it. Effective solutions require multi-disciplinary and cross-domain cooperation that includes information sharing and joint development of comprehensive solutions, as well as support for a long-term research agenda.

> implant /ɪmˈplɑːnt/ v. to put sth. (usually sth. artificial) into a part of the body for medical purposes, usually by means of an operation
> connectivity /ˌkənekˈtɪvɪti/ n. the ability to make and maintain a connection between two or more points in a telecommunications system
> activate /ˈæktɪveɪt/ v. to make sth. such as a device or chemical process start working
> sequential /sɪˈkwɪnʃəl/ adj. following in order of time or place
> sustain /səsˈteɪn/ v. to make sth. continue for some time without becoming less
> domain /dəˈmeɪn/ n. an area of knowledge or activity; especially one that sb. is responsible for
> agenda /əˈdʒendə/ n. a list of items to be discussed at a meeting
> foreseeable /fɔːˈsiːəbəl/ adj. that you can predict will happen; that can be foreseen
> volatile /ˈvɒlətaɪl/ adj. (of a situation) likely to change suddenly; easily becoming dangerous
> survivability /səˌvaɪvəˈbɪlɪti/ n. the capability of a system to fulfill its mission in a timely manner, even in the presence of attacks or failures

The nature of threats to the Internet is changing rapidly and will continue to do so for the foreseeable future. The combination of rapidly changing technology, rapidly expanding use, and the continuously new and often unimagined uses of the Internet creates a volatile situation in which the nature of threats and vulnerabilities is difficult to assess and even more difficult to predict.

To help ensure the survivability of the Internet, and the information infrastructure as a whole, it is essential to continuously monitor and analyze cyber security threats and vulnerabilities and to identify trends in intrusion activity. The organization doing this should collect, analyze, and report on quantity, trends, and character of cyber security incidents. To obtain the required information, the organization must be well trusted throughout the community. Given the universal concerns about privacy and confidentiality

> infrastructure /ˈɪnfrəˌstrʌktʃə/ n. the basic systems and services that are necessary for a country or an organization, for example, buildings, transport, water and power supplies and administrative systems
> monitor /ˈmɒnɪtə/ v. to watch and check sth. over a period of time in order to see how it develops, so that you can make any necessary changes
> confidentiality /ˌkɒnfɪˌdenʃɪˈælɪti/ n. a situation in which you expect sb. to keep information secret

and the inherently voluntary nature of reporting, the collection organization should be neither government nor commercial. Nor can it be responsible for public policy, investigation, enforcement, or other activities perceived as conflicting. Organizations that have suffered attacks are often unwilling to discuss their problems for fear of loss of confidence by their customers.

> enforcement /ɪnˈfɔːsmənt/ *n.* the act of enforcing; ensuring observance of or obedience
> expertise /ˌekspɜːˈtiːz/ *n.* expert knowledge or skill in a particular subject, activity or job
> disseminate /dɪˈsemɪneɪt/ *v.* to spread information, knowledge, etc. so that it reaches many people
> capitalize /ˈkæpɪtəlaɪz/ *v.* to provide a company etc. with the money it needs to function

Among the ways to gain a global view of threats are to use the experience and expertise of incident response teams to identify new threats and vulnerabilities. Ongoing operation and expansion of open, wide area networks will benefit from stronger response teams and response infrastructures.

Similarly, it is important to encourage Internet service providers to develop security incident response teams and other security improvement services for their customers. Many network service providers are well positioned to offer security services to their clients. These services should include helping clients install and operate secure network connections as well as mechanisms to rapidly disseminate vulnerability information and corrections.

As noted earlier, the security of each system on the Internet depends on the security of all other systems on the network. The interconnectedness and interdependency of systems pose a serious threat to commerce.

The combination of easy access and user-friendly interfaces have drawn users of all ages and from all walks of life. As a result, many users of the Internet have no more understanding of the technology than they do of the engineering behind other infrastructures. Similarly, many system administrators lack adequate knowledge about the network and about security, even while the Internet is becoming increasingly complex and dynamic. To encourage "safe computing," there are steps we believe the government could take.

The Internet has proven to be an engine that is driving a revolution in the way government, companies, and individuals conduct their business. Capitalizing Internet opportunities, however, brings a new set of risks—risks that must be effectively managed. Because of the interconnectedness and interdependence among computer systems on the Internet, the security of each system depends on the security of all other systems on the network. For a country to thrive on the Internet, cyber security efforts need to focus on reporting and monitoring threats and vulnerabilities, education and training, and research and development.

Better Know More

1. Richard D. Pethia

Director of the CERT Coordination Center at Carnegie Mellon University (a center of Internet security expertise).

2. silver bullet

The metaphor of the silver bullet applies to any straightforward solution perceived to have extreme effectiveness.

Check Your Understanding

Answer the following questions based on the text you have just learned.

1. Why is it difficult to ensure the integrity, availability, and privacy of information on the Internet?
2. What was the Internet originally designed to be?
3. What are required to understand the workings and the vulnerabilities of the Internet?
4. Why can even unsophisticated intruders use intruder programs?
5. Why does the use of the Internet replace other forms of electronic communication?
6. Why is successful apprehension and prosecution of computer criminals unlikely?
7. What are the factors leading to the exposure of sensitive data and risk to safety-critical systems?
8. What can result in vulnerabilities that intruders can exploit?
9. Why may resolution and restoration of systems be time-consuming?
10. What creates a volatile situation?
11. What should be done to help ensure the survivability of the Internet, and the information infrastructure as a whole?
12. What need cyber security efforts to focus on?
13. After reading the text, what is your opinion of Internet security?
14. What do you think should be done to make the Internet less vulnerable?

A Sip of Word Formation

Locative Prefixes

Sub-, *inter-*, *trans-* are locative prefixes.

1. *Sub-* means "under" (*subway*, *submarine*,), or "less than" (*sub-zero temperature*, *sub-standard*)
2. *Trans-* means "across", examples, *transcontinental, transmigrate*
3. *Inter-* means "between", examples, *interbreed, intergalactic*

Build Your Vocabulary

A. Find the word in column I that matches each meaning in column II.

I	II
crossing the Atlantic Ocean	sub-normal
below normal	international
between countries	sub-zero
below zero	transatlantic
between sb. and sb.	transcontinental
below the surface layer	suborbital
less than one orbit of the earth, moon	transoceanic
between the lines	interlinear
crossing an ocean	subsoil
crossing a continent	intermediary

B. Give examples to the following locative prefixes.

sub- means "under": _____ _____ _____ _____
sub- means "less than": _____ _____ _____ _____
sub- means "lower in rank": _____ _____ _____ _____
trans- means "across": _____ _____ _____ _____
inter- means "between": _____ _____ _____ _____

You'd Like to Be

A Skilled Text Weaver

Complete each sentence with one of the words listed below. Make changes where necessary.

vulnerability	administer	harness	simultaneously
apprehension	deterrent	misconfigure	legitimate
traverse	sequentially	vocatile	put at risk
foreseeable	confidentially	disseminate	

1. The problem that solar energy researchers face is how to _____ the sun's energy effectively and inexpensively.
2. It's fairly easy to _____ your firewall if you don't have strong technology expertise among your staff.
3. It is a manager's responsibility to intervene and manage a potentially _____ situation.
4. The myth is _____ throughout the southwest of the country.
5. He is the _____ heir to the property.
6. According to Australian scientists, vision and hearing loss happens almost _____ in older people.
7. America's ports are still among the most _____ to terrorist attack.
8. Five years is unacceptable and we need specific answers on why the _____ of these particular criminals are not continuing with all the force and determination it had before investigation.
9. Recently, a major news telecast talked with a group of experts as to their views of world events in the _____ future.
10. We anticipate that State agencies that _____ the school meal programs will work.
11. _____ is an important principle in health and social care because it functions to impose a boundary on the amount of personal information and data that can be disclosed without consent.
12. Capital punishment used to be a major _____. It made the violent robber think twice before pulling the trigger.
13. Hundreds of patients have been _____ after a computer glitch caused parts of their medical notes to disappear and attach to other patients' records.
14. I have often wondered why God would allow Jesus to _____ the desert for 40 days, dusty, hungry and thirsty.
15. While we read articles _____, we read them with more than one sequence.

A Sharp Interpreter

Paraphrase the following sentences, referring to the contexts in which the sentences are located.

1. The Internet was designed to be "open," with distributed control and mutual trust among users.
2. Traditional physical "rules" are difficult or impossible to apply.
3. The current state of Internet security is the result of many additional factors.
4. Internet sites have become so interconnected and intruder tools so effective that the security of any site depends, in part, on the security of all other sites on the Internet.
5. Although an organization may be able to "harden" its own systems to help prevent having its systems used as part of a distributed attack, there is essentially nothing a site can do with currently available technology to prevent becoming a victim of, for example, a coordinated network flood.
6. The combination of easy access and user-friendly interfaces has drawn users of all ages and from all walks of life.

A Solid Sentence Constructor

Complete each sentence with one of the phrases listed below. Make changes where necessary.

be associated with	give priority to	in addition to
the bottom line	be subject to	benefit from
all walks of life	thrive on	

1. Food scientist says, "Moderate coffee consumption may _____ a reduction in the risk of certain diseases."
2. Singapore Prime Minister said Sunday evening that Southeast Asia will benefit from expanding economic exchanges with China and _____ China's prosperity.
3. Peasants used to _____ the local landowners.
4. If your partner has a pet that she adores, at Christmas, _____ buying a gift for your partner, buy a small present for her pet.
5. Most Americans perceive that poor countries do not really _____ international trade.
6. No longer is _____ a primary consideration. Instead, the focus is on patients who need help regardless of their age, occupation, etc.
7. With help from the government and from people in _____, many welfare homes own fairly advanced medical equipment to meet the basic needs of their children.
8. You can interrupt the current job to _____ an urgent job.

A Careful Writer

Study the following synonyms and complete the sentences.

> arrest   capture   catch   seize

1. Hong Kong police _____ their largest haul of weapons and ammunition in 20 years after smashing a crime syndicate.
2. We will stop you, we will _____ you and we will punish you.
3. A suspect has been _____ in connection with the recent series of letter bomb attacks, police said today.
4. The criminal was _____ when trying to escape from the city.

> consent (*n.*)   approve   grant   agree   admit

5. He was not _____ to the club because he wasn't a member.
6. The two countries have _____ on the date for next talk.
7. The boy slipped out of the room and headed for the swimming pool without his parents' _____.
8. I don't _____ of your way of looking at things.
9. The firm finally _____ him a pension.

> compel   oblige   force   constrain

10. The two noblemen _____ him to their carriage and took him to a lonely house.
11. I feel _____ to apologize to you now.
12. Can they _____ obedience from us?
13. The government was considering making laws to _____ all truck drivers to install rear close circuit television system.
14. I was _____ to give up the plan.
15. He was _____ by illness to suspend his experiment.

A Superb Bilingualist

Translate the following sentences into English, using the words given in the brackets.

1. 那个色盲的男孩不得不放弃成为服装设计师的理想。(compel)
2. 这个地区利用河流发电。(harness)
3. 在过去的十年当中,摩天大楼在芝加哥和纽约同时发展起来。(simultaneously)

4. 我不太清楚，在可预见的将来印度是否会成为超级大国。(foreseeable)
5. 宣传者利用因特网把他们的信条传播至全球。(disseminate)
6. 核武器对一个国家可能产生极大的政治威慑。(deterrent)

Text B

Internet Evolution: Cyber Youth Culture in China

By Erica Schlaikjer
(Abridged and Edited)

I'm sitting at an Internet café—or *wang ba*, in Chinese—and I feel like I'm involved in some shady, underground operation. The lights are turned off, the rusty chairs don't match, and the computers are falling apart. My keyboard keeps sticking, and I'm sweating, thanks to today's smoggy Shanghai weather. Dusty fans whir in the background as teenaged
5 boys click away on their mouses. But instead of planning some illegal scheme, they're just fighting Anime characters in an online game. One guy next to me fingers a cigarette in one hand as he hawks something slimy onto the cracked tile floor.

I came to China to learn about the Inter-
10 net and youth culture. Before I left, I read articles about Internet addiction treatment clinics for game-loving teens, government crackdowns on instant messaging, illegal "naked chatting," and online dissidence.
15 While all of the news was true, it was also somewhat over-hyped and "makes China out to be a really scary place," as one student told me. Political or subversive activities are actually confined to only a small minority.

20 The majority of China's Internet users, however, are young, well-educated males with high-paying jobs, who log on primarily for information or entertainment purposes, according to a November 2005 survey report by Guo
25 Liang, a professor at the Chinese Academy of Social Sciences in Beijing.

> **whir** /wɜː/ *v.* to make a continuous low sound like the parts of a machine moving
> **hawk** /hɔːk/ *v.* to get phlegm in your mouth when you cough
> **slimy** /ˈslaɪmi/ *adj.* like or covered with slime
> **tile** /taɪl/ *n.* a flat, usually square, piece of baked clay, carpet or other material that is used in rows for covering walls and floors
> **crackdown** /ˈkrækdaʊn/ *n.* severe action taken to restrict the activities of criminals or of people opposed to the government or authorities
> **dissidence** /ˈdɪsɪdəns/ *n.* disagreement, especially disagreement with the government
> **hype** /haɪp/ *v.* to advertise sth. a lot and exaggerate its good qualities, in order to get a lot of public attention for it
> **scary** /ˈskeəri/ *adj.* frightening
> **subversive** /səbˈvɜːsɪv/ *adj.* trying or likely to destroy or damage a government or political system by attacking it secretly or indirectly
> **confine** /kənˈfaɪn/ *v.* to keep sb./sth. inside the limits of a particular activity, subject, area, etc.
> **log on/in** to perform the actions that allow you to begin using a computer system

109

The number of Internet users in China hit 111 million at the end of 2005, a 17 million increase since the previous
30 year, according to the China Internet Network Information Center (CNNIC). By

subscriber /səbˈskraɪbə/ n. a person who pays to receive a service
constraint /kənˈstreɪnt/ n. a thing that limits or restricts sth., or your freedom to do sth.

the time this article is published, the number will no doubt soar even higher.

As of now, the number of Internet users in China comprises only 8.5 percent of the country's total population, but it ranks second in the world, following the United States, in terms
35 of total broadband subscribers.

Only about a third of users have had more than five years of Internet experience, with television still being the dominant media, but survey results show that the Internet is gaining popularity. Since 1995, when the Internet first became commercially available to Chinese individuals, the majority of users log on for general browsing and reading the news, communi-
40 cating in chat rooms and instant messaging systems, and hanging out in Internet cafés to play games and download music. They are less likely to use the Internet for e-mail, banking or online shopping.

"All these statistics show that rather than being an information highway, the Internet in China is more like an entertainment highway," Professor Guo writes.

45 While the Internet in China is still in its preliminary stages of development, it shows exciting promise among at least 51 percent of users, who say it will "make the world a better place," according to Guo's report.

During my travels to different Chinese cities, I held informal conversations with Chinese youth to better understand how the Internet plays a role in their lives. From the country's
50 first-ever Chinese Bloggers Conference in Shanghai to a coffee shop discussion about Wikipedia in Beijing, I began to identify different sub-cultures of Internet users.

Perhaps the following categories over-generalize the population, but they also provide

some useful clues about the day-to-day online habits of Chinese youth, which are not so different from how
55 my American friends and I use the Web, but that certainly exist in a different social and political context.

Through my research, I could tell the impact of the Internet in China was significant. Everyone I talked to seemed so excited about this "new" technol-
60 ogy. Unfortunately, my time constraints and limited language skills made it difficult to understand the real depth of the situation.

One thing is clear: There's no turning back now. As the rest of China continues to get wired, as online business grows, and as information overwhelms, there's bound to be widespread change. But it's too early to determine exactly what direction that change will take.

The Chinese version of the free, online encyclopedia that anyone can edit, Wikipedia, known as Wei Ji Bai Ke in Mandarin, is home to more than 48,000 registered users contributing nearly 59,000 articles. But it is still relatively small compared to other versions, such as the one in English, which has more than one million users.

"Wiki is such a good information tool," a student says. "You can share knowledge and develop your interests, meet people, and learn new things. There's never been anything like it before."

The young Wikipedian admits that his online hobby puts him in the minority. Most educated Chinese youth are pressured by their parents and teachers to make money with "practical" careers, like electronics, business, or medicine, rather than waste their time contributing articles for free online. Plus, uneducated youth usually don't have access to computers to begin with, or they would rather just play games.

One user, who writes under the pen name Neverland, says he is proud to be a "geek."

"There are a lot of young people online, but all they do is chat, play games and flirt with girls," Neverland says. "They don't like using the Internet for things that take a lot of effort. It's too tiring."

"Wiki is also amusement for us," he continues, "just not in the same way as amusement is for them."

The total Internet market in China was valued at about 11.3 billion RMB (US$1.3 billion) in 2004, and 35 percent of that was spent on gaming, according to Guo's report.

Many gamers frequent Internet cafés, where an hour of computer time generally costs less than 40 cents. For people who crave amusement but don't have Internet access at home, these cafés are an escapist's haven.

"There are three types of people that like to visit the *wang ba*," one girl told me. "Boys who like to play games, people who like to chat with friends, and people who just like to waste time."

> encyclopedia /ɪnˌsaɪkləˈpiːdiə/ *n.* a book or set of books giving information about all areas of knowledge or about different areas of one particular subject, usually arranged in alphabetical order; a similar collection of information
>
> geek /giːk/ *n.* a person who is boring, who wears clothes that are not fashionable
>
> flirt /flɜːt/ *v.* to behave towards sb. as if you find them sexually attractive, without seriously wanting to have a relationship with them
>
> frequent /ˈfriːkwənt/ *v.* to visit a particular place often
>
> crave /kreɪv/ *v.* to have a very strong desire for sth.
>
> haven /ˈheɪvən/ *n.* a place that is safe and peaceful where people go to rest or to be protected from sth.

The majority of patrons I met were between the ages of 16 and 24. Technically, city regulations make it illegal for minors under 18 to enter, and all users must present state identification to log on. Internet café owners are required to register with the government and install filtering software to control "subversive" elements, like pornography or "state secrets." And illegal underground establishments may be shut down or forced to pay severe penalties.

One 14-year-old girl, Li Xiafei, told me that stories of Internet café violence and even child abduction are common hearsay. "Most of the time I can convince my parents that they don't need to worry," she says.

Extraordinary rumors aside, Internet addiction is a legitimate concern. "Little kids don't understand," one Shanghai café owner said. "It will affect their studies."

In an informal survey I conducted, most people said they stayed at cafés for about two to three hours at a time, but some confessed to logging on for up to 12 hours in one sitting! Beijing, the nation's capital, opened an officially licensed Internet addiction clinic in the summer of 2005, right before I began my research, to treat the Web's most obsessed users.

Other than providing entertainment, the Internet has also given Chinese youth the opportunity to express themselves. At the country's first Chinese Bloggers Conference in Shanghai, "Everybody is Somebody," according to the event's motto. Hardcore bloggers praised the Internet's contributions to society. Isaac Mao, one of the pioneers of blogging in China and founder of CNblog.org, said today's bloggers will create a "social brain."

"The combination of all these small voices will make our society smarter," he said.

Mao spoke of the "pro-ams," or "professional amateurs," a powerful minority of online writers who prove that you don't need a college degree to be an expert on something.

But not all expression is necessarily news-based and informative. Afterall, China's blogosphere is home to some of the country's biggest celebrities, like Furong JieJie ("Sister Lotus") and Muzi Mei, two

---

patron /ˈpeɪtrən/ *n.* a person who uses a particular shop/store, restaurant, theatre, etc.

pornography /pɔːˈnɒgrəfi/ *n.* books, videos, etc. that describe or show naked people and sexual acts in order to make people feel sexually excited, especially in a way that many other people find offensive

penalty /ˈpenlti/ *n.* a punishment for breaking a law, rule or contract

abduction /əbˈdʌkʃən/ *n.* the criminal act of taking of a person by force

hearsay /ˈhɪəseɪ/ *n.* things that you have heard from another person but do not (definitely) know to be true

rumor /ˈruːmə/ *n.* a piece of information, or a story, that people talk about, but that may not be true

addiction /əˈdɪkʃən/ *n.* the condition of being addicted to sth.

legitimate /lɪˈdʒɪtɪmɪt/ *adj.* for which there is a fair and acceptable reason

confess /kənˈfes/ *v.* to admit sth. that you feel ashamed or embarrassed about

obsess /əbˈses/ *v.* to completely fill your mind so that you cannot think of anything else

motto /ˈmɒtəʊ/ *n.* a short sentence or phrase that expresses the aims and beliefs of a person, a group, an institution, etc. and is used as a rule of behavior

hardcore /ˈhɑːdkɔː/ *adj.* having a belief or a way of behaving that will not change

blogosphere /ˈblɒgɒksfɪə/ *n.* blogs and their interconnections

women who rose to fame by posting self-indulgent photos and journal entries of their sexual escapades and other personal experiences.

Adding to the trend of cyber self-expression
145 is the popularity of podcasting, a fusion of Apple's "iPod" and "broadcasting," which allows virtually anyone with an Internet connection to create and share audio or visual recordings—everything from news talk shows to amateur music
150 videos. In China, thanks to companies like Toodou.com, the country's first podcasting service, people have seized the "do-it-yourself" attitude to explore their creativity and, on occasion, create their own stardom.

For example, a couple of college guys from the Guangzhou Arts Institute created a video
155 spoof of Backstreet Boys music videos. The hilarious duo, dubbed "The Back Dorm Boys," catapulted into Internet fame, and they were soon rumored to strike a promo deal with Motorola, the mobile phone company.

In a Sohu.com survey of more than 2,000 bloggers in China, about 83 percent said they hope to increase their Internet fame, and 86 percent sought economic benefits, which suggests
160 that blogging and other forms of online expression can be a rather selfish enterprise.

Sometimes, it's all about the yuan. In January 2005, Hong Kong native Edwyn Chan founded Concept Idea Technologies (CIT), a company based in Chengdu and Beijing that specializes in Web 2.0 tech-
165 nologies, such as RSS feeds, blogs, and other social networking tools.

"I'm online 15 hours a day—it's like an addiction," says Chan, 24, a graduate of New York University's Stern
170 School of Business.

Chan says he is less concerned with things like free expression than he is about maintaining high traffic on his Web site and attracting advertisers.

175 "I'm not a journalist, I'm a business person," he says, emphasizing that even his personal blogs, which cover subjects like Internet advertising and web en

self-indulgent /ˌselfɪnˈdʌldʒənt/ *adj.* allowing yourself to have or do things that you like, especially when you do this too much or too often
escapade /ˈeskəpeɪd/ *n.* an exciting adventure (often one that people think is dangerous or stupid) podcasting
fusion /ˈfjuːʒən/ *n.* the process or result of joining two or more things together to form one
stardom /ˈstɑːdəm/ *n.* the state of being famous as an actor, a singer, etc.
spoof /spuːf/ *n.* a humorous copy of a film/movie, television program, etc. that exaggerates its main features
hilarious /hɪˈleəriəs/ *adj.* extremely funny
duo /ˈdjuːəʊ/ *n.* two people who perform together or are often seen or thought of together
dub /dʌb/ *v.* to give sb./sth. a particular name, often in a humorous or critical way
catapult /ˈkætəpʌlt/ *v.* to throw sb./sth. or be thrown suddenly and violently through the air
promo /ˈprəʊməʊ/ *n.* promotion
yuan /jʊˈɑːn/ *n.* the unit of money in China

trepreneurship, are merely for "investor relations."

"I never think about how it affects people," he says.

One of the core businesses of CIT is blogkumedia, a blog media network similar to Gawker Media in the U.S., which publishes blogs using the conventional business model of print magazines.

Chan says he created blogkumedia to provide entertaining, customized content that you can't find online anywhere else.

"There's a lot of stuff that traditional media skips out on, like really weird, niche stuff," Chan says.

> blogkumedia /blɔk'miːdjə/ *n.* blog media
> weird /wɪəd/ *adj.* unusual or different; not normal
> niche /nɪtʃ/ *n.* an opportunity to sell a particular product to a particular group of people
> hassle /'hæsəl/ *n.* a situation that is annoying because it involves doing sth. difficult or complicated that needs a lot of effort
> sift /sɪft/ *v.* to separate sth. from a group of things
> crap /kræp/ *n.* something of bad quality
> savvy /'sævi/ *adj.* having practical knowledge and understanding of sth.; having common sense
> celebrity /sə'lebrəti/ *n.* a famous person
> underexposed /ˌʌndərɪk'spəʊzd/ *adj.* providing with too little publicity
> flip side the opposite side
> copycat /'kɒpɪkæt/ *v.* to imitate closely; to mimic

To relieve browsers of the hassle of sifting through all the "crap" in cyberspace, Chan says his blogkumedia site targets net-savvy consumers who only want the "necessary info."

The site hosts five blogs, covering consumer gadgets, gaming, humor, celebrity gossip, and movies. Each blog is written by young people, aged 18 to 26, who must apply to be accepted as full-time bloggers. This screening process, which Chan oversees, runs contrary to the notion that blogging should be open to everyone. In other words, it's controlled free speech.

"Everybody is an expert on something and should have the chance to express their knowledge," Chan says. "I'm not taking away their chance to do that; I'm just doing it in a more organized way."

Chan's business model is a relatively underexposed concept in China's blog media landscape, which is mainly dominated by personal blogs, and on the flip side, a sophisticated system of Internet monitoring and filtering to control sensitive material. But with creative people like Chan taking the lead, young money-hungry entrepreneurs are bound to copycat his profit-making success, and ultimately change the structure and content of China's media.

No matter where you live in the world, the Internet inevitably paves the way for access to new knowledge, economic markets, foreign influence, self-expression and expanded social networks. And in a rapidly developing country like China, the long-term impact of the Internet is even more profound. And its full effects remain to be seen.

Notes

1. Erica Schlaikjer

A senior editor for "Abroad View," interned at "Shanghai Talk" in China during the fall of 2005 through Teaching and Projects Abroad. Her research on the Internet and Chinese youth culture was made possible by The Medill School of Journalism's Eric Lund Global Research and Reporting grant.

2. Chinese Academy of Social Sciences

The Chinese Academy of Social Sciences (CASS) is the highest academic research organization in the fields of philosophy and social sciences as well as a national center for comprehensive studies in the People's Republic of China.

3. China Internet Network Information Center (CNNIC)

It is authorized by the Ministry of Information Industry as domain name registration administrative organ, namely domain name registry. The CNNIC is responsible for the management of the country code top level domain of China and Chinese domain name system. It maintains the central database.

4. Chinese Bloggers Conference

Shanghai played host to the first Chinese Blogger Conference.

5. Apple's "iPod"

iPod is a brand of portable media players designed and marketed by Apple and launched in 2001.

6. Toodou.com

Launched on April 15, 2005, Toodou.com is one of the leading video sharing companies in China. It is a multimedia podcasting website that allows Internet users to share original audio and video clips and then post them to their websites and blogs. Gary Wang is the founder of Toodou.

7. Backstreet Boys

A quintet of hunkalicious singing vocalists, the Backstreet Boys is, probably the most popular vocal group outside the United States.

8. The Back Dorm Boys

The Back Dorm Boys refer to a Chinese male duo who gained fame for their lip sync videos to songs by the Backstreet Boys and other pop stars.

9. Concept Idea Technologies (CIT)

CIT's vision is to enable internet users to have an alternative method to search engines for finding information online.

10. RSS feeds

RSS stands for Really Simple Syndication. Also called web feeds, RSS is a content delivery vehicle. It is the format used when you want to syndicate news and other web content. When it distributes the content it is called a feed. You could think of RSS as your own personal wire service.

11. Gawker Media

Gawker Media is an online media company founded and owned by Nick Denton. It is considered to be one of the most visible and successful blog-oriented media companies.

Comprehension Questions

1. What is the Internet café like in China according to the author in the first paragraph?
2. According to a November 2005 survey report by Guo Liang, a professor at the Chinese Academy of Social Sciences in Being, who are the majority of China's Internet users?
3. How many Internet users in China at the end of 2005?
4. How many users have had more than five years of Internet experience?
5. Since 1995, when the Internet first became commercially available to Chinese individuals,

what did the majority of users do using the Internet?
6. What is Wiki like in a student's eye?
7. What are most educated Chinese youth pressured to do by their parents and teachers?
8. What are the three types of people that like to visit the wang bas, according to one girl?
9. Why is Internet addiction a legitimate concern?
10. How did Furong JieJie and Muzi Mei rise to fame according to the author?
11. What is podcasting?
12. Which company is China's first podcasting service?
13. Why does Chan say "I'm not a journalist, I'm a business person?"
14. What does Chan's blogkumedia target in order to relieve browsers of the hassle of sifting through all the "crap" in cyberspace?
15. What is the impact of the Internet in the world?

Writing Practice

As a class, brainstorm current technology controversies. Some examples might include Internet file sharing (Napster, pirated films, etc.), Internet censorship vs. free speech (pornography, hate crimes), the Microsoft monopoly controversy, and student plagiarism through the Internet (Web sites that provide term papers and projects to students). Encourage students to analyze the controversial or divisive nature of each topic. Are there deeper ethical, legal or constitutional questions underlying these debates? Create a list on the board of suggestions, along with some key points about each. Divide class into groups of four, assigning each group a technology controversy from the brainstorm. Instruct groups to research their topics, using the following questions as guidelines:

—What are the major positions in this debate?

—What facts or evidence does each side use to support its position?

—What famous or influential people have expressed opinions in this debate? How have their opinions affected the debate?

—What have been some of the proposed or implemented solutions to the problems posed in this debate? How do people feel about these solutions?

After researching and analyzing responses to the above questions, have each group write an essay about its topic.

Further Study

Through the picture above we will be introduced to the darker side of chatting. Use your imagination to describe the picture and comment on it. After description, discuss with your fellow students what is your opinion on internet-chatting? How to go carefully with the chatters?

Unit 7

Biography

Unit Goals

After completing the lessons in this unit, students will be able to:
- ☞ read short (or sections of) biographies/autobiographies/memoirs and answer both technical and comprehension questions in order to understand the difference between a(n) biography/autobiography/memoir;
- ☞ describe significant life events and interests;
- ☞ extend their vocabulary through recognition of prefixes of time and order.

Before Reading

Hands-on Activities

1. A good biography brings the person to life and makes us care about what he or she did. Search the library or surf the internet, and find biographies of presidents, athletes, entertainers, world leaders, etc. Choose one of them that you like most and learn how he or she becomes a famous person. Here are some famous people listed for you, Jimmy Carter, John Nash, Lillian Hellman, Katharine Hepburn, David Beckham and Yaoming.
2. Browse the website http://www.biography.com/ and read one or two biographies.

Brainstorming

Brainstorm the following questions. Work in Pairs or groups to discuss these questions.

1. What is a biography? What makes it different from an autobiography or memoirs?
2. Have you ever read works written by Earnest Hemingway? Make a list of Hemingway's works in a chronological order.

3. Do you think it is necessary to learn about the life experiences of the writers if you want to get a good understanding of their works? Why?

A Glimpse at Words and Expressions

Please read the following sentences. Pay attention to the underlined part in each sentence and see how these expressions are used in the context, and then write down their meanings in the blanks provided.

1. In this context, Hemingway's childhood pursuits <u>fostered the interests</u> which would blossom into literary achievements. (   )
2. Hemingway also <u>had an aptitude for</u> physical challenge that engaged him through high school. (   )
3. Fighting on the Italian front <u>inspired</u> the plot of *A Farewell to Arms* in 1929. (   )
4. This time of stylistic development for Hemingway <u>reached its zenith</u> in 1923. (   )
5. At this point he had no writing that <u>was not committed to</u> publication. (   )
6. "Papa" was both a legendary celebrity and a sensitive writer, and his influence, as well as some unseen writings, <u>survived his passing</u>. (   )
7. …the passions of the man <u>are equaled</u> only by those in his writing. (   )

Text A

Earnest Hemingway

Anonymous

Ernest Hemingway was born on July 21, 1899, in suburban Oak Park, IL to Dr. Clarence and Grace Hemingway. Ernest was the second of six children to be raised in the quiet suburban town. His father was a physician and his mother was devout and musical. In this context, Heming-

> **physician** /fɪˈzɪʃən/ *n.* (formal especially AmE) a doctor, especially one who is a specialist in general medicine and not surgery
> **devout** /dɪˈvaʊt/ *adj.* (of a person) believing strongly in a particular religion and obeying its laws and practices

way's childhood pursuits fostered the interests which would blossom into literary achievements.

Although Grace hoped her son would be influenced by her musical interests, young Hemingway preferred to accompany his father on hunting and fishing trips. This love of outdoor adventure would be reflected later in many of Hemingway's stories, particularly those featuring protagonist Nick Adams.

Hemingway also had an aptitude for physical challenge that engaged him through high school, where he both played football and boxed. Because of permanent eye damage contracted from numerous boxing matches, Hemingway was repeatedly rejected from service in World War I. Boxing provided more material for Hemingway's stories, as well as a habit of likening his literary feats to boxing victories.

Hemingway also edited his high school newspaper and reported for the Kansas City Star, adding a year to his age after graduating from high school in 1917.

After this short stint, Hemingway finally was able to participate in World War I as an ambulance driver for the American Red Cross. He was wounded on July 8, 1918, on the Italian front near Fossalta di Piave. During his convalescence in Milan, he had an affair with nurse Agnes von Kurowsky. Hemingway was given two decorations by the Italian government, and he joined the Italian infantry. Fighting on the Italian front inspired the plot of *A Farewell to Arms* in 1929. Indeed, war itself is a major theme in Hemingway's works. Hemingway would witness firsthand the cruelty and stoicism required of the soldiers he would portray in his writing when covering the Greco-Turkish War in 1920 for the *Toronto Star*. In 1937 he was a war correspondent in Spain, and the events of the Spanish Civil War inspired *For Whom the Bell Tolls*.

Upon returning briefly to the United States

---

foster /'fɒstə/ v. to encourage sth. to develop

blossom /'blɒsəm/ v. to produce blossom

protagonist /prəʊ'tægənɪst/ n. (formal) the main character in a play, film/movie or book

aptitude /'æptɪtjuːd/ n. natural ability or skill at doing sth.

challenge /'tʃælɪndʒ/ n. a new or difficult task that tests sb.'s ability and skill

engage /ɪn'ɡeɪdʒ/ v. (formal) to succeed in attracting and keeping sb.'s attention and interest

permanent /'pɜːmənənt/ adj. lasting for a long time or for all time in the future; existing all the time

reject /rɪ'dʒekt/ v. to refuse to accept or consider sth.

stint /stɪnt/ n. a period of time that you spend working somewhere or doing a particular activity

ambulance /'æmbjʊləns/ n. a vehicle with special equipment, used for taking sick or injured people to hospital

convalescence /ˌkɒnvə'lesəns/ n. a period of time when you get well again after an illness or a medical operation; the process of getting well

decoration /ˌdekə'reɪʃən/ n. a medal that is given to sb. as an honour

infantry /'ɪnfəntri/ n. soldiers who fight on foot

stoicism /'stəʊɪˌsɪzəm/ n. (formal) the fact of not complaining or showing what you are feeling when you are suffering

correspondent /ˌkɒrɪ'spɒndənt/ n. a person who reports news from a particular country or on a particular subject for a newspaper or a television or radio station

after the First World War, Hemingway worked for the *Toronto Star* and lived for a short time in Chicago. There, he met Sherwood Anderson and married Hadley Richardson in 1921. On Anderson's advice, the couple moved to Paris, where he served as foreign correspondent for the *Star*. As Hemingway covered events on all of Europe, the young reporter interviewed important leaders such as Lloyd George, Clemenceau, and Mussolini.

The Hemingways lived in Paris from 1921—1926. This time of stylistic development for Hemingway reached its zenith in 1923 with the publication of *Three Stories and Ten Poems* by Robert McAlmon in Paris and the birth of his son John. This time in Paris also inspired the novel *A Moveable Feast*, published posthumously in 1964.

In January 1923 Hemingway began writing sketches that would appear in *In Our Time*, which was published in 1924. In August of 1923 he and Hadley returned to Toronto where he worked once again for the *Star*. At this point he had no writing that was not committed to publication, and in the coming months his job kept him from starting anything new. But this time off from writing gave him renewed energy upon his return to Paris in January of 1924.

During his time in Toronto he read Joyce's *Dubliners*, which forever changed his writing career. By August of 1924 he had the majority of *In Our Time* written. Although there was a period when his publisher Horace Liverwright wanted to change much of the collection, Hemingway stood firm and refused to change even one word of the book.

In Paris, Hemingway used Sherwood Anderson's letter of introduction to meet Gertrude Stein and enter the world of expatriate authors and artists who inhabited her intellectual circle. The famous description of this "lost generation" was born of an employee's remark to Hemingway, and it became immortalized as the epigraph for his first major novel, *The Sun Also Rises*.

This "lost generation" both characterized the postwar generation and the literary movement it produced. In the 1920s, writers such as Anderson, F. Scott Fitzgerald, James Joyce, Ezra Pound, and Gertrude Stein decried the false ideals of

---

zenith /ˈzenɪθ/ *n.* (formal) the time when sth. is strongest and most successful

posthumous /ˈpɒstjʊməs/ *adj.* happening, done, published, etc. after a person has died

sketch /sketʃ/ *n.* a short report or story that gives only basic details about sth.

commit /kəˈmɪt/ *v.* to promise sincerely that you will definitely do sth., keep to agreement or arrangement, etc.

expatriate /eksˈpætriət/ *adj.* of a person living in a country that is not their own

inhabit /ɪnˈhæbɪt/ *v.* to live in a particular place

immortalize /ɪˈmɔːtəlaɪz/ *v.* to prevent sb./sth. from being forgotten in the future, especially by mentioning them in literature, making films/movies about them, painting them, etc.

epigraph /ˈepɪɡrɑːf/ *n.* a line of writing, short phrase, etc. on a building or statue, or as an introduction to part of a book

decry /dɪˈkraɪ/ *v.* (formal) to strongly criticize sb./sth., especially publicly

patriotism that led young people to war, only to the benefit of materialistic elders. These writers held that the only truth was reality, and thus life could be nothing but hardship. This tenet strongly influenced Hemingway.

The late 1920s were a time of many publications for Hemingway. In 1926, *The Torrents of Spring* and *The Sun Also Rises* were published by Charles Scribner's Sons.

In 1927 Hemingway published a short story collection, *Men Without Women*. In the same year he divorced Hadley Richardson and married Pauline Pfieffer, a writer for *Vogue*. In 1928 they moved to Key West, where sons Patrick and Gregory were born in 1929 and 1932. 1928 was a year of both success and sorrow for Hemingway. In this year *A Farewell to Arms* was published, and his father committed su icide. Clarence Hemingway had been suffering from hypertension and diabetes. This painful experience is reflected in the pondering of Robert Jordan in *For Whom the Bell Tolls*.

In addition to personal experiences with war and death, Hemingway's extensive travel in pursuit of hunting and other sports provided a great deal of material for his novels. Bullfighting inspired *Death in the Afternoon*, published in 1932. In 1934, Hemingway went on safari in Africa, which gave him new themes and scenes on which to base *The Snows of Kilamanjaro* and *The Green Hills of Africa*, published in 1935.

In 1937 he traveled to Spain as a war correspondent, and he published *To Have and Have Not*. After his divorce from Pauline in 1940, Hemingway married Martha Gelhorn, a writer. They toured China before settling in Cuba at Finca Vigia (Look-out Farm). *For Whom the Bell Tolls* was published in the same year.

patriotism /ˌpætriˈɒtɪzəm/ *n.* love of your country and willingness to defend it
materialistic /məˌtɪəriəˈlɪstɪk/ *n.* caring more about money and possessions than anything else
tenet /ˈtenɪt/ *n.* (formal) one of the principles or beliefs that a theory or larger set of beliefs is based on
diabetes /ˌdaɪəˈbiːtiːz/ *n.* a medical condition, caused by a lack of insulin, which makes the patient produce a lot of urine and feel very thirsty
ponder /ˈpɒndə/ *v.* (written) to think about sth. carefully for a period of time
submarine /ˈsʌbməriːn/ *n.* a ship that can travel underwater
spotter /ˈspɒtə/ *n.* a person who looks for a particular type of thing or person, as a hobby or job

During World War II, Hemingway volunteered his fishing boat and served with the U.S. Navy as a submarine spotter in the Caribbean. In 1944, he traveled through Europe with the Allies as a war correspondent and participated in the liberation of Paris. Hemingway divorced again in 1945 and then married Mary Welsh, a correspondent for *Time* magazine, in 1946. They lived in Venice before returning to Cuba.

In 1950 he published *Across the River and Into the Trees*, though it was not

120 received with the usual critical acclaim. In 1952, however, Hemingway proved the comment "Papa is finished" wrong, in that *The Old Man and the Sea* won the Pulitzer Prize in 1953. In 1954, he won the Nobel Prize for Lit-
125 erature.

In 1960, the now aged Hemingway moved to Ketchum, Idaho, where he was hospitalized for uncontrolled high blood pressure, liver disease, diabetes, and depression.

130 On July 2, 1961, he died of self-inflicted gunshot wounds. He was buried in Ketchum. "Papa" was both a legendary celebrity and a sensitive writer, and his influence, as well as some unseen writings, survived his passing. In 1964, *A Moveable Feast* was published; in 1969, *The Fifth Column and Four Stories of the Spanish Civil War*; in 1970, *Islands in*
135 *the Stream*; in 1972, *The Nick Adams Stories*; in 1985, *The Dangerous Summer*; and in 1986, *The Garden of Eden*.

> safari /səˈfɑːri/ *n.* a trip to see or hunt wild animals, especially in East Africa
> acclaim /əˈkleɪm/ praise and approval for sb./sth., especially an artistic achievement
> hospitalize /ˈhɒspɪtlaɪz/ *v.* to send sb. to a hospital for treatment
> inflict /ɪnˈflɪkt/ *v.* to make sb./sth. suffer sth. unpleasant
> celebrity /sɪˈlebrɪti/ *n.* a famous person
> fascinating /ˈfæsɪneɪtɪŋ/ *adj.* extremely interesting and attractive
> flamboyant /flæmˈbɔɪənt/ *adj.* (of people or their behavior) different, confident and exciting in a way that attracts attention

Hemingway's own life and character are as fascinating as any in his stories. On one level, Papa was a legendary adventurer
140 who enjoyed his flamboyant lifestyle and celebrity status. But deep inside lived a disciplined author who worked tirelessly in pursuit of literary perfection. His success in both living and writing is reflected in the fact
145 that Hemingway is a hero to intellectuals and rebels alike; the passions of the man are equaled only by those in his writing.

Better Know More

1. Nick Adams

The protagonist of more than a dozen of Ernest Hemingway's short stories written in the 1920s and 30s, such as *In Our Time* (1925), *Men Without Women* (1927), *Winner Take Nothing* (1933). Most of the stories were collected in a 1972 book entitled "The Nick Adams Stories."

2. Greco-Turkish War (1919–1922)

Also called the War in Asia Minor, and in Turkey considered a part of the Turkish War of Independence, was a war between Greece and Turkey fought in the wake of World War I.

3. The Toronto Star

Founded in 1892, the Canada's largest daily newspaper.

4. The Spanish Civil War (1937–1939)

A major conflict in Spain that started after an attempted coup d'état committed by parts of the army against the government of the Second Spanish Republic. During the war Spain became a battleground for fascists and socialists from all countries.

5. Sherwood Anderson (1876–1941)

Is one of the representatives of American writers of Modernism. He published his masterpiece *Winesburg, Ohio* in 1919.

6. Lloyd George (1863–1945)

In December 1916, Lloyd George became prime minister of Britain.

7. Clemenceau (1841–1929)

Georges Clemenceau was born in Vendée, France, on 28th September, 1841. In November 1917 the French president, Raymond Poincare appointed Clemenceau as prime minister.

8. Benito Mussolini (1883–1945)

Over the course of his lifetime went from Socialism—he was the editor of *Avanti*, a socialist newspaper—to the leadership of a new political movement called "fascism"

Mussolini came to power after the "March on Rome" in 1922, and was appointed Prime Minister by King Victor Emmanuel.

9. Joyce's *Dubliners*

James Joyce (1882–1941), one of best-known novelists of the "stream of consciousness" school in Britain. *Dubliners* is a collection of 15 short stories.

10. Gertrude Stein (1874–1946)

American writer, an eccentric whose Paris home was a salon for the Cubist and experimental artist and writers.

11. Lost Generation

The Lost Generation is a term used to describe a group of American writers who were rebelling against what America had become by the 1900's.

12. F. Scott Fitzgerald (1896–1940)

Francis Scott Key Fitzgerald was a Jazz Age novelist and short story writer who is considered to be among the greatest twentieth-century American writers.

13. Ezra Pound (1885–1972)

American poet and critic, is generally considered the poet most responsible for defining and promoting a modernist aesthetic in poetry.

Check Your Understanding

Choose the best answer to each of the following questions based on the text you have just learned.

1. The love of outdoor adventure would be reflected in many of Hemingway's stories, particularly those featuring protagonist_____.
    A. Jake Barnes   B. Nick Adams
    C. Robert Jordan   D. Frederic Henry
2. Which of the following writers didn't belong to the Lost Generation?
    A. Earnest Hemingway.   B. F. Scott Fitzgerald.
    C. Gertrude Stein.   D. William Faulkner.

3. Which of the following events happened forever changed Hemingway's writing style?
   A. When he was in Chicago, he met Sherwood Anderson in 1921.
   B. During his time in Toronto, he read Joyce's *Dubliners*.
   C. In Paris, Hemingway used Sherwood Anderson's letter of introduction to meet Gertrude Stein and enter the world of expatriate authors and artists who inhabited her intellectual circle.
   D. *Three stories* and *Ten poems* were published in 1923.
4. Which of the following statements is **Not** true according to the text?
   A. Fighting on the Italian front inspired the plot *A Farewell to Arms*.
   B. The events of the Spanish Civil War inspired *For Whom the Bell Tolls*.
   C. The painful experience of suffering from hypertension and diabetes is reflected in the pondering of Robert Jordan.
   D. Bullfighting inspired *The Green Hills of Africa*.
5. By which of the following novels, Hemingway proved the comment "Papa is finished" wrong?
   A. *For Whom the Bell Tolls*   B. *A Farewell to Arms*
   C. *The Old Man and the Sea*   D. *The Sun Also Rises*
6. Which of the following novels was published when he was still alive?
   A. *A Moveable Feast*   B. *To Have and Have Not*
   C. *The Nick Adams Stories*   D. *The Garden of Eden*

A Sip of Word Formation

Prefixes of Time and Order

Pre-, *post-*, *ex-*, *re-* are prefixes of time and order.
1. *Pre-* is added to nouns, adjectives, verbs with the meaning of *before*.
   For example: pre-marital, prehistory
2. *Post-* is added to nouns, verbs and adjectives with the meaning of *after*.
   For example: post-graduate, post-war
3. *Ex-* is added to nouns with the meaning of *former*.
   For example: ex-boyfriend, ex-wife.
4. *Re-* is added to nouns, verbs, adjectives, adverbs with the meaning of *again*.
   For example: re-fuel, re-examine.

Build Your Vocabulary

A. Decide which form of the negative prefix to use to make each word. Add the prefix and write the whole word.

condition		cover	
criminal		draw	
conceive		distribute	
requisite		war	
script		husband	
construction		modernism	

B. Complete each of the following sentences with proper form of the word given in brackets.

1. Smith said _____ babies had problems with motor skills, learning and eyesight later in life. (mature)
2. In the _____ or service-society, structure will have a much shorter life-span; therefore education has to provide knowledge that is relevant for future markets of great volatility. (industrial)
3. South African _____ Nelson Mandela said he was hoping for a safer and more caring world in the new century. (President)
4. A strong public outcry forced him to _____ his decision. (consider)
5. "These factors _____ to large extent the outcome" Jessica Mitford said. (determine)
6. The _____ infection rate of 541 patients was 2.98%. (operative)
7. _____ David Beckham is one of the world's most recognized sportsmen. (football player)
8. The writer tries to _____ the sights and sounds of his children. (create)
9. But it is to be seen if we have eyes to notice without _____. (judge)
10. Zhejiang University set up the _____ station in 1985 which was initially approved by Ministry Personnel all over the country. (doctoral)
11. _____ is the reprocessing of materials into new products. (cycle)
12. George W. Bush was _____ as American President in 2004. (elect)

You'd Like to Be

A Skilled Text Weaver

A. *Replace the underlined words or expressions in the following sentences with words or expressions from the text that best keep the original meaning.*

1. He studied abroad for a two-year period after he graduated from university.
2. He was a faithful Christian.
3. Some of his works were published after he died.
4. The measure was strongly criticized in public as useless.
5. The work was praised publicly as a masterpiece.
6. He is so strong that four week's recovering from illness is enough for him.
7. He played a leading role in a film directed by a famous director, which made him a famous person overnight.
8. They surveyed the damage suffered from the storm.
9. The club's aim is to develop better relations within the community.
10. He is at the highest peak of his career.
11. They planned to live there for a long time.

B. *Complete the following sentences with the help of the first letter(s). Fill in each blank with one word only.*

1. Nick Adams is the p_____ of more than a dozen of Ernest Hemingway's short stories written in the 1920s and 30s.
2. Some of the rare species i_____ the area.
3. She endured her long illness with s_____.
4. Now China has set up a modern i_____ property system.
5. The "Lost Generation" criticized the false idea of p_____ that led young people to war.
6. Their friendship b_____ into love.
7. Earnest Hemingway ever was a war c_____ in Spain during the Spanish Civil War.
8. It is f_____ to see how different people deal with the same problem.
9. Advertisers and marketers are turning our children into m_____ monsters.
10. E_____ Chinese in the world celebrate Spring Festival in their own special way.

11. In literature, an e_____ is a phrase, quotation, or poem that is set at the beginning of a document or component.
12. Many p_____ and surgeons work long, irregular hours.
13. Hemingway was a legendary adventurer who enjoyed his f_____ lifestyle and celebrity.

A Sharp Interpreter

Paraphrase the following sentences with your own words, pay attention to the underlined expressions.

1. In this context, Hemingway's childhood pursuits fostered the interests which would blossom into literary achievements.
2. Because of permanent eye damage contracted from numerous boxing matches, Hemingway was repeatedly rejected from service in World War I.
3. In the 1920s, writers such as Anderson, F. Scott Fitzgerald, James Joyce, Ezra Pound, and Gertrude Stein decried the false ideals of patriotism that led young people to war, only to the benefit of materialistic elders.
4. This painful experience is reflected in the pondering of Robert Jordan in *For Whom the Bell Tolls*.
5. In 1950 he published *Across the River and Into the Trees*, though it was not received with the usual critical acclaim. In 1952, however, Hemingway proved the comment "Papa is finished" wrong, in that *The Old Man and the Sea* won the Pulitzer Prize in 1953.

A Solid Sentence Constructor

Combine the following sentences.

Example: In January 1923 Hemingway began writing sketches that would appear in *In Our Times*.
In Our Times was published in 1924.
→ In January 1923 Hemingway began writing sketches that would appear in *In Our Times*, which was published in 1924.

1. The meeting will be put off until next month. We will have made all the preparations at that time.
2. The performance was a great success. People had expected that.
3. We stood at the top of the hill. We could see the town from the top of the hill.
4. There are about seven million people taking part in the election. Most of them are well educated.

5. Copper offers very little resistance. Cooper is used so widely for carrying electricity.
6. A young man had a new girl friend. He wanted to impress her.
7. The accused has the right to defense. The right to defense is guaranteed by the constitution.

A Careful Writer

Study the following synonyms and complete the sentences.

reject refuse decline

1. She _____ to stand up for a white man and was arrested by the police.
2. The prisoner's plea for pardon was _____.
3. I offered to give them a lift but they _____.
4. People who _____ to comply with the law will be punished.
5. I will definitely _____ the view that human beings need animal protein to remain healthy.
6. I _____ to do something so low and beneath my dignity.
7. We regret we have to _____ your offer.

zenith peak crest

8. When the sun was at its _____, the glare was not as strong as at sunrise and sunset.
9. Mt. Jolmolungma is the world's highest _____.
10. A surfboard fin sliced the _____ of a wave.
11. A point on the celestial sphere directly below the observer, diametrically opposite the _____.
12. Traffic reaches the _____ about five o'clock.
13. At its _____ the Rome Empire covered almost the whole of Europe.
14. The biggest flood _____ on the Yangtze River this year has passed through the Three Georges Dam, and the middle and lower reaches of the Yangtze were protected.

decry criticize denounce

15. They _____ him to the police as a criminal.
16. He _____ me for not finishing the work in time.
17. The mayor _____ gambling in all forms.
18. At the meeting people _____ him as a traitor.
19. He shut all _____ out.

20. The founder of the Children's Defense Fund, Marian Wright Edelman, strongly _____ the lack of financial and moral support fo children in America today.

A Superb Bilingualist

Translate the following sentences into English with the phrases or expressions given below. Change the form where necessary.

1. 应聘者需要有把握和掌握新兴技术的天分。(have an aptitude for)
2. 我们没有采纳他关于成立音乐俱乐部的想法,而是决定成立艺术俱乐部。(reject)
3. 他仔细考虑了那个建议,最终决定接受它。(ponder over)
4. 环境的破坏是我们面临的最严峻的挑战之一。(challenge)
5. 暴风雨使该地遭受严重损失。(inflict)
6. 承德避暑山庄 (The Mountain Resort in Chengde) 植物配置的 (the plant disposition) 艺术特色是追求古朴体现自然。(in pursuit of)
7. 他妈妈因血压过高被送往医院治疗。(hospitalize)
8. 警察呼吁凡是目击这一事故的人与他们联系。(witness)

Text B

Joseph Heller

Anonymous

American writer, who gained world fame with his satirical, anti-war novel *CATCH-22* (1961), set in the World War II Italy. The book was partly based on Heller's own experiences and influenced among others Robert Altman's comedy *Mash*, and the subsequent long-running TV series, set in the Korean War. The phrase "catch-22" has entered the English language to signify a no-win situation, particularly one created by a law, regulation or circumstance.

"All over the world, boys on every side of the bomb line were laying down their lives for what they had been told was their country, and no one seemed to mind, least of all the boys who were laying down their young lives. There was no end in sight." (from *Catch-22*)

Joseph Heller was born in Brooklyn, New York, as the son of poor Jewish parents. His Russian-born father, who was a bakery truck driver, died in 1927. After graduating from Abraham Lincoln High School in 1941,

> **regulation** /ˌreɡjʊˈleɪʃən/ *n.* an official rule made by a government or some other authority

Heller joined the Twelfth Air Force. He was stationed in Corsica, where he flew 60 combat missions as a B-25 bombardier. In 1949 Heller received his M.A. from Columbia University. He was a Fulbright scholar at Oxford in 1949–1950. Heller worked as a teacher at Pennsylvania State University (1950 – 1952), copywriter for the magazines *Time* (1952 – 1956), *Look* (1956 – 1958), and promotion manager for *McCall's*. He left *McCall's* in 1961 to teach fiction and dramatic writing at Yale University and the University of Pennsylvania.

His first stories Heller sold already during his student times. They were published in such magazines as *Atlantic Monthly* and *Esquire*. In the early 1950s he started working on *Catch-22*. At that time Heller was employed as a copywriter at a small advertising agency. Most of the book he wrote in the foyer of a West End Avenue apartment. "As I've said and repeated, I wrote the first chapter in longhand one morning in 1953, hunched over my desk at the advertising agency (from ideas and words that had leaped into my mind only the night before); the chapter was published in the quarterly *New World Writing #7* in 1955 under the title "Catch-18." (I received twenty-five dollars. The same issue carried a chapter from Jack Kerouac's *On the Road*, under a pseudonym.)" (from *Now and Then*, 1998) The novel went largely unnoticed until 1962, when its English publication received critical praise. And in *The New York World-Telegram* Richard Starnes opened his column with the prophetic words: "Yossarian will, I think, live a very long time." An earlier reviewer called the book "repetitious and monotonous", and another "dazzling performance that will outrage nearly as many readers as it delights."

The protagonist is Captain John Yossarian, lead bombardier of the 256th squadron, who is stationed at an airstrip on the fictitious island off the coast of Italy during WW II. Other characters in-

---

combat /ˈkɒmbæt/ *n.* fighting or a fight, especially during a time of war
mission /ˈmɪʃən/ *n.* a flight into space
bombardier /ˌbɒmbəˈdɪə/ *n.* the person on a military plane in the US air force who is responsible for aiming and dropping bombs
promotion /prəˈməʊʃən/ *n.* activities done in order to increase the sales of a product or service; a set of advertisements for a particular product or service
foyer /ˈfɔɪə/ *n.* an entrance hall in a private house or flat/apartment
longhand /ˈlɒŋhænd/ *n.* ordinary writing; not typed or written in shorthand
hunch /hʌntʃ/ *v.* to bend the top part of your body forward and raise your shoulders and back
pseudonym /ˈsjuːdənɪm/ *n.* a name used by sb., especially a writer, instead of their real name

---

prophetic /prəˈfetɪk/ *adj.* (formal) correctly stating or showing what will happen in the future
repetitious /ˌrepɪˈtɪʃəs/ *adj.* involving sth. that is often repeated
monotonous /məˈnɒtənəs/ *adj.* never changing and therefore boring
dazzling /ˈdæzəlɪŋ/ *adj.* of impressing sb. a lot with your beauty, skill, knowledge, etc.
outrage /ˈaʊtreɪdʒ/ *v.* to make sb. very shocked and angry
squadron /ˈskwɒdrən/ *n.* a group of military aircraft or ships forming a section a military force
airstrip /ˈeəˌstrɪp/ *n.* a narrow piece of cleared land that an aircraft can land on
fictitious /fɪkˈtɪʃəs/ *adj.* invented by sb. rather than true

> **conman** /ˈkɒnmæn/ n. (informal) a man who tricks others into giving him money, etc.
> **mess** /mes/ n. food or a meal served to a group of people, usually soldiers or sailors
> **lieutenant** /lefˈtenənt/ n. an officer of middle rank in the army, navy, or air force
> **evict** /ɪˈvɪkt/ v. to force sb. to leave a house or land, especially when you have the legal right to do so
> **sanity** /ˈsænɪti/ n. the state of having a normal healthy mind
> **discharge** /dɪsˈtʃɑːdʒ/ n. the act of officially allowing sb., or of telling sb., to leave somewhere, especially sb. in a hospital or the army
> **insane** /ɪnˈseɪn/ adj. seriously mentally ill and unable to live in normal society
> **relieve** /rɪˈliːv/ v. to dismiss sb. from a job, position, etc.
> **irrational** /ɪˈræʃənəl/ adj. not based on, or not using, clear logical thought
> **desert** /dɪˈzɜːt/ v. to leave the armed force without permission
> **chronological** /ˌkrɒnəˈlɒdʒɪkəl/ adj. (of a number of events) arranged in the order in which they happened
> **fragmented** /ˈfrægməntɪd/ adj. of breaking or making sth. break into small pieces or parts
> **narrative** /ˈnærətɪv/ n. (formal) a description of events, especially in a novel
> **surreal** /səˈrɪəl/ adj. very strange; more like a dream than reality, with ideas and images mixed together in a strange way

clude the conman Milo Minderbinder, company mess officer, who creates a successful black-market business, Major Major, Lieutenant Scheisskopf, who wants to turn his men into perfect parade ground robots, Chief White Halfoat, whose family is constantly chased and evicted by oil companies, and mail clerk Wintergreen, who is really running the war. Jossarian, struggles to retain his sanity and hopes to get a medical discharge by pretending to be insane. The story centers on the USAF regulation which suggests that willingness to fly dangerous combat missions must be considered insane, but if the airmen seek to be relieved on grounds of mental reasons, the request proves their sanity. Heller's absurd world follows the rules of Samuel Beckett and Lewis Carroll's Wonderland: "'Oh, you can't help that,' said the Cat: 'we're all mad here. I'm mad. You're mad.' 'How do you know I'm mad?' said Alice. 'You must be,' said the Cat, 'or you wouldn't have come here.'" And as Alice, Yossarian eventually rejects the irrational logic of his rabbit hole after his friends are killed or missing. But instead of waking up, Yossarian decides to desert to Sweden. The non-chronological, fragmented narrative underlines the surreal experience of the characters and the contrast between real life and illogicalities of war. It has been noted, that Heller's characters have similarities with Louis Falstein's novel *The Sky is a Lonely Place*, which was published earlier. Falstein depicts combat missions above Mediterranean during WW II. However, Heller's tone is comic. The publication of *Catch-22* signaled a more experimental approach to the war novel, anticipating such works as Thomas Pynchon's *V*.

(1963) and Kurt Vonnegut's *Slaughterhouse-Five* (1969). Heller also expressed the emerging rebelliousness of the Vietnam generation and criticism of mass society.

Catch-22 has enjoyed a steady sale since its publication. Mike Nichols's movie version of the novel from 1970 is considered disappointing, although its good cast tried its best. Nichols emphasized the absurdity of war, and as Heller, he rejected American militarism. Orson Welles, who also was interested in filming the book, was in the role of General Dreedle. After writing *Catch-22*, Heller worked on several Hollywood screenplays, such as *Sex and the Single Girl*, *Casino Royale*, and *Dirty Dingus Magee*, and contributed to the TV show "McHale's Navy" under the pseudonym Max Orange. In the 1960s Heller was involved with the anti-Vietnam war protest movement.

Heller waited 13 years before publishing his next novel, *Something Happened* (1974). It portrayed a corporation man Bob Slocum, who suffers from insomnia and almost smells the disaster mounting toward him. Slocum's life is undramatic, but he feels that his happiness is threatened by unknown forces. "When an ambulance comes, I'd rather not know for whom." He does not share Yossarian's rebelliousness, but he act cynically as a "wolf among a pack of wolves". Heller's play-within-a-play, *We bombed in New Haven* (1968), was written in part to express his protest against the Vietnam war. It was produced on Broadway and ran for 86 performances. *Catch-22* has also been dramatized. It was first performed at the John Drew Theater in East Hampton, New York, July 13, 1971.

Heller's later works include *Good as Gold* (1979), where the protagonist Bruce Gold tries to regain the Jewishness he has lost. Readers hailed the work as a return to puns and verbal games familiar from Heller's first novel. *God Knows* (1984) was a modern version of the story of King David and an allegory of what it is like for a Jew to survive in a hostile world. David has decided that he has been given one of the best parts of

---

cast /kɑːst/ *n.* all the people who act in a play or film/movie

absurdity /əbˈsɜːdəti, -ˈzɜːdəti/ *n.* being completely ridiculous; not being logical and sensible

militarism /ˈmɪlɪtərɪzəm/ *n.* the belief that a country should have great military strength in order to be powerful

insomnia /ɪnˈsɒmniə/ *n.* the condition of being unable to sleep

cynically /ˈsɪnɪkəli/ *adv.* believing that people only do things to help themselves rather than for good or honest reasons

regain /rɪˈɡeɪn/ *v.* to get back sth. you no longer have, especially an ability or quality

hail /heɪl/ *v.* to describe sb./sth. being very good or special, especially in newspaper, etc.

pun /pʌn/ *n.* the clever or humorous use of a word that has more than one meaning, or of words that have different meanings but sound the same

allegory /ˈælɪɡəri/ *n.* a story, play, picture, etc. in which each character or event is a symbol representing an idea or a quality, such as truth, evil, death, etc.; the use of such symbols

survive /səˈvaɪv/ *v.* to continue to live or exist in spite of a dangerous event or time

hostile /ˈhɒstaɪl/ *adj.* very unfriendly or aggressive and ready to argue or fight

the Bible. "I have suicide, regicide, patricide, homicide, fratricide, infanticide, adultery, incest, hanging, and more decapitations than just Saul's."

No Laughing Matter (1986), written with Speed Vogel, was a surprisingly cheerful account of Heller's experience as a victim of Guillain-Barré syndrome. During his recuperation Heller was visited among others by Mario Puzo, Dustin Hoffman and Mel Brooks. *Closing Time* (1994) is a sequel to *Catch-22*, depicting the current lives of its heroes. Yossarian is now 40 years older and as preoccupied with death as in the earlier novel. "Thank God for the atom bomb," says Yossarian. *Now and Then* (1998) is Heller's autobiographical work, evocation of his boyhood home, Brooklyn's Coney Island in the 1920s and 30's. "It has struck me since—it couldn't have done so then—that in *Catch-22* and in all my subsequent novels, and also in my one play, the resolution at the end of what narrative there is evolves from the death of someone other than the main character." (from *Now and Then*)

Heller had two children by his first marriage. His divorce was recounted in *No Laughing Matter*. In 1989 Heller married Valerie Humphries, a nurse he met while ill. Heller died of a heart attack at his home on Long Island on December 13, 1999. His last novel, *Portrait of an Artist as an old Man* (2000), was about a successful novelist who seeks an inspiration for his book. "A lifetime of experience had trained him never to toss away a page he had written, no matter how clumsy, until he had gone over it again for improvement, or had at least stored it in a folder for safekeeping or recorded the words on his computer." (from *Portrait of an Artist as an Old Man*)

---

regicide /ˈredʒɪsaɪd/ *n.* (formal) the crime of killing a king or queen; a person who is guilty of this crime
patricide /ˈpætrɪsaɪd/ *n.* (formal) the crime of killing your father; a person who is guilty of this crime
fratricide /ˈfrætrɪsaɪd/ *n.* (formal) the crime of killing your brother or sister; a person who is guilty of this crime
infanticide /ɪnˈfæntɪsaɪd/ *n.* (formal) the crime of killing a baby; a person who is guilty of this crime
adultery /əˈdʌltəri/ *n.* sex between a married person and sb. who is not their husband or wife
incest /ˈɪnsest/ *n.* involving sex between two people in a family who are very closely related
decapitation /dɪˌkæpɪteɪʃən/ *n.* cutting off sb.'s head
syndrome /ˈsɪndrəʊm/ *n.* a set of physical conditions that show you have a particular disease or medical problem
recuperation /rɪˌkjuːpəreɪʃən/ *n.* getting back your health, strength or energy after being ill/sick, tired, injured, etc.
sequel /ˈsiːkwəl/ *adj.* a book, film/movie, play, etc. that continues the story of an earlier one
depict /dɪˈpɪkt/ *v.* to describe sth. in words, or give an impression of sth. in words or with a picture
evocation /ˌevəʊˈkeɪʃən/ *n.* bringing a feeling, a memory or an image into your mind
recount /rɪˈkaʊnt/ *v.* (formal) to tell sb. about sth., especially sth. that you have experienced
toss /tɒs/ *v.* to throw sth. lightly or carelessly
clumsy /ˈklʌmzi/ *adj.* (of actions and statements) done without skill or in a way that offends people
folder /ˈfəʊldə/ *n.* a cardboard or plastic cover for holding loose papers, etc.

Notes

1. Robert Altman (1925–2006)

The famous director in USA. *Mash* was directed by him in 1970.

2. Fulbright scholar

Sponsored by the US Department of State, Fulbright is the largest US international exchange program offering opportunities for students, scholars and professionals to undertake international graduate study, advanced research.

3. *Look*

Look magazine is the name of a number of publications: *Look* is a weekly, general-interest magazine published in the United States.

4. Pulitzer Prize

The Pulitzer Prize is an American award regarded as the highest national honor in print journalism, literary achievements, etc.

5. Samuel Beckett (1906–1989)

Irish novelist and playwright, one of the great names of Absurd Theatre, although recent study regards Beckett as postmodernist. His plays are concerned with human suffering and survival, and his characters are struggling with meaninglessness and the world of the nothing. Beckett was awarded the Nobel Prize for Literature in 1969.

6. Lewis Carroll (1832–1898)

The pseudonym of the English writer and mathematician Charles Lutwidge Dodgson, known especially for *ALICE'S ADVENTURES IN WONDERLAND* (1865) and *THROUGH THE LOOKING GLASS* (1872).

7. Thomas Pynchon (1937–)

American novelist and short-story writer whose works combine black humour and fantasy to depict human alienation in the chaos of modern society. In 1963 Pynchon won the Faulkner Foundation Award for his first novel, *V.* (1963), a whimsical, cynically absurd tale of a middle-aged Englishman's search for "V", an elusive, supernatural adventuress appearing in various guises at critical periods in European history.

8. Kurt Vonnegut

Kurt Vonnegut is a legendary author, WW II veteran, humanist, artist, smoker and *In These Times* senior editor. His classic works include *Slaughterhouse-Five, Breakfast of Champions, Cat's Cradle*.

Comprehension Questions

Choose the best answer for each of the following questions.

1. Which of the following statements is NOT true about the novel *Catch-22*?
   A. It's an anti-war novel.
   B. It's set in the World War II Italy.
   C. It's based on Joseph Heller's own experience.
   D. Its protagonist is Captain John Yossarian.
2. Joseph Heller ever worked as _____.
   A. copywriter　　　B. teacher　　　C. bombardier　　　D. all of the above
3. Which of the following statements about the phrase "catch-22" is **Not** true according to your understanding?
   A. A difficult situation from which there is no escape because you need to do one thing before doing a second, and you can't do the second thing before doing the first.
   B. Between the devil and the deep sea.
   C. Making you feel shy, awkward or ashamed.
   D. Dilemma faced by sb. who is bound to suffer, whichever course of action he takes.
4. Which of Joseph Heller's later works is regarded as a return to puns and verbal games familiar from Heller's *Catch-22*?
   A. *Something Happened*　　　　B. *Good as Gold*
   C. *Closing Time*　　　　　　　 D. *Now and Then*

Writing Practice

Talent alone cannot make a writer. —Ralph Waldo Emerson.
Give some tips on **How to Become a Good Writer.**

Further Study

Usually, writers are categorized to a certain school, try to find that which school Earnest Hemingway and Joseph Heller belong to? How are these schools born and what the characteristics of each school? List other writers that belong to these schools.

Unit

Reflections on Life

Unit Goals

After completing the texts in this unit, students will be able to:
- know how to deal with difficulties in life;
- develop the ability to work independently of the teacher;
- extend vocabulary through recognition of conversion prefixes.

Before Reading

Hands-on Activities

1. Try to find as much information as possible to prove that "Attitude is everything" —how we see the world affects how we feel, our relationships and every aspect of our day-to-day existence. Then share the information with your fellow students in class.
2. Read some stories on Zhang Haidi, who is a good example to students, and reflect on how she overcomes difficulties in life and finally realizes her value in society.

Brainstorming

Brainstorm the following questions. Work in pairs or groups to discuss these questions.

1. What do you expect will happen in your future life?
2. If life doesn't go as what you have expected (for example, if you failed in your career), what will you do to face the problem?
3. Do you believe that "attitude is everything?" Can you give an example of the story of success led by positive attitude?
4. What is your understanding of "life is a journey?"

A Glimpse at Words and Expressions

Please read the following sentences. Pay attention to the underlined part in each sentence and see how these expressions are used in the context, and then write down their meanings in the blanks provided.

1. He graciously accepted and sat down in one of the cushioned chairs, albeit slightly uneasy. (   )
2. He sighed, took a sip of his coffee and began to tell me how much he was becoming disillusioned with work and the whole scheme of things. (   )
3. It seemed that the bottom line of the matter was that he was tired of pulling the weight for his family and wanted out. (   )
4. The spark has gone out of my marriage and I see no other alternative than to end it. (   )
5. "What has happened here is that when you first got married, you had the tendency to think 'outside of the square'." (   )
6. Basically, Elmer, you're a walking time bomb, ready to explode anytime and it doesn't have to be that way. (   )
7. "You've got a point there," he said. (   )
8. I see not having to worry over bills and having a chance to enjoy life instead of always fretting over what's going to get paid this month and what isn't. (   )
9. After that, I joined a gym and chewed the fat with my buddies there. I've never been happier! (   )
10. I watched Elmer walk back to his house and it could have been my imagination, but I do believe there was a step in his gait that wasn't there before. (   )

Text A

Think Inside the Square to Keep Those Love Fires Burning

By Dorothy Thompson
(Abridged and Edited)

I was sitting in my **sanctuary** in my back yard **contemplating** the world's mysteries and minding my own business when a fellow neighbor walked up to me and started a conversation. As he looked a little **distressed**, I invited him into my little spiritual **oasis** and offered him a cup of coffee. He **graciously** accepted and sat down in one of the **cushioned** chairs, **al-**
5 **beit** slightly uneasy. I could tell by looking at him that he was troubled and I asked him what the matter was. He sighed, took a **sip** of his coffee and began to tell me how much he was becoming **disillusioned** with work and the whole **scheme** of things. It seemed that the bottom line of the matter was that he was tired of
10 pulling the weight for his family and wanted out.

"Elmer," I said, "how long have you been married?"

"Too long," was his reply. "I'm working
15 two jobs while she's sitting home, doing nothing. The **spark** has gone out of my marriage and I see no other **alternative** than to end it."

He took a sip of his coffee and put it back down on the **patio** table. The worry in his eyes
20 was evident and I felt the urge to fix things, as was my nature when it comes to helping people not only find their soul mates, but keep them as well.

"Elmer," I began, "when I tell you this,
25 you have to keep in mind that I'm telling you from a professional **standpoint** and not as a friend. You understand, don't you?"

"I'm listening," he said.

---

sanctuary /ˈsæŋktʃuəri/ *n.* a safe place, especially one where people who are being chased or attacked can stay and be protected
contemplate /ˈkɒntəmpleɪt/ *v.* to think deeply about sth. for a long time
distressed /dɪˈstrest/ *adj.* upset and anxious
oasis /əʊˈeɪsɪs/ *n.* a pleasant place or period of time in the middle of sth. unpleasant or difficult
graciously /ˈɡreɪʃəsli/ *adv.* elegantly
cushion /ˈkʊʃən/ *v.* to make sth. soft with a cushion
albeit /ɔːlˈbiːɪt/ *conj.* (formal) although
sip /sɪp/ *n.* a very small amount of a drink that you take into your mouth
disillusioned /ˌdɪsɪˈluːʒənd/ *adj.* disappointed because the person you admired or the idea you believed to be good and true now seems without value
scheme /skiːm/ *n.* a plan or system for doing or organizing sth.
spark /spɑːk/ *n.* a special quality of energy, intelligence or enthusiasm that makes sb. very imaginative, amusing, etc.
alternative /ɔːlˈtɜːnətɪv/ *n.* a thing that you can choose to do or have out of two or more possibilities
patio /ˈpætiəʊ/ *n.* a flat hard area outside, and usually behind, a house where people can sit
standpoint /ˈstændpɔɪnt/ *n.* a point of view or way of thinking about ideas or situations

"You remember when you married Fran and all the world was a happy and blissful place?" I asked him.

"Sure, I remember."

"What has happened here is that when you first got married, you had the tendency to think 'outside of the square'" I said.

"Outside of the square?"

"Yes, instead of focusing on yourself, you took on responsibilities such as caring for your family and all those other obligations that entails when one agrees to marry. You put your own needs aside to make sure that your wife and children were well cared for. What has happened is reality crashed down upon you and you have no inner resources left in which to restore things to the way they were. Basically, Elmer, you're a walking time bomb, ready to explode anytime and it doesn't have to be that way."

> blissful /'blɪsfəl/ *adj.* extremely happy; showing happiness
> tendency /'tendənsi/ *n.* if sb./sth. has a particular tendency, they are likely to behave or act in a particular way
> obligation /ˌɒblɪ'ɡeɪʃən/ *n.* the state of being forced to do sth. because it is your duty, or because of a law, etc.
> entail /ɪn'teɪl/ *v.* to involve sth. that cannot be avoided
> explode /ɪk'spləʊd/ *v.* to burst or make sth. burst loudly and violently, causing damage
> mortgage /'mɔːɡɪdʒ/ *n.* a legal agreement by which a bank or similar organization lends you money to buy a house, etc., and you pay the money back over a particular number of years; the sum of money that you borrow
> tuition /tjuˈɪʃən/ *n.* the money that you pay to be taught, especially in a college or university
> fret /fret/ *v.* to be worried or unhappy and not able to relax

"It doesn't?"

"Of course, it doesn't. It's time to think 'inside the square', Elmer. It's time you focused on what makes you happy in order to make the rest of your family happy."

"You've got a point there," he said.

"You've got to begin with what makes Elmer happy," I continued. "Look at you. You're working two jobs and you come home and all you can do is eat a little dinner and go to bed. Then, you get back up and do it all over again. It's no wonder that you're distressed. What we have here, Elmer, is not disillusionment with your marriage; it's disillusionment with yourself and you don't even realize it."

"But, I have to work two jobs," he interrupted. "There's the mortgage, the kid's college tuition, car payments."

"Elmer, stop right there," I interrupted. "What you are doing is looking 'outside of the square' again. Look 'inside of the square' and what do you see?"

Elmer stopped and thought for a moment. "I see someone who wants good things in life," he said. "I see not having to worry over bills and having a chance to enjoy life instead of always fretting over what's going to get paid this month and what isn't."

"Okay, Elmer," I said, "what can you do to make this happen for you?"

"Tell my wife to get a job?"

"Yes, that would certainly help, but we're not talking about your wife right now; we're talking about you. What can you do for yourself to keep your marriage alive and become a happier person within?"

"Accept the things I cannot change and focus on the things I can?"

"And how do you do that?" I asked.

"By looking 'inside the square' and not blaming others for my unhappiness?"

"Exactly."

Elmer is but one of the millions of people in the world that think running away from their problems is the solution to finding happiness within themselves. And they're dead wrong. Running away only prolongs the problem and, in fact, can intensify the very problem that you need to fix. Once Elmer understands what he has to fix about himself, only positive energy will flow, which will eradicate the negativities in his life.

I saw Elmer a week later while I was pruning my shrubs and he stopped for a bit to tell me his good news.

"I just have to tell you," he said, out of breath. "I took your advice and started thinking 'inside the square'. I took up cycling like I used to do in my twenties. After that, I told my wife that from now on, I'm going to do this twice a week. She looked at me in astonishment, but then said, 'Elmer, that's wonderful!' I was so surprised that she would approve of this. After that, I joined a gym and chewed the fat with my buddies there. I've never been happier!"

"That's wonderful, Elmer," I said. "And, how is your marriage?"

"Oh, that's the best part," he said, excitedly. "My wife looks at me like I'm a new man. It seems my positive attitude was contagious and even her own attitude has changed. She's thinking of joining me for a long-distance cycling trip to the mountains! And, even better than that, she's willing to join me for a budgeting class so that we can manage our bills better!"

"I'm so happy for you, Elmer," I said. "Just remember this—whenever things start getting bad, think 'inside the square' and do

---

dead /ded/ *adv.* completely; exactly

prolong /prə'lɒŋ/ *v.* to make sth. last longer

intensify /ɪn'tensɪfaɪ/ *v.* to increase in degree or strength; to make sth. increase in degree or strength

eradicate /ɪ'rædɪkeɪt/ *v.* to destroy or get rid of sth. completely, especially sth. bad

negativity /ˌnegə'tɪvɪti/ *n.* a tendency to consider only the bad side of sth./sb.; a lack of enthusiasm or hope

prune /pruːn/ *v.* to cut off some of the branches from a tree, bush, etc. so that it will grow better and stronger

shrub /ʃrʌb/ *n.* a large plant that is smaller than a tree and that has several stems of wood coming from the ground

buddy /'bʌdi/ *n.* a friend

contagious /kən'teɪdʒəs/ *adj.* spreading or tending to spread from one to another; infectious

105 something good for yourself. The positive attitude will offset any negative energies that might arise and through
bonding with your wife again, you will find that over time,
it can only get better."

    I watched Elmer walk back to his house and it could
110 have been my imagination, but I do believe there was a step in his gait that wasn't there before.

    Sometimes life gets in the way of maintaining a positive outlook on life, but if you stop for a moment and "fix" things within your own self, everything will come together not only for you, but for the loved ones in your family, too!

> **offset** /ˈɒːfset/ v. to use one cost, payment or situation in order to cancel or reduce the effect of another
>
> **gait** /ɡeɪt/ n. a way of walking

Better Know More

About the author

Dorothy Thompson is a syndicated advice columnist, soul mate relationship coach and compiler/editor of the book that is going to change the way we view soul mates, "*Romancing the soul—true stories of soul mates from around the world and beyond*". She is also the author of the e-book, "*How to Find and Keep Your Soul Mate*" and runs a highly successful advice blog called "Are you my soul mate?" at http://www.soulmateadvice.blogspot.com.

For more information, visit her home on the web at http://www.dorothythompson.net.

Check Your Understanding

Answer the following questions based on the text you have just learned.

1. What was the author doing when a fellow neighbor walked up to her and started a conversation?
2. Why did the author invite him into her little spiritual oasis and offer him a cup of coffee?
3. Why could the author know that the neighbour was troubled?
4. What does "think 'outside the square'" mean in the text?

5. Why did the author say to the neighbour "What has happened is reality crashed upon you and you have no inner resources left in which to restore things to the way they were?"
6. What did the author mean by saying "you're a walking time bomb?"
7. Why did the author say that it was not disillusionment with marriage, but disillusionment with the neighbor himself?
8. Why did the neighbor have to work two jobs?
9. What can the neighbor do for himself to keep his marriage alive and become a happier person within?
10. Is running away from problems the solution to finding happiness within oneself? If yes, why? If not, why not?
11. How is the neighbor's marriage going after he took the author's advice?
12. Why did the author believe that there was a step in his gait that wasn't there before?

A Sip of Word Formation

Conversion Prefixes

Prefixes modify the meaning of the stem, but usually do not change the part of speech of the original word. Exceptions are the prefixes "*be-*" and "*en (m)-*". *Be-* and *en-* change the part of speech of the stem when they are attached to the original word.

1. *be-*   benumb   befriend
2. *en- (em-)*   enslave   enable   embody   empower
3. *a-*   asleep   ablaze

Build Your Vocabulary

A. Try to complete each sentence with the right form of the word given at the end of each sentence.

1. Pakistani President Pervez Musharraf vowed to support reforms to _____ women in the male-dominated society, but said the ultimate responsibility for change lay with women. **(power)**
2. She was _____ after she had found her own parents. **(noble)**
3. Mark Twain keeps away from those who try to _____ his ambitions. **(little)**
4. How to _____ and assess the value of technology has been the focus of researchers

and practitioners. (body)
5. The people _____ the plane are from all works of life. (board)
6. The ship was listing badly but still kept _____. (float)
7. At the sight of her matchless beauty, both the princes were _____. (witch)
8. _____ the lake and on the side stand five beautiful pavilions connected to one another. (cross)

B. Decide which form of the conversion prefix to use to make each word. Add the prefix and write the whole word. Then give the part of speech of each new word and make a sentence with each new word.

wake		case	
camp		code	
little		slave	
circle		rage	
large		courage	
sleep		drift	
blaze		rich	

You'd Like to Be

A Skilled Text Weaver

Fill in each blank with the right word or phrase listed below. Make changes where necessary.

fret	alternative	fellow	chew the fat
oasis	mortgage	contagious	contemplate
sanctuary	offset	pull one's weight	spark

1. As we sit on the threshold of a new millennium it seems only natural to reflect on the past and _____ the future.
2. Based in the heart of England and busy city life, the show proposes an escape from modern day living and retreat to a spiritual _____.
3. A healthy and positive attitude is _____ but don't wait to catch it from others. Be a carrier.
4. Don't _____, we will get there on time.
5. The fleeing rebels found a _____ in the nearby church.

6. You have the _____ of marrying or remaining a bachelor.
7. We are having difficulty keeping up our _____ payments.
8. Mr. Green urged the electronics industry to foster the planting of trees to _____ the effect on the environment.
9. There is a life waiting for you—a life blazing with enthusiasm—and it all starts with a _____.
10. On the contrary if we get to know our neighbors well we can build up community spirit among our _____ residents, so that all neighbors can work together to everybody's benefit.
11. As the oldest of seven children, Andy was expected to _____ and was often put in charge of his younger siblings around the farm.
12. If you _____ with someone, you chat with them in an informal and friendly way about things that interest you.

A Smart Word Player

Look up the dictionary and explain the meanings of the italicized words in the following sentences.

1. I invited him into my little *spiritual oasis* and offered him a cup of coffee.
2. He *graciously* accepted and sat down in one of the *cushioned chairs*, *albeit* slightly uneasy.
3. You remember when you married Fran and all the world was a happy and *blissful* place?
4. There's the *mortgage*, the kid's college *tuition*, car payments.
5. Running away only *prolongs* the problem and, in fact, can *intensify* the very problem that you need to fix.
6. After that, I joined a gym and *chewed the fat* with my *buddies* there.

A Sharp Interpreter

Paraphrase the following sentences. Change the sentence structure if necessary.

1. It seemed that the bottom line of the matter was that he was tired of pulling the weight for his family and wanted out.
2. The worry in his eyes was evident and I felt the urge to fix things.
3. What has happened is reality crashed down upon you and you have no inner resources left in which to restore things to the way they were.
4. Elmer is but one of the millions of people in the world that think running away from their problems is the solution to finding happiness within themselves.
5. It seems my positive attitude was contagious and even her own attitude has changed.

6. The positive attitude will offset any negative energies that might arise and through bonding with your wife again.
7. Sometimes life gets in the way of maintaining a positive outlook on life, but if you stop for a moment and "fix" things within your own self, everything will come together not only for you.

A Careful Writer

Study the following synonyms and complete the sentences. Make changes where necessary.

contemplate   study   consider   meditate

1. We need time to _____ a suitable answer.
2. She lay on the grass, _____ the high, blue sky.
3. She _____ for two days before giving her answer.
4. His success is not surprising if you _____ his excellent training.

distressed   disturbed   worried   uneasy

5. We meet in _____ times but we must not be _____. We must be calm and peaceful, for peace cannot come from hearts _____ and angry.
6. The curious look from the strangers around her made her feel _____.
7. They are constantly tense and _____, apparently without valid reasons.
8. He was too _____ and confused to answer their questions.

evident   manifest   apparent

9. You don't seem to have any _____ experience in working with large aquatic appliance.
10. It is _____ that he is guilty; his fingerprints were found at the crime scene.
11. Her ability is _____, but she is not attractive.

A Superb Bilingualist

Translate the following sentences into English, using the words or phrases given in brackets.

1. 我们的底线是必须增加销售额,否则就减工资。(the bottom line)
2. 他厌倦了为家庭尽职责,想退出了。(pull one's weight)
3. 你没有打扰我们。我们只是在闲聊。(chew the fat)
4. 你在烦躁什么？烦躁也是无补的。(fret about)

5. 真相其实只是一个幻象,虽然这个幻象相当顽固。(albeit)
6. 他对生活的热情具有感染力。(contagious)

Text B

Learn How to Face Difficulty

By Deanna Mascle

(Abridged and Edited)

"*It is not because things are difficult that we do not dare; it is because we do not dare that they are difficult.*"

—Seneca the Younger

This is a great quote to both contemplate and to apply to your life.

5   How often do you hear people complain? Pick a topic—love, friendship, careers, etc. The list of issues that people complain about is endless. You and I are no different. Perhaps we don't complain about each of these things but more than likely there is something that we complain 10 about with great regularity.

Now, sometimes complaints are simply a way to vent some frustration at the moment but we don't really want anything to change in this area. However, more often than not, someone regularly complains about one specific problem.

15   If I had a dollar for every time I heard one friend complain about the difficulty of finding a good man I could throw her a huge wedding bash or perhaps simply buy her a husband in some small third-world country. When I thought about my friend Donna's problem and applied Seneca's quote to it a 20 light bulb suddenly appeared above my head just like in the cartoons!

It was true! Donna is having difficulty finding a good man simply because she isn't daring enough. Sure she goes out on dates and tries 25 to maintain an active social life, however she holds herself aloof emotionally. She isn't willing to dare much at all when it comes to her

---

quote /kwəʊt/ *n.* quotation

contemplate /ˈkɒntəmpleɪt/ *v.* to think deeply about sth. for a long time

vent /vent/ *v.* to express feelings, especially anger, strongly

more often than not usually; in a way that is typical of sb./sth.

bash /bæʃ/ *n.* a large party or celebration

daring /ˈdeərɪŋ/ *adj.* brave; willing to do dangerous or unusual things; involving danger or taking risks

aloof /əˈluːf/ *adj.* not friendly or interested in other people

heart—so how can she hope that someone else will do so for her? Sure, there might be someone, somewhere, but she is also missing out on relationships, at least friendships, with some really great guys simply because she is too afraid to dare to care.

That is sad. We all know that love is marvelous but it is also frightening, however we have to take risks in order to experience it fully. Sometimes we might get hurt, however, more often than not, we will find the rewards outweigh the risks. There is no guarantee that Donna opens herself up and dares to love and that she will find the love of her life—however, there is certainly a guarantee that a life filled with love is more rewarding than one that is not.

> guarantee /ˌgærən'tiː/ n. something that makes sth. else certain to happen
> horrible /'hɒrɪbəl/ adj. very bad or unpleasant; used to describe sth. that you do not like
> doom /duːm/ v. to make sb./sth. certain to fail, suffer, die, etc.
> complaisant /kəm'pleɪzənt/ adj. ready to accept other people's actions and opinions and to do what other people want

I have another friend who is also afraid to dare. Jeff hates his job. No, that's not exactly right. He loves the work itself but he really hates the company that he works for. He finds the management very difficult to work for (and if even a small percentage of the stories he tells are true then he's right, it is a horrible place to work).

However, every time I suggest he look for a job somewhere else he comes up with some excuse about how difficult it would be. True the job market isn't great, but he's a skilled worker in a high-demand field so I'm sure he could find something. He's doomed his job search before he even started it because he's not daring enough.

It wouldn't be fair to share my friends' examples without pointing to my own shortcomings. Probably the greatest difficulty in my own life is within my marriage and that is simply because I don't dare enough emotionally there. I have become too complaisant and take my husband and marriage for granted. I need to dare more emotionally.

So think about the difficulties in your own life and apply Seneca's rule then decide if you can be more daring! All the best!

Notes

  Deanna Mascle

Deanna Mascle is an inspirational freelance writer. You can find more inspiration at *Inspiration* by Dawggone and her inspirational ezines *Words of Inspiration Online* and *Daily Quote Online*.

Comprehension Questions

1. Can you give an example to explain the quote by Seneca?
2. What does the author mean by "You and I are no different?"
3. What is the function of complaints sometimes?
4. According to the author, why did Donna have difficulty in finding a good man?
5. What is characteristic of love?
6. Does Jeff really hate his job? Why?
7. What is the real reason that Jeff has doomed his job search?
8. What is the greatest difficulty in the author's own life?

Writting Practice

Read the following short passage and write a composition of your understanding in about 100 words.

Teacher Debbie Moon's first-graders were discussing a picture of a family. One little boy in the picture had different color hair from other family members. One child suggested that he was adopted, and a little girl named Jocelyn said, "I know all about adoptions because I'm adopted." "What does it mean to be adopted?" asked another child. "It means," said Jocelyn, "that you grew in your mother's heart instead of her tummy."

Further Study

1. Visit http://www.chinaenglish.com.cn/n7887c76.aspx and read the story entitled *The Girl on the Train*. What is your impression on the blind girl? What is her attitude towards life? What can you learn from her stories?
2. After learning the lessons in this unit, does your attitude towards life change to be positive and full of enthusiasm? If yes, try to write down this process of the change of your ideas and feelings.

Unit 9

Ambition

Unit Goals

After completing the lessons in this unit, students will be able to:
- know the importance of ambition and have a better understanding of the essence of life;
- develop the ability to self-evaluate and strengthen personal traits and develop a personal professional plan;
- extend vocabulary through recognition of noun suffixes.

Before Reading

Hands-on Activities

Make full use of your school library and read at least three articles about how important people (such as, Zhou Enlai, Madam Curie) do in their life to realize their ambition.
- get a better understanding of the importance of ambition;
- have your own ambition in mind before preparing the lessons in this unit.

Brainstorming

Brainstorm the following questions. Work in pairs or groups to discuss these questions.

1. What is your dream or ambition?
2. Are you an ambitious person? If yes, to what degree? If not, why?
3. Have you ever made a five-year or ten-year plan towards your future development?
4. Is ambition good or bad for one's development? Why?
5. If you have dreams, what should you do to achieve them?

6. Are dreams essential or necessary to one's development in life or career?

A Glimpse at Words and Expressions

Please read the following sentences. Pay attention to the underlined part in each sentence and see how these expressions are used in the context, and then write down their meanings in the blanks provided.

1. Why are some people born with <u>a fire in the belly</u>? ( )
2. Every buffalo you kill for your family is one less for somebody else's; every acre of land you occupy <u>elbows out</u> somebody else. ( )
3. For every person <u>consumed with the need</u> to achieve, there's someone content to accept whatever life brings. ( )
4. People with goals but no energy are the ones who <u>wind up sitting on the couch</u> saying "One day I'm going to build a better mousetrap." ( )
5. Is the successful musician to whom melody comes naturally more driven than the unsuccessful one who <u>sweats out</u> every note? ( )
6. Most troubling of all, what about when enough ambition <u>becomes way too much</u>? ( )
7. They have by no means <u>thrown the curtain all the way back</u>, but they have begun to part it. ( )
8. The phlegmatic child who never really showed much <u>go</u>. ( )
9. But if it's genes that run the show, what accounts for the Shipps, who didn't <u>bestir themselves until the cusp of adulthood</u>? ( )
10. It's members of the upper middle class, reasonably safe economically but not so safe that a bad break couldn't <u>spell catastrophe</u>, who are most driven to improve their lot. ( )

Text A

Ambition: Why Some People Are Most Likely to Succeed

By Jeffrey Kluger
(Abridged and Edited)

You don't get as successful as Gregg and Drew Shipp by accident. Shake hands with the 36-year-old fraternal twins who co-own the sprawling Hi Fi Personal Fitness club in Chicago,  and it's clear you're in the presence of people who thrive on their drive. But that wasn't always the case. The twins' father founded the Jovan perfume company, a glamorous business that spun off the kinds of glamorous profits that made it possible for the Shipps to amble through high school, coast into college and never much worry about getting the rent paid or keeping the fridge filled. But before they graduated, their sense of drift began to trouble them. At about the same time, their father sold off the company, and with it went the cozy billets in adult life that had always served as an emotional backstop for the boys.

That did it. By the time they got out of school, both Shipps had entirely transformed themselves, changing from boys who might have grown up to live off the family's wealth to men consumed with going out and creating their own. "At this point," says Gregg, "I consider myself to be almost maniacally ambitious."

It shows. In 1998 the brothers went into the gym trade. They spotted a modest health club doing a modest business, bought out the owner and transformed the place into a luxury facility where private trainers could reserve space for top-dollar clients. In the years since, the company has outgrown one building, then another, and the brothers are about to move a third time. Gregg, a communications major at college, manages the club's clients, while

---

fraternal /frəˈtɜːnl/ *adj.* connected with the relationship that exists between brothers
sprawling /ˈsprɔːlɪŋ/ *adj.* spreading in an untidy way
glamorous /ˈɡlæmərəs/ *adj.* especially attractive and exciting, and different from ordinary things or people
spun off to happen or to produce sth. as a new or unexpected result of sth. that already exists
amble /ˈæmbəl/ *v.* to walk at a slow relaxed speed
coast (into) to be successful at sth. without having to try hard
maniacal /məˈnaɪəkəl/ *adj.* wild or violent

Drew, a business major, oversees the more hardheaded chore of finance and expansion.

"We're not sitting still," Drew says. "Even now that we're doing twice the business we did at our old place, there's a thirst that needs to be quenched."

Why is that? Why are some people born with a fire in the belly, while others—like the Shipps—need something to get their pilot light lit? And why do others never get the flame of ambition going? Is there a family anywhere that doesn't have its overachievers and underachievers—its Jimmy Carters and Billy Carters, its Jeb Bushes and Neil Bushes—and find itself wondering how they all could have come splashing out of exactly the same gene pool?

> quench /kwentʃ/ v. to drink so that you no longer feel thirsty
> portfolio /pɔːtˈfəʊljəʊ/ n. a thin flat case used for carrying documents, drawings, etc.
> zero-sum game n. a situation in which what is gained by one person or group is lost by another person or group
> buffalo /ˈbʌfələʊ/ n. a large animal of the cow family
> punch out to record the time you leave work by putting a card into a special machine
> anthropologist /ˌænθrəˈpɒlədʒɪst/ n. a person who studies anthropology
> eccentricity /ˌeksenˈtrɪsɪti/ n. behavior that people think is strange or unusual; the quality of being unusual and different from other people

Of all the impulses in humanity's behavioral portfolio, ambition—that need to grab an ever bigger piece of the resource pie before someone else gets it—ought to be one of the most democratically distributed. Nature is a zero-sum game, after all. Every buffalo you kill for your family is one less for somebody else's; every acre of land you occupy elbows out somebody else. Given that, the need to get ahead ought to be hard-wired into all of us equally.

And yet it's not. For every person consumed with the need to achieve, there's someone content to accept whatever life brings. For everyone who chooses the 80-hour workweek, there's someone punching out at 5.

Men and women—so it's said—express ambition differently; so do Americans and Europeans, baby boomers and Gen Xers, the middle class and the well-to-do. Even among the manifestly motivated, there are degrees of ambition.

Not only do we struggle to understand why some people seem to have more ambition than others, but we can't even agree on just what ambition is. "Ambition is an evolutionary product," says anthropologist Edward Lowe at Soka University of America, in Aliso Viejo, Calif. "No matter how social status is defined, there are certain people in every community who aggressively pursue it and others who aren't so aggressive."

Dean Simonton, a psychologist at the University of California, Davis, who studies genius, creativity and eccentricity, believes it's more complicated than that.

"Ambition is energy and determination," he says. "But it calls for goals too. People with goals but no energy are the ones who wind up sitting on the couch saying 'One day I'm going to build a better mousetrap.' People with energy but no clear goals just dissipate themselves in one desultory project after the next."

Assuming you've got drive, dreams and skill, is all ambition equal? Is the overworked lawyer on the partner track any more ambitious than the overworked parent on the mommy track? Is the successful musician to whom melody comes naturally more driven than the unsuccessful one who sweats out every note? We may listen to Mozart, but should we applaud Salieri?

Most troubling of all, what about when enough ambition becomes way too much? Grand dreams unmoored from morals are the stuff of tyrants—or at least of Enron. The 16-hour workday filled with high stress and at-the-desk meals is the stuff of burnout and heart attacks. Even among kids, too much ambition quickly starts to do real harm. In a just completed study, anthropologist Peter Demerath of Ohio State University surveyed 600 students at a high-achieving high school where most of the kids are triple-booked with advanced-placement courses, sports and after-school jobs. About 70% of them reported that they were starting to feel stress some or all of the time.

Anthropologists, psychologists and others have begun looking more closely at these issues, seeking the roots of ambition in family, culture, gender, genes and more. They have by no means thrown the curtain all the way back, but they have begun to part it. "It's fundamentally human to be prestige conscious," says Soka's Lowe. "It's not enough just to be fed and housed. People want more."

If humans are an ambitious species, it's clear we're not the only one. Many animals are known to signal their ambitious tendencies almost from birth. Even before wolf pups are weaned, they begin sorting themselves out into alphas and all the others. The alphas are quicker, more curious, greedier for space, milk, Mom—and they stay that way for life. Alpha wolves wander widely, breed annually and may live to a geriatric 10 or 11 years old. Lower-ranking wolves enjoy none of these benefits—staying close to home,

---

mousetrap /'maʊstræp/ *n.* a trap with a powerful spring that is used, for example in a house, for catching mice

dissipate /'dɪsɪpeɪt/ *v.* to waste sth., such as time or money, especially by not planning the best way of using it

desultory /'desəltəri/ *adj.* going from one thing to another, without a definite plan and without enthusiasm

melody /'melədi/ *n.* a tune, especially the main tune in a piece of music written for several instruments or voices

moor /mʊə/ *v.* to attach a boat, ship, etc. to a fixed object or to the land with a rope, or anchor it

prestige /pre'stiːʒ/ *n.* the respect and admiration that sb./sth. has because of their social position, or what they have done

pup /pʌp/ *n.* a young animal of various species

wean /wiːn/ *v.* to gradually stop feeding a baby or young animal with its mother's milk and start feeding it with solid food

alpha wolf a top-ranking wolf; the leader of a wolf pack

geriatric /ˌdʒeri'ætrɪk/ *n.* an old person, especially one with poor physical or mental health

breeding rarely and usually dying before they're 4.

Humans often report the same kind of temperamental determinism. Families are full of stories of the inexhaustible infant who grew up to be an entrepreneur, the phlegmatic child who never really showed much go. But if it's genes that run the show, what accounts for the Shipps, who didn't bestir themselves until the cusp of adulthood? And what, more tellingly, explains identical twins—precise genetic templates of each other who ought to be temperamentally identical but often exhibit profound differences in the octane of their ambition?

Ongoing studies of identical twins have measured achievement motivation—lab language for ambition—in identical siblings separated at birth, and found that each twin's profile overlaps 30% to 50% of the other's. In genetic terms, that's an awful lot. But that still leaves a great deal that can be determined by experiences in infancy, subsequent upbringing and countless other imponderables.

But even if something as primal as the reproductive impulse wires you one way, it's possible for other things to rewire you completely. Two of the biggest influences on your level of ambition are the family that produced you and the culture that produced your family.

When measuring ambition, anthropologists divide families into four categories: poor, struggling but getting by, upper middle class, and rich. For members of the first two groups, who are fighting just to keep the electricity on and the phone bill paid, ambition is often a luxury. For the rich, it's often unnecessary. It's members of the upper middle class, reasonably safe economically but not so safe that a bad break couldn't spell catastrophe, who are most driven to improve their lot.

But some societies make you more anxious than others. The U.S. has always been a me-first culture, as befits a nation that grew from a scattering of people on a fat saddle of continent where land was often given away. That have-it-all ethos persists today, even though the resource freebies are long since gone. Other countries came of age differently, with the need to cooperate getting etched into the cultural DNA. The American model has produced wealth, but it has come at a price—with ambition sometimes turning back on the ambitious and

---

temperamental /ˌtempərəˈmentl/ *adj.* connected with sb.'s nature and personality
phlegmatic /flegˈmætɪk/ *adj.* not easily made angry or upset
bestir /bɪˈstɜː/ *v.* to start doing things after a period during which you have been doing nothing
telling /ˈtelɪŋ/ *adj.* having a strong or important effect; effective
template /ˈtempleɪt/ *n.* a thing that is used as a model for producing other similar examples
imponderable /ɪmˈpɒndərəbl/ *n.* something that is difficult to measure or estimate
primal /ˈpraɪml/ *adj.* connected with the earliest origins of life; very basic
wire /waɪə/ *v.* to join things together using wire
spell /spel/ *v.* to have sth., usually sth. bad, as a result; to mean sth., usually sth. bad
catastrophe /kəˈtæstrəfi/ *n.* an event that causes one person or a group of people personal suffering, or that makes difficulties
befit /bɪˈfɪt/ *v.* to be suitable and good enough for sb./sth.
ethos /ˈiːθɒs/ *n.* the moral ideas and attitudes that belong to a particular group or society
freebie /ˈfriːbiː/ *n.* something that is given to sb. without payment, usually by a company
etch /etʃ/ *v.* to engrave

consuming them whole.

Ultimately, it's that very flexibility—that multiplicity of possible rewards—that makes dreaming big dreams and pursuing big goals worth all the bother. Ambition is an expensive impulse, one that requires an enormous investment of emotional capital. Like any investment, it can pay off in countless different kinds of coin. The trick, as any good speculator will tell you, is recognizing the riches when they come your way.

> impulse /ˈɪmpʌls/ *n.* something that causes sb./sth. to do sth. or to develop and make progress

Better Know More

1. Jeffrey Kluger

Jeffrey Kluger is a senior writer for *TIME*. He joined *TIME* as a contributor in 1996, and was named a senior writer in 1998. He has written a number of cover stories, including reports on the connection between sex and health, the Mars Pathfinder landing, the loss of the shuttle Columbia and the collision aboard the Mir space station.

2. Jimmy Carter and Billy Carter

Jimmy Carter, the first President born in a hospital on Oct. 1, 1924, was the 39th President of the United States.

Billy Carter was neither the first nor the last brother to embarrass a president, but he was surely the most colorful. From the time Jimmy Carter started running for president to the end of his term in office, his younger brother was never far from the spotlight. In 1976 he provided humor and a charming contrast to his straight-laced candidate sibling. But by 1980, Billy's act had worn thin, and a major controversy over his dealings with the Libyan government cast a shadow over a Carter White House that could ill-afford another problem.

former President Jimmy Carter

Billy Carter

3. Jeb Bush and Neil Bush

They are brothers. John Ellis "Jeb" Bush, born on February 11, 1953, in Midland, Texas, was the 43rd Governor of Florida, in the United States, as well as the first Republican to be re-elected to that office. Jeb Bush is a brother of President George Walker Bush and son of former President George Walker Bush.

Neil Bush, born on January 22, 1955, is a brother of President George Walker Bush and former Florida Governor Jeb Bush and the son of former President George Herbert Walker Bush and Barbara Bush.

Jeb Bush

Neil Bush

4. Soka University of America

It is a private four-year liberal arts college and graduate school located in Orange County, California. Soka offers undergraduate, graduate and international study abroad programs as part of the tuition.

5. Aliso Viejo, Calif.

Aliso Viejo is a city in Orange County, California, United States.

6. Mozart

Mozart is among the most enduring popular of European composers and many of his works are part of the standard concert repertoire. He is generally considered to be one of the greatest composers of classical music.

7. Salieri

Autonio Salieri (August 18, 1750—May 7, 1825), born in Legnago, Italy, was a composer and conductor. As the Austrian imperial Kapellmeister from 1788 to 1824, he was one of the most important and famous musicians of his time.

Check Your Understanding

Answer the following questions based on the text you have just learned.

1. After you have read the first paragraph, why do you think the author says "you don't get as successful as Gregg and Drew Shipp by accident?"
2. What did the brothers do in 1998? How did their career develop after 1998?
3. Why does the author say "nature is a zero-sum game?"
4. Why does the anthropologist Edward Lowe say "ambition is an evolutionary product?"
5. Find the evidence in the passage to show that "many animals are known to signal their ambitious tendencies almost from birth."
6. What is the result of the studies of identical twins which have measured achievement motivation?
7. What are two of the biggest influences on your level of ambition?
8. What are the four categories of families divided by anthropologists when measuring ambition?
9. According to the author, who are most driven to improve their lot?
10. What is the price of the wealth produced by the American model?
11. Why is ambition an expensive impulse?
12. Why does the author say that ambition is "like investment?"

A Sip of Word Formation

Noun Suffixes: Person

-er (*-or*)*, -eer, -ist, -ant* are person noun forming suffixes.

1. *-er*

    The suffix can be seen as closely related to *-ee*, as its derivatives frequently signify entities that are active or volitional participants in an event (e.g. teacher, singer, writer etc.). This is, however, only a sub-class of *-er* derivatives, and there is a wide range of forms with quite heterogeneous meanings.

    -er (*-or*) frequently signifies entities that are active or volitional participants in an event. That is perfomers of actions.

Examples: *teacher, singer, writer*, etc.

-er (-or) signifies instrument nouns.

Examples: *blender, mixer, steamer, toaster*, etc.

-er (-or) can be used to denote entities associated with an activity.

Examples: *diner, lounger, trainer* and *winner* (in the sense "winning shot"), etc.

Furthermore, *-er* is used to create person nouns indicating place of origin or residence.

Examples: *Londoner, New Yorker, Highlander, New Englander*, etc.

The orthographic variant *-or* occurs mainly with Latinate bases ending in /s/ or /t/,

Examples: *conductor, oscillator, compressor*, etc.

2. *-eer*

This is another person noun forming suffix, whose meaning can be paraphrased as "person who deals in, is concerned with, or has to do with X", as evidenced in forms such as *auctioneer, budgeteer, cameleer, mountaineer, pamphleteer*. Many words have a depreciative tinge. The suffix *-eer* is autostressed and attaches almost exclusively to bases ending in a stressed syllable followed by an unstressed syllable.

3. *-ist*

This suffix derives nouns denoting persons, mostly from nominal and adjectival bases (*ballonist, careerist, fantasist, minimalist*). All nouns in *-ism* which denote attitudes, beliefs or theories have potential counterparts in *-ist*. The semantics of *-ist* can be considered underspecified "person having to do with X", with the exact meaning of the derivative being a function of the meaning of the base and further inferencing. Thus, a balloonist is someone who ascends in a balloon, a careerist is someone who is chiefly interested in her/his career, while a fundamentalist is a supporter or follower of fundamentalism.

4. *-ant*

This suffix forms count nouns referring to persons (often in technical or legal discourse, cf. *applicant, defendant, disclaimant*) or to substances involved in biological, chemical, or physical processes (*attractant, dispersant, etchant, suppressant*). Most bases are verbs of Latinate origin.

Build Your Vocabulary

A. Decide which form of the noun suffix to use to make each word. Add the suffix and write the whole word.

train		mob	
employ		export	
refuge		mountain	
gang		fundamental	
manage		conduct	
arrange		absent	
drift		supervise	
dump		pamphlet	
dwell		assist	
elect		racket	
entertain		auction	
exhibit		survive	
explore		stroll	
offend		market	
material		depend	
occupy		career	

B. The word at the end of the following sentences can be used to form a word that fits suitably in the blank space. Fill in each blank this way.

Example: He said "Good morning" in a most *friendly* way. (friend)

1. "I can't say that I'm glad I had cancer, but I'm grateful for what I've learned from cancer." said Lucy, "It's better to be a cancer survivor than a cancer _____." (suffer)

2. When most people hear the word _____, they think of a confident, fast-talking person standing behind a podium, gavel in hand, chanting "going once, going twice, and sold!" (auction)

3. In order to balance the unequal relationship between _____ and _____ and to make the interview situation less artificial, it might be a good idea for the _____ to share some stories with _____ and contribute to the conversation. (interview)

4. After more than a decade of involvement in programmes for seriously violent _____, we decided to reassess the empirical evidence underpinning violence rehabilitation in adult. (offend)

5. Prosecutors arrested a _____ yesterday who is said to be at the heart of a growing scandal involving the Japanese brokerage firm Nomura Securities. (racket)

6. We created a series of tools for the player who wants to log in and role-play as an _____ or just chat with friends while hanging out in a social environment. (entertain)

7. A _____ is a historical term for someone who creates or distributes pamphlets in order to get people to vote for their favorite politician or to articulate a particular political ideology. A famous _____ of the American Revolutionary War was Thomas Paine.

(pamphlet)

8. _____ is a slang term for a person who participates in organized crime, which is known as belonging to the Mob. In western stories and movies, cowboys as _____ are known as outlaws. (mob)

9. I was looking at it from above, it was nothing but amazing. The player looked at the notes in front of them, and they looked closely at the _____. (conduct)

10. Because computers are increasingly used to record and organize data, many financial _____ are spending more time developing strategies and implementing the long-term goals of their organization. (manage)

You'd Like to Be

A Skilled Text Weaver

Complete the following sentences with words given. Make changes where necessary.

| fraternal | anthropologists | dissipate | desultory | wean |
| phlegmatic | bestir | telling | imponderables | freebies |

1. In fact, I do not myself intend to _____ baby by feeding her formula.
2. She had better _____ herself and give more thought and attention to what she was doing at present.
3. My six-year old sister's attitude towards smoking provides a _____ demonstration of the success of the anti-smoking movement to date.
4. You will find _____ and free stuff such as free coupons, cards, graphics, fonts, game, etc. on this website.
5. _____ twins do not share any more similarities generically than any other siblings, but they share a bond that is unique nonetheless.
6. This is one of the few hobbies that can _____ money faster than photography.
7. _____ have new evidence that ancient farmers in Mexico were cultivating an early form of maize, the forerunner of modern corn, about 7300 years ago—1200 years earlier than scholars previously thought.
8. I lunched with him on Saturday and had some _____ talk.
9. When all is said and done, the college should encourage each student to develop the capacity to judge wisely in matters of life and conduct. Time must be taken for exploring ambiguities and reflecting on the _____ of life.

10. A _____ person is calm and unemotional. _____ means pertaining to phlegm, corresponds to the season of winter.

A Sharp Interpreter

Paraphrase the following sentences, referring to the contexts in which the sentences are located.

1. You don't get as successful as Gregg and Drew Shipp by accident.
2. By the time they got out of school, both Shipps had entirely transformed themselves.
3. Of all the impulses in humanity's behavioral portfolio, ambition—that need to grab an ever bigger piece of the resource pie before someone else gets it—ought to be one of the most democratically distributed.
4. But even if something as primal as the reproductive impulse wires you one way, it's possible for other things to rewire you completely.
5. The U.S. has always been a me-first culture.
6. Like any investment, it can pay off in countless different kinds of coin.

A Solid Sentence Constructor

Complete each sentence with one of the phrases listed below. Make changes where necessary.

in the presence of	spin off	sell off	consumed with
buy out	zero-sum game	punch in	punch out
on impulse			

1. Every day the employees _____ at eight o'clock in the morning and _____ at six o'clock in the afternoon.
2. Girls should be able to express their own perspectives _____ boys.
3. As Duke Energy Company prepares to _____ its natural gas business in January, investors are starting to see its stock as an unusually attractive energy play.
4. I used to buy things _____ due to my shop-aholic addiction, and thus my room is now kind of packed with many things.
5. His life has been _____ sorrow and misery ever since his father died.
6. He decided to _____ his tobacco holdings in the company.
7. In a two-player _____, whatever one player wins, the other loses. Therefore, the players share no common interests.
8. The company will issue £189 million shares, worth £154 million at yesterday's closing share

price, to _____ its partners.

A Careful Writer

Study the following synonyms and complete the sentences. Make changes where necessary.

> roam   wander   stroll   ramble   amble

1. They _____ here and there in the woods.
2. The little boy is _____ along the road.
3. He has nothing to do, so he is _____ along the street.
4. The poor tramp _____ every day.
5. A group of people _____ down to the east.

> smart   brilliant   intelligent   ingenious

6. The brains of highly _____ children develop in a different pattern from those with more average abilities, researchers have found after analyzing a series of imaging scans collected over many years.
7. Dolphins are very _____.
8. It is very difficult for anyone to become a _____ star.
9. Not everyone has an _____ mind.

A Superb Bilingualist

Translate the following sentences into English, using the words or phrases given in brackets.

1. 世人欲成功须努力发奋,夜以继日。(bestir oneself)
2. 他出于一时冲动让那个陌生人搭了车。(impulse)
3. 他心里充满了负罪感,耻辱和尴尬。(consume)
4. 她设法使好朋友戒掉毒品。(wean sb. off sth.)
5. 他在失败面前没有气馁。(in the presence of)
6. 瓶中之酒不解渴。(quench thirst)
7. 不要再浪费你的精力。(dissipate)
8. 精心研究几部书胜过随意地读许多书。(desultory)

Text B

The Roots of My Ambition

By Russell Baler

(Abridged and Edited)

My mother, dead now to this world but still roaming free in my mind, wakes me some mornings before daybreak. "If there's one thing I can't stand, it's a quitter."

I have heard her say that all my life. Now, lying in bed, coming awake in the dark, I feel the fury of her energy fighting the good-for-nothing idler within me who wants to go back to sleep instead of tackling the brave new day.

Silently I protest: I am not a child anymore I have made something of myself. I am entitled to sleep late.

"Russell, you've got no more initiative than a bump on a log."

She has hounded me with these battle cries since I was a boy in short pants.

"Make something of yourself!"

"Don't be a quitter!"

"Have a little ambition."

The civilized man of the world within me scoffs at materialism and strives after success: He has read the philosophers and social critics. He thinks it is vulgar and unworthy to spend one's life pursuing money, power, fame, and...

"Sometimes you act like you're not worth the powder and shot it would take to blow you up with."

Life had been hard for my mother ever since her father died, leaving nothing but debts. The family house was lost, the children scattered. My mother's mother, fatally ill with tubercular infection, fell into a suicidal depression and was institutionalized. My mother, who had just started college, had to quit and look for work.

---

quitter /ˈkwɪtə/ *n.* (often disapproving) a person who gives up easily and does not finish a task they have started

fury /ˈfjʊəri/ *n.* extreme anger that often includes violent behavior

tackle /ˈtækl/ *v.* to make a determined effort to deal with a difficult problem or situation

initiative /ɪˈnɪʃətɪv/ *n.* the ability to decide and act on your own without waiting for sb. to tell you what to do

bump /bʌmp/ *n.* a part of a flat surface that is not even, but raised above the rest of it

log /lɔg/ *n.* a thick piece of wood that is cut from or has fallen from a tree

hound /haʊnd/ *v.* to keep following sb. and not leave them alone, especially in order to get sth. from them or ask them questions

scoff /skɒf/ *v.* to talk about sb./sth. in a way that makes it clear that you think they are stupid or ridiculous

strive /straɪv/ *v.* to try very hard to achieve sth. or to defeat sth.

vulgar /ˈvʌlgə/ *adj.* not having or showing good taste; not polite, elegant or well behaved

tubercular /tjuˈbɜːkjulə/ *adj.* relating to, or covered with tubercles; tuberculate

infection /ɪnˈfekʃn/ *n.* the act or process of causing or getting a disease

suicidal /ˌsuːɪˈsaɪdəl/ *adj.* people who are suicidal feel that they want to kill themselves

institutionalize /ˌɪnstɪˈtjuːʃənəlaɪz/ *v.* to send sb. who is not capable of living independently to live in a special house (=an institution) especially when it is for a long period of time

Then, after five years of marriage and three babies, her husband died in 1930, leaving my mother so poor that she had to give up her baby
35 Audrey for adoption. Maybe the bravest thing she did was give up Audrey, only ten months old, to my Uncle Tom and Aunt Goldie. Uncle Tom, one of my father's brothers, had a good job with the railroad and could give Au-
40 drey a comfortable life.

My mother headed off to New Jersey with my other sister and me to take shelter with her brother Allen, poor relatives dependent on his goodness. She eventually found work patching
45 grocers' smocks at ten dollars a week in a laundry.

Mother would have like it better if I could have grown up to be President or a rich businessman, but much as she loved me, she did not deceive herself. Before I was out of pri-
50 mary school, she could see I lacked the gifts for either making millions or winning the love of crowds. After that she began nudging me toward working with words.

Words ran in her family. There seemed to be a word gene that passed down from her maternal grandfather. He was a school-teacher, his daughter Lulie wrote poetry, and his son Charlie became New York correspondent for the Baltimore, Maryland, Herald. In
55 the turn-of-the-century American South, still impoverished by the Civil War, words were a way out.

The most spectacular proof was my mother's first cousin Edwin. He was managing editor of the *New York Times*. He had traveled all over Europe, proving that words could take you to places so glorious and so far from the place you
60 came from that your own kin could only gape in wonder and envy. My mother used Edwin as an example of how far a man could go without much talent.

"Edwin James was no smarter than anybody else, and look where he is today," my mother said, and
65 said, and said again, so that I finally grew up thinking Edwin James was a dull clod who had a lucky break. Maybe she felt that way about him, but she was saying something deeper. She was telling me I didn't have to be brilliant to get where Edwin had go to, that the way to

---

patch /pætʃ/ *v.* to cover a hole or a worn place, especially in clothes, with a piece of cloth or other material

smock /smɒk/ *n.* a long loose piece of clothing worn over other clothes to protect them from dirt, etc.

deceive /dɪˈsiːv/ *v.* to refuse to admit to yourself that sth. unpleasant is true

nudge /nʌdʒ/ *v.* to push sb./sth. gently or gradually in a particular direction

gene /dʒiːn/ *n.* a unit inside a cell which controls a particular quality in a living thing that has been passed on from its parents

maternal /məˈtɜːnl/ *adj.* related through the mother's side of the family

impoverish /ɪmˈpɒvərɪʃ/ *v.* to make sb. poor

spectacular /spekˈtækjʊlə/ *adj.* very impressive

kin /kɪn/ *n.* your family or your relatives

gape /ɡeɪp/ *v.* to stare at sb./sth. with your mouth open because you are shocked or surprised

clod /klɒd/ *n.* (informal) a stupid person

get to the top was to work, work, work.

When my mother saw that I might have the word gift, she started trying to make it grow. Though desperately poor, she signed up for a deal that supplied one volume of "World's Greatest Literature" every month at 39 cents a book.

I respected those great writers, but what I read with joy were newspapers. I lapped up every word about monstrous crimes, dreadful accidents and hideous butcheries committed in faraway wars. Accounts of murderers dying in the electric chair fascinated me, and I kept close track of last meals ordered by condemned men.

In 1947 I graduated from Johns Hopkins University in Baltimore and learned that the Baltimore Sun needed a police reporter. Two or three classmates at Hopkins also applied for the job. Why I was picked was a mystery. It paid $30 a week. When I complained that was insulting for a college man, my mother refused to sympathize.

"If you work hard at this job," she said, "maybe you can make something of it. Then they'll have to give you a raise."

Seven years later I was assigned by the Sun to cover the White House. For most reporters, being White House correspondent was as close to heaven as you could get. I was 29 years old and puffed up with pride. I went to see my mother's delight while telling her about it. I should have known better.

"Well, Russ," she said, "if you work hard at this White House job, you might be able to make something of yourself."

Onward and upward was the course she set. Small progress was no excuse for feeling satisfied with yourself. People who stopped to pat themselves on the back didn't last long. Even if you got to the top, you'd better not take it easy. "The bigger they come, the harder they fall" was one of her favorite maxims.

During my early years in the newspaper business, I began to entertain childish fantasies of revenge against Cousin Edwin. Wouldn't

lap up *v.* to accept or receive sth. with great enjoyment, without thinking about whether it is good, true or sincere

monstrous /ˈmɒnstrəs/ *adj.* considered to be shocking and unacceptable because it is morally wrong or unfair

dreadful /ˈdredfəl/ *adj.* causing fear or suffering

hideous /ˈhɪdiəs/ *adj.* very ugly or unpleasant

butchery /ˈbʊtʃəri/ *n.* cruel, violent and unnecessary killing

condemned /kənˈdemd/ *adj.* pronounced to be wrong, guilty, worthless, or forfeited; adjudged or sentenced to punishment, destruction, or confiscation

sympathize /ˈsɪmpəθaɪz/ *v.* to feel sorry for sb.; to show that you understand and feel sorry about sb.'s problems

be puffed up with pride *v.* to be too full of pride

pat sb./yourself on the back *v.* to praise sb. or yourself for doing sth. well

maxim /ˈmæksɪm/ *n.* a well-known phrase that expresses sth. that is usually true or that people think is a rule for sensible behavior

entertain /ˌentəˈteɪn/ *v.* to consider or allow yourself to think about an idea, a hope, a feeling, etc.

revenge /rɪˈvendʒ/ *n.* something that you do in order to make sb. suffer because they have made you suffer

it be delightful if I became such an outstanding reporter that the Times hired me without knowing I was related to the great Edwin? Wouldn't it be delicious if Edwin himself invited me into his huge office and said, "Tell me something about yourself, young man?" What exquisite vengeance to reply, "I am the only son of your poor cousin Lucy Elizabeth Robinson."

What would one day happen was right out of my wildest childhood fantasy. The Times did come knocking at my door, though Cousin Edwin had departed by the time I arrived. Eventually I would be offered one of the gaudiest prizes in American journalism: a column in the *New York Times*.

It was not a column meant to convey news, but a writer's column commenting on the news by using different literary forms: essay devices, satire, burlesque, sometimes even fiction. It was proof that my mother had been absolutely right when she sized me up early in life and steered me toward literature.

The column won its share of medals, including a Pulitzer Prize for journalism in 1979. My mother never knew about that. The circuitry of her brain had collapsed the year before, and she was in a nursing home, out of touch with life forevermore.

I can only guess how she'd have responded to news of the Pulitzer. I'm pretty sure she would have said, "That's nice, Buddy. It shows if you buckle down and work hard, you'll be able to make something of yourself one of these days."

In time there would be an attack on the values my mother preached and I have lived by. In the 1960s and 70s, people who admitted to wanting to amount to something were put down as materialists idiotically wasting their lives in the "rat race."

I tried at first to roll with the new age. I decided not to drive my children, as my mother had driven me, with those corrupt old demands that they amount to something.

The new age exalted love, self-grati-

---

exquisite /'ekskwɪzɪt/ *adj.* (of feeling) strongly felt
vengeance /'vendʒəns/ *n.* (formal) the act of punishing or harming sb. in return for what they have done to you, your family or friends
depart /dɪ'pɑːt/ *v.* to leave one's job
gaudy /'ɡɔːdi/ *adj.* too brightly coloured in a way that lacks taste
convey /kən'veɪ/ *v.* to make ideas, feelings, etc. known to sb.
burlesque /bɜː'lesk/ *n.* a performance or piece of writing which tries to make sth. look ridiculous by representing it in a humorous way
fiction /'fɪkʃən/ *n.* a type of literature that describes imaginary people and events, not real ones
size sb. up *v.* to form a judgement or an opinion about sb.

circuitry /'sɜːkɪtri/ *n.* a system of electrical circuits or the equipment that forms this
collapse /kə'læps/ *v.* to fail suddenly or completely
buckle down *v.* (informal) to start to do sth. seriously
preach /priːtʃ/ *v.* to tell people about a particular religion, way of life, system, etc. in order to persuade them to accept it
idiotic /ˌɪdi'ɒtɪk/ *adj.* very stupid
rat race *n.* a difficult, tiring, often competitive activity or routine
corrupt /kə'rʌpt/ *adj.* containing changes or faults, and no longer in the original state
exalt /ɪɡ'zɔːlt/ *v.* to praise sb./sth. very much

fication and passive Asian philosophies that aimed at helping people resign themselves to the status quo. Much of this seemed preposterous to me, but I conceded that my mother might
150 have turned me into a coarse materialist (one defect in her code was its emphasis on money and position), so I kept my heretical suspicions to myself.

And then, realizing I had failed to fire my
155 own children with ambition, I broke. One evening at dinner, I heard my self shouting, "Don't you want to amount to something?"

The children looked blank. Amount to something? What a strange expression. I could
160 see their thoughts: That isn't Dad yelling. That's those martinis he had before dinner.

It wasn't the gin that was shouting. It was my mother. The gin only gave me the courage to announce to them that yes, by God, I had
165 always believed in success, had always believed that without hard work and self-discipline you could never amount to anything, and didn't deserve to.

It would turn out that the children's bleak
170 school reports did not forebode failure, but a refusal to march to the drumbeat of the ordinary, which should have made me proud. Now they are grown people with children of their own, and we like one another and have good times when we are together.

So it is with a family. We carry the dead generations within us and pass them on to the
175 future aboard our children. This keeps the people of the past alive long after we have taken them to the graveyard.

"If there's one thing I can't stand, Russell, it's a quitter."

Lord, I can hear her still.

---

gratification /ˌɡrætɪfɪˈkeɪʃən/ *n.* the state of feeling pleasure when sth. goes well for you or when your desires are satisfied; sth. that gives you pleasure

resign oneself to *v.* to accept sth. unpleasant that cannot be changed or avoided

status quo *n.* the situation as it is now, or as it was before a recent change

preposterous /prɪˈpɒstərəs/ *adj.* completely unreasonable, especially in a way that is shocking or annoying

concede /kənˈsiːd/ *v.* to admit that sth. is true, logical, etc.

coarse /kɔːs/ *adj.* rude and offensive

defect /dɪˈfekt/ *n.* a fault in sth. or in the way it has been made which means that it is not perfect

heretical /hɪˈretɪkəl/ *adj.* characterized by, revealing, or approaching departure from established beliefs or standards

suspicion /səˈspɪʃən/ *n.* the feeling that you cannot trust sb./sth.

blank /blæŋk/ *adj.* showing no feeling, understanding or interest

martini /mɑːˈtiːni/ *n.* a type of vermouth

gin /dʒɪn/ *n.* an alcoholic drink made from grain flavoured with juniper berries

bleak /bliːk/ *adj.* (of a situation) not hopeful or encouraging

forebode /fɔːˈbəʊd/ *v.* to indicate the likelihood of; to portend

drumbeat /ˈdrʌmbiːt/ *n.* the sound that a beat on a drum makes

Notes

1. Russell Baler

The author is a famous columnist in the United States. The article is written in his later years. In this article, he talks about his old days and the background of his successful career.

2. Johns Hopkins University

The Johns Hopkins University was the first research university in the United States. Founded in 1876, it was an entirely new educational enterprise. Its aim was not only to advance students' knowledge, but also to advance human knowledge generally, through discovery and scholarship. The university's emphasis on both learning and research—and on how each complements the other—revolutionized U.S. higher education. Today, Johns Hopkins has ventured from its home in Baltimore to countries throughout the world—China, Italy and Singapore, among many others. It remains a world leader in teaching, patient care and discovery.

3. The Baltimore Sun

Maryland's leading online source for local, state, national, entertainment and sports news, plus jobs, real estate, cars and shopping information, primarily from the Baltimore Sun.

Comprehension Questions

1. What do you think of the characteristics of the author's mother when she says "if there's one thing I can't stand, it's a quitter?"
2. What is the life like after the death of the author's grandfather?
3. What does the author mean by "working with words?"
4. Who is Edwin? What is his job? What can his traveling all over Europe prove?
5. Why does the author take Edwin for example?
6. After graduation from John Hopkins University, what kind of job did the author begin to do?

7. When the author was picked, how much did he earn every week?
8. When was the author assigned by the Sun to cover the White House?
9. What kind of column in the *New York Times* that the author was offered?
10. What values did the mother preach and the author live by?
11. What did the new age exalt?
12. Why did the author at first decide to roll with the age, then become very angry at his children?
13. What did the children's bleak school reports forebode?

Writing Practice

Study the following essay carefully and write a summary in about 80 words.

We continue to share with our remotest ancestors the most tangled and evasive attitudes about death, despite the great distance we have come in understanding some of the profound aspects of biology. We have as much distaste for talking about personal death as for thinking about it; it is an indelicacy, like talking in mixed company about venereal disease or abortion in the old days. Death on a grand scale does not bother us in the same special way: we can sit around a dinner table and discuss war, involving 60 billion volatilized human deaths, as though we were talking about bad weather; we can watch abrupt bloody death every day, in color, on films and television, without blinking back a tear. It is when the numbers of dead are very small, and very close, that we begin to think in scurrying circles. At the very center of the problem is the naked cold deadness of one's own self, the only reality in nature of which we can have absolute certainty, and it is unmentionable, unthinkable. We may be even less willing to face the issue at first hand than our predecessors because of a secret new hope that maybe it will go away. We like to think, hiding the thought, that with all the marvelous ways in which we seem now to lead nature around by the nose, perhaps we can avoid the central problem if we just become, next year, say, a bit smarter. (246 words)

Further Study

1. Ambition is very important in our life, and it can inspire people to achieve their goals. Visit http://englishreading.info/main/goal-setting/20545.php for more information about the realization of one's dream. After reading the article, compare it with Text B to see the similarities and differences between the two articles.
2. September 11th is a day of disaster. In order to better understand the process of September 11th with the background information and pictures of the World Trade Center and the Pentagon, visit http://zombietime.com/wtc_9-13-2001/ and http://911research.wtc7.net/pentagon/analysis/index.html.

Unit 10

China Today

Unit Goals

After completing the lessons in this unit, students will be able to:
- ☞ familiarize themselves with the development of China in modern history;
- ☞ familiarize themselves with the current situations of China and the West;
- ☞ extend vocabulary through recognition of diminutive suffixes.

Before Reading

Hands-on Activities

1. Make a list of what we should learn from the West and what should be abandoned.
2. Make a list of the new developments of China.

Brainstorming

Brainstorm the following questions. Work in pairs or groups to discuss these questions.

1. At present, in terms of Western culture and our traditional culture, there are two opposing camps: one advocates we should absorb more from the West while the other thinks that we should develop our traditional cultural fully. What do you think? Give your reasons.
2. Some international observers view China's rise as a world power as a threat to the status quo and to the hegemony of the United States. Is China a threat or an opportunity? Supply evidence to your answer.

A Glimpse at Words and Expressions

Please read the following sentences. Pay attention to the underlined part in each sentence and see how these expressions are used in the context, and then write down their meanings in the blanks provided.

1. In the end, we did not have much choice, as the country was being caught up with successive conflicts. (   )
2. This declaration accurately captured the mood of the country. (   )
3. We had been knocked down several times but we refused to give in, and were now making a comeback. (   )
4. The only comparable rise of a major economy in terms of its proportion to world Gross Domestic Product (GDP) is that of the United States between the late 1800s and World War I. (   )
5. ...but Chinese officials stress that continued Chinese growth requires peaceful stability, open trade routes to the West, and clear access to oil and other energy sources in the Middle East, Africa, Southeast Asia and elsewhere. (   )
6. Chinese sources say that the only thing that could provoke a furious Chinese military response would be any attempt by Taiwan to declare itself an independent republic no longer affiliated with China. (   )
7. But on a per capita basis, China will remain in the middle-income bracket. (   )
8. We now have a renewed confidence in our own cultural identity, but remain firmly committed to the cause of modernization. (   )
9. Like any other culture on the planet, it grew out of necessity and habit handed down from one generation to another. (   )
10. The chances are that they will succeed. (   )

Text A

China: Past and Prensent

By Anonymous
(Abridged and Edited)

China is a great nation, it struggled to survive after being attacked by Western powers and reduced to semi-colonial status in the latter part of the nineteenth century. In that process we did a lot of painful soul-searching. One of the conclusions we arrived at was that we had to learn from the West, with the only difference being whether we did it in a wholesale or
5 selective manner.

In the end, we did not have much choice, as the country was being caught up with successive conflicts, civil wars, famines, and hyperinflation. Stark reality forced us to adopt and adapt, improvising with whatever came along. All the time we had to admit that we were backward, poor and ignorant, although we knew deep in our hearts that the descendents of the dragon could not be that bad.

For a whole century, the proud people of this great country suffered from a great shame and agony that few outsiders could possibly understand. In October 1949, when Chairman Mao Zedong announced the establishment of the People's Republic of China and proclaimed to the world that "the Chinese people have stood up," this declaration accurately captured the mood of the country. We had been knocked down several times but we refused to give in, and were now making a comeback. Nevertheless, we still had to wait another 30 years for the launch of the reform and opening up under the late leader Deng Xiaoping to seriously start to fulfill this collective aspiration.

In the subsequent quarter of a century China has broken one development record after another. Never in human history have so many people enjoyed such a period of uninterrupted progress. Rapid economic growth has brought vast improvements in the quality of life throughout China over the past three decades. Life expectancy rose to 71 years by 2000, the last time China conducted a full census, and estimates in 2007 put the figure at 72.6 years (74.5 for females and 70.5 for males). Life expectancy at birth is a measure of overall quality of life in a country and is a clear indication that life is getting better for most Chinese. Adult illiteracy, high by any standards before 1949, sank to only seven percent in 2006. The country's rapid growth and its government's targeted policies has reduced the share of the rural population living below its poverty line by nearly ninety percent, from more than 250 million in 1978 to only 26 million in 2004.

China's stunning transformation into a global economic and political power is one of the seminal events of the modern era. China's rise has drastically altered the glob-

---

famine /'fæmɪn/ *n.* a lack of food during a long period of time in a region

hyperinflation /ˌhaɪpərɪn'fleɪʃən/ *n.* the rise in the prices of services and goods in a particular country seriously, resulting in a fall in the value of money; the rate at which this happens

stark /stɑːk/ *adj.* unpleasant; real, and impossible to avoid

improvise /'ɪmprəvaɪz/ *v.* to make or do sth. using whatever is available, usually because you do not have what you really need

agony /'ægəni/ *n.* extreme physical or mental pain

census /'sensəs/ *n.* the process of officially counting sth., especially a country's population, and recording various facts

illiteracy /ɪ'lɪtərəsi/ *n.* the condition not knowing how to read or write

seminal /'semnəl/ *adj.* very important and having a strong influence on later developments

al economic and political balance of power. China has already become the "factory workshop" for the entire world, sending inexpensive and increasingly higher quality goods to consumers throughout the developed world while simultaneously forcing nations like the United States to rationalize and restructure their domestic economies. What happens in China both directly and indirectly affects the lives of billions of people around the world.

The world has rarely seen a major power grow as fast as China. Its economy in 2006 is a full nine times larger than it was in 1978, making it the world's fourth largest economy behind the United States, Japan, and Germany. The only comparable rise of a major economy in terms of its proportion to world Gross Domestic Product (GDP) is that of the United States between the late 1800s and World War I. China's growth propelled 400 million Chinese out of poverty during the last two decades of the twentieth century. Between 1978 and 2003, China's per capita income rose by a multiple of six. The world's greatest domestic migration in modern times doubled the proportion of Chinese living in towns and cities to over forty percent. As many as 150 million workers have moved to China's booming cities. It is a stunning achievement.

The Chinese model of development, popularly known as the "Beijing consensus," is now being recognized as being superior to the "Washington consensus," the model proposed by the United States to Latin America.

Some international observers view China's rise as a world power as a threat to the status quo and to the hegemony of the United States, but Chinese officials stress that continued Chinese growth requires peaceful stability, open trade routes to the West, and clear access to oil and other energy sources in the Middle East, Africa, Southeast Asia and elsewhere. Chinese sources say that the only thing that could provoke a furious Chinese military response would be any attempt by Taiwan to declare itself an independent republic no longer affiliated with China.

China remains a developing country. Her economy is the world's fourth-largest, and is

rationalize /ˈræʃənəlaɪz/ v. to make changes to a business, system, etc. in order to make it more efficient, especially by spending less money
propel /prəˈpel/ v. to move, drive or push sth. forward or in a particular direction
per capita adj. for each person
migration /maɪˈɡreɪʃən/ n. the movement of large numbers of people, birds or animals from one place to another
consensus /kənˈsensəs/ n. an opinion that all members of a group agree with
hegemony /hɪˈɡeməni/ n. control by one country, organization, etc. over other countries, etc. within a particular group
provoke /prəˈvəʊk/ v. to cause a particular reaction or have a particular effect
furious /ˈfjʊəriəs/ adj. very angry
affiliated /əˈfɪlieɪtɪd/ adj. closely connected to or controlled by a group or an organization

predicted to be number-one in about 20 years' time. But on a per capita basis, China will remain in the middle-income bracket.
85 Bearing in mind the fact that on the eve of the Opium War in 1840, which started the nation's downward spiral, China used to account for one-third of global GNP, this is nothing to boast about. Nevertheless, we have
90 already gone so far, we have somewhat vindicated ourselves.

At one time, many Chinese people worshipped Western culture as the symbol of modernity. We now have a renewed confi-
95 dence in our own cultural identity, but remain firmly committed to the cause of modernization. The Chinese people are now perhaps the most inquisitive in the world. Lacking any traditional burdens and inhibitions, we are
100 free to sample all the goodies, and are also prepared to throw out those we do not like, no matter whether they are local or imported. Now we can understand the situation a little better, and can put it into proper perspective. We can sort out fact from fiction, and we tend
105 not to over-generalize and mystify.

bracket /ˈbrækɪt/ n.	price, age, income, etc. ~ prices, etc. within a particular range
spiral /ˈspaɪərəl/ n.	a continuous harmful increase or decrease in sth., that gradually gets faster and faster
vindicate /ˈvɪndɪkeɪt/ v.	to prove that sth. is true or that you were right to do sth., especially when other people thought differently
inquisitive /ɪnˈkwɪzɪtɪv/ adj.	very interested in learning about many different things
inhibition /ˌɪnhɪˈbɪʃən/ n.	the act of restricting or preventing a process or an action
goody /ˈɡʊdi/ n.	anything that is attractive and that people want to have
mystify /ˈmɪstɪfaɪ/ v.	to make sb. confused because they do not understand sth.
mold /məʊld/ v.	to strongly influence the way sb's character, opinions, etc.
obesity /əʊˈbiːsɪti/ n.	(of people) a kind of disease due to eating too much
hypertension /ˌhaɪpəˈtenʃən/ n.	high blood pressure
emulation /ˌemjʊˈleɪʃən/	the competition with others
havoc /ˈhævək/ n.	a situation in which there is a lot of damage, destruction or disorder
idiosyncrasy /ˌɪdɪəˈsɪŋkrəsi/ n.	a person's particular way of behaving, thinking, etc., especially when it is unusual; an unusual feature
slanted /ˈslɑːntɪd/ adj.	sloping in one direction

With that, we gradually establish our own perspectives, a healthy, open and balanced one. We can now face any country in the world as equals, and, more importantly, we can also face our ancestors and look at them straight in the eye. There is in fact nothing wrong with Chinese culture. Like any other culture on the planet, it grew out of necessity and
110 habit handed down from one generation to another. Like it or not, we are being surrounded and molded by our culture, and there is no way we can cut ourselves away from it.

With that also comes the realization that the blind Westernization of the recent past has done us great damage. The adaptation of a high-protein diet has resulted, just like what is happening in the West, in a high incidence of obesity, hypertension, diabetes and cancer.
115 The emulation of an automobile society is bringing us havoc and pollution. We have determined to find our own way, taking reference from around the world. The world is rich with cultural diversity, and we are proud to maintain our own idiosyncrasies. Slanted eyes are equally as beautiful as round ones.

Currently it is fashionable for middle-class people to celebrate Western festivals. Many send cards at Christmas and flowers on Valentine's Day, forgetting that Lunar New Year is our day of family reunions. We also have our Lover's Day, with equally, if not more, romantic legends behind it. Some Chinese are now advocating making major traditional festivals public holidays. The chances are that they will succeed.

China is beginning to send instructors all over the world to teach people our language, one that is the mother tongue of over 20 percent of humankind, and that is fast becoming the second language in an increasing number of countries and schools. Very soon, there will be 100 Confucius Institutes around the world. Some say that this is the projection of China's "soft power." We do not see it this way. We have never wanted to dominate the world, and we have never sought power. We are China and we are proud of our identity.

> projection /prəˈdʒekʃən/ n. (technical) the act of imagining that sb. else is thinking the same as you and is reacting in the same way

Better Know More

1. Chairman Mao Zedong (1893–1976)

Mao Zedong or Mao Tse Tung is the founder of the People's Republic of China in 1949 and one of the founders of the Chinese Communist Party in 1921. He is recognized as one of the most prominent Communist theoreticians. He is also known as a great poet.

2. Deng Xiaoping (1904–1997)

The Chinese communist leader, China's most important figure from the late 1970s until his death. He made great contributions to the development of China, proposing the "Reform and Open Policy" and "One Country, Two Systems," etc.

3. Gross Domestic Product (GDP)

The total value of all the goods and services produced by a country in one year.

4. Washington Consensus

The phrase "Washington Consensus," coined by John Williamson, is today a very popular and often pilloried term in debates about trade and development. It is often seen as synonymous with "neoliberalism" and "globalization."

5. Lunar New Year

It is a traditional festival of China, starting with the New Moon on the first day of the new year and ends on the full moon 15 days later. New Year's Eve and New Year's Day are celebrated as a family affair, a time of reunion and thanksgiving.

6. Lover's Day

Lover's Day also known as Valentine's Day, is on February 14, a time beloved of romantics.

7. Confucius Institutes

It is also named "Confucius Course," aimed at promoting friendly relationship with other countries and enhancing the understanding of the Chinese language and culture among world Chinese learners as well as providing good learning conditions for them.

Check Your Understanding

Answer the following questions based on the text you have just learned.

1. In the first paragraph, what does "western powers" refer to?
2. In terms of two ways "in a wholesale or selective manner", which one should we take?
3. Mao Zedong is a great leader and makes great contributions to liberating the sufferers. Could you give a short description?
4. Deng Xiaoping is another great leader. Please list some contributions he has made to China's development.
5. Why do Chinese people worship Western culture as the symbol of modernity?
6. In the last paragraph, do you agree with the phrase "soft power" to describe the spread of culture and knowledge of one country?
7. Combined with current international context, what measures should our country take to hold a firm position in the world?

A Sip of Word Formation

Diminutive Suffixes

-let, *-ette*, *-ess*, *-ling*, *-y* and *-ie* are noun suffixes, representing diminutive and feminine. The diminutive, the opposite of augmentative, conveys a slight degree of root meaning, smallness of the object named, intimacy and endearment.

1. *-let* is added to noun meaning "small, not very important."
   For example: filmlet, piglet
2. *-ette* can be interpreted into two meanings (1) "small", (2) "female."
   For example: kitchenette, usherette
3. *-ess* the suffix is used to indicate the "female."
   For example: actress
4. *-ling* the suffix means "small."
   For example: birdling, duckling
5. *-y or -ie* these two suffixes mean "small" and "dear."
   For example: doggy, sweetie

Build Your Vocabulary

A. Check what suffixes can the following words be added to, and then give the Chinese meaning.

author_____	gos_____	disk_____
cigar_____	eye_____	dear_____
cat_____	pig_____	book_____
lion_____	sweet_____	leather_____

B. According to the first letter, fill in the blanks to complete the following sentences.

1. We a_____ for hours about which wallpaper to buy.
2. The pianist forgot his music and had to i_____ the accompaniment.
3. You must be i_____ if you've never heard of Marx.
4. She r_____ her decision to abandon her baby by saying she could not afford to keep it.
5. Those rights and obligations are based on an unstated c_____.
6. Such tendentious statements are likely to p_____ strong opposition.

7. The two footballers a_____ themselves with the same club.
8. Our society permits people to sue for libel so that they may v_____ their reputations.
9. The i_____ of growth in one species of plants by chemicals produced by another species.
10. I'm completely m_____ about what happened in the hotel the other day.
11. The initial design development stage wherein, at first, it is certain that errors will be discovered which will require design changes. It is in this period that design aids, e_____ techniques, and supportive design techniques are essential to quick design.
12. I can now afford a new car, holidays abroad and lots of other g_____.

You'd Like to Be

A Skilled Text Weaver

Choose the appropriate words to fill in the blanks and change their forms if necessary.

struggle to	reduce	arrive at	catch up with	suffer from
force	on the eve of	account for	affiliate oneself with	

1. _____ the conference the main speaker backed out.
2. It took Harry only a few minutes to _____ a solution.
3. Most southern towns have _____ the reckless depredation of the armed gang.
4. The government will be looking to _____ inflation by a further two percent this year.
5. Petrochemicals today _____ one fourth of all the chemicals made, in ten years this amount is expected to double.
6. I _____ get out of the observation to inform on the stealer.
7. A Soviet crash program to _____ the West in designing powerful new computers is beginning to pay off, but the Russians still lag far behind, according to industry reports.
8. After being ill I didn't feel like eating but I managed to _____ something down.
9. The minority of students criticized _____ themselves _____ a group of bad boys.
10. He'll have to _____ where every cent goes.

A Sharp Interpreter

Paraphrase the following sentences. Change the sentence structure if necessary.

1. One of the conclusions we arrived at was that we had to learn from the West, with the only

difference being whether we did it in a wholesale or selective manner.
2. We had been knocked down several times but we refused to give in, and were now making a comeback.
3. Never in human history have so many people enjoyed such a period of uninterrupted progress.
4. Chinese sources say that the only thing that could provoke a furious Chinese military response would be any attempt by Taiwan to declare itself an independent republic no longer affiliated with China.
5. Our economy is the world's fourth-largest, and is predicted to be number-one in about 20 years' time.
6. Lacking any traditional burdens and inhibitions, we are free to sample all the goodies, and are also prepared to throw out those we do not like, no matter whether they are local or imported.
7. We can sort out fact from fiction, and we tend not to over-generalize and mystify.
8. Some say that this is the projection of China's "soft power."

A Solid Sentence Constructor

Complete each sentences with one of the expressions listed below. Make changes where necessary.

insist on	die for	in return	to one's amazement
keep company with	fell on one's knees	endeavor to	have no intention to
weary of	set out	keep up with	

1. Endeavor, as much as you can, to _____ people above you. _____ Chesterfield.
2. My phone rang. It was my wife. I _____ crying when I heard her voice.
3. He confessed that he _____ from Pakistan on June 26th and arrived in Abidjan on July 28th.
4. If you _____ your price and refuse to make any concession, there will be not much point in further discussion.
5. When a Party intends to innovate, it shall _____ take into account the views expressed by other Parties regarding any potential problems.
6. The bargain they reached with their employers was to reduce their wage claim _____ a shorter working week.
7. Man is ready to _____ an idea, provided that idea was not quite clear to him.
8. He was never _____ experimenting with different ways of planting his crops.
9. I _____ deceive her, which was forced by others.

10. _____, Jim who dislikes studying has passed the final examination.
11. I can't _____ all the changes in computer technology.

A Careful Writer

Study the following synonyms and complete the sentences.

> reduce   decrease   diminish

1. They are making every effort to _____ military spending.
2. The sheep must of necessity be scattered, unless the great Shepherd of souls oppose, or some of his delegates _____ and direct us.
3. Nobody can _____ the great contribution the constructors have made to the development of the country.

> suspect   distrust   doubt   mistrust

4. He was beyond all _____ the greatest statesmen of his day.
5. Everything he says seems to be pervaded with a _____ of the company.
6. Negotiations between management and the work force are made more difficult by mutual _____.
7. Nothing makes a man _____ much, more than to know little; and therefore men should remedy suspicion by procuring to know more.

> tolerable   tolerant

8. The maltreatment the slaves had suffered made them barely _____, therefore they took the arms.
9. As for the demerits of the others, he holds a _____ attitude.
10. They have a _____ degree of success in introducing the foreign capital.

A Superb Bilingualist

Translate the following sentences into English.

1. 那纯粹是障眼法，用以分散人们对他真正意图的注意力。(distract)
2. 因为我谎称钱仍在我处，所以他们要我交出时，我很尴尬。(corner)

3. 一个人的好奇心越强,他取得的成就就越大。(the more..., the more)
4. 那个男孩儿给拐走了,想想看他父母得多伤心那。(suffer)
5. 因为有大量的石油收入,该酋长国为世界上人均收入最高的国家之一。人口约242,975。(per capita)
6. 他受到他们嘲笑恼羞成怒,说了一些过头的话。(provoke)
7. 财务负责人必须说明交给他的钱是怎样用的。(account for)
8. 灭草剂用来摧毁或抑制植物,尤指杂草生长的化学物质。(inhibit)
9. 我希望他不再把哥哥作为自己的学习榜样。(emulate)

Text B

Cultural Healing

By Julia Carnine

(Abridged and Edited)

I was teetering along the boulevard in Shanghai in my new shoes, navigating the overwhelming heat, sun and uneven pavement when we met. Amid the horns and staccato Shanghai-ese chirping, I faltered when I heard, "What time is it please?"

The sound of my native language summoned me to the present. Glancing over at the
5 small granny with three plastic shopping bags in her hand, I answered her as best as I could, in my poor Mandarin. The light turned, and we stepped together across the street through the maniacal traffic.

Once safely landed, she drew me out with questions in English, guessing my nationality
10 and my profession (isn't every young white woman in China an English teacher from the U.S.). I offered affirmative answers in Mandarin. We were starting a conversation that I had become very used to after one year in China.
15 We were equally staunch in our ability to use what little foreign language we had; in my schoolgirl Mandarin I wanted to show her that I knew where this could go. I couldn't help remembering the expatriate stories of similar
20 street meetings throughout this country that

---

teeter /ˈtiːtə/ *v.* to stand or move in an unsteady way so that you look as if you are going to fall
boulevard /ˈbuːlvɑːd/ *n.* a wide city street, often with trees on either side
horn /hɔːn/ *n.* a device in a vehicle for making a loud sound as a warning or signal
staccato /stəˈkɑːtəʊ/ *adj.* with each note played separately in order to produce short, sharp sounds
chirp /tʃɜːp/ *v.* to speak in a lively and cheerful way
falter /ˈfɔːltə/ *v.* to speak in a way that shows that one is not confident
maniacal /məˈnaɪəkəl/ *adj.* wild and violent
staunch /stɔːntʃ/ *adj.* strong and loyal in one's opinions and attitude
expatriate /eksˈpætriət/ *adj.* [only before noun] living in a country that is not their own

ended up in sticky obligations to teach someone's cousin's child good English, to lend a copy of your passport to aid in buying stocks, or to write the famous letter of invitation to your country. But then she told me she was a doctor, a Traditional Chinese Medicine doctor, and

she taught foreigners her secrets. I took a hot,
25 exhaust-filled breath from the tip of my aching toes, realizing then that someone else was monkeying with my day.

How I wanted to be healed, spirit-filled, and touched that day in the sprawling mess
30 of Shanghai. Then I paused, and she paused in the shade of the lonely tree, next to the stoplight, across the street from the U.S. funded "Portman Hotel Complex," where Clinton had stayed and where cappuccinos and clean immunization shots are sold. My misguided idea of salvation that lonesome Saturday
35 was the hairdresser behind those air-conditioned doors. I knew I had to take this chance.

The heated street went into soft focus as I followed her singsong English. She had been to the States to teach and administer medicine. Her fiery eyes startled me when she stopped in her tracks and exclaimed, "Jacksonville, Florida! That is a marvelous place. I would live there." The air of entitlement fueling this quote suggested her age (about sixty-five) and the
40 fact the she was likely born before Mao. And her claim to Jacksonville revealed her double vision—she could see outside of China.

It was her medical trade that took her around the world, to San Francisco, Florida, New York and Washington. She specialized in teaching techniques of Chinese medicine that worked when Western medicine failed. I asked
45 her in the way I had heard so many young women address their elders: "Auntie, what's your name?"

She answered me without stopping, letting me naturally assume a Chinese girl's role. Then
50 she flamboyantly added, "Christine, en francais." She was showing off, how splendid!

Christine adjusted her sweaty grasp on her collection of plastic bags. She had stayed in Paris for a study on several middle aged men who had
55 high blood pressure. "We used Chinese medicine, massage and musk to treat them. And then change the diet, and exercise," she added firmly. "One man do not follow and he still have problem,

monkey /ˈmʌŋki/ v. to play a joke
sprawling /ˈsprɔːlɪŋ/ adj. [only before noun] spreading in an untidy way
cappuccino /ˌkæpʊˈtʃiːnəʊ/ n. a kind of coffee made with hot frothy milk and sometimes with chocolate powder on the top
immunization /ˌɪmjʊnaɪˈzeɪʃən/ n. a protection system of human from the disease
fiery /ˈfaɪəri/ adj. showing strong emotions
entitlement /ɪnˈtaɪtlmənt/ n. the official right to have or do sth.
flamboyantly /flæmˈbɔɪəntli/ adv. fatuously, jazzily or ostentatiously
massage /ˈmæsɑːʒ/ n. the action of rubbing and pressing a person's body with hands to reduce pain in the muscles and joints
musk /mʌsk/ n. a substance with a strong smell that is used in making some perfumes

others they follow—no cigarettes, no wine. They better."

My chuckle fell out of my mouth. "Those French men were not too happy about that." I imagined the drooping shrugs and lips, the frustrated functionaries under Christine's watch.

With this, her nimble left index finger took on its age-old role, arching up at the patient. "Yes, but the body was happy. That is the most important thing: first, Health; second, Knowledge; third, Relationships. With these things of course you will have a good life and money."

The boldness of voice and finger showed conviction. She raised her hands and put her fingers next to my eyes. Feeling the wrinkles forming there, she gently rubbed the creases. "You need something; you have age here." Her touch was like that of a butterfly, incredibly warm and kind. I stood awaiting her prognosis, sure that her mystical words alone would save my fair skin and me.

"Johnsons, yes, one for babies no chemicals." Her scolding finger re-emerged: "Trouble in life makes you old, when you think outside of life, you are old." In my American-in-China mode, I found myself dumbfounded again. Today the shock was sweltering sidewalk therapy in halting phrases. My gaze refocused on the Hard Rock Café across the street opening its doors, the limousines with diplomatic plates carrying money, speeding away. I, myself, exalted by a tiny woman, with bad eyeliner and yellowed teeth, who chose today to preach to me in the center of the city.

"Many Chinese, they are happy. They have few things but they are happy. Do you know why? Because health. They have health."

I was still smiling, pleased at my karmic ability to run into such an improbable situation, but I was not sure I entirely agreed with her. I was thinking, this is the shtick they want to hear in Jacksonville?

"Stay in the shade, inside when the weather is cold and wet, exercise and eat good things and then dancing. Dancing and singing is so good, no think."

How many images I could conjure of ballroom dancing at every Chinese park I have visited, when the sun is a lacy print through the trees, where middle aged and old folks in all

---

drooping /'druːpɪŋ/ adj. sad and depressed
functionary /'fʌŋkʃənəri/ n. a person with official duties
nimble /'nɪmbəl/ adj. able to move quickly and easily
conviction /kən'vɪkʃən/ n. the feeling or appearance of believing sth. strongly and of being sure about it
prognosis /prɒg'nəʊsɪs/ n. an opinion, based on medical experience, of the likely development of a disease or an illness
dumbfounded /dʌm'faʊndɪd/ adj. unable to speak because of surprise
swelter /'sweltə/ v. to be very hot in a way that makes you feel uncomfortable
therapy /'θerəpi/ n. the treatment of a physical problem or an illness
limousine /'lɪməziːn/ n. a large expensive comfortable car
exalt /ɪg'zɔːlt/ v. to praise sb./sth. very much
eyeliner /'aɪˌlaɪnə/ n. a type of make-up, usually black, that is put around the edge of the eyes to make them more noticeable and attractive
shtick /ʃtɪk/ n. a style of humor that is typical of a particular performer
conjure /'kʌndʒə/ v. to make sth. appear as a picture in your mind
lacy /'leɪsi/ adj. made of or looking like lace

their splendor twist and swing each other around. No inhibition, shame or worry. They are not old here.

"It is a pity you have no time today," she cooed. "I would teach you some self-massage."

I was riveted. I had exactly an hour before my hair appointment. I had time. My excited toes forgot their chosen confinement and ached anew, but I managed to squeak, "Oh, but I have one hour, Auntie, and I want to learn."

We crossed the street and entered the Communist Exhibition Hall Complex. "No good space inside," Christine muttered. We were rounding our way toward the garden in the middle of the complex in the middle of a city of 13 million people when she cried, "Oh, a magnolia, a pine! We will sit in the shade." She stopped me from sitting directly on the cement bench, putting down a sheet of paper before offering me my seat. Having just visited the Hall's abominable toilets, I noted the irony, while she took out a book from her purse.

Christine used her whole body to teach. As she traced my arms, I learned that the fingers correspond with channels of "chi," or energy, which run through the body. You can start at a finger and follow the channel home. Then she whipped out a small pot: "Tiger Balm, you know this?" and I was whisked back to college massages in the dorm lounge, stories of Asian adventures. She unscrewed the top, and the camphoric odors found my nose. Grandma Rose used to feed an American spin-off of this balm, VIC's Vapo-rub, to my father with sugar on a spoon. What would my newfound Chinese angel think of that?

Soon my temples, chin, nose and cheekbones were pounding and red and thundering with her touch.

"For a clear mind," she said, massaging the sharp odor into my head, working her fingers back and forth along my cheekbones. "Then you need no makeup!"

"The ear," she showed me in the book,

inhibition /ˌɪnhɪˈbɪʃən/ n. a shy or nervous feeling that stops you from expressing your real thoughts or feelings

rivet /ˈrɪvɪt/ v. to hold sb's interest or attention so completely that they cannot look away or think of anything else

confinement /kənˈfaɪnmənt/ n. the state of being force to stay in a closed space, prison, etc., the act of putting sb there

squeak /skwiːk/ v. to only just manage to win sth., pass a test, etc.

mutter /ˈmʌtə/ v. to speak or say sth. in a quite voice that is difficult to hear, especially because you are annoyed about sth.

magnolia /mæɡˈnəʊliə/ n. a tree with large white, pink or purple flowers that smell sweet

pine /paɪn/ n. a tall forest tree with leaves like needles

cement /sɪˈment/ n. the hard substance that is formed when cement dry and hard

abominable /əˈbɒmɪnəbəl/ adj. extremely unpleasant and causing disgust

whisk /wɪsk/ v. to take sb/sth. somewhere very quickly and suddenly

camphoric /kæmˈfɒrɪk/ adj. relating to or derived from or containing camphor

"is just like the body." In the diagram, there were several numbers that corresponded to places in the body, energy spots that can be stimulated by massaging the ear. "Sixty-two is the earring place. Why women do that? See, it is for eyes." She gestured to the grid on the following page, nodding with satisfaction.

She rubbed hard, bunching my ears into awkward shapes and squeezing, moving her fingers into the opening, applying pressure throughout. "Vigorous," she smiled. "When they are red you stop."

> fervor /ˈfɜːvə/ n. very strong feelings about sth.
> spastic /ˈspæstɪk/ adj. an offensive word, sometimes used by children to mean 'stupid'
> whack /wæk/ v. to hit sb./sth. very hard
> invigorate /ɪnˈvɪɡəreɪt/ v. to make sb. feel healthy and full of energy
> momentarily /ˈməʊməntərɪli/ adv. for a very short time
> suspend /səˈspend/ v. to officially stop sth. for a time; to prevent sth. from being active, used, etc. for a time
> limbo /ˈlɪmbəʊ/ n. a situation in which you are no certain what to do next, can not take action, etc., especially because you are waiting for sb. else to make a decision
> opaque /əʊˈpeɪk/ adj. difficult to understand; not clear

I was relieved that she was taking note of the changed quality of my skin, her hurried touch at once rough and sweet. She was rolling through what seems to be her well-rehearsed routine. "Hearing!" she cried, "follow me!" and she inserted her index fingers repeatedly into each ear, each time crying, "hard, hard, hard!"

I was delighted by this simplistic treatment, something I would have subjected my baby-doll Amos to in my early years.

"Now, you HEAR good!" She seemed certain of my success and of my confidence in her teachings. Some folks wandering through the garden paused for the show that we were providing. I eagerly followed, actually pleased to not know what was coming.

Increasing her fervor, she explained that each side of our body has an opposite charge, *yin* and *yang*, and that we need to force these two sides to interact in order to achieve balance. I obediently imitated her spastic moves, whacking myself on the right side with a flat, clapping left hand and likewise for the other side. We had become a bit of a spectacle, me and my new shoes feeling their groundlessness again, a 4-foot-tall drill sergeant leading me in my battle toward cosmic health. Breathing heavily, she showed me how I should massage my own shoulders and chest, invigorating the lungs. Then came the most unexpected of all. Maintaining the same teacherly mode, she grabbed my breasts, one in each hand, pulsing through the tissues. I almost lost my breath from shock. A second later she gently grazed my nipples and kept her fingers there another instant, gently moving in circles. "This is an important place for energy, vital. You should touch it daily."

I have always believed, and always teach my students, that crossing cultures creates a new realm where rules are bent and transformed, where judgement should be at least momentarily suspended. Looking back at hazy Shanghai on that afternoon, it is easy for me to recreate the thick limbo, the opaque lack of conclusion I felt when Christine left me in the Communist garden. She was 50 kuai richer, though she wanted me to pay her more than the less-than-five dollar equivalent for her teachings. I sat quietly and smiled, saying, "xie xie."

She disappeared, and after a few minutes, I gathered the piece of paper I was sitting on and made my way to the hair salon.

Notes

1. Julia Carnine

Julia Carnine received her B.A. in French and sociology and anthropology from Lewis and Clark College and her M.S. in educational technology from Long Island University. Julia was director for Friends World Long Island, University study abroad program in Hangzhou, China from 1998–2001 and has been the academic director for the School for International Training's Intensive Language and Culture program in Toulouse, France since 2002.

2. Portman Hotel Complex

A brand new hotel has opened with a new service strategy: import to America Asian-style service using a butler-like employee group called the personal valets.

3. Jacksonville, Florida

Jacksonville is located in the First Coast region of northeast Florida, on banks of the St. Johns River.

4. Hard Rock Café

Hard Rock Cafe is a chain of casual dining restaurants. It was founded in 1971 by Isaac Tigrett and Peter Morton, and their first Hard Rock Café opened near Hyde Park Corner in London.

5. En francais

a French phrase, means "in French."

6. Communist Exhibition Hall Complex

This Soviet designed structure, with its star-topped spire, occupies a huge area opposite the Shanghai Centre on Nanjing Xi Lu. It was originally known as the Hall of Sino-Soviet Friendship and was built with Soviet help in the late 1950s to commemorate the 10th anniversary of the Chinese communist victory in 1949.

7. Chi

Called as "Qi" or "Ki", is a Chinese word used to describe "the natural energy of Universe". This energy, though called "natural", is spiritual or supernatural, and is part of a metaphysical.

8. Tiger Balm

Tiger Balm is a world famous topical pain relieving ointment. A versatile external medication, Tiger Balm provides effective relief for most symptoms of bodily aches and pains including headaches, rheumatism, arthritic pains, and muscle strains and sprains.

9. Grandma Rose

The character of "Tending Roses" written by Lisa Wingate, who drew upon her relationship with her grandmother for inspiration in writing this book.

10. VIC's Vapo-rub

Vic's Vapo rub is in fact, a sort of aromatherapy, which is the buzzword these days—and essentially it is the use of aromatic plant essences to bring about positive changes or effects in the mind and body.

11. Energy Spot

It is a human energy field and energy works such as Reiki and Emotional Freedom Technique.

12. Amos

Amos was set up in 2002 by James Jarvis, Sofia Prantera and Russell Waterman. James had previously been designing toys for fashion brand Silas, beginning with the now legendary Martin figure, released back in 1998. Along with Bounty Hunter in Japan, Silas unwittingly became one of the pioneers of the soft vinyl designer toy revolution.

Amos is also home for the curious tales from Green Fuzz. Will Sweeney's story of food abuse, kidnap, pillage and general mayhem has so far spawned a handful of comic books and limited vinyl figures.

13. Yin and Yang

Yin and Yang are famous symbols of the Tao & Taoism. They are the dynamic force of the Tao, constantly interacting with one another.

14. Kuai

A measuring unit of money equivalent to "yuan."

15. Xie Xie

"xie xie" means "thank you."

Comprehension Questions

Decide which of the following statements are True (T) or False (F) according to Text B.

1. (   ) From the text, we conclude that "I"'s mandarin is not very good.
2. (   ) From the passage, we can infer that "I" is a white woman working as an English teacher.
3. (   ) Two persons in the text are two foreigners.
4. (   ) "I", at the beginning, planned to have a haircut.
5. (   ) According to the author, conventions and laws of one country are infeasible in another country.
6. (   ) Chinese traditional medicines are more effective than western medicine in curing diseases.
7. (   ) In Christine's opinion, health is a more influential factor in terms of affecting people's life.

Writing Practice

Since the establishment of New China, it has experienced several developing phases. Nowadays, China has entered a new era when contact among countries becomes more and more frequent. Every country, as an indispensable component, can't keep themselves away from the sophisticated world, instead, they should participate on their own initiative in introducing advanced technologies on the one hand; having their own countries known on the other hand, so should China. Based on what texts mentioned, combined with China's current situation, can you expound how China can more deeply immerge into the changeable world? (You could touch upon economic and politic policies etc.)

Further Study

    Nowadays, with economic globalization and integration, the relation ship among countries becomes more and more intimate, not only the politics, economy but also culture, ideology, etc. Due to this, some take this point that the spread of one country's culture is another way to conquer other countries. As for this topic, students can go to library (or other sources) to collect materials. Furthermore, students can read newspaper or research on internet to get further understanding of changeable international relations.

Unit 11

Friendship

Unit Goals

After completing the lessons in this unit, students will be able to:
- ☞ extend and analyze what they have learned from looking at the main characters by discussing what it means to be a friend;
- ☞ apply and connect this knowledge to their own lives by brainstorming ways to make and keep friends;
- ☞ extend vocabulary through recognition of suffixes of status and domain.

Before Reading

Hands-on Activities

1. Search the library or surf the internet, and find materials related to friendship (movies, lyrics, songs, or short stories).
2. "Of friendship", an essay, is one of Bacon's essays, search it in the library or surf it on the net. And try to mime its writing technique and write an essay alike.

Brainstorming

Brainstorm the following questions. Work in pairs or groups to discuss these questions.

1. How do you define friendship?
2. What is the nature of friendship?
3. How to value and justify friendship?
4. Think about what friendship means to you by finishing the statements below.
   - Friendship means...

- A good friend always...
- A good friend never...
- It's good to have friends because...

A Glimpse at Words and Expressions

Please read the following sentences. Pay attention to the underlined part in each sentence and see how these expressions are used in the context, and then write down their meanings in the blanks provided.

1. It seems to me that for most people, the very mention of a certain name will bring back <u>a rush of</u> childhood memories. (   )
2. I think the best <u>estimate</u> we have for the stability of friendships is that they last—on the average—a few months. (   )
3. We conducted a solemn wedding ceremony for two of her teddy bears and <u>spied on</u> the neighborhood boys as they played outside. (   )
4. I was always a bit tall and lanky for my age, and called a "<u>show-off</u>" on more than one occasion. (   )
5. But clearly it <u>goes beyond</u> that if you're dealing with friendships that have lasted a while. (   )
6. Some nights after the sun had long since <u>retired</u>. (   )
7. We <u>double-dated to prom</u>, just as we'd always planned. (   )
8. My childhood friend was <u>a close second</u>. (   )

Text A

The Value of Friendship

By Tara Swords

It seems to me that for most people, the very mention of a certain name will bring back a rush of childhood memories—memories of summer days spent together barefoot and of deep secrets passed from behind a guarding hand cupped to the mouth. Memories that turn up the corners of your lips in a slight smile and make you squint your eyes as though doing so will give a clearer

> cup /kʌp/ *v.* to place one's curved hand or hands around
> squint /skwɪnt/ *v.* to partly close (one's eyes)

197

view of the past. For me, that name is Joelle.

I met her when I was just 6. Joelle was 5, and we both made our way to the same baby-sitter's house every school morning at 7:00 a.m. She always wore her school jacket with the sleeves stylishly pushed up to her elbows. For no particular reason, we didn't like each other.

But two years later, when my parents bought a house on the other side of our small, central Illinois town, we found ourselves next-door neighbors. One cool spring night, shortly after my family had moved in, I saw her playing in her driveway, the sleeves of her St. Mary's school jacket pushed confidently up to her elbows. I nervously approached her with a pair of shoes that no longer fit me. She accepted the peace offering, and agreed to a bike ride around the block.

Our first conversation:

"Do you like fish?" she asked me as we neared the end of our street.

"Yes," I said. "Do you?"

"No!"

But we agreed that bike rides were fun, cats were cute and acrobats were the coolest. So on that spring evening as we rode toward the cornfield bordering the southeast side of tiny Metamora, Illinois, and chatted about inane subjects, a friendship was born.

Psychologists often disagree about the impact childhood friendships like this one have on the development of kids' personalities. But quite often, the truth of the matter is that friends come and go while children are young, and that is perfectly healthy.

Thomas Berndt, professor of psychology at Purdue University, says what forms childhood friendships is "a similarity in social circumstances: living in the same neighborhood, riding the same bus. If those circumstances change, so do the friendships. From the ages of 5 through 10, I think the best estimate we have for the stability of friendships is that they last—on the average—a few months."

So Joelle and I weren't typical. In fact, after that first ride around the block, almost every part of my childhood involved Joelle. We played outside every night after school, attempting to perfect cartwheels and backflips until our mothers called us in at dark. We choreographed dances to all the best wham songs and became masters of the swingset in her backyard. We conducted a solemn wedding

---

stylishly /ˈstaɪlɪʃli/ *adv.* fashionably
driveway /ˈdraɪvweɪ/ *n.* a short private road leading to a house
inane /ɪˈneɪn/ *adj.* extremely foolish; irrational
choreograph /ˈkɒriəɡrɑːf/ *v.* to compose the sequence of steps and moves for (a dance performance)
backflip /ˈbækflɪp/ *n.* a backward somersault
swingset /ˈswɪŋset/ *n.* a frame for children to play on, including one or more swings

ceremony for two of her teddy bears and spied on the neighborhood boys as they played outside.

Yet we were different—at least in the ways that might keep some children from becoming friends. We attended different elementary schools; Joelle, a St. Mary's Falcon, and I, a Metamora Redbird, were cross-town rivals by day. She was quiet and shy; I often talked too much and, according to my exasperated grandmother, was "too rambunctious." Joelle was small and petite and a bit serious, with freckles that made adults coo over her cuteness. I was always a bit tall and lanky for my age, and called a "show-off" on more than one occasion.

We had some ferocious fights. Joelle's mother watched out for me during the summer when school was out and both my parents were at work, and if we got into an argument, I would run into my empty house and lock the door. Joelle and her little brother would gleefully ring our doorbell until the battery died or the circuit shorted—whichever happened first. Yet there was always an unstated understanding between us that we were friends, and that was unchangeable.

"Kids care more about friendship at a young age than they are able to say," says Berndt. "If you ask them, they say a friend is someone you play with, who you give your toys to, and who doesn't fight with you. But clearly it goes beyond that if you're dealing with friendships that have lasted a while." That was true for us. I think we understood the value of our friendship, but rarely talked about it.

Some evenings after dark, when we were assumed to be taking baths or doing homework in our own homes, I would sneak over to her house and enter through the garage door that led to the basement—just so we could talk a while longer. I now know that there is something ferocious and innocent in that time when young girls will steal away into the night just to spend time with a best friend, something that—when later replaced with late-night phone calls to boys—can never be reclaimed.

Some nights after the sun had long since retired, we would march a mile or two into

teddy /'tedi/ n. (pl. teddies) (also teddy bear) a soft toy bear
exasperate /ɪgˈzɑːspəreɪt/ v. to irritate intensely
rambunctious /ræmˈbʌŋkʃəs/ adj. uncontrollably exuberant
petite /pəˈtiːt/ adj. (of a woman) attractively small and dainty
freckle /ˈfrekəl/ n. a small light brown spot on the skin, caused and made more pronounced by exposure to the sun
coo /kuː/ v. (of a person) to speak in a soft gentle voice
lanky /ˈlæŋki/ adj. (lankier, lankiest) awkwardly thin and tall
ferocious /fəˈrəʊʃəs/ adj. savagely fierce, cruel, or violent
gleefully /ˈɡliːfəli/ adv. joyfully
circuit /ˈsɜːkɪt/ n. a system of conductors and components forming a complete path for an electric current
reclaim /rɪˈkleɪm/ v. to retrieve or recover

the cornfields that stretched out behind our subdivision as far as the eye could see. After about 45 minutes of walking huddled together with the flashlight beam jumping nervously, we would reach a tiny, century-old graveyard tucked away and forgotten in the middle of the field. Half amazed and half scared to death, we would shine the beam on the crumbling tombstones to read the names and dates, wondering what sort of people had lived there before us. We always felt most sad when the dates on the stones were too close together. Though we were but children ourselves, it must have made us confront our own mortality, and there was comfort in not doing that alone. I remember feeling horror at the idea that of all the important events in our lives, only the dates of two would serve as evidence that we had existed.

As we grew, we stayed close and served as role models for each other. Both of us always got high grades, and probably motivated each other to excel in school as a result. While today I delight in some of the harmless mischief we instigated, we were good kids that listened to our parents on the big issues, and never did anything that could get us into real trouble. In a way, we were our own support system for doing the right thing when parents weren't physically there to guide us.

And now, my memories of her are too many to count—a kind of animated collage: The day her house caught on fire, she grabbed her cat and ran to the safety of my bedroom; She taught me to shave my legs; I was the one driving her mother's car with Joelle sitting beside me when we crashed into a truck that had run a stop sign; We cried together as we rode in the ambulance to the hospital, and I was glad that I hadn't gotten blood on the shirt that she had let me borrow that day; We double-dated to prom, just as we'd always planned.

Now, college degrees later and miles away, we are still close. We live in different cities and work different jobs. And while I realize that my parents had the most important role in molding the person I was to eventually become, my childhood friend was a close second. It makes me wonder about the future, about my "someday" children and the people who will have an unforgettable impact on their lives, regardless of me. I will help nurture those friendships, knowing that their quality of life will be so enriched. The effects of a good, true friendship never fade: As children, Joelle and I explored and exploited the freedoms of being young and carefree; and as adults, the mere remembrance of that fact is enough to make me cherish the good in my life.

subdivision /ˌsʌbdɪˈvɪʒən/ n. an area of land divided into plots
huddle /ˈhʌdl/ v. to crowd together
tuck /tʌk/ v. (often tuck away) to store in a secure or secret place
crumble /ˈkrʌmbəl/ v. to break or fall apart into small fragments
motivate /ˈməʊtɪveɪt/ v. to stimulate the interest of
excel /ɪkˈsel/ v. to be exceptionally good at an activity or subject
instigate /ˈɪnstɪɡeɪt/ v. to bring about or initiate
animated /ˈænɪmeɪtɪd/ adj. lively
collage /ˈkɒlɑːʒ/ n. a combination or collection of various things
prom /prɒm/ n. a formal dance, especially one at a high school or college
nurture /ˈnɜːtʃə/ v. to cherish (a hope, belief, or ambition)
remembrance /rɪˈmembrəns/ n. a memory

Better Know More

1. Tara Swords

Tara Swords is an iParenting associate editor. Iparenting is famous for its Media Awards Program which provides a credible and objective method of determining the best products in the marketplace and then honors them with the most prestigious consumer award.

2. Purdue University

Purdue University is a coeducational, state-assisted system in Indiana. Founded in 1869 and named after benefactor John Purdue, the University is one of the nation's leading research institutions with a reputation for excellent and affordable education.

3. Wham!

Wham (often written WHAM!) was a top band formed in 1981 in Britain composed of George Michael and Andrew Ridgeley. They were briefly known in the United States as Wham.

Check Your Understanding

Choose the best answer to each of the following questions based on the text you have just learned.

1. What forms childhood friendship according to Thomas Berndt, professor of psychology at Purdue University?
   A. A similarity in social circumstances.   B. Living in the same neighborhood.
   C. Riding the same bus.   D. All of the above.
2. Why did the author say "after first ride around the block, almost every part of my childhood involved Joelle." Which of the following statements is TRUE according to the text?
   A. They had so many similarities.
   B. The author gave us examples to illustrate that they had a good time together.
   C. Joelle often helped me study.
   D. Joelle often took good care of me.

3. What were their dispositions according to the author?

   A. Joelle talked too much while I was quiet.

   B. They were both introvert.

   C. Joelle was quiet and shy while I often talked too much.

   D. They were both extrovert.

4. What's the meaning of the word "but" in "Though we were but children ourselves…?"

   A. only
   B. except
   C. besides
   D. apart from

5. Which of the following is the summary of the last paragraph?

   A. Although they lived in different cities, they still contacted each other.

   B. Jolle played an important role in molding the author's personality.

   C. The author told us the effects of a good, true friendship.

   D. The friendship made the author wonder about her "someday" children.

6. Which of the following statements is **Not** true according to the text?

   A. When Joelle and I met for the first time, we liked each other.

   B. The author couldn't remember their first conversation when they became the neighbors.

   C. They understood the value of friendship but rarely talked about it.

   D. After they had some ferocious fight, they would be angry with each other and ignore each other at once.

A Sip of Word Formation

Noun Suffixes: Status, Domain

1. *-hood*

   Similar in meaning to *-dom*, *-hood* derivatives express concepts such as "state" (as in *adulthood*, *childhood*, *farmerhood*), and "collectivity" (as in *beggarhood*, *Christianhood*, *companionhood*). As with other suffixes, metaphorical extensions can create new meanings, for example the sense "area" in the highly frequent *neighborhood*, which originates in the collectivity sense of the suffix.

2. *-ship*

   The suffix *-ship* forms nouns denoting "state" or "condition", similar in meaning to derivatives in *-age*, *-hood* and *-dom*. Base words are mostly person nouns as in *friendship*, *membership*, *statesmanship*, *vicarship*. Extensions of the basic senses occur, for example "office", as in *postmastership*, or "activity", as in *courtship* "courting" or *censorship* "censoring."

3. *-dom*

The native suffix *-dom* is semantically closely related to *-hood*, and *-ship*, which expresses similar concepts. *-dom* attaches to nouns to form nominals which can be paraphrased as "state of being X" as in *apedom, clerkdom, slumdom, yuppiedom*, or which refers to collective entities, such as *professordom, studentdom*, or denote domains, realms or territories as in *kingdom, cameldom, maoridom*.

Build Your Vocabulary

A. Decide which form of the noun suffix to use to make each word. Add the suffix and write the whole word.

ape		apprentice	
beggar		camel	
Christian		clerk	
clerk		friend	
earl		postmaster	
professor		slum	
statesman		student	
vicar		yuppie	

B. Complete each of the following sentences with proper form of the word given in brackets.

1. A liar begins with making _____ appear like truth, and ends with making truth itself appear like _____. (false)
2. The main theme of discussion was press _____. (censor)
3. A federal law enforcement official says investigators in Britain have found at least one _____ tape at the home of a suspect. (martyr)
4. I realized then that they had probably learnt their _____ at one of those mass children's classes dear to Maoist theory. (musician)
5. I keep _____ with my old friends. (companion)
6. This humiliation came on the heels of an earlier encounter with _____. (official)
7. Not only was everything that he had taken away from him, but also his German _____. (citizen)
8. It is commonly believed that a lie in childhood may lead to a crime in _____.(adult)
9. The King is the most important person in a _____. (king)
10. The Party must be on full alert against corrosion by all decadent ideas and maintain the purity of its _____. (member)

You'd Like to Be

A Skilled Text Weaver

Replace the underlined words or expressions in the following sentences with words or expressions from the text that best keep the original meaning.

1. Drouet had a habit, characteristic of his kind, of looking after <u>fashionably</u> dressed or pretty women on the street and remarking upon them.
2. She is a bit <u>crazy</u>; she always makes a regular exhibition of herself by raging at almost everybody.
3. And sweet little Dorete is so <u>small and thin</u>! They both love to eat meat and wheat, but they never smell their dirty stinky feet!
4. This <u>lively</u> picture suggests immediately some explanations for the more obvious properties of gases.
5. When the monkey saw the bananas, he was delighted, and ran <u>joyfully</u> to welcome the third man.
6. He <u>half closed his eyes</u> in the bright sunlight.
7. She looked curiously at this <u>awkwardly thin and tall</u> man with his bony stooped shoulders, his pinkish hair and calm unwavering eyes.
8. I became completely uninterested in my upcoming graduation, the senior-class play and the <u>dance</u>.
9. His object was to <u>bring about</u> a little rebellion on the part of the bishop.
10. My boy is such a <u>practical joke</u> maker. I am at my wits' end with him.
11. The <u>violent</u> winds seemed about to tear the ship to pieces.

A Solid Sentence Constructor

A. Complete each of the following sentences with proper form of the words given in brackets.

1. The government has taken a measure to maintain the _____ of prices. (stable)
2. They are discussing the _____ of abortion. (moral)
3. It is generally thought that traveling abroad can _____ one's knowledge. (rich)
4. In _____ of the battle, we set up a museum. (remember)
5. He persuaded them to join him by the sheer magnetism of his _____. (personal)
6. These days I have heard many _____ students and working adults alike express

a strong desire to take an English course and a computer course. (exasperate)

7. A _____ old church building needed remodeling, so, during his sermon, the preacher made an impassioned appeal looking directly at the richest man in town. (crumble)

8. Perhaps this _____ does not meet completely the point of view of scientifically exact systematics. (subdivide)

9. Parents play an important role in _____ the person their children are to eventually become. (mold)

10. It is the duty of every citizen to make the country rich and powerful, I consider this an _____ truth. (change)

B. Fill in the blanks in the following sentences with the words given below. Change the form where necessary.

| driveway | choreograph | rambunctious | circuit | huddle | motivate |
| collage | fade | coo | acrobat | elbow | |

1. The audience held their breath as the _____ walked along the tightrope.
2. The boys _____ together in the cave to keep warm.
3. You have to be able to listen well if you are going to _____ the people who work for you.
4. When the team turned into the _____ to the ranch house, Hilma uttered a little cry, clasping her hands joyfully.
5. Their _____ son always got into trouble.
6. The switches close the contacts and complete the _____.
7. There was some carefully _____ flag-waving as the President drove by.
8. As the pretty girl passed by, people _____ over her cuteness.
9. He fractured his _____ because of the traffic accident.
10. The painting comes from his private _____.
11. As evening came the coastline _____ into darkness.

A Sharp Interpreter

Paraphrase the following sentences. Change the sentence structure where necessary.

1. It seems to me that for most people, the very mention of a certain name will bring back a rush of childhood memories—memories of summer days spent together barefoot and of deep secrets passed from behind a guarding hand cupped to the mouth.

2. If we got into an argument, I would run into my empty house and lock the door. Joelle and her little brother would gleefully ring our doorbell until the battery died or the circuit shorted.

3. Some evenings after dark, when we were assumed to be taking baths or doing homework in our own homes, I would sneak over to her house and enter through the garage door that led to the basement—just so we could talk a while longer.

4. Half amazed and half scared to death, we would shine the beam on the crumbling tombstones to read the names and dates, wondering what sort of people had lived there before us.

5. Both of us always got high grades, and probably motivated each other to excel in school as a result.

A Careful Writer

Study the following synonyms and complete the setences.

stylish   fashionable   dashing

1. He made a _____ appearance.
2. She lives in a very _____ part of London.
3. Such thinking is _____ among right-wing politicians at the moment.
4. It was _____ performance by the two famous artists.
5. One of Darcy's acquaintances is a _____ young officer, George Wickham.
6. His wife was blonde and _____ thin.
7. His _____ good looks attracted many young women.

gleeful   jolly   happy

8. Mr. Smith was _____ over the achievements they had made.
9. The magnificent sights collect a _____ crowd.
10. You will be _____ in future if you follow my advice.
11. After they made the little girl cry, the naught boys ran away _____.
12. My boss is a _____ dog.
13. A _____ thought struck her.

excel   exceed   surpass

14. She has always _____ in her study.

15. The output this month _____ what we anticipated.
16. As a child he _____ at music.
17. His knowledge of history _____ mine.
18. The result _____ our hopes.
19. He was unable to _____ the limitation of his ability.

A Superb Bilingualist

Translate the following sentences into English with the words in brackets. Change the form where necessary.

1. 作为音乐家,她花费了多年的心血在技巧上精益求精。(perfect)
2. 他从人群中挤了过来。(elbow)
3. 他把我讲的故事加以改进,讲了一个更好的故事。(cap)
4. 农夫一边挤奶一边吹口哨。(milk)
5. 这张照片显示她和父母在一起。(picture)
6. 他们只是在空中喊口号。(mouth)
7. 在湖里游泳后,我们感到凉快了。(cool)

Translate the following sentences into English with the phrases or expressions given in brackets. Change the form where necessary.

1. 看来彼得是以他人的痛苦为快乐。(delight in)
2. 他们在各自的领域里都是出类拔萃的。(excel in)
3. 她假装着悲伤的样子。(assume)
4. 那个农场隐蔽在群山之中。(tuck away)
5. 他感到血一下涌到了脸上。(a rush of)
6. 谜语的要素在于谜底与谜面之间的比较。(unstated)
7. 你也许有权要求退回去年你交的部分税金。(reclaim)
8. 我认为那架飞机只有坠入海里,别无选择。(crash into)
9. 杰克受雇于警察,在暗中监视他的同事。(spy on)
10. 我们要想一想买新房子的事了,时机即将来临。(approach)
11. 詹姆斯喜欢溜到妹妹身后吓她一大跳。(sneak)
12. 我们想支持这个新工程,不想破坏它。(nurture)

Text B

All Un-Alone in the City

Why the lastest chatter about friendship doesn't feel very relevant to New York?

By Liesl Schillinger

It's not polite to talk about numbers: But how many men and/or women have you added to your list since you've lived in New York? Are we talking single digits? Double digits? Triple digits? How many of them were long-term, how many short-term, and how many turned out to be one-week (or one-night) wonders? Do you still keep in touch with them, and
5 do you remember their names? Do they remember yours?

We're talking, of course, about friends—a topic of joy, anxiety, and competition in the city that invented Friends, Seinfeld, and Sex and the City; a city in which invidious comparison is available with the flick of the remote, or with a glance into any restaurant window. A city in which, at the moment, it is August, and many of the people we count as
10 friends are away for weekends, or weeks at a time, leading to a sudden slip-off phone calls and e-mails that produces the existential question: Do I exist when the hulk of my friends are absent? It's like a dip in the Force.

In June, sociologists at Duke and the University of Arizona released a study that showed that, over the past twenty years, the number of people that the average American has
15 heart-to-heart talks with (or, in shorthand, "friends") has dropped by one-third, from about three people in 1985 to about two in 2004. For many people, the only confidant left is a spouse. Then, last month, Joseph lipstein, the Chicagoan taxouomist of American social
20 mores, released a book called Friendship: An Exposé, in which he addressed the broad topic of friends much as an exterminator might address the broad spectrum of pests, suggesting it was high time that Hallmark came out with
25 a card that read on the cover: "We've been friends for a very long time," and continued on the inside, "What do you say we stop?"

Assuming (which may not be entirely fair) that people have the friends they deserve,

---

invidious /ɪnˈvɪdɪəs/ *adj.* unpleasant and unfair; likely to offend sb. or make them jealous

flick /flɪk/ *n.* a quick look through the pages of a book, magazine, etc.

hulk /hʌlk/ *n.* a very large person, especially one who is not very grateful

dip /dɪp/ *n.* a decrease in the amount or success of sth., usually for only a short period

release /rɪˈliːs/ *v.* to make sth. available to the public

spouse /spaʊz/ *n.* a husband or a wife

exterminator /ɪkˈstɜːmɪneɪtə/ *n.* a person who destroys completely (a race or group of people or animals)

spectrum /ˈspektrəm/ *n.* a complete or wide range of related qualities, ideas, etc.

deserve /dɪˈzɜːv/ *v.* if sb. deserves sth., it is right that they should have it, because of the way they have behaved or because of what they are

and that, given human nature, if they really wanted more, they'd make an effort to socialize beyond their lawns. New Yorkers are once again faced with evidence that the priorities of the average American may have little to do with our own. For us, not having a spouse is acceptable; not having friends is anathema—a sign that your neuroses are so beyond—Woody Allen that only a shrink would take your calls. And when we marry, the comfort and reassurance of family life are constantly weighed against the stimulation and temptations of urban life and the preexisting bonds of longtime friendships. A hundred years ago (and earlier), before modern transportation made it easy for people to carom across the continent(s) at will, people largely stayed where they were dropped, leading to the invention of such strategies as "etiquette," which is, essentially, the art of not alienating the people you are constrained to live among. But New Yorkers are unusual in that they still stay put (except in August), though not so much through constraint as through choice. The result of staying put is that the old-fashioned art of cultivating and maintaining your circle is as necessary here as it was in a small town in Indiana in 1875 or 1975.

I remember, arriving alone in Manhattan at the tail end of the eighties, being alarmed that I lacked the built-in friend base that my New York-born contemporaries had. Having grown up in Indiana, I had witnessed the efforts that adults went to in low-population zones to whip up a social whirl: gourmet clubs, canoeing expeditions, picnics, car races. Activities changed—my mother would joke about going to a "dog shoot in Fowler" (a nearby hamlet) to pad the schedule—but friends remained the same.

In New York, there was no need to resort to dog shoots, but how did an absolute beginner go about finding a plus-one, much

---

priority /praɪˈɒrɪti/ *n.* something that you think is more important than other things and should be dealt with first

anathema /əˈnæθəmə/ *n.* a thing or an idea which you hate because it is the opposite of what you believe

neuroses /njʊˈrəʊsɪs/ *n.* (plural of neurosis) a mental illness which a person suffers strong feelings of fear and worry

shrink /ʃrɪŋk/ *n.* (slang, humorous) a psychologist or a psychiatrist

reassurance /ˌriːəˈʃʊərəns/ *n.* the fact of giving advice or help that takes away a person's fears or doubts

constantly /ˈkɒnstəntli/ *adv.* repeatedly, all the time

stimulation /ˌstɪmjʊleɪʃən/ *n.* sensory/intellectual/sexual/visual/physical

temptation /tempˈteɪʃən/ *n.* the desire to do or have sth. that you know is bad or wrong

preexisting /ˌpriːɪɡˈzɪstɪŋ/ *adj.* existing from an earlier time

carom /ˈkærəm/ *v.* to strike and rebound

etiquette /ˈetɪket/ *n.* the formal rules of correct or polite behavior in society or among members of a particular profession

alienate /ˈeɪliəneɪt/ *v.* to make sb. less friendly or sympathetic towards you

constrain /kənˈstreɪn/ *v.* to force sb. to do sth. or behave in a particular way

whip sb./sth. up to deliberately try and make people excited or feel strongly about sth.

whirl /wɜːl/ *n.* a number of activities or events happening one after the other

gourmet /ˈɡʊəmeɪ/ *n.* a person who knows a lot about good food and wines and who enjoys choosing, eating and drinking them

pad /pæd/ *v.* to tread, trudge, or tramp along

less a plus-posse, when everyone seemed so **dazzlingly** unavailable? At work, in those early days, I **furtively** filled out a Rolodex card with the names and numbers of nearly everyone I spoke to for more than ten minutes, wondering if they would mystically **morph** into Friends. I labeled the card "Amici" and filed it under A, so that if the Rolodex **flapped** open, nobody would guess the meaning of my hopeful jottings. Over time, thankfully, I was able to shred the card. There is no idiot's guide to how to make friends in New York, but if there were one, it would have to include a thorough classification chart of the indigenous friend varieties.

dazzlingly /ˈdæzəlɪŋli/ *adv.*	to impress sb. a lot with your beauty, skill, knowledge, etc.
furtively /ˈfɜːtɪvli/ *adv.*	behaving in a way that shows you want to keep sth. secret and do not want to be noticed
morph /mɔːf/ *v.*	to alter or animate by transformation
flap /flæp/ *v.*	to strike with a sudden blow
workaholism /ˌwɜːkəˈhɒlɪzəm/ *n.*	the condition of being a workaholic
claustrophobic /ˌklɔːstrəˈfəʊbɪk/ *adj.*	giving you claustrophobia, suffering from claustrophobia
breezy /ˈbriːzi/ *adj.*	having or showing a cheerful and relaxed manner
masochist /ˈmæsəkɪst/ *n.*	a person who exhibits or is given to masochism
borough /ˈbʌrə/ *n.*	a town or part of a city that has its own local government
supplant /səˈplɑːnt/ *v.*	to take the place of sb./sth. (especially sb./sth. older or less modern)
interloper /ˈɪntələʊpə/ *n.*	a person who is two events during which sth. different happens
spur /spɜː/ *n.*	a fact or an event that makes you want to do sth. better or more quickly
infidelity /ˌɪnfɪˈdelɪti/ *n.*	the act of not being faithful to your wife, husband or partner, by having sex with sb. else

There are the friends-from-the-office, whom you see most often, because of the **workaholism** of this town, but don't necessarily hang with outside of work (a subset of this is the office "marriage"); there are the "tribe" friends, the essential, familially **claustrophobic** pack everybody depends on; the drop-of-a-hat friends, tireless explorers of the city's delights whom you ring up when your tribe members are King low; activity-friends, whom you round up for poker games or bike rides; too-busy friends (which can include married friends), who E you and phone you and suggest meetings that they generally, sheepishly, cancel; friends you only see at parties; old lovers (popular among the **breezy**, the thick-skinned, and **masochists**); old friends, who include schoolmates, college roommates, family, and anyone who knew you before you were employed; new friends, who come and go like junior-high crushes; and friends-of-the-heart (who can be drawn from any of the above groups, and who can change).

In five **boroughs**, holding some 8 million people, the risk of being crossed off someone's mental "friends" list, or **supplanted** by a fascinating **interloper**, is an ever-present **spur** to comradely effort. Proust wrote that the threat of **infidelity** hovers over successful marriages; in the same way, the **expendability** of local friendships keeps players on their toes. And when a friendship dies, its casualties cannot easily avoid each other, given the persistence of social circuits-leading to **confrontations** out of Choderlos de Laclos-men **flinging** drinks and fists at one another, women cutting each other dead. To escape the awkwardness, you'd have to leave town for good ... another kind of death.

> **expendability** /ɪkˈspendəbiliti/ *n.* getting rid of things when they are no longer needed, or thinking it is acceptable if they are killed or destroyed
>
> **confrontation** /ˌkɒnfrənˈteɪʃən/ *n.* a situation in which there is an angry disagreement between people or groups who have different opinions
>
> **fling** /flɪŋ/ *v.* to throw sb./sth. somewhere with force, especially because you are angry

To Epstein, friendship seems to be no big whoop. "Friendship does not arise out of necessity, but out of preference," he chin-strokingly opines. Yes and no. I have never come across a New Yorker who does not regard friends as a necessity; and while making friends may happen out of choice, keeping them over time requires the same tact and harmonizing of egos that occur in family life. How New Yorkers pull off this delicate balancing act, while holding down their jobs, is one of the city's enduring mysteries. In fact, in seventeen years of socializing in this town, at thousands of social occasions (breakfast, lunch, brunch, dinner, book party, party party), I have found only one rule of friendship etiquette that remains constant: Maximum number of times you can meet somebody on second introduction, forget their name, yet still become friends. Maximum number of times you can meet somebody on second introduction, forget their face, yet still become friends.

Notes

1. Liesl Schillinger

Liesl Schillinger is a New York-based arts writer, a regular contributor to *the Book Review*. She was born and raised in college towns across the Midwestern United States, chiefly Indiana and Oklahoma. She attended Yale University, where she studied Comparative Literature. She worked at *The New Yorker* from 1988 to 2005, first as a fact checker, then as theatre and dance editor for the magazine's Goings On About Town section. Since 1991, she has written for many publications in the United States and Britain, chiefly *The New York Times, The New Yorker, the Washington Post,* and *the London Independent on Sunday,* where she wrote a column about New York life in 1996-98. She now writes full time, and is pursuing the goal of living like an expat in her own city.

2. Friends

One of the most watched television shows of the 1990s, it's a comedy series based in Manhattan about 6 young people, on their own and struggling to survive in the real world, finding the companionship, comfort and support they get from each other to be the perfect antidote to the pressures of life.

3. Seinfeld

An Emmy Award-winning sitcom that originally aired on NBC from July 5, 1989, to May 14, 1998, running a total of 9 seasons. It is a true-to-life comedy series that follows the events of a group of friends.

4. Sex and the City

A sensuous and ironic sitcom about four young, desirable, virtually inseparable New York bachelor girls who lead and confide in each-other their ever changing and confusing sex lives, as different as their natures.

Comprehension Questions

1. In the second paragraph, what does the writer say about friends?
2. What did the study released by the sociologist Duke and the University of Arizona show about friendship?
3. How is etiquette invented? What is its essence?
4. In Indiana, how do the adults socialize?
5. How many kinds of friends are mentioned in the passage?
6. According to Epstein, how does friendship arise in the last paragraph?

Writing Practice

Write a short passage on friendship. You have two choices.

1. You can write a three-paragraph composition according to the following requirements.
   You are to write in three parts. In the first part, state clearly what your view is. In the second part, support your view with details. In the last part, bring what you have written

to a natural conclusion with a summary or suggestion.
2. Write a story on friendship, it can be your own experiences or others.

Further Study

Interest in children's friendships has increased dramatically in recent years. Most of the research relating to children's friendships has focused on children's construct of friendship and on their conceptions of friendship. In addition to these main research areas, some researchers have attempted to examine the developmental process of children's friendship. Past research highlights a general trend in children's reflective understanding of friendship. Age differences are found in children's descriptions of friends or peers whom they like. The concrete features of common activities and propinquity are already apparent by four or five years of age, while relational features (e.g., liking and sharing and helping) increase in saliency around six and seven. The awareness of intimacy increases from middle childhood to adolescence. Older mutual friends have greater awareness of each other's individual differences than younger friends. In this key point in children's friendship development is the construction of reciprocity. Reciprocity means that sharing and playing can be initiated by either peer for younger children, whereas adolescents stress psychological attributes and general forms of interacting. Conduct further research on the differences between children's conception of friendship and that of adults'.

Unit 12

Honesty

Unit Goals

After completing the lessons in this unit, students will be able to:
- have a good understanding of the both sides of keeping honest;
- extend vocabulary through recognition of noun suffixes;
- show ways in which individuals learn behavior and values from groups in the community.

Before Reading

Hands-on Activities

1. Conduct a survey in your school or class asking questions like the following: Do you think people are honest enough? What are some examples of dishonesty you really dislike? What are some examples of honesty that you especially appreciate? Compile the results into a report and give a presentation in class.
2. Keep an "Honesty-Dishonesty" journal for one week. In this journal, document examples of honesty and dishonesty in everyday life. Keep track of all the times you hear or tell "white lies". Pay particular attention to the local media. See what role honesty plays in stories covered in the news. Note how often dishonesty is at the core of TV sitcoms and dramas. At the end of a week, write your conclusions and share them with the class. What did you learn about your own behavior from doing this project?
3. Visit the web: http://www.school-for-champions.com/character/honesty.htm and find out what honesty means.

Brainstorming

Brainstorm the following questions. Work in pairs or groups to discuss these questions.

1. As a class, brainstorm all the excuses and rationalizations people give for lying, cheating, and stealing, and then have a discussion about them. How valid are they? What's wrong with each of them?
2. Discuss in groups:
   (1) Do you consider yourself to be an honest person? Why?
   (2) What would you do if you found $10,000 on the shelf beneath an ATM machine and nobody saw you find it?
   (3) People often rationalize their own dishonesty by saying, "That's the way the world is, so why should I be different?" What do you think of this reasoning?
   (4) Is there anything wrong with a "small" lie to parents or friends to keep from upsetting them?
   (5) When people are dishonest with you, how does it make you feel?
   (6) If you discover your classmates are cheating on an important exam, does that make it okay for you to cheat, too?

A Glimpse at Words and Expressions

Please read the following sentences. Pay attention to the underlined part in each sentence and see how these expressions are used in the context, and then write down their meanings in the blanks provided.

1. The legends in the making involve mad, all-night scrambles to launch a web site. (   )
2. Their favorite stories touch on a theme that hardly ever takes center stage in Silicon Valley. (   )
3. If we're going to be the kind of company that people trust, we've got to keep our promises. (   )
4. Plenty of companies are prepared to cut a few ethical corners in order to move faster. (   )
5. But wiggling away from the truth can be disastrously expensive in the long run. (   )
6. But they came across as very reliable, trustworthy people. (   )
7. That may make it a little harder to wrap up recruiting efforts in a hurry. (   )
8. But Mann's honesty usually pays off when tough times arise. (   )
9. Perhaps the most common failing of a young, ambitious Internet executive is the tendency to squeeze every possible advantage out of negotiations with an outsider. (   )

10. A more even-handed approach may be the best bet.   (   )
11. Who might have ended up getting a smaller stake in the company.   (   )

Text A

Honesty Is the Best Policy

By George Anders

It's always fascinating to step inside a Silicon Valley startup and ask the people there to share stories about what makes their company special. The anecdotes that rank-and-file employees tell a visitor tend to reflect the way that their company views its character and its culture.

5 At some companies, the legends in the making involve mad, all-night scrambles to launch a web site or to release a new piece of software. At other companies, the best lore involves relentless efforts to line up customers. And if a company is attracting favor from venture capitalists or from public shareholders, it's a safe bet that at least one story will involve the shock and delight of employees upon realizing how valuable the business has
10 become.

Employees at CenterBeam Inc., based in Santa Clara, California, could tell variants of all of these stories. Since April 1999, CenterBeam's main service—taking charge
15 of small companies' computer departments by installing networks of wireless, internet-oriented machines—has attracted hundreds of customers. While CenterBeam hasn't yet gone public, it has attracted ever-
20 higher valuations from VCs and strategic investors. But those aren't the stories that CenterBeam's employees want to tell. Their favorite stories touch on a theme that hardly ever takes center stage in Silicon Valley: in-
25 tegrity—that is, the make-or-break importance of simply keeping your word.

Early on, for example, CenterBeam was

---

startup /ˈstɑːtʌp/ *n.* connected with starting a new business or project

rank-and-file *n.* the ordinary members of an organization

scramble /ˈskræmbəl/ *n.* a situation in which people push, fight or compete with each other in order to get or do sth.

release /rɪˈliːs/ *v.* to make sth. available to the public

lore /lɔː/ *n.* knowledge and information related to a particular subject, especially when this is not written down; the stories and traditions of a particular group of people

relentless /rɪˈlentləs/ *adj.* not stopping or getting less strong

venture /ˈventʃə/ *n.* a business project or activity, especially one that involves taking risks

bet /bet/ *n.* an opinion about what is likely to happen or to have happened

integrity /ɪnˈtegrɪti/ *n.* the quality of being honest and having strong moral principles

make-or-break *adj.* to be the thing that makes sb./sth. either a success or a failure

on a hiring spree, trying to recruit enough people to carry out its rapid expansion plans. The company offered a job to one candidate, but before that person could accept, a résumé from an absolutely dazzling contender arrived. Could the first offer be rescinded, managers wanted to know, so that the company could hire this superstar instead? The answer from Sheldon Laube, 49, CenterBeam's chairman and CEO: No way. "We made a promise to the first candidate," Laube recalls. "If we're going to be the kind of company that people trust, we've got to keep our promises."

Around that same time, CenterBeam executives ordered $500,000 worth of tape drives from a distributor. Those drives (vital equipment that the company uses to back up customer-data files) soon arrived at CenterBeam's headquarters. But before engineers could unpack the merchandise, they learned that a rival distributor was offering comparable machines at a price that would save CenterBeam $93,000 a year. A few engineers wanted to refuse delivery of the more-expensive machines. But CenterBeam executives treated the shipment as binding. Instead, they asked the distributor to take back the expensive system and then bought the cheaper system from the same distributor—at a cost that was roughly $50,000 more than the rival distributor was charging.

What's the road to success for a startup? For many companies, it's whatever road leads them to the most business in the least amount of time. The Internet economy worships at the altar of fast action, fast growth, and fast results. Plenty of companies (and the people who lead them) are prepared to cut a few ethical corners in order to move faster: not gross violations, such as accounting manipulations or outright fraud, but day-to-day dilemmas—leadership moments in which you do either the right thing or the expedient thing.

> spree /spriː/ n. a short period of time that you spend doing one particular activity that you enjoy, but often too much of it; a period of activity, especially criminal activity
> recruit /rɪˈkruːt/ v. to find new people to join a company, an organization, the armed forces
> contender /kənˈtendə/ n. a person who takes part in a competition or tries to win sth.
> rescind /rɪˈsɪnd/ v. to officially state that a law, contract, decision, etc. is no longer valid
> distributor /dɪsˈtrɪbjʊtə/ n. a person or company that supplies goods to shops/stores, etc.
> binding /ˈbaɪndɪŋ/ adj. that must be obeyed because it is accepted in law
> altar /ˈɔːltə/ n. a holy table in a church or temple
> outright /ˈaʊtraɪt/ adj. complete and total; open and direct
> fraud /frɔːd/ n. the crime of deceiving sb. in order to get money or goods illegally
> dilemma /dɪˈlemə/ n. a situation which makes problems, often one in which you have to make a very difficult choice between things of equal importance
> expedient /ɪkˈspiːdiənt/ adj. useful or necessary for a particular purpose, but not always fail or right

Are you aboveboard with investors when you know that the next quarter may be disappointing? Will you say anything to recruit a great job candidate, or are you honest about the risks involved in an assignment?

If this were a Sunday-school lesson, the answers would be obvious. Virtue would triumph, and cheaters would be vanquished by truth tellers. But the startup business is not so simple. There's a widespread feeling among entrepreneurs and venture capitalists that if a new company doesn't display a bit of bluster and outright exaggeration in its launch phase, it won't be taken seriously—and it won't get a chance to change the world. What fun is starting a company if you can't be a little devious?

Yet if hubris was a winning strategy in the past, its perils have recently become all too clear. Many of the Net companies that went public on the strength of extravagant promises have stumbled badly. In some cases, signs of a credibility gap are so severe that they ooze from companies' financial statements—and translate into plummeting stock prices.

"It's amazing how many employees have come up to me and said, 'It's great to work at a company that has integrity,'" says Laube. "Many employees tell me that at their old companies, 'people promised things that they just didn't deliver.'" Yolanda Gonzalez, 48, VP of human resources at CenterBeam, estimates that two-thirds of the company's new hires tell her that they were uncomfortable with the low ethical standards that prevailed at their former employers.

Some of the clearest thinking about integrity in the Internet economy comes from Darlene Mann, 39, a general partner at Onset Ventures, in Menlo Park, California. Her firm has bankrolled dozens of startups, and she has worked inside numerous high-tech companies. If executives want "integrity" to be more than just a buzzword in a mission statement, she says, they need to think hard about three issues: the growth goals that they promise to customers and investors, the career opportunities that they promise to employees, and the tone that they strike in day-to-day negotiations with business partners. In some cases, Mann acknowledges, keeping one's word carries extra short-term costs. But wiggling away from the truth can be disastrously expensive in the long run.

The point, says Mann, isn't that startups need to let go of their ambitious dreams. But they do need to ensure that promises made to the outside world are believable to their

---

vanquish /'væŋkwɪʃ/ v. to defeat sb. completely in a competition, war, etc.
entrepreneur /ˌɒntrəprə'nɜː/ n. a person who makes money by starting or running businesses, especially when this involves taking financial risks
bluster /'blʌstə/ v. to talk in an aggressive or threatening way, but with little effect
exaggeration /ɪɡˌzædʒə'reɪʃən/ n. a statement or description that makes sth. seem larger, better, worse or more important than it really is; the act of making a statement like this
devious /'diːviəs/ adj. behaving in a dishonest or indirect way, or deceiving people, in order to get sth.
hubris /'hjuːbrɪs/ n. the fact of sb. being too proud
peril /'perɪl/ n. serious danger
extravagant /ɪk'strævəɡənt/ adj. spending a lot more money or using a lot more of sth. than you can afford or than is necessary
credibility /ˌkredɪ'bɪlɪti/ n. the quality that sb./sth. has that makes people believe or trust them
ooze /uːz/ v. to emit a particular essence or quality
plummet /'plʌmɪt/ v. to decline suddenly and steeply
bankroll /'bæŋkrəʊl/ v. to support sb./sth. financially
buzzword /'bʌzwɜːd/ n. a word or phrase, especially one connected with a particular subject, that has become fashionable and popular and is used a lot in newspapers, etc.
wiggle /'wɪɡəl/ v. to move from side to side or up and down in short quick movements; to make sth. move in this way

own people. Otherwise, they will be built on a foundation of cynicism and distrust.

What's more, in the current culture of hype, companies that undersell their strengths can win remarkable loyalty. Last year, when Carl Russo was CEO of Cerent Corp., an optical-networking company, he signed up Calico Commerce to build his company's web site. "Unlike everyone else, they were very subdued in what they promised us," recalls Russo, 44, now a VP and a general manager at Cisco Systems, which recently acquired Cerent. "But they came across as very reliable, trustworthy people." Russo had a good experience with Calico, and now he is one of that company's most valuable customer references.

As the Internet sector undergoes a shakeout of sorts, people are paying a lot of attention to the explicit or implicit promises that companies make to employees and managers. No one ever said that working for an Internet startup was a lifetime job. But some top executives and board members have done a good job of communicating, each step of the way, what could go right and what could go wrong—a practice that makes it easy to regroup when times change. By contrast, other business leaders have opportunistically hired what they thought was a winning growth team, making grand promises without building the kind of stability that gets a company through hard times.

At Onset Ventures, Mann tells some executive recruits to work in their new job for a few months, and to make sure that it will work out, before relocating their families. She also preps candidates on the risks that come with taking a given job. That may make it a little harder to wrap up recruiting efforts in a hurry, but Mann's honesty usually pays off when tough times arise. A person who knows the risks of a job up front, says Mann, "is much more likely to be a good hire in a difficult situation."

Less dramatic, but every bit as challenging, is the issue of how high-tech startups treat their business partners. Perhaps the most common failing of a

---

cynicism /ˈsɪnɪsɪzəm/ *n.* a scornful, bitterly mocking attitude or quality

hype /haɪp/ *n.* (informal, disapproving) advertisements and discussion on television, radio, etc. telling the public about a product and about how good or important it is

undersell /ˌʌndəˈsel/ *v.* to sell goods or services at a lower price than your competitors

optical /ˈɒptɪkəl/ *adj.* connected with the sense of sight or the relationship between light and sight

subdue /səbˈdjuː/ *v.* to bring sb./sth. under control, especially by using force; to calm or control your feelings

sector /ˈsektə/ *n.* a part or division, as of a city or a national economy

shakeout /ˈʃeɪkaʊt/ *n.* a situation in which people lose their jobs and less successful companies are forced to close because of competition and difficult economic conditions

opportunistic /ˌɒpəˈtjuːnɪstɪk/ *adj.* taking immediate advantage, often unethically, of any circumstance of possible benefit.

prep /prep/ *v.* to prepare sb./sth.

young, ambitious Internet executive is the tendency to squeeze every possible advantage out of negotiations with an outsider—whether the deal in question involves a $40,000 supply contract or a $20 million marketing alliance. That's just not wise, says Ram Shriram, 43, a former Amazon.com vice president who is now an angel investor. It leaves an undercurrent of bitterness—and a very small list of partners that will want to continue doing business with such a razor-sharp deal maker.

In the long run, argues Scott Sandell, 35, a partner at New Enterprise Associates, a Menlo Park-based venture-capital firm, a more even-handed approach may be the best bet—even in the fast-paced world of Internet negotiations. To illustrate his point, Sandell tells a story of the financing negotiations that got CenterBeam in business. New Enterprise had planned on being one of two firms that would bankroll the business. But at the last moment, a third firm, Accel Partners, swooped in.

That was good news for CenterBeam and for its CEO, Sheldon Laube—but potentially bad news for the earlier investors, who might have ended up getting a smaller stake in the company. Rather than unilaterally reworking CenterBeam's financing terms, Laube asked his early backers if they were willing to add Accel to the financing group. And he didn't revise the deal until they said yes.

According to Sandell, it's all too easy to think that because everything moves so fast in the Internet economy, there just isn't enough time to fuss over the fine points of integrity. In fact, he says, the urgency of Internet-based business means that "there is no time for lack of integrity. Without it, everything becomes more complicated, because you can't depend on people to do what they say they will do."

Sure, we live and work in a world where "the Internet changes everything." But it's heartening to see that some of the Web's smartest mavericks believe that honesty is still the best policy.

---

alliance /əˈlaɪəns/ *n.* an agreement between countries, political parties, etc. to work together in order to achieve sth. that they all want

undercurrent /ˈʌndəˌkʌrənt/ *n.* a feeling, especially a negative one, that is hidden but whose effects are felt

razor-sharp *adj.* extremely sharp; showing that sb. is extremely intelligent

swoop /swuːp/ *v.* (of a bird or plane) to fly quickly and suddenly downwards, especially in order to attack sb./sth.

stake /steɪk/ *n.* an important part or share in a business, plan, etc. that is important to you and that you want to be successful

unilateral /ˌjuːnɪˈlætərəl/ *adj.* done by one member of a group or an organization without the agreement of the other members

fuss /fʌs/ *v.* to do things, or pay too much attention to things, that are not important or necessary

maverick /ˈmævərɪk/ *n.* a person who does not behave or think like everyone else, but who has independent, unusual opinions

Better Know More

1. George Anders
A Fast Company senior editor based in Silicon Valley.

2. Silicon Valley
Silicon Valley is the southern part of the San Francisco Bay Area in Northern California in the United States.

3. CenterBeam Inc
A California-based IT outsourcing company, focuses *exclusively* on serving small and medium sized organizations and offers a new way to outsource the base IT support functions.

4. Santa Clara
Founded in 1777 and incorporated in 1852, is a city in Santa Clara County, in the U.S. state of California. The city is the site of the eighth of 21 California missions, Mission Santa Clara de Asís, and was named after the mission. The Mission and Mission Gardens are located on the grounds of Santa Clara University.

5. VCs
Venture capital, money made available for investment in innovative enterprises or research, especially in high technology, in which both the risk of loss and the potential for profit may be considerable. It also called risk capital.

6. CEO
Abbr. Chief Executive Officer.

7. VP
Abbr. Vice President.

8. Onset Venture
A company engages in early-stage investments in information, communication, and medical technology.

9. Menlo Park

A city in San Mateo County, California in the United States of America.

10. Cerent Corp

An optical-networking company, acquired by Cisco Systems in 1999.

11. Calico Commerce

Headquartered in San Jose, Calif. and with offices throughout the United States and Europe, is a provider of software and services that enable customers to engage in eCommerce by selling complex products and services over the Internet.

12. Cisco Systems

The leading supplier of networking equipment & network management for the Internet. Products include routers, hubs, ethernet, LAN/ATM switches, dial-up access servers and software.

13. New Enterprise Associates

Is one of the world's leading venture capital firms focused on information technology and healthcare investments.

14. Accel Partners

Accel Partners is a venture capital firm that has been dedicated to supporting entrepreneurs who possess the unique insight to define new categories and build world-class technology companies.

Check Your Understanding

Answer the following questions based on the text you have just learned.

1. According to the rank-and-file employees of Silicon Valley startups, what makes their companies special?
2. What do the legends at some companies in the making involve according the article?
3. What are the stories that the CenterBeam's employees want to tell?
4. If you were CEO of CenterBeam, what would you do when you encounter such situation occurred in paragraph 4? And why?

5. Do you support the executives of CenterBeam about their deal with the distributor? If not, what would you do?
6. In your own opinion, what's the road to success for a new company?
7. If a startup can't be a little devious, will it get a chance to change the world?
8. What do you think of the reasons of the Internet companies' wanting integrity? Do they want it just for the sake of itself?
9. What's the best bet for a company in treating its business partners?
10. What can you deduce from the last paragraph?

A Sip of Word Formation

Noun Suffixes

Nominal suffixes are often employed to derive abstract nouns from verbs, adjectives and nouns. *-ful*, *-ion*, *-ment*, *-al*, *-age*, *-ness*, *-ity*, *-ant* are nominal suffixes.

1. The nominal suffix *-ful* derives measure partitive nouns (similar to expressions such as a lot of, a bunch of) from nominal base words that can be construed as containers: *cupful*.
2. The Latinate suffix *-ion* has three allomorphs: when attached to a verb in *-ify*, the verbal suffix and *-ion* surface together as *-ification* (personification). When attached to a verb ending in *-ate*, we find the allomorph *-ation* in all other cases (*starvation*). Derivatives in *-ion* denote events or results of processes. As such, verbal bases are by far the most frequent, but there is also a comparatively large number of forms where *-ation* is directly attached to nouns without any intervening verb in *-ate*. These forms are found primarily in scientific discourse with words denoting chemical or other substances as bases (e.g. sediment—*sedimentation*).
3. The suffix *-ment* derives action nouns denoting processes or results from (mainly) verbs, with a strong preference for monosyllables or disyllabic base words with stress on the last syllable (e.g. *assessment, endorsement*).
4. The suffix *-al* is used to mean a process or state of (e.g. *survival, approval*).
5. The suffix *-age* derives nouns that express an activity (or its result) as in coverage, and nouns denoting a collective entity or quantity, as in *acreage*. Due to inherent ambiguities of certain coinages, the meaning can be extended to include locations, as in *orphanage*.
6. The suffix *-ness* can attach to practically any adjective, and apart from adjectival base words we find nouns as in *thingness*, pronouns as in *us-ness* and frequently phrases as in *over-the-top-ness, all-or-nothing-ness*.
7. The suffix *-ity* is used to form nouns. Words belonging to this morphological category are

nouns denoting qualities, states or properties usually derived from Latinate adjectives (e.g. *curiosity, productivity*).

8. The suffix *-ant* forms count nouns referring to persons (often in technical or legal discourse, cf. *applicant*) or to substances involved in biological, chemical, or physical processes (*attractant, dispersant*).

📖 Build Your Vocabulary

A. Decide which form of the nominal suffixes introduced above to use to make each word a noun. Add the suffix and write the whole word.

disarm		parent	
arrive		deter	
contribute		profound	
arm		silly	
leak		renew	
polite		appease	
pure		anticipate	
assist		spoon	
glass		hand	
classify		complete	
agree		treat	
refer		recite	
break		spill	
blind		dry	
odd		solid	
inhabit		defend	

B. The word in brackets at the end of each of the following sentences can be used to form a word that fits suitably in the blank space. Fill in each blank this way.

Example: Please give me three <u>cupfuls</u> of water. (cup)

1. This is the entire _____ of the upcoming game "Spore" given by Will Wright. (demonstrate)
2. To our great _____, it rained every day of the trip. (appoint)
3. _____ voting is any voting system that allows many voters to express formal _____ simultaneously, in a system where they all share some power. (approve)
4. Poor circulation and _____ of blood in the leg arteries produces an aching, tired, and

sometimes burning pain in the legs. (block)

5. At least have the _____ to look at me when I'm talking to you. (good)
6. _____ is a subjectively defined characteristic, assigned to those with rare or dysfunctional conditions. Defining who is normal or abnormal is a contentious issue in abnormal psychology. (normal)
7. We're a very small group of editors, teachers and MBAs from Stanford, Columbia and UCLA who have worked with business school _____ for the last eight years. (apply)
8. It is even more important to arouse people's national integrity, oppose _____ and treason, heighten their courage to fight the enemy and foster their confidence in victory. (vacillate)
9. He spoken openly about his _____ with the actress. (involve)
10. Human _____ is part of our human condition, found in all families, cultures and communities, and is woven within the very fabric of our society. (denigrate)

You'd Like to Be

A Skilled Text Weaver

Fill in each blank with an appropriate word from the text.

1. You also tried to _____ the objective case from its thralldom to the preposition, and it is written that servants should obey their masters.
2. Don't be so _____; spend your money more carefully.
3. Then the members of the committee tried to withdraw their admission, and Sergey Ivanovitch began to prove that they must logically admit either that they had verified the accounts or that they had not, and he developed this _____ in detail.
4. The difficulty of tactical maneuvering consists in turning the _____ into the direct, and misfortune into gain.
5. These are the four useful branches of military knowledge which enabled the Yellow Emperor to _____ four several sovereigns.
6. Come, D'Artagnan, don't let us play a sidelong game; your hesitation, your evasion, tells me at once on whose side you are; for that party no one dares openly to _____, and when people _____ for it, it is with averted eyes and humble voice.
7. But Glinda was now really angry, and sent word to Jinjur that the _____ was discovered and she must deliver up the real Mombi or suffer terrible consequences.
8. I may _____ to assert the same of every aspect of the story, while I confess that the

particular typhoon of the tale was not a typhoon of my actual experience.

9. For instance, the upright man takes his character from the possession of the quality of _____, but the name given him is not derived from the word "_____."

10. Lady Susan finds it necessary that Frederica should be to blame, and probably has sometimes judged it _____ to excuse her of ill-nature and sometimes to lament her want of sense.

11. There was what appeared to be a _____ and a rush rather than any regulated movement.

12. They are now on terms of the most particular friendship, frequently engaged in long conversations together; and she has contrived by the most artful coquetry to _____ his judgment to her own purposes.

13. He was _____ in worrying him about his soul's concerns, and about ruling his children rigidly.

A Sharp Interpreter

Paraphrase the following sentences, refer to the contexts in which the sentences are located.

1. The anecdotes that rank-and-file employees tell a visitor tend to reflect the way that their company views its character and its culture.
2. Their favorite stories touch on a theme that hardly ever takes center stage in Silicon Valley.
3. For many companies, it's whatever road leads them to the most business in the least amount of times.
4. In some cases, Mann acknowledges, keeping one's word carries extra short-term costs.
5. Perhaps the most common failing of a young, ambitious Internet executive is the tendency to squeeze every possible advantage out of negotiations with an outsider.
6. But it's heartening to see that some of the Web's smartest mavericks believe that honesty is still the best policy.

A Solid Sentence Constructor

A. Complete each sentences with one of the expressions listed below. Make changes where necessary.

in the making	line up	touch on	keep one's word	keep one's promise
in the long run	let go	come across	wrap up	pay off
end up	fuss over	the best bet		

1. It became clear that this was a disaster _____ and we had no way of coping with it.
2. It's a mistake to _____ your computer.
3. They would _____ in all they owned, but they could not _____ against exhaustion; and many a man gave out in these battles with the snowdrifts, and lay down and fell asleep.
4. I began work as an accountant and _____ writing advertising.
5. I have found out, beyond any doubt whatever, that disobedient boys are certainly far from happy, and that, _____, they always lose out.
6. Lee had already _____ a good lawyer to handle his case.
7. It takes a while to build up the trust necessary for him to know that I intend to _____ when I say I'm going to do something and vice versa.
8. He longed to question her, to hear more about the life of which her careless words had given him so illuminating a glimpse; but he feared to _____ distressing memories, and before he could think of anything to say she had strayed back to her original subject.
9. I was looking through a magazine and _____ an interesting article on American artists.
10. He heard her, and tried to pull down the sail; but the wind would not _____ of the broad canvas and the ropes had become tangled.
11. Miss Dearborn asked us what is the object of education and I said the object of mine was to help _____ the mortgage.
12. Cars are also major polluters, so your _____ is to take a train or a bus.

B. Finish each of the following sentences in such a way that it means the same as the sentence printed before it.

1. It's a safe bet that at least one story will involve the shock and delight of employees upon realizing how valuable the business has become.
   _____ is that _____.
2. Plenty of companies are prepared to cut a few ethical corners in order to move faster.
   Plenty of companies _____ they can move faster.
3. Rather than unilaterally reworking CenterBeam's financing terms, Laube asked his early backers if they were willing to add Accel to the financing group.
   Laube asked his early backers _____
   _____.
4. And he didn't revise the deal until they said yes.
   _____ he didn't revise the deal.
5. It's all too easy to think that because everything moves so fast in the Internet economy.
   It's so much _____.

6. Their favorite stories touch on a theme that hardly ever takes center stage in Silicon Valley: integrity.

   Their favorite stories _____ theme—integrity, _____ it ever take center stage in Silicon Valley.

A Careful Writer

Study the following synonyms and complete the sentences.

| honesty   honor   integrity |

1. "Never give in except to convictions of _____ and good sense." (Winston S. Churchill)
2. _____ is the best policy.
3. "_____ without knowledge is weak and useless, and knowledge without _____ is dangerous and dreadful." (Samuel Johnson)

| defeat   conquer   vanquish   beat   subdue |

4. The forces of Napoleon were _____ at Waterloo.
5. "To win battles ... you _____ the soul ... of the enemy man." (George S. Patton)
6. "A _____ army on the border will not be halted by the power of eloquence." (Otto von Bismarck)
7. "Whether we _____ the enemy in one battle, or by degrees, the consequences will be the same." (Thomas Paine)
8. "It cost the Romans two great wars, and three great battles, to _____ that little kingdom [Macedonia]." (Adam Smith)

| peril   danger   risk |

9. He stayed up so late that he was afraid that he was in _____ of oversleeping and being late for work.
10. Mrs Anne Sterling did not think of the _____ she was taking when she ran through a forest after two men.
11. Passengers ignore the importance these results at their _____.

A Superb Bilingualist

Translate the following sentences into English.

1. 看上去只是抢夺和混乱，而不是有秩序地运动。(scramble)
2. 这免除了他们的个人责任。(release)
3. 我要为周六准备些东西，因为我们有可能要去博物馆。(line up)
4. 他在谈话中提到了拉丁美洲的局势。(touch on)
5. 州长因没能履行竞选时的一项承诺而受到新闻界的抨击。(keep a promise)
6. 别急！如果你想干得出色，就不能只图简便。(cut corners)
7. 那装潢已精致到了奢华的地步。(extravagant)
8. 这孩子紧紧抓住汤姆不放。(let go)
9. 她完全迷上了他，连他的缺点也看不见了。(wrap up)
10. 我不想为这种小事大惊小怪。(fuss over)

Text B

To Lie or Not to Lie?

Anonymous
(Abridged and Edited)

Some fibs benefit others, but Lilliputians teach lesson of societal responsibility.

Those who never lie or cheat can stop reading. Most likely, we all lie in some way or another. Completely honest individuals tell the truth at all times... even when it causes discomfort. Honest people speak up when their silence could mislead others. They tell the grocery store
5 checker about his mistake when the error is in their favor.

Yet, even extremely honest people might lie for the purpose of convenience —to simplify or speed up conversations. How often do you tell people, "I'm fine" when you're actually not doing so well? Is anyone completely honest?

Dishonesty comes in varying complexities. Obvious forms of dishonesty include perjury
10 and intentional deception. Some people make up stories for shock value. Some lie to hide shameful or embarrassing secrets. They are afraid of what others will think, and the lies become so internalized that it's difficult

---

fib /fɪb/ *n.* a statement that is not true; a lie about sth. that is not important

perjury /ˈpɜːdʒəri/ *n.* (law) the crime of telling a lie in a court of law

internalize /ɪnˈtɜːnəlaɪz/ *v.* to make a feeling, an attitude, or a belief part of the way you think and behave

to stop lying. Yet, blatant fabrication is detrimental to others, society and oneself.

Other forms of dishonesty are more subtle because they don't involve outright lies—but they still involve harmful deception:

"I didn't tell the checker he gave me extra change because it makes up for those high prices" or "because I didn't want to cause a commotion and hold up the line." But didn't you hold up the line last week when you were shortchanged or overcharged? Let's face it: Selective honesty has its benefits.

However, is that falsely acquired $2 really a benefit? In retrospect, is a guilty conscience worth $2? Is a guilty conscience even worth that $500 you fudged when you did your taxes? Perhaps some of us don't pay attention to our consciences, so guilt is not an issue.

> blatant /ˈbleɪtənt/ adj. (disapproving)(of actions that are considered bad) done in an obvious and open way without caring if people object or are shocked
> fabricate /ˈfæbrɪkeɪt/ v. to invent false information in order to deceive people
> detrimental /ˌdetrɪˈmentl/ adj. harmful
> outright /ˈaʊtraɪt/ adj. complete and total; open and direct
> commotion /kəˈməʊʃən/ n. sudden noisy confusion or excitement
> retrospect /ˈretrəspekt/ n. thinking about a past event or situation, often with a different opinion of it from the one you had at the time
> fudge /fʌdʒ/ v. to avoid giving clear and accurate information, or a clear answer
> proctor /ˈprɒktə/ v. (=invigilate) to watch people while they are taking an exam to make sure that they have everything they need, that they keep to the rules, etc.
> twinge /twɪndʒ/ n. a sudden short feeling of pain; a sudden short feeling of an unpleasant emotion
> snitch /snɪtʃ/ v. (informal, disapproving) to tell parent, teacher, etc. about sth. wrong that another child has done

"I have to cheat because this class is graded on a curve, and I know at least 10 people who have seen the exam." If you had the opportunity to view an exam before it is proctored, would you? Even though you may feel a twinge of guilt, would you cast aside honesty and join your cheating classmates? Does academic survival justify dishonesty?

Further, if you decided not to cheat, would you tell the professor about the others? Should we go out of the way to snitch on dishonest individuals? Maybe not. The point is to be responsible for your own honesty and to encourage others to follow your example—not to act as some kind of honesty police officer on a mission.

"I knew the accident was my fault, but I wasn't going to admit it. You're supposed to let the insurance companies work it out." Here, dishonesty does include the withholding of truth because you are personally responsible.

These cases of subtle dishonesty weigh the truth-telling process against its outcome. Whether or not to lie or cheat becomes a question of how it will benefit us: We gain $2 or an A grade.

As dishonesty's boundaries become blurred, we assign value to honesty based on its outcome instead of its intrinsic worth. If the outcome of telling the truth is negative for us, we justify a lie: "It won't hurt anyone." "If I tell the truth, I'm in trouble." We want to protect ourselves from the negative consequences of speaking truth, such as punishment. But the ultimate goal should be to uphold honesty, whether the result suits our fancy, or not.

However, when it involves the feelings of others, honesty can be a brutal choice. In these cases, unlike in those of personal benefit or pain, the outcome can be taken into consideration when you decide to "break the truth." How do you tell your friend that you don't like her new haircut when she asks you? Sometimes there are ways to soften the truth, to deliver it gently and still avoid a lie.

Parents find themselves in this predicament when they want to encourage their children in a particular endeavor. It would be cruel to tell your child he was a disaster in the school play. You might scar him for life and shatter his dream. Parents recognize potential when they "lie" to their children, and this kind of lie is not considered deception. Parents have a nurturing role to fulfill, and a little positive dishonesty will not harm their kids, but rather build self-confid-ence.

So, there are exceptions to the famous maxim ("Honesty is the best policy"). However, selfish dishonesty is harmful to society. Instances of dishonesty are so pervasive we lose a clear understanding of what constitutes a lie. We change its name to white lie, fib or half-truth. In addition, because lies are second nature to most people, the concept of conscience loses its effect, and we fail to clearly discern our own dishonesty. We rationalize untruths with all sorts of "good reasons."

And the problem with all of this is that when deceit exists on so many planes, and when we, ourselves, partake in it, we question whether or not we can trust others. Trust builds personal, political, casual, business and family relationships. Society's lenient attitude toward dishonesty ultimately breaks down trust. Dishonesty is so commonplace, it is accepted as a normal part of life.

> blur /blɜː/ v. to become less clear
> intrinsic /ɪnˈtrɪnsɪk/ adj. belonging to or part of the real nature of sth./sb.
> predicament /prɪˈdɪkəmənt/ n. a difficult or unpleasant situation, especially one where it is difficult to know what to do
> scar /skɑː/ v. (of an unpleasant experience) to leave sb. with a feeling of sadness or mental pain
> discern /dɪˈsɜːn/ v. to know, recognize or understand sth., especially sth. that is not obvious
> rationalize /ˈræʃənəlaɪz/ v. to find or try to find a logical reason to explain why sb. thinks, behaves, etc. in a way that is difficult to understand
> partake /pɑːˈteɪk/ v. to take part in an activity
> lenient /ˈliːniənt/ adj. not as strict as expected when punishing sb. or when making sure that rules are obeyed

In a perfect world, we would be certain that people were telling us the truth. Doubt would not exist. Lilliput, in Jonathan Swift's Gulliver's Travels, comes close to such a world.

The people of Lilliput, Gulliver relates, "look upon fraud as a greater crime than theft ... for they allege that care and vigilance, with a very common understanding, may preserve a man's goods from thieves; but honesty hath no fence against superior cunning."

> fraud /frɔːd/ n. the crime of deceiving sb. in order to get money or goods illegally
> allege /əˈledʒ/ v. to state sth. as a fact but without giving proof
> vigilance /ˈvɪdʒɪləns/ n. alert watchfulness
> transgression /trænzˈgreʃən/ n. a violation of law, command or duty
> vulnerable /ˈvʌlnərəbəl/ adj. weak and easily hurt physically or emotionally
> hinder /ˈhɪndə/ v. to make it difficult for sb. to do sth. or sth. to happen
> sneak /sniːk/ v. to go somewhere secretly, trying to avoid being seen

Lilliputians see fraud, a form of dishonesty, as a far worse transgression against fellow humans than theft, because those who trust are completely vulnerable. They have no way of securing themselves against deceit. To paraphrase Swift, trusting individuals expect that others use language to serve its purpose as a means of communication. Lying defeats language in that it hinders understanding.

Thus, honesty is immensely crucial in maintaining trust and communication. Society needs role models to set standards of behavior. Role models are people who remind us to practice honesty, people who aren't afraid to speak up and challenge those who would lie or cheat, people who refuse to sneak into movie theaters—at the risk of exclusion from their friends. We can look for role models in the people we trust. Better yet, we can look to be role models ourselves.

Notes

1. Lilliput and Blefuscu

Lilliput and Blefuscu are two fictional island nations that appear in the 1726 novel *Gulliver's Travels* by Jonathan Swift. Both are portrayed as being in the South Indian Ocean and are inhabited by tiny people who are "not six inches high". The two are separated by a channel eight hundred yards wide. The tiny people of Lilliput and Blefuscu contrast with the giants of Brobdingnag whom Gulliver also met.

2. Jonathan Swift

Jonathan Swift (November 30, 1667–October 19, 1745) was an Irish priest, satirist, essayist, political pamphleteer, and poet, famous for works like *Gulliver's Travels, A Modest*

Proposal, A Journal to Stella, The Drapier's Letters, The Battle of the Books, and *A Tale of a Tub.* Swift is probably the foremost prose satirist in the English language, although he is less well known for his poetry. Swift published all of his works under pseudonyms—such as Lemuel Gulliver, Isaac Bickerstaff, M.B. Drapier—or anonymously.

Comprehension Questions

1. For what purpose might extremely honest people lie?
2. In what complexities does dishonesty come?
3. How do people defend their lie?
4. Do you think survival in any circumstance justify dishonesty?
5. Do you think it's your responsibility to act as some kind of honesty police officer? Will you snitch on dishonest individuals? If not, why?
6. Do you think it's really hard to choose between telling the truth and avoiding hurting other people's feelings?
7. Why do the parents find themselves in a predicament when they want to encourage their children in a particular endeavor?
8. Do you think we should be an extremely honest people just for the sake of honesty itself?
9. Do you like to live in a perfect world in which doubt does not exist?
10. How do you understand the author's statement in last paragraph? Does "Role Model" really work in society in maintaining trust?

Writing Practice

Sometimes being honest involves risks, and at other times being dishonest can be beneficial. Write a story to illustrate how someone is hurt by being honest or how someone benefits from being dishonest.

Further Study

Honesty implies truthfulness, fairness in dealing with others, and refusal to engage in fraud, deceit, or dissembling; honor implies principled uprightness of character and a worthy adherence to a strict moral or ethical code. You can find something different in one word in different cultures. Please visit http://en.wikipedia.org/wiki/Honesty or go to your university library's philosophy or life section to get a glimpse of the theories of honesty. Conduct further research and compare the west views and Confucius view on honesty.

Unit 13

Sports

Unit Goals

After completing the lessons in this unit, students will be able to:
☞ get some knowledge of sports and cheerleading through a series of reading, listening, speaking and writing activities related to the theme of the unit;
☞ develop the ability to use a variety of information from diverse sources and to work cooperatively;
☞ extend vocabulary through recognition of verb suffixes.

Before Reading

Hands-on Activities

1. Try the website www.mlb.com for some basic knowledge about baseball and the baseball teams.
2. Try the website http://encyclopedia.thefreedictionary.com to get some ideas about the organization of the baseball sports.
3. Baseball is the second most popular sport in the USA and it has a completely different atmosphere than other sports games. However, baseball is not so popular in many other countries, please find out the reasons.

Brainstorming

Brainstorm the following questions. Work in pairs or groups to discuss these questions.

1. Sports can be categorized into individual sports, sports that require two players and team sports. How many kinds of sports do you know? Work together in groups and list as many items as possible.

Individual Sports	Sports That Require Two Players	Team Sports

2. Describe your favorite sports star, Chinese or international, and tell us what you think of star atheletes.

3. Do you participate in any sports? If yes, which ones? And how do you benefit from them? If not, what reasons would you give for not participating in any sports?

A Glimpse at Words and Expressions

Please read the following sentences. Pay attention to the underlined part in each sentence and see how these expressions are used in the context, and then write down their meanings in the blanks provided.

1. Some of the top pitchers in the post season rely on ... wait for it... keeping hitters off-balance. ( )

2. At the same time, he has to be confident enough to go against a pitcher's every instinct. ( )

3. Every postseason, fans hear the same old gushing about power pitchers. ( )

4. This year, it's Mariano Rivera and his unhittable cutter, Joel Zumaya and his invisible fastball and Joe Nathan and his slick-as-snot slider. ( )

5. More than a handful of pitchers including such stars as Trevor Hoffman, Greg Maddux and Tom Glavine—will help determine their teams' success by slowing things down. Way down. ( )

6. Men want to overpower other men, especially when those other men wield wooden clubs. ( )

7. Chalk it up as one more deception in a career built on false appearances. ( )

8. Hoffman remains effective because hitters can't tell the two pitches apart. ( )

9. That means pitchers who rely more on power or the trickery of changeups have a better chance of getting hitters out. ( )

10. Many in baseball suggest the change can work in any count. ( )

Text A

A Change Will Do Them Good

By Matt Crossman
(Abridged and Edited)

Some of the top pitchers in the postseason rely on..., wait for it..., keeping hitters off-balance.

A changeup is like a sense of humor. Both require
5 humility and confidence and can be sexy. Both require impeccable timing and can be disastrous if used improperly. A pitcher has to be humble enough to acknowledge his need for the pitch, that his fastball isn't good enough by itself. At the same time, he has to be confident enough
10 to go against a pitcher's every instinct: He must intentionally throw the ball slower.

> pitcher /ˈpɪtʃə/ n. the player who throws the baseball from the mound to the batter
> humility /hjuːˈmɪlɪti/ n. the quality of not thinking that you are better than other people; the quality of being humble
> impeccable /ɪmˈpekəbəl/ adj. without mistakes or faults; perfect
> acknowledge /əkˈnɒlɪdʒ/ v. to accept that sth. is true
> instinct /ˈɪnstɪŋkt/ n. an inborn pattern of behavior that is characteristic of a species and is often a response to specific environmental stimuli
> intentional /ɪnˈtenʃənəl/ adj. done deliberately, intended
> gush /gʌʃ/ v. to make an excessive display of sentiment or enthusiasm
> slick /slɪk/ adj. done quickly and smoothly; smooth and difficult to hold or move on
> snot /snɒt/ n. (informal) a word that some people find offensive, used to describe the liquid produced in the nose
> slider /ˈslaɪdə/ n. a fast pitch that breaks in the same direction as a curve ball at the last moment
> obsess /əbˈses/ v. [usually passive] to completely fill your mind so that you cannot think of anything else
> changeup /ˈtʃeɪndʒʌp/ n. a type of pitch in baseball

Every postseason, fans hear the same old gushing about power pitchers. This year, it's Mariano Rivera and his
15 unhittable cutter, Joel Zumaya and his invisible fastball and Joe Nathan and his slick-as-snot slider. Enough already. Let's throw the power-obsessed, a changeup by celebrating the changeup. More than
20 a handful of pitchers including such stars as Trevor Hoffman, Greg Maddux and Tom Glavine—will help determine their teams' success by slowing things down. Way down.

25   You have to love a pitch designed to keep hitters honest by deceiving them. Changeups are made, not born. Few, if any, pitchers throw good changeups before they have to. Who needs

a changeup when you have testosterone flowing through your veins? Men want to overpower other men, especially when those other men wield wooden clubs. The wise pitcher realizes hitters eventually stop swinging at every pitch. The wise pitcher realizes he can't blow every fastball past every hitter, maybe not even any fastball past any hitter. But he can make the hitter think he's trying to.

A tall, skinny man with sharp features sits in the visitors' dugout at Busch Stadium. He looks a lot like Trevor Hoffman, and the back of his Padres warm-up shirt says Hoffman. Just 18 hours earlier, Hoffman had set the career major league saves record. So who could blame a few members of the St. Louis media for approaching him? But looks can be deceiving. The man is not Trevor Hoffman, owner of the best changeup in baseball. It's his brother, third base coach Glenn Hoffman.

Chalk it up as one more deception in a career built on false appearances.

For 14 years, Trevor Hoffman has thrived by tricking hitters into thinking his changeup is his fastball. Now, he hopes to propel his team deep into the postseason by continuing to hoodwink hitters.

Hoffman's changeup is, in fact, a palm ball. And though his fastball has caught down to his changeup as he has gotten older, Hoffman remains effective because hitters can't tell the two pitches apart.

The postseason often punishes finesse pitchers because umpires' strike zones tend to get smaller. That means pitchers who rely more on power or the trickery of change-ups have a better chance of getting hitters out. A good changeup needs to be located properly; it darts out of the strike zone when it looked for all the world as if it were going to be a strike. A pitcher's mechanics and release point for his changeup and fastball must be identical. A changeup is successful when it is considerably slower or has a completely different movement pattern than a fastball. "What ends up happening is a batter swings at an arm motion instead of the speed of the ball," says Steve Lyons, FOX analyst and former big-leaguer.

In the regular season, changeups work best against aggressive, free-swinging teams.

---

testosterone /teˈstɒstərəʊn/ *n.* a hormone produced in men's testicles that causes them to develop the physical and sexual features that are characteristic of the male body
overpower /ˌəʊvəˈpaʊə/ *v.* to defeat or gain control over sb. completely by using greater strength
wield /wiːld/ *v.* to have and use power, authority; to hold sth., ready to use it as a weapon or tool
dugout /ˈdʌɡaʊt/ *n.* a shelter by the side of a football or baseball field where a team's manager, etc. can sit and watch the game
chalk up *v.* used to say that you should think of a failure as being sth. that you can learn from
chalk up sth. *v.* to achieve or record a success, points in a game, etc.
chalk sth. up to sth. *v.* to consider that sth. is caused by sth.
propel /prəˈpel/ *v.* to force sb. to move in a particular direction or to get into a particular situation
hoodwink /ˈhʊdˌwɪŋk/ *v.* to trick sb.
umpire /ˈʌmpaɪə/ *n.* (in sports such as tennis and baseball) a person whose job is to watch a game and make sure that rules are not broken
dart /dɑːt/ *v.* to move suddenly and quickly in a particular direction
identical /aɪˈdentɪkəl/ *adj.* similar in every detail
aggressive /əˈɡresɪv/ *adj.* behaving in a very determined and forceful way in order to succeed

(Cough, cough, Detroit Tigers, cough, cough.) In the postseason, every at-bat is more important, every pitch more scrutinized. Even the most experienced batters grip the handle a little more tightly and jump a little earlier when a pitcher releases the ball. Pitchers with good changeups can use that aggressiveness against hitters. "In postseason play, when that pitch is on, it's tough to get players to relax," Padres general manager Kevin Towers says.

There are many more variations of changeups than fastballs. Johan Santana, the Twins' ace, has a great changeup because its speed is so different from his fastball. "The bottom falls out of it," says Cardinals shortstop David Eckstein. "And it just never gets there."

Tigers reliever Fernando Rodney's changeup is similar. Everything about him oozes power—his build, his appearance, his demeanor, the cockeyed setting of his hat, his vicious fastball. All of that is contradicted by his changeup.

"It gets to the plate and stops," says a major league scout.

Maddux and Glavine, who rely on superior control, use their changeups differently from Rodney. Neither throws as hard as he once did, though neither ever threw gas, either. Their changeups succeed because they are deceptive and have movement—in Maddux's case, incredible movement.

There also are guys like Kirk Saarloos. An A's right-hander, Saarloos pitches like a lefthander. His circle changeup acts like a screwball. It doesn't matter what a changeup does, as long as it does it well.

"Changeups can be as effective as the best fastball if you execute them properly," the scout says. Many in baseball suggest the change can work in any count. Maddux, for example, won't hesitate to throw one at 3-2.

Relievers have more success with the pitch because they face hitters less frequently. Only pitchers with the very best changeups throw more than one per at-bat, and only the very best changeups are used as out pitches. More often, the changeup is used to mess with a batter's timing and bat

---

scrutinize /ˈskruːtɪnaɪz/ v. to look at or examine sb./sth. carefully

grip /ɡrɪp/ v. to hold sth. tightly

fastball /ˈfɑːstbɔːl/ n. a pitch thrown at the pitcher's maximum speed

shortstop /ˈʃɔːtstɒp/ n. the field position between second and third base

demeanor /dɪˈmiːnə/ n. the way that sb. looks or behaves

vicious /ˈvɪʃəs/ adj. violent and cruel

scout /skaʊt/ n. one who is employed to discover and recruit talented persons, especially in the fields of sports and entertainment

deceptive /dɪˈseptɪv/ adj. likely to make you believe sth. that is not true

screwball /ˈskruːbɔːl/ n. a strange or crazy person

count /kaʊnt/ n. the number of balls and strikes that an umpire has called against a batter

batter /ˈbætə/ n. the player at bat in baseball and cricket

speed. The pitch induces a lot more groundouts and popouts than strikeouts. Exciting? No. Effective? Absolutely.

"It's a gutsy pitch. It's not glamorous. It's not overpowering. It needs to be perfect in location," Trevor Hoffman says. "I'd love to be able to rear back and throw 98 mph past somebody. That's an amazing feeling. It doesn't always have that feel when you rear back and throw a changeup."

> induce /ɪnˈdjuːs/ v. to cause sth.
> groundout /ˈɡraʊndaʊt/ n. a play in which a batter is put out at first base after hitting a ground ball to an infielder
> strikeout /ˈstraɪkaʊt/ n. (in baseball) a situation in which the player who is suppose to be hitting the ball is out and has to stop because he or she has tried to hit the ball three times and failed
> mutter /ˈmʌtə/ v. to speak or say sth. in a quiet voice that is difficult to hear, especially because you are annoyed about sth.
> cuss /kʌs/ v. to swear at sb.

Maybe not, but for Hoffman, the result is the same. A hitter walks to the dugout muttering to himself, probably cussing out Hoffman. And his brother.

Better Know More

1. Matt Crossman

Matt Crossman. Since joining Sporting News in 2000, Matt Crossman has written cover stories on all of the big stars in NASCAR plus Donovan McNabb, Albert Pujols and Carson Palmer.

In the last two National Motorsports Press Association writing contests, Crossman has won five awards, including magazine writer of the year for 2005.

2. Postseason

In sports with playoffs, they generally occur after the regular season is finished. A select number of teams, generally the ones with the best overall record (most wins, fewest losses) from the regular season, enter into a playoff tournament. Each sport may use one of many playoff systems to determine the champion. The teams compete against each other for the top prize of their league.

3. Padres Warm Up Shirt

Padres here means San Diego Padres. The San Diego Padres ("The Friars") are a Major League Baseball team based in San Diego, California. They are in the National League West. "Warm-up" here means the clothing, such as a sweat suit, made or designed to be worn before or after participation in an athletic event.

4. Saves

Baseball to preserve (another pitcher's win) by protecting one's team's lead during a stint of relief pitching.

5. Strike Zones

In baseball, the strike zone is a conceptual rectangular area over home plate which defines the boundaries through which a pitch must pass in order to count as a *strike* when the batter does not swing.

6. Reliever

A relief pitcher or reliever is a baseball or softball pitcher who enters the game after the starting pitcher is removed due to injury, ineffectiveness or fatigue.

7. At-bat

In *baseball* a player's official turn to bat, counted in figuring a batting average unless the catcher interferes or unless the player is hit by the ball, makes a sacrifice hit, or is walked.

8. Pop-out

In baseball, refers to an act of being put out by a fielder catching a ball that has been hit high in the air, or "popped-up."

Check Your Understanding

Answer the following questions based on the text you have just learned.

1. Why is this article entitled "A Change Will Do Them Good?"
2. How do you understand the comparison between the changeup and the fastball?
3. What's the author's attitude towards the changeup?
4. Why the author claimed that the changeup is made, not born?
5. How to throw a good and successful changeup? And, how the successful changeup deceived the hitter?
6. Why pitchers with good changeups can use aggressiveness against hitters of those aggressive, free-swinging teams?
7. How many variations of changeups can you tell? And can you demonstrate them to your classmates?
8. How many advantages of the changeups can you illustrate in a baseball game?

9. Can you make any difference about the changeups of Fernando Rodney, Maddux and Glavine, and Kirk Saarloos?
10. How do you understand Trevor Hoffman's words in the second paragraph from the bottom?

A Sip of Word Formation

Verb Suffixes

There are four suffixes which derive verbs from other categories (mostly adjectives and nouns), *-ify*, *-ize*, *-en* and *-ate*.

1. *-ate* means to give the thing or quality mentioned to, as in regulate (regular), there are also some examples of non-canonical formations as in the back-formation (*formate* < *formation*).
2. The Germanic suffix *-en* attaches mostly to adjectives (e.g. *blacken*, *ripen*), but a few nouns can also be found (e.g. *lengthen*). The meaning of *-en* formations is "to make" or "become."
3. *-ify* usually attaches to some adjectives, as in *purify*, *specify*, it means "to make" or "become."
4. *-ize* means "to become", "make" or "make like", as in *Americanize*, *fossilize*.

Build Your Vocabulary

A. Add a suffix to each word to make it match the meaning given. Write the new word you have made.

solid _____ (to make solid or hard)
private _____ (to sell a business so that it is no longer owned by the government)
broad _____ (to become wider)
active _____ (to make sth. such as a device start working)
concentration _____ (to give all your attention to sth.)
strength _____ (to become stronger; to make sb./sth. stronger)
theory _____ (to form a theory about sth.)
specific _____ (to state explicitly or in detail)
memory _____ (to commit to memory, learn by heart)
fright _____ (to make sb. suddenly feel afraid)

B. *The word in brackets at the end of each of the following sentences can be used to form a word that fits suitably in the blank space. Fill in each blank this way.*

Example: The government thought the native people needed to assimilate and <u>Americanize</u>. (American)

1. We must promote civilized running and use of the Internet and _____ the Internet environment. (pure)
2. Everybody thinks that they know what people think or how they feel. I just want to _____ my knowledge of psychology on 43 things. (formal)
3. It doesn't _____ me but I do find a worrying trend of people accepting media depictions as accurate and perhaps more worrying the fact the producers are willing to change things on a whim(奇想) or other reasons. (sad)
4. China is drafting new rules to _____ large-scale shopping outlets, which could impede the expansion plans of foreign retailers such as Wal-Mart Stores Inc. and Carrefour SA, the *Wall Street Journal* reported. (regular)
5. China will _____ the development of bioindustry, making it the leading industry of the national economy. (quick)
6. His childhood-father in prison, factory work as a boy—both haunted (萦绕) and _____ him, and he wrote on a grand scale and worked his way free. (energy)
7. Having a chance to get to know neighbors not only has been fun, but it's also helped us further _____. (simple)
8. While lifting the performance of all schools, we must _____ the importance of strengthening those institutions serving. (emphasis)
9. Leg _____ and shortening are types of surgery to treat children who have legs of unequal lengths. (length)
10. China is to _____ supportive policies to push forward agricultural insurance and encourage insurance companies to provide better services. (formulation)

You'd Like to Be

A Skilled Text Weaver

Fill in each blank with an appropriate word from the text.

1. Another trait of eastern culture is _____ in learning.

2. He grew up in Sweden, but he writes _____ English.
3. Chinese and US researchers have said illegal blood donation is to _____ high levels of hepatitis(肝炎) C infection in rural China. Although illegal blood donation practices were stopped by the Chinese government in the late 1990s.
4. Children do not know by _____ the difference between the right and wrong.
5. Americans deserve to know where their money is being spent, and how money allocated for friends and technology shared with friends can all too easily _____ in the wrong hands, threatening all parties involved.
6. Unfortunately, Arthur Stoke will never make a good salesman. He rubs people up the wrong way with his _____ attitude.
7. Our team has _____ a record score for the season.
8. Being is desirable because it is _____ Beauty, and Beauty is loved because it is Being.
9. _____ coloration is when an organism's color fools either its predators or prey.
10. Don't let them _____ us _____ another war. Yes, Iran does need fuel. The Bush administration has alternately said that Iran has a secret nuclear weapons program or wants one.
11. She's dead. And you're still _____.
12. A philosophical movement of the 18th century that emphasized the use of reason to _____ previously accepted doctrines and traditions and that brought about many humanitarian reforms.
13. What many local experts lack is a _____ audience, a point at which I try to rectify by listening more than I talk. When I failed with my first tomato crop several years ago, I went to Mr. Kalm to inquire about the matter.
14. There's a new virus which was found recently which will erase the whole C drive. if you get a mail with the subject "Economic _____ in US" please delete that mail right away.
15. These magazines should be talking about US, the people behind the pictures, and about the personal ethics and the guiding principles that _____ us to do what we do in the world.

A Sharp Interpreter

Paraphrase the following sentences, refer to the contexts in which the sentences are located.

1. Changeups are made, not born.
2. He looks a lot like Trevor Hoffman, and the back of his Padres warm-up shirt says Hoffman.

3. In the regular season, changeups work best against aggressive, free-swinging teams.
4. It doesn't matter what a changeup does, as long as it does it well.
5. Many in baseball suggest the change can work in any count.

A Solid Sentence Constructor

Complete each sentences with one of the phrases listed below. Make changes where necessary.

| rely on | a handful of | trick sb. into doing sth. | tell apart |
| tend to | instead of | mess with | go against |

1. We were genuinely surprised to hear investors and commentators alike were shocked to find that during periods of intense market stress, like last week, that markets would _____ _____ move together in the same direction.
2. The Taliban is now claiming that they really tried to _____ the Vice President via a homicide bomber at the entry to the base where Cheney was making a surprise visit.
3. The Chief Executive said he would not _____ the wishes of the majority of Hong Kong people on universal suffrage.
4. But such was either the hatred or avarice of this man, that _____ doing us the good offices he pretended, he advised the King to refuse our present, which he might draw from us something more valuable.
5. With this the Prime Minister poured _____ soil into Vincent Lingiari's hands. Vincent replied: "We are all mates now."
6. Maybe we can't _____ existing moderate Muslims, but that doesn't mean they don't exist. The bigotry expressed by many commenters in this thread is unfortunately all-too-typical.
7. Scientists have found a way to _____ cancer cells _____ committing suicide.
8. I have known the twins for a year now and I still find it hard to _____ them _____.

A Careful Writer

Study the following synonyms and complete the sentences.

| humble | modest | shy |

1. After reading the comment left by Bengbeng, I have some _____ opinions to share here.

2. _____ people tend to perceive their own shyness as a negative trait and many people are uneasy with shyness.
3. Through a touch of self-seeking that _____ artist of solid merit became untrue to his temperament.

> acknowledge   admit   confess

4. There are some faults which men readily _____, but others not so readily.
5. I have to _____ that I lied to you about her age.
6. He _____ that the purchase had been a mistake.

> intentional   voluntary   willful

7. In whatsoever houses I enter, I will enter to help the sick, and I will abstain from all _____ wrongdoing and harm.
8. If anything, this episode points out that management is wholly responsible for the behavior of its employees—especially when one repeatedly demonstrates _____ violations of safety procedures resulting in gross errors.
9. Ignorance, when it is _____, is criminal.

> demeanor   manner

10. We immediately asked the waiter (Min-Ho Yoon) to return the dish, he acted in a very arrogant _____ and he informed us that the chief said that was impossible.
11. The President's outward _____ was genial and relaxed.

📖 A Superb Bilingualist

Translate the following sentences into English with the help of the words given in the bracket.

1. 他开始认为任何和他有关系的人最后都会进监狱。(end up)
2. 许多孩子害怕讲英语时犯错误而受责备。(blame for)
3. 在如今这个竞争激烈的社会,一个生意人必须要有积极的进取精神。(aggressive)
4. 警察有权向嫌疑人询问他们想到的任何问题,甚至可以诱使嫌疑人招供。(trick into)
5. 一些社会学家似乎并不认可这种个案研究。(acknowledge)
6. 这位医生虽然治好了许多人的病,但他对他的工作仍很谦逊。(humble)

7. 你若要逆潮流而行, 创立自己的风格, 并不是一件容易的事。(go against)

8. 他将他的成功归因于他夜以继日地努力工作。(chalk up)

Text B

Cheerleading

Anonymous
(Abridged and Edited)

Contrary to popular lore, cheerleading is not a product of the deep South. Even though the most famous cheerleading crew of all time belongs to the Dallas Cowboys, and the sport's perennial national high school champions are from Kentucky, cheerleading has purebred New England roots. No, they didn't wave pom-poms on the Mayflower (Goooooo Plymouth! Rock, rock,
5 rock!), but they were full o' pep at Princeton University in the Nineteenth Century. Way back in the 1870s, Princeton organized the first pep club, we presume to celebrate their tremendous wealth. And in the 1880s, the first organized yell was recorded at Princeton:

Ray, Ray, Ray!
10 Tiger, Tiger, Tiger!
Sis, Sis, Sis!
Boom, Boom, Boom!
Aaaaah! Princeton, Princeton, Princeton!

15 Okay, so it's not Robert Frost, but it was the first time anyone organized a crowd to cheer at a college football game.

But of course, Princeton coul-
20 dn't dominate this, or any other sport, for very long. In 1884, a Princeton graduate by the name of Thomas Peebles exported the yell and the sport of football to the University of
25 Minnesota. It was in the cold Mid-

---

cheerleading /ˈtʃɪəˌliːdɪŋ/ *n.* an athletic activity that uses organized routines made up of elements from dance, gymnastics, and stunting to cheer on sports teams at games and matches, and/or as a "competitive sport"

perennial /pəˈrenɪəl/ *adj.* lasting or active through the year or through many years; lasting an indefinitely long time; enduring

purebred /ˈpjʊəbred/ *adj.* of or belonging to a recognized strain established by breeding individuals of unmixed lineage over many generations

pom-pom /ˈpɒmpɒm/ *n.* artillery designed to shoot upward at airplanes

pep /pep/ *n.* energy and high spirits; vim

presume /prɪˈzjuːm/ *v.* to suppose that sth. is true, although you do not have actual proof

west that crowds first took a keen interest in hopping around and shouting no doubt to survive the chill and pathetic athletics and in 1898, Johnny Campbell made cheerleading what it is today. As an undergrad at Minnesota, Campbell directed the crowd in the
30 still-used cheer:

Rah, Rah, Rah!
Sku-u-mah, Hoo-rah, Hoo-rah!
Varsity, Varsity!
35 Minn-e-so-tah!
From there, cheerleading took off.

Minnesota again pioneered innovations in the sport in the 1920s, when women first became active cheerleaders—prior to that time, boys had all the fun. In fact, some of our most famous
40 male cheerleaders have included such studs as Dwight D. Eisenhower and Jimmy Stewart. But let's not kid ourselves... Charlie's Angel Cheryl Ladd and Miss America Phyllis George have also led their fair share of cheers.

It was not until the middle of the Twentieth Century that pom-poms were developed as a vital prop. Cheerleaders incorporated tumbling and gymnastics into their routines around the same
45 time. The sport reached the big time in 1978, when CBS first televised the National Collegiate Cheerleading Championships, and by that time, universities began offering scholarships, college credit, and four-year letter programs in the sport. Today, cheerleading pervades all American athletics, from friendly football to professional athletics.

50   2. Get In Shape

To have a good chance of making your cheerleading squad (at any level), your first order of business must be to get in good shape. While it may not be obvious that
55 cheerleading involves an awful lot of work, over the course of a game or a competitive routine, cheerleaders require enormous cardiovascular stamina and a good deal of strength. Before you try out, follow our
60 pointers to develop the most important physical aspects of the activity.
    Stamina
    Strength

hop /hɒp/ v. to move with light bounding skips or leaps
pathetic /pəˈθetɪk/ adj. arousing or capable of arousing sympathetic sadness and compassion
undergrad /ˈʌndəgræd/ n. equals undergraduate
varsity /ˈvɑːsɪti/ n. the principal team representing a university, college, or school in sports, games, or other competitions
tumbling /ˈtʌmblɪŋ/ n. gymnastics, such as somersaults, rolls, and handsprings, performed without the use of specialized apparatus
cardiovascular /ˌkɑːdiəʊˈvæskjʊlə/ adj. of, relating to, or involving the heart and the blood vessels
stamina /ˈstæmɪnə/ n. physical or moral strength to resist or withstand illness, fatigue, or hardship; endurance

Flexibility

Stamina

Perhaps the key physical requirement for cheerleading is stamina. When performing a competitive routine, you will expend an enormous amount of energy; but well before any competition, cheerleaders will practice their routines countless times, over and over. To practice at this kind of level—which is crucial to developing the necessary precision—you will have to be in great aerobic shape.

There are a number of things you can do to improve your endurance, but perhaps the best is to participate in a sport. Training for training's sake is very difficult to do, but taking part in a fun game is much easier. So while you can take up jogging or suffering through the Stairmaster, organized athletics are a great option too. Soccer and basketball are excellent team sports that will get you in great shape pretty quickly. Sports like racquetball, tennis, and squash can also be quite demanding, if you play against strong competition. If you take the easy way out, you're only hurting your own chances, so be sure to push yourself a little no matter what activity you choose.

When you have chosen an aerobic activity, begin by training for around 30 minutes a day, three days a week. You won't get in great shape in a few days, but killing yourself at the start won't help either. Choose a manageable regimen like we have below, focusing on increasing the amount of time you train each week. To start, try a program such as this:

Time Activity Frequency 30 minutes Light jogging or energetic walking Twice during the week & once on the weekend.

Work toward but don't go beyond:

Time Activity Frequency One hour Stairmaster, treadmill, or organized sports. Three times during the week & twice on the weekend.

Ultimately, your stamina will allow you to coast through the rigors of tumbling runs, elaborate lifts, and frenetic dance routines.

Strength

An often overlooked asset to any cheerleader is strength. Whether you are a base, whose job is to lift other cheerleaders and to support pyramids, or a flyer, who climbs atop these constructions, you'll need to be able to lift yourself and others into the air. Top-flight cheerleaders are built much like Olympic gymnasts, with powerful lower bodies for tumbling and jumping.

The best way to add strength training to your workout regimen is by incorporating modest

---

aerobic /eəˈroʊbɪk/ *adj.* involving or improving oxygen consumption by the body

endurance /ɪnˈdjʊərəns/ *n.* the act, quality, or power of withstanding hardship or stress

racquetball /ˈrækɪtbɔːl/ *n.* a game played on a four-walled handball court by two or four players with short-handled rackets and a hollow rubber ball 2¼ inches (5.7 centimeters) in diameter

squash /skwɒʃ/ *n.* a racket game played in a closed walled court with a rubber ball

regimen /ˈrɛdʒɪmɪn/ *n.* a course of intense physical training

treadmill /ˈtrɛdˌmɪl/ *n.* an exercise device consisting of an endless moving belt on which a person can walk or jog while remaining in one place

frenetic /frɪˈnɛtɪk/ *adj.* wildly excited or active; frantic; frenzied

weights. So, for instance, if you spend time on the Stairmaster or jogging, consider holding light free weights in your hands. Even small amounts of weight will add muscle to your arms when you add this resistance over a high number of repetitions. Do not, however, add weights to your feet, ankles, or legs during aerobic exercise, as these can place injurious strain on your important supporting joints. The best way to add strength to your lower body is to perform targeted and individual repetitions on weight machines.

These days, every decent gym has several machines designed solely to strengthen the lower body. Work this equipment into your routine, but concentrate on controlled movements during your workout. Adding a ton of weight, but then swinging it around with momentum is not going to help. Choose a lighter weight that you can slowly and carefully raise and lower; this will provide the resistance training most beneficial for cheerleading.

Strength training is particularly important for male cheerleaders, as they are usually the ones lifting people onto their shoulders or tossing people into the air. But a bit of strength training benefits all cheerleaders.

Flexibility

Cheerleaders are famously flexible, often kicking their legs impossibly high during their routines and frequently performing the splits on the ground and in the air. Flexibility is not something you can schedule in for a couple of intensive sessions—you must give a little bit of time to it every day. Don't panic, this won't become all-consuming, but it is a very good idea to stretch a little each day, perhaps after you wake up or right before you go to bed. Your ligaments need constant reminders to stay elasticated and limber.

The best way to stretch is through constant pressure, never bouncing. Try to hold each stretch for at least 30 seconds, and work up to about a minute. Push yourself to attempt difficult stretches, but don't get to the point of pain. Avoid spending all your time on the stretches you can already do well—we're all tempted to stick to the comfortable, but you want to ensure that you're comprehensively flexible. Draw up a list of stretches to do, starting with your feet and working all the way up to your neck. Be sure to spend some time on all the major muscle groups, such as your calves, quads, hamstring,

---

splits /'splɪts/ *n.* an acrobatic feat in which the legs are stretched out straight in opposite directions at right angles to the trunk

ligament /'lɪgəmənt/ *n.* a sheet or band of tough, fibrous tissue connecting bones or cartilages at a joint or supporting an organ

elasticated /ɪ'læstɪkeɪtɪd/ *adj.* made using elastic material that can stretch

calves /kɑːvz/ *n.* the fleshy, muscular back part of the human leg between the knee and ankle

quads /kwɒdz/ *n.* muscle of the thigh that extends the leg

hamstring /'hæm,strɪŋ/ *n.* any of the tendons at the rear hollow of the human knee

140 groin, triceps, and traps. A fantastic way to stretch your entire body without injuring yourself is to start taking yoga classes. We have a couple tips here to help you find one.

A great tip for making stretching easier
145 is to focus on your breathing—many of us are tempted to hold our breath while doing something physically demanding, but all exercise is improved by circulating oxygen and relaxing, both of which are aided by careful.

150   3. Be Sure You're Qualified

Once you've prepared your body for the rigors of a tryout and a long cheerleading season—which can last from September until April—you'll want to make sure you satisfy all the other requirements too. Many schools require that cheerleaders, like all other students who perform in school activities, maintain certain grade point averages. While you may not see a connection be-
155 tween doing well in school and being a good cheerleader, it doesn't matter. Your school says that you need a certain GPA to participate, and if you don't make the grade, you won't be doing any cheerleading. How's that for a connection!

As well as good grades, most schools and clubs will require you to meet a few technical requirements too. The two most prevalent involve getting your parents' permission if you're under
160 eighteen, and signing a waiver that releases your cheerleading organization from any liability if you get hurt while practicing or performing.

We've provided an example of a Parental Permission Form and a Waiver. Now you can check them out here to know what's coming. In fact, it may be a good idea to let your parents know about these requirements before the season begins, just to prepare them, since you'll need
165 their signatures on these forms.

Finally, you have to make sure that you have the time to participate. While cheerleaders in teen movies seem to have the most exciting social lives on the planet, actual cheerleading squads often have to give up 25+ hours a week to practice . . . not to mention going to the actual games to do the cheerleading. It's a huge time commit-
170 ment, so be 100% sure that you have the time to devote to it.

groin /grɔɪn/ *n.* the crease or hollow at the junction of the inner part of each thigh with the trunk, together with the adjacent region and often including the external genitals

triceps /ˈtraɪseps/ *n.* a large three-headed muscle running along the back of the upper arm and serving to extend the forearm

trap /træp/ *n.* (slang) the human mouth

waiver /ˈweɪvə/ *n.* the document that evidences such relinquishment

   4. Succeed At Tryouts

Obviously the crucial step in becoming a
175 cheerleader is to succeed at the tryouts. Most programs hold their tryouts towards the end of spring, so that the new squad will be chosen before the

summer holiday; over summer break, many cheerleading teams attend cheerleader summer camp together to improve their skills under the direction of professional and collegiate experts.

> cartwheel /ˈkɑːtwiːl/ n. a handspring in which the body turns over sideways with the arms and legs spread like the spokes of a wheel

The typical schedule for tryouts can take as long as two weeks and usually consists of several steps. First, the current cheerleading squad often organizes a pre-tryout meeting, where you will be told about the rules and the schedule of the tryouts and where you will meet the current cheerleading squad. The members of that squad, often the graduating cheerleaders, will then help to teach you a few cheers and routines. You will need to learn these for the actual tryouts. You may also be taught a few basic jumps and gymnastic stunts. These, too, will be important for the tryouts. This is the ideal time for you to ask all the questions you have about how to perform the routines or stunts, so that you can have the confidence to practice these maneuvers at home and then execute them well at the tryouts. You should be honest, however, about what you can and cannot do. If you tell them that you can do a perfect cartwheel, they'll expect to see it. Remember, they're not looking for what you already know, but for the potential you have to learn.

The tryouts themselves will often be broken into at least two stages: semifinals and finals. That means that after one session, the pack will be cut down to a small number, and then the actual members of the team will be chosen from the finalists. At these two or more sessions, you will be judged on the quality of your execution of the routines and stunts you were taught at the pre-tryout session. Obviously, practice is key to succeeding, so draw up a comprehensive practice schedule to ensure that you set aside time each day to work on various aspects of the routines in the time leading up to the tryouts.

Next, you'll want to do the actual practice. This can be a difficult task to perform diligently, so you may improve your dedication by rehearsing with a friend. Another good tip for doing well is to ask current and former cheerleaders questions to find out exactly what takes place during the tryouts. The best way to calm your nerves is to gather a clear idea of exactly what is going to happen. Then you can relax and focus on getting better.

Now, at the tryouts themselves, we recommend a few pointers for doing well:

Be sure that you warm up. You may be so nervous or excited that you don't take the time to stretch properly or to get your blood pumping, but be sure you do so. This is a good time to visualize the moves in your head, and to focus on your breathing, which will calm your nerves.

Dress correctly. One option is to come dressed in your school colors, which is always a nice touch. If not, then consider black shorts and a white top (it makes it easier for the selection committee to see your basic form during routines).

> repertoire /ˈrepətwɑː/ *n.* the range or number of skills, aptitudes, or special accomplishments of a particular person or group

Be enthusiastic. Often, people can focus so much on remembering steps that they will look lost or introverted... not a good thing in cheerleading. Remind yourself to be energetic; just don't overdo it and end up like a Saturday Night Live sketch.

Come with a few stock chants of your own. If you get nervous, you need something to fall back on, and yelling, "Go team! Defense! Defense!" can make you look spirited.

Make eye contact with the judges. It's tempting to stare into the middle distance so that you are not distracted by external things, but again, cheerleading involves making a connection with the crowd. A great way to do that is to look people in the eye.

Keep your hair out of your face. Tie it back in a ponytail if this is a potential problem.

Smile. This is key and we shouldn't have to explain. You're trying to be a cheerleader for God's sake. Even if you screw up a little during your tryout, keep showing them your pearly whites. The judges are not only looking for how well you do the steps, but how you generally handle yourself in front of a group of people.

Be loud. That doesn't mean shrieking or screaming, but project from your stomach. You'll have to be heard above a noisy crowd, so work on your projection.

Don't "woo!" It's so tempting to walk in and just go "Wooooooooo!" for two hours, but it really gets judges annoyed. They'd much prefer to hear you actually say words of spirit and encouragement, or even some stock chants.

Don't be afraid of looking dumb. A lot of people feel silly cheering away like a freak in front of a small tryout committee. Well, cheerleading involves a lot of acting (for instance, acting like you care who wins the big swim meet, or acting like the team is still in the football game, even when they're 60 points behind). The tryout committee will want to see that you can turn on the juice, no matter what the circumstances are. If you hold back because you're afraid of looking dumb, then you will look dumb. Just go for it.

Have fun. It's contagious.

5. Learn About Different Types Of Cheering

A good cheerleader must have a wide repertoire of skills, which should include precision movements, gymnastics and tumbling, lifting and pyramids, and dancing ability. These techniques all involve coordination and timing, but each has its own distinctive flavor too. Most competitive teams have cheerleaders who specialize in one or another of these skills, so if you have one that is your favorite, you may be able to become a specialist in it. First, though, you should be sure you know and try each of them, if only to get a sense of what your options are.

Precision movements

Nowadays, many cheerleaders are excellent dancers, but the classic cheerleader spends a good deal of time performing precision movements. These involve strict timing and sharp, defined motions. There are only a few basic arm movements: daggers, vertical-up, high v, horizontal, low v, vertical-down, hands on hips, punch, and diagonal. It's like synchronized swimming, but on a muddy football field. But by adding small variations to the position of your hands, and varying what you do with each arm, you can build a huge array of motions. You'll want to practice these motions in a mirror to work on your precision. Also be aware of your presentation, which should always involve your smiling, keeping your head up, keeping the motions sharp and snappy, and refraining from staring at one point.

> **punctuate** /ˈpʌŋktʃueɪt/ *v.* to interrupt sth. in intervals
> **synchronize** /ˈsɪŋkrənaɪz/ *adj.* to occur at the same time; be simultaneous
> **snappy** /ˈsnæpi/ *adj.* clever or amusing and short
> **handspring** /ˈhændsprɪŋ/ *n.* a gymnastic feat in which the body is flipped completely forward or backward from an upright position, landing first on the hands and then on the feet
> **tuck** /tʌk/ *n.* a bodily position used in some sports, such as diving, in which the knees are bent, the thighs are drawn close to the chest, and the hands are clasped around the shins
> **mainstay** /ˈmeɪnsteɪ/ *n.* a person or thing that is the most important part of sth. and enables it to exist or be successful
> **spotter** /ˈspɒtə/ *n.* one who is responsible for watching and guarding a performer during practice to prevent injury, as in gymnastics or weightlifting

Gymnastics

Gymnastics and tumbling are skills that are sports in their own right, and we can't hope to tell you how to do them here. Because they add so much to any cheerleader's skills, though, we recommend that you pursue these skills with specialists. The most spectacular movements are often tumbling runs involving back-to-back handsprings, but you'll want to be sure to have a trained coach educate you. You can, however, work a variety of jumps into your routine without specialized training. There are ten classic jumps: tuck, c, spread, herkie, stag, toe touch, split, hurdler, pike, and doubles. Again, you can add to these any variety of hand motions to make your routines unique.

Lifting

Working with a partner can open up an even broader range of cheerleading movements, and many excellent squads rely on partner and double stunts as a mainstay of their routines. These are best practiced with the assistance of trained coaches and spotters, as the risks of injury are high for novices. The most exciting thing about working on these motions is that they can quickly lead to elaborate pyramids if you combine various partner pairs. There are a few basic rules to keep in mind whenever you attempt a pyramid:

Be sure you have plenty of experienced spotters.

Build the pyramid one level at a time; don't move up until the entire base is formed.

Plan out the building order beforehand and disassemble the pyramid in the reverse order that you built it.

Keep your cheer progressing as you build, using various new levels to accentuate parts of the cheer.

²⁹⁵ Always finish with a flourish, emphasizing the final words of the cheer.

> **choreograph** /ˈkɒriəɡrɑːf/ *v.* to design and arrange the steps and movements in dances, especially in ballet or show

Oh, and always smile, you want this to look easy.

Dance

Dance in many ways is the opposite of precision movement. Rather than punctuating ³⁰⁰ each motion as a separate move, dance focuses on smooth and flowing routines. Many cheerleading squads combine dance with precision movements, by using dance moves for the legs, for instance, while using the arms for precision movements. Many schools now have entirely different squads for cheerleading and for dance, which demonstrates how different these two disciplines can be. But music can be such an excellent asset for any routine, that every squad ³⁰⁵ should consider choreographing a few dance moves.

No matter what element of cheerleading you choose to specialize in, you and your squad will benefit a great deal if you take the time to experiment with all your possibilities. If you have a background in gymnastics, you should have a friend teach you some dance moves. Similarly, if you've never participated in any strength moves, you may discover that you have a great ³¹⁰ skill with partner movements and building pyramids. So explore all your options, and become the best cheerleader you can be.

Notes

1. Dallas Cowboys

The Dallas Cowboys are a professional American football team based in the Dallas/Fort Worth metropolitan area in North Texas.

2. Robert Frost

Robert Lee Frost (March 26, 1874–January 29, 1963) was an American poet. His work frequently drew inspiration from rural life in New England, using the setting to explore complex social and philosophical themes. A popular and often-quoted poet, Frost was highly honored during his lifetime, receiving four Pulitzer Prizes.

3. CBS

Columbia Broadcasting System.

4. Stairmaster

The name of a line of exercise machines, which includes stepping machines and revolving stairs. Their original product, the Stairmill, was introduced in 1983. The Stairmaster dual-step machine was very popular in the 1980s, but it has been somewhat supplanted by elliptical trainers, which are less stressful on the knees.

5. GPA

Grade point average. A measure of a student's academic achievement at a college or university; calculated by dividing the total number of grade points received by the total number attempted.

6. Saturday Night Live

Saturday Night Live (SNL) is a weekly late night 90-minute American comedy-variety show based in New York City which has been broadcast by NBC nearly every Saturday night since its debut on October 11, 1975. It is one of the longest-running network entertainment programs in American television history. Each week, the show's cast is joined by a guest host and a musical act.

7. Herkie

A cheerleading jump named after Lawrence R. Herkimer, the founder of the National Cheerleader's Association. This jump is similar to a side-hurdler, except that instead of both arms being in a "T" motion, both arms are opposite of what the leg beneath them is doing.

Comprehension Questions

1. How to try out to be a cheerleader?
2. From the narration, can you tell where cheerleading comes from? Will you introduce some detailed information about its origin?
3. When did cheerleading begin to pervade in America?
4. What is the key physical requirement for cheerleading? And how to practice it?
5. In strength training, on what aspects should the cheerleader pay attention to?
6. Can flexibility be scheduled in for a couple of intensive sessions? And why? How to be flexible according to the author?
7. Can you see a connection between doing well in school and being a good cheerleader? What is it?

8. How to succeed at the tryouts?
9. How many types of cheering? What are they?
10. Can you understand all the movements of cheering? And can you perform some of them?

Writing Practice

Précis Writing

Précis is one of the most important forms of retelling; it states briefly the essential thought of the passage. Depending on the main contents, a précis can be a as short as one sentence or a few pages long. It is a group of coherently stated sentences that summarize the essence of the passage.

Précis writing demands care and thought when we read, we should distinguish between the trifling details and the main thought; we should grip the heart of the whole matter. Précis writing also requires clearness, preciseness and conciseness when we write.

Try to write a précis of A CHANGE WILL DO THEM GOOD.

A Change Will Do Them Good is narrative. There is an adequate amount of description in it as well, the variations of the changeup. You can write the précis in two ways, in one single sentence or a passage.

Further Study

As we all know, sport is one aspect of a country's culture. It is worth noting that America's most popular sports—football, baseball, and basketball—aren't played by many people in other countries. The sport that evokes more nostalgia among Americans than any other is baseball. Baseball is called the "National Pastime" of the United States because it is so popular. If you look into the different taste of people for different sports games in different countries, you can get valuable perspective of the country's culture. The websites http://usinfo.state.gov/usa/infousa/facts/factover/ch11.htm http://sports.sohu.com/2004/02/19/27/news219122790.shtml can help you find more in analyzing the reasons of the baseball's being popular in America. If you want to get further details of the research of the meaning of the sports in America, you can try the book *The Meaning Of Sports: Why Americans Watch baseball, Football, and Basketball and What They See When They Do* by Michael Mandelbaum.

Unit 14

Science

Unit Goals

After completing the lessons in this unit, students will be able to:
- ☞ learn some knowledge about the universe and the future technology and get a general idea about the writing style of science articles;
- ☞ develop the ability to describe and discuss current trends in technology with respect to the social, economic forces within a society;
- ☞ extend vocabulary through learning adjective suffixes.

Before Reading

Hands-on Activities

Search the library or surf the internet, and find materials concerning the development of science and technology, find materials on any of the following topics:

There have been many technological developments in the 20th century. e.g. computer and electric power. Find materials on the changes they have brought about.

As is known to all, modern technology makes life more convenient, find materials on the changes that technology has brought to us.

Brainstorming

Brainstorm the following questions. Work in pairs or groups to discuss these questions.

1. Which area do you hope hi-tech can benefit us most, why?
3. Which is more powerful, the brain or the computer? Compare the advantages and disadvantages of the brain and the computer.

4. Some people say that exploration of outer space has many advantages; other people feel it is a waste of money, which viewpoints do you agree? Why?

A Glimpse at Words and Expressions

Please read the following sentences. Pay attention to the underlined part in each sentence and see how these expressions are used in the context, and then write down their meanings in the blanks provided.

1. Our perceptions may be distorted by training and prejudice or merely because of the limitations of our sense organs, which, of course, perceive directly but a small fraction of the phenomena of the world. (   )
2. ...how it is possible for the body to convert yesterday's lunch into today's muscle and sinew... (   )
3. Every culture has posed such questions in one way or another. (   )
4. And sometimes we hear pronouncements from scientists who confidently state that everything worth knowing will soon be known—or even is already known—... (   )
5. Let us approach a much more modest question: not whether we can know the universe or the Milky Way Galaxy or a star o a world. Can we know, ultimately and in detail, a grain of salt? (   )
6. So in this sense the universe is intractable, astonishingly immune to any human attempt at full knowledge. (   )
7. Those creatures who find everyday experience a muddled jumble of events with no predictability, no regularity, are in grave peril. (   )
8. Every restriction corresponds to a law of nature, a regulation of the universe. (   )

Text A

Can We Know the Universe-Reflections on a Grain of Salt

By Carl Sagan

> "Nothing is rich but the inexhaustible wealth of nature. She shows us only surfaces, but she is a million fathoms deep."
>
> —Ralph Waldo Emerson

Science is a way of thinking much more than it is a body of knowledge. Its goal is to find out how the world works, to seek what regularities there may be, to penetrate the connections of things—from subnuclear particles, which may be the constituents of all matter, to living organisms, the human social community, and thence to the cosmos as a whole. Our intuition is by no means an infallible guide. Our perceptions may be distorted by training and prejudice or merely because of the limitations of our sense organs, which, of course, perceive directly but a small fraction of the phenomena of the world. Even so straightforward a question as whether in the absence of friction a pound of lead falls faster than a gram of fluff was answered incorrectly by Aristotle and almost everyone else before the time of Galileo. Science is based on experiment, on a willingness to challenge old dogma, on an openness to see the universe as it really is. Accordingly, science sometimes requires courage—at the very least the courage to question the conventional wisdom.

penetrate /'penɪtreɪt/ *v.* to go into or through sth.
particle /'pɑːtɪkəl/ *n.* a very small part of matter, such as an electron or proton, that is part of an atom
constituent /kənˈstɪtʃuənt/ *n.* one of the parts of sth. that combine to form the whole
organism /'ɔːɡənɪzəm/ *n.* a living thing, especially one that is extremely small
thence /ðens/ *adv.* (old use or formal) form that place, following that
cosmos /'kɒzmɒs/ *n.* the universe, especially when it is thought of as an ordered system
intuition /ˌɪntjuˈɪʃən/ *n.* the ability to know sth. by using your feelings rather than considering the facts
infallible /ɪnˈfæləbəl/ *adj.* that never fails, always doing what it is supposed to do
perception /pəˈsepʃən/ *n.* (formal) an idea, a belief or an image you have as a result of how you see or understand sth.
distort /dɪsˈtɔːt/ *v.* to twist or change facts, ideas, etc, so that they are no longer correct or true
straightforward /ˌstreɪtˈfɔːwəd/ *adj.* easy to do or to understand; not complicated
friction /'frɪkʃən/ *n.* the resistance (= the force that stops sth. moving) of one surface to another surface or substance moving over or through it
fluff /flʌf/ *n.* small pieces of wool, cotton, soft animal fur or bird feathers
dogma /'dɒɡmə/ *n.* a belief or set of beliefs held by a group or organization, which others are expected to accept without argument

Beyond this the main trick of science is to really think of something: the shape of clouds and their occasional sharp bottom edges at the same altitude everywhere in the sky; the formation of the dewdrop on a leaf; the origin of a name or a word—Shakespeare, say, or "philanthropic"; the reason for human social customs—the incest taboo, for example; how it is that a lens in sunlight can make paper burn; how a "walking stick" got to look so much like a twig; why the Moon seems to follow us as we walk; what prevents us from digging a hole down to the center of the Earth; what the definition is of "down" on a spherical Earth; how it is possible for the body to convert yesterday's lunch into today's muscle and sinew; or how far is up—does the universe go on forever, or if it does not, is there any meaning to the question of what lies on the other side? Some of these questions are pretty easy. Others, especially the last, are mysteries to which no one even today knows the answer. They are natural questions to ask. Every culture has posed such questions in one way or another. Almost always the proposed answers are in the nature of "Just So Stories," attempted explanations divorced from experiment, or even from careful comparative observations.

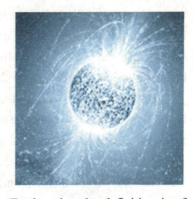

But the scientific cast of mind examines the world critically as if many alternative worlds might exist, as if other things might be here which are not. Then we are forced to ask why what we see is present and not something else. Why are the Sun and the Moon and the planets spheres? Why not pyramids, or cubes, or dodecahedra? Why not irregular, jumbly shapes? Why so symmetrical, worlds? If you spend any time spinning hypotheses, checking to see whether they make sense, whether they conform to what else we know, thinking of tests you can pose to substantiate or deflate your hypotheses, you will find yourself doing science. And as you come to practice this habit of thought more and more you will get better and better at it. To penetrate into the heart of the thing—even a little thing, a

altitude /ˈæltɪtjuːd/ n. the height above sea level
philanthropic /ˌfɪlənˈθrɒpɪk/ adj. of the practice of helping the poor and those in need, especially by giving money
taboo /təˈbuː/ n. a cultural or religious custom that does not allow people to do, use or talk about a particular thing as people find it offensive or embarrassing
twig /twɪg/ n. a small very thin branch that grows out of a larger branch on a bush or tree
spherical /ˈsferɪkəl/ adj. shaped like a sphere
convert /kənˈvɜːt/ v. to be able to be changed from one form, purpose, or system to another
sinew /ˈsɪnjuː/ n. a strong band of tissue in the body that joins a muscle to a bone
pose /pəʊz/ v. to create a threat, problem, etc. that has to be dealt with
alternative /ɔːlˈtɜːnətɪv/ adj. that can be used instead of sth. else
dodecahedra /ˌdəʊˌdekəˈhiːdrə/ n. a solid or hollow figure with twelve equal square sides
conform /kənˈfɔːm/ v. to agree with or match sth.
substantiate /səbˈstænʃieɪt/ v. (formal) to provide information or evidence to prove that sth. is true
deflate /ˌdiˈfleɪt/ v. to make sb. feel less confident; to make sb./sth. feel or seem less important

blade of grass, as Walt Whitman said—is to experience a kind of exhilaration kikothat, it may be, only human beings of all the beings on this planet can feel. We are an intelligent species, and the use of our intelligence quite properly gives us pleasure. In this respect the brain is like a muscle. When we think well, we feel good. Understanding is a kind of ecstasy.

But to what extent can we really know the universe around us? Sometimes this question is posed by people who hope the answer will be in the negative, who are fearful of a universe in which everything might one day be known. And sometimes we hear pronouncements from scientists who confidently state that everything worth knowing will soon be known—or even is already known—and who paint pictures of a Dionysian or Polynesian age in which the zest for intellectual discovery has withered, to be replaced by a kind of subdued languor, the lotus eaters drinking fermented coconut milk or some other mild hallucinogen. In addition to maligning both the Polynesians, who were intrepid explorers (and whose brief respite in paradise is now sadly ending), as well as the inducements to intellectual discovery provided by some hallucinogens, this contention turns out to be trivially mistaken.

Let us approach a much more modest question: not whether we can know the universe or the Milky Way Galaxy or a star of a world. Can we know, ultimately and in detail, a grain of salt? Consider one microgram of table salt, a speck just barely large enough for someone with keen eyesight to make out without a microscope. In that grain of salt there are about 10^{16} sodium and chlorine atoms. That is a 1 followed by 16 zeros, 10 million billion atoms. If we wish to know a grain of salt we must know at least the threedimensional positions of each of these atoms. (In fact, there is much more to be known—for example, the nature of the forces between the atoms—but we are making only a modest calculation.) Now, is this number more or less than the number of things which the brain can know?

How much can the brain know? There are perhaps 10^{11} neurons in the brain, the circuit elements and switches that are responsible in their electrical and chemical activity for the functioning of our minds. A typical brain neuron has perhaps a

exhilaration /ɪgˌzɪləˈreɪʃən/ *n.* making sb. feel very happy and excited

ecstasy /ˈekstəsɪ/ *n.* a feeling or state of very great happiness

pronouncement /prəˈnaʊnsmənt/ *n.* (formal) a formal public statement

wither /ˈwɪðə/ *v.* to become less or weaker, especially before disappearing completely

subdued /səbˈdjuːd/ *adj.* (of a person) usually quiet, and possibly unhappy

languor /ˈlæŋɡə/ *n.* the state of feeling lazy and without enery

lotus /ˈləʊtəs/ *n.* a fruit that is supposed to make you feel happy and relaxed when you have eaten it, as if in a dream

ferment /ˈfɜːment/ *v.* to experience a chemical change because of the action of yeast or bacteria, often changing sugar to alcohol; to make sth. change in this way

hallucinogen /ˌhæluːˈsɪnədʒən/ *n.* a drug, such as LSD, that affects people's minds and makes them see and hear things that are not really there

malign /məˈlaɪn/ *v.* (written) to say bad things about sb./sth. publicly

intrepid /ɪnˈtrepɪd/ *adj.* very brave, not afraid of danger or difficulties

sodium /ˈsəʊdɪəm/ *n.* a chemical element

chlorine /ˈklɔːriːn/ *n.* a chemical element

thousand little wires, called dendrites, which connect it with its fellows. If, as seems likely, every bit of information in the brain corresponds to one of these connections, the total number of things knowable by the brain is no more than 10^{14}, one hundred trillion. But this number is only one percent of the number of atoms in our speck of salt.

So in this sense the universe is intractable, astonishingly immune to any human attempt at full knowledge. We cannot on this level understand a grain of salt, much less the universe.

But let us look a little more deeply at our microgram of salt. Salt happens to be a crystal in which, except for defects in the structure of the crystal lattice, the position of every sodium and chlorine atom is predetermined. If we could shrink ourselves into this crystalline world, we would see rank upon rank of atoms in an ordered array, a regularly alternating structure-sodium, chlorine, sodium, chlorine, specifying the sheet of atoms we are standing on and all the sheets above us and below us. An absolutely pure crystal of salt could have the position of every atom specified by something like 10 bits of information. This would not strain the information-carrying capacity of the brain.

If the universe had natural laws that governed its behavior to the same degree of regularity that determines a crystal of salt, then, of course, the universe would be knowable. Even if there were many such laws, each of considerable complexity, human beings might have the capability to understand them all. Even if such knowledge exceeded the information-carrying capacity of the brain, we might store the additional information outside our bodies—in books, for example, or in computer memories—and still, in some sense, know the universe.

Human beings are, understandably, highly motivated to find regularities, natural laws. The search for rules, the only possible way to understand such a vast and complex universe, is called science. The universe forces those who live in it to understand it. Those creatures who find everyday experience a muddled jumble of events with no predictability, no regularity, are in grave peril. The universe belongs to those who, at least to some degree, have figured it out.

dendrite /ˈdendraɪt/ n. (a stone, mineral, etc. bearing) a natural treelike or mosslike marking
immune /ɪˈmjuːn/ adj. not affected by
lattice /ˈlætɪs/ n. a structure of laths or strips of metal etc. crossed and fastened together, with open spaces left between, used as a screen, e.g. in window openings
shrink /ʃrɪŋk/ v. to move back or away from sth. because you are frightened or shocked
crystalline /ˈkrɪstəlaɪn/ adj. made of or similar to crystal
exceed /ɪkˈsiːd/ v. to be greater than a particular number or amount
muddled /ˈmʌdld/ adj. confused
jumble /ˈdʒʌmbəl/ n. an untidy or confused mixture of things
peril /ˈperɪl/ n. serious danger

> **stunning** /ˈstʌnɪŋ/ *adj.* extremely attractive or impressive
> **testimony** /ˈtestɪməni/ *n.* a thing that shows that sth. else exists or is true
> **velocity** /vɪˈlɒsɪti/ *n.* (formal) high speed
> **quantum** /ˈkwɒntəm/ *n.* a very small quantity of electromagnetic energy

It is an astonishing fact that there are laws of nature, rules that summarize conveniently—not just qualitatively but quantitatively—how the world works. We might imagine a universe in which there are no such laws, in which the 10^{80} elementary particles that make up a universe like our own behave with utter and uncompromising abandon. To understand such a universe we would need a brain at least as massive as the universe. It seems unlikely that such a universe could have life and intelligence, because beings and brains require some degree of internal stability and order. But even if in a much more random universe there were such beings with an intelligence much greater than our own, there could not be much knowledge, passion or joy.

Fortunately for us, we live in a universe that has at least important parts that are knowable. Our common-sense experience and our evolutionary history have prepared us to understand something of the workaday world. When we go into other realms, however, common sense and ordinary intuition turn out to be highly unreliable guides. It is stunning that as we go close to the speed of light our mass increases indefinitely, we shrink towards zero thickness in the direction of motion, and time for us comes as near to stopping as we would like. Many people think that this is silly, and every week or two I get a letter from someone who complains to me about it. But it is a virtually certain consequence not just of experiment but also of Albert Einstein's brilliant analysis of space and time called the Special Theory of Relativity. It does not matter that these effects seem unreasonable to us. We are not in the habit of traveling close to the speed of light. The testimony of our common sense is suspect at high velocities.

Or consider an isolated molecule composed of two atoms shaped something like a dumbbell—a molecule of salt, it might be. Such a molecule rotates about an axis through the line connecting the two atoms. But in the world of quantum mechanics, the realm of the very small, not all orientations of our dumbbell molecule are possible. It might be that the molecule could be oriented in a horizontal position, say, or in a vertical position, but not at many angles in between. Some rotational positions are forbidden. Forbidden by what? By the laws of nature. The universe is built in such a way as to limit, or quantise, rotation. We do not experience this directly in everyday life; we would find it startling as well as awkward in sitting-up exercises, to find arms

outstretched from the sides or pointed up to the skies permitted but many intermediate positions forbidden. We do not live in the world of the small, on the scale of 10-13 centimeters, in the realm where there are twelve zeros between the decimal place and the one. Our common-sense intuitions do not count. What does count is experiment—in this case observations from the far infrared spectra of molecules. They show molecular rotation to be quantized.

> infrared /ˌɪnfrəˈred/ *adj.* having or using electromagnetic waves which are longer than those of red light in the spectrum, and which can't be seen
>
> encompass /mˈkʌmpəs/ *v.* to surround or cover sth. completely
>
> theologian /ˌθiːəˈləʊdʒən/ *n.* a person who studies theology

The idea that the world places restrictions on what humans might do is frustrating. Why shouldn't we be able to have intermediate rotational positions? Why can't we travel faster than the speed of light? But so far as we can tell, this is the way the universe is constructed. Such prohibitions not only press us toward a little humility; they also make the world more knowable. Every restriction corresponds to a law of nature, a regulation of the universe. The more restrictions there are on what matter and energy can do, the more know- ledge human beings can attain. Whether in some sense the universe is ultimately knowable depends not only on how many natural laws there are that encompass widely divergent phenomena, but also on whether we have the openness and the intellectual capacity to understand such laws. Our formulations of the regularities of nature are surely dependent on how the brain is built, but also, and to a significant degree, on how the universe is built.

For myself, I like a universe that includes much that is unknown and, at the same time, much that is knowable. A universe in which everything is known would be static and dull, as boring as the heaven of some weak-minded theologians. A universe that is unknowable is no fit place for a thinking being. The ideal universe for us is one very much like the universe we inhabit. And I would guess that this is not really much of a coincidence.

Better Know More

1. The author

Carl Edward Sagan (1934–1998), an American astronomer and pioneer exobiologist, was born in New York City and studied astrophysics at the University of Chicago. After his study he got a job at the NASA. Afterwards, he became researcher at Berkeley University, assistant professor Genetics at Stanford, Professor of Astrono

my at Harvard University, and finally, at the end of the sixties of the twentieth century, he became Professor of Astronomy and Space Sciences at Cornell University, and he kept that job until he died in 1996.

Sagan has always wanted to tell the man in the street about science. His research was directed toward evidence of life in outer space. He wrote lots of articles and books, i.e. Broca's Brain (1979), Contact (1985) and The Dragons of Eden (1977), of which the last one got him the Pulitzer Prize. In 1980 he produced the successful television series Cosmos, in thirteen parts, which popularized science even more. Cosmos has even been broadcasted in the Netherlands. The book of the same name has been a bestseller for over seventy weeks. Sagan was awarded in 1994 with NASA's Public Welfare Medal, its highest decoration. He died of pneumonia on 20 December 1996.

2. Walt Whitman (1819–1892)

Walt Whitman was an American poet and essayist. His famous collection of poems *Leaves of Grass* expresses the poet's pleasure in observing nature in which a blade of grass is a tiny pan.

Check Your Understanding

Answer the following questions based on the text you have just learned.

1. What are the goals of science? Can we rely on our intuition or perception to achieve these goals?
2. What are the bases of scientific study of the world around us?
3. What does "Just So Stories" mean in paragraph 2? Can we count on explanations divorced from experiment, or from careful comparative observations?
4. What are the characteristics of a scientific mind?
5. Is science something that only scientists are concerned about? Why does the author mention Walt Whitman?
6. Why are some people fearful of a universe in which everything might one day be known?
7. What is the author's attitude towards those who confidently state that everything worth knowing will soon be known?
8. What kinds of atoms is a grain of salt composed of?
9. Why, in paragraph 6, does the author tell us the number of neurons in the human brain? What is he trying to show?
10. What is characteristic of the structure of a grain of salt according to paragraph 8? For what

purpose does the writer explain the characteristics of the structure of a grain of salt?
11. What is the importance of finding regularities and natural laws?
12. What kind of universe is an ideal universe in the author's opinion?
13. What kind of universe do human beings inhabit now?
14. Is the concluding paragraph encouraging or discouraging to the scientific mind? In what way?

A Sip of Word Formation

Adjective Suffixes

-ful, *-less*, *-ly*, *-y*, *-ish*, *-some*, *-able*, *-al*, *-ous*, *-ic*, *-ive* are adjective suffixes. Suffixes usually change the part of speech of the original word.

1. *-ful* is usually added to nouns with the meaning of (1) *full of.* (2) *having the qualities of.* (3) *tending to.* *-less* is a negative suffix with the meaning of (1) *without* (2) *not doing; not affected by.* Usually they can be added to the same root while having the opposite meaning. For example: helpful→helpless

2. *-ly* is added to the end of nouns with the meaning of *having the qualities of.* Hourly, daily, weekly and monthly can be adjective or adverbs.
   For example: friendly, scholarly

3. *-y* is added to the end of nouns and changes the nouns into adjectives.
   For example: greedy, salty.

4. *-ish* is added to the end of nouns with the meaning of (1) *from the country mentioned.* (2) (sometimes disapproving) *having the mature of; like.* (3) *fairly, approximately.*
   For example: turkish, childish, thirtyish

5. *-some* is added to the end of a certain word with the meaning of *producing, likely to.*
   For example: fearsome, quarrelsome

6. *-able* (BRE, also *-ible*) often means that something can be done.
   For example: This sweater is washable. (= This sweater can be washed.)
   But not all adjectives in *-able/-ible* have this meaning.
   For example: pleasurable (= giving pleasure), valuable (= worth a lot).

7. *-al* can be added to a noun with the meaning of *connected with.*
   For example: magical, verbal

8. *-ous* combines with nouns meaning *having the nature or quality of.*
   For example: dangerous, famous

9. *-ic* is added to a certain word with the meaning of 1 *connected with* 2 *that performs the*

action mentioned.

For example: *scenic, artistic*

10. *-ive* is usually combined with a certain noun word with the meaning of (1) *tending to.*
(2) *having the nature of.*

For example: *explosive, prescriptive*

Build Your Vocabulary

A. Write the antonyms of the following words with the same roots.

1. hopeful _____
2. powerful _____
3. careful _____
4. helpful _____
5. useful _____
6. meaningful _____
7. painful _____
8. cheerful _____
9. artful _____

B. Give adjectives of the following words with suffixes -ly, -y, -able, -al, -ish, -ic, -some.

1. coward _____
2. order _____
3. wealth _____
4. craze _____
5. sweet _____
6. book _____
7. quarrel _____
8. trouble _____
9. notice _____
10. change _____
11. wash _____
12. industry _____
13. origin _____
14. luxury _____
15. poison _____
16. energy _____
17. photograph _____
18. effect _____
19. act _____
20. value _____

C. Study the meaning of the words given below and then complete the following sentences with the proper forms of these words.

| peaceful | worthy | sensitive | sensible | sluggish | Irelandish |
| practicable | courageous | mountainous | economic | informative | |

1. He bought a cup of _____ coffee for her.
2. She is very _____ about her weight.
3. David Krieger ever put forward 100 ideas for creating a more _____ world.
4. _____ growth is the increase in value of the goods and services produced by an economy.
5. He felt very heavy and _____ after the meal.
6. He is the man _____ of praise.

7. I hope people will be _____ enough to speak out against this injustice.
8. The center of Hainan Island is _____ with a range that extends southwards in contrast to the relatively lower lying northern regions.
9. A professional conference call should attempt to be courteous, respectful and _____.
10. If something is _____, it can be carried out, or put into practice.
11. I think it's a very _____ idea.

You'd Like to Be

A Skilled Text Weaver

A. Fill in the blanks in the following sentences with the words given below. Change the form where necessary.

| dogma | alternative | wither | malign | jumble | divergent |
| intrepid | ecstasy | intuition | altitude | ferment | |

1. The goal of _____ thinking is to generate any different ideas about a topic in a short period of time.
2. Men tend to explain everything in everyday life, and like to talk about the philosophy of life. Women tend to lead a life on their _____.
3. The major theme of the film is about modern people regaining their faith in God, and the danger in faith being confused with _____.
4. The plane was then flying at an _____ of 8000 feet.
5. The frost has _____ the plants.
6. For her _____ conduct nursing the wounded during the war, Florence Nightingale was honored by Queen Victoria.
7. We were in _____ at the thought of going home.
8. Free translation is an _____ approach which is used mainly to convey the meaning and spirit of the original without trying to reproduce its patterns or figures of speech.
9. This politician has been _____ by the newspaper.
10. PIMs help put your life in order while rescuing your desktop from a _____ of business cards, paper scraps and calendar scribbles.
11. We _____ the grapes for a very long time to achieve high alcohol content.

B. *Fill in the blanks in the following sentences with the words in the brackets. Change the form where necessary.*

1. He finally concluded that the _____ gases must exist in the form of tiny particles or atoms and that these must be completely mixed together in the atmosphere. (constitute)
2. My _____ of the problem is quite different. (percept)
3. There was a sense of _____ about being alone on the beach. (exhilarate)
4. You _____ the scheme completely. (muddle)
5. Anselm is the outstanding _____ of the medieval period. (theology)
6. You're very _____. What's wrong? (subdue)
7. There has been no official _____ yet on the state of the president's death. (pronounce)
8. The president's trip will _____ good relations with the former enemy country. (substantiate)
9. All the criticism had left her feeling totally _____. (deflate)
10. The article gave a _____ picture of his childhood. (distort)
11. The cotton boll is white, roughly _____ and fluffy. (sphere)

A Sharp Interpreter

Paragraph the following sentences. Change the sentence structure where necessary.

1. Our intuition is by no means an infallible guide.
2. If you spend any time spinning hypotheses, checking to see whether they make sense, whether they conform to what else we know, thinking of tests you can pose to substantiate or deflate your hypotheses, you will find yourself doing science.
3. So in this sense the universe is intractable, astonishingly immune to any human attempt at full knowledge.
4. Those creatures who find everyday exprience a muddled jumble of events with no predictability, no regularity, are in grave peril.
5. The testimony of our common sense is suspect at high velocities.
6. The idea that the world places restrictions on what humans might do is frustrating.

A Solid Sentence Constructor

Fill in the blanks in the following sentences with proper prepositions.

1. This increase in imports bears testimony _____ the successes of industry.

2. The written record of the conversation doesn't correspond _____ what has actually said.
3. San Diego has joined a growing list of cities nationwide to place restrictions _____ large retail developments—a move that pits the city squarely against Wal-Mart, the nation's largest retailer.
4. The testimony of our common sense is suspect _____ high velocities.
5. Researchers Zheng Cui and Mark Willingham, and a team of eight others, have discovered a strain of mice that are immune _____ cancer.
6. The priest converted many natives _____ Christianity.
7. Now, the corruption in Santaphrax has placed that city and Undertown _____ grave peril.

A Careful Writer

Study the following synonyms and complete the sentences.

> penetrate   permeate   pervade

1. He strained his eyes to _____ beyond the thick cloud of dust.
2. Water will easily _____ a cotton dress.
3. There was a smell of coffee _____ the atmosphere.
4. The sunshine could not _____ where the trees were thickest.
5. This error _____ all present-day systems.
6. The rain _____ the grind swiftly.

> convert   change   transform

7. The priest _____ many natives into Christianity.
8. The photochemical reactions _____ the light into electrical impulses.
9. She used to be terribly shy, but a year abroad have completely _____ her.
10. He _____ into a new suit.
11. We'll soon _____ him to our way of thinking.
12. Let me _____ the dollar bill for coins.
13. I watched his face _____ color as he heard the news.

> shrink   contract   condense   deflate

14. Washing wool in hot water will make it _____.

15. The heart muscles _____ to expel the blood.
16. He _____ his report from 2000 words to 1000.
17. Don't _____ from the thought of obstacle.
18. I felt quite _____ by your nasty remark.
19. Glass _____ as it cools.
20. The steam has been _____ into a few drops of water.
21. Moisture in the atmosphere _____ into dew during the night.
22. The government decided to _____.
23. I _____ the balloon to let air escape from inside of it.

A Superb Bilingualist

A. Translate the following sentences with as if/even if.

1. He felt as if _____. (他感觉唯独他一个要承担责任。)
2. He speaks to us as if _____. (他给我们讲的好像他去过那里。)
3. She cried as if _____. (她哭的好像心都碎了。)
4. Alan talked about Rome as if _____. (艾伦谈起来罗马来好像他是个罗马人。)
5. Nothing could have saved your father, even if _____. (即使医生按时抵达,也无法挽救你父亲。)
6. Even if _____, she would have helped us. (即使当时她很忙,她还是会来帮我们。)
7. Even if _____, you shouldn't give up. (即使你再次失败,你也不应放弃。)
8. Even if _____, Margaret could not have done anything either. (即使玛格瑞特去过那,她也不能做任何事情。)

B. Translate the following sentences into English with the phrases or expressions given below. Change the form where necessary.

1. 没有几个人识破他的伪装。(penetrate)
2. 第一步的时间相当地长,绝不是一朝一夕所能完成的。(by no means)
3. 美国政府宣称核试验将给地区稳定造成严重威胁。(pose a threat to)
4. 写作时既要遵守语法规则,又要符合习惯用法。(conform to)
5. 该产品的需求超过供给。(exceed)
6. 当他的影响减小时,他的财富也缩小。(shrink)
7. 汽车是导致空气污染的原因。(be responsible for)
8. 我一定要你给我一个直截了当的回答。(straightforward)

9. 马戏团给观众们带来了精彩的表演。(stunning)
10. 每个人都会犯错误,但是有些人自认为不会犯错误。(infallible)
11. 课程将包括物理、化学和生物学。(encompass)

Text B

Future Tech

By Dennis Behreandt
(Abridged and Edited)

Since the close of World War II, the world has been experienced an age of progress that is nearly unequaled in human history. More people have more food, more shelter, more access to medical care, more access to transportation, to education, and to technology than ever before. Of course, problems remain to be solved and progress is yet to be made in a number of areas. But advances since World War II—leading to such marvels as the Internet, personal computing, and synthetic materials, to name but a few—have allowed millions to live in greater comfort and dignity than ever before. The lesson of the last 50 years is that the future is brighter than the naysayers will have people believe as technology allows people the chance to enjoy and pursue other endeavors, including what is truly important. Looking forward, then, here are three major areas in which rapid technological advance will improve the way people live.

1. Life Expectancy

The current life expectancy in the United States is 77.6 years. This is a remarkable number. Even as recently as 100 years ago, life spans in the United States were remarkably lower than they are now. According to economists Stephen Moore and Julian Simon, "In 1900 the average life expectancy in the

---

unequaled /ʌnˈiːkwəld/ *adj.* better than all others

access /ˈækses/ *n.* the opportunity or right to use sth. or to see sb./sth.

transportation /ˌtrænspɔːˈteɪʃən/ *n.* a vehicle or method of travel

marvel /ˈmɑːvəl/ *n.* a wonderful and surprising person or thing

synthetic /sɪnˈθetɪk/ *adj.* artificial; made by combining chemical substances rather than being produced naturally by plants or animals

dignity /ˈdɪɡnɪti/ *n.* the fact of being given honor and respect by people

naysayer /ˈneɪseɪə/ *n.* a refuser; a person who votes against sth.

pursue /pəˈsjuː/ *v.* (formal) to do sth. or try to achieve sth. over a period of time

endeavor /ɪnˈdevə/ *n.* (formal) an attempt to do sth., especially new or difficult

expectancy /ɪkˈspektənsi/ *n.* the state of expecting or hoping that sth., especially sth. good or exciting will happen

remarkable /rɪˈmɑːkəbəl/ *adj.* unusual or surprising in a way that causes people to take notice

span /spæn/ *n.* the length of time that sth. lasts or is able to continue

United States was just under 50 years," This figure is, of course, based in part on statistics stemming from the formerly high rates of infant mortality experienced even in the United States. Nevertheless, it also reflects deficiencies in diet, sanitation, work conditions, and healthcare that have been improved over time.

So, have we reached the limits of life expectancy? In 2002, researchers Jim Oeppen and James W. Vaupel argued in the pages of *Science* magazine that the answer is no. They pointed out that experts have repeatedly asserted that life expectancy is approaching a ceiling: "these experts have repeatedly been proven wrong."

In the near future, gains in life expectancy will come through an improved understanding of biology. Scientists are now studying intriguing genetic possibilities. In one study, Cynthia Kenyon, at the University of California in San Francisco, found that by altering the function of one gene, the life span of a species of roundworm could be increased from the usual two weeks to a month.

Another study with roundworms found that certain anticonvulsant drugs had a substantial impact on life expectancy. The drugs lengthened the life of the worms by up to 50 percent. The research has fueled speculation that there soon may be drugs available that could have related life-extending effects in humans. "What's very encouraging is that these drugs were developed to treat humans, and they are well understood," said Kerry Kornfield, a geneticist.

These discoveries come on the tail of research from 2001 pointing to genes located on the fourth chromosome in humans that play a role in extending life. But for researchers studying aging,

---

mortality /mɔːˈtælɪti/ *n.* the number of deaths in a particular situation or period of time

deficiency /dɪˈfɪʃənsi/ *n.* the state of not having, or not having enough of, sth. that is essential

sanitation /ˌsænɪˈteɪʃən/ *n.* the equipment and systems that keep places clean, especially by removing human waste

assert /əˈsɜːt/ *v.* to state clearly and firmly that sth. is true

intriguing /ɪnˈtriːɡɪŋ/ *adj.* very interesting because of being unusual or not having an obvious answer

alter /ˈɔːltə/ *v.* to become different; to make sb./sth. different

roundworm /ˈraʊndwɜːm/ *n.* a small worm that lives in the intestines of pigs, humans and some other animals

anticonvulsant /ˌæntɪkənˈvʌlsənt/ *adj.* (a drug) used to control seizers or stop an ongoing series of seizers

substantial /səbˈstænʃəl/ *adj.* large in amount or value; important

speculation /ˌspekjʊˈleɪʃən/ *n.* the act of forming opinions about what has happened or what might happen without knowing all the facts

geneticist /dʒɪˈnetɪsɪst/ *n.* a scientist who studies genetics

chromosome /ˈkrəʊməsəʊm/ *n.* one of the very small parts like threads in the nuclei of animal and plant cells, that carry the genes

there is still much left to learn. "Somehow ... neutral activity seems to regulate the aging of all of the body... the skin, musculature, and reproductive tract," Kornfeld told *National Geographic*, "Somehow the nervous system coordinates the progress of all these issues, evidently, through the life stages. But we don't know how it does that." Nevertheless, as science begins to uncover the hidden control mechanisms behind aging, it is likely that rapid advances in life expectancy will be the norm.

2. Regenerative Medicine

According to the American Heart Association, there are almost 500,000 deaths from heart attacks each year in the United States alone. Some estimates indicate that as many as 6.5 million Americans suffer from angina or chest pain stemming from heart disease. Currently, heart disease is treated by drugs or, in more serious cases, with bypass surgeries and angioplasties. In worst cases, heart transplants may extend life. These treatments may soon be supplemented with or supplanted by a new, innovative technology.

Tissue engineers are now growing and testing heart "patch" that someday soon could be used to repair damaged heart tissue, essentially returning the heart to pre-heart attack functionality. According to *Health Day* reporter E.J. Mundell, the patches are grown in a "cardiac environment inside a special tissue-growing chamber called a bioreactor." Of course, much work remains on techniques to implant such patches within the heart, but some trials in animals on aspects of the problem are already underway. Perhaps in the next decade, say scientists, damaged tissues will be replaced by custom-grown replacements.

The most exciting part of the research into regenerative therapies is the prospect that future regenerative treat-

---

musculature /ˈmʌskjʊlətʃə/ *n.* the system of muscles in the body or part of the body

reproductive /ˌriːprəˈdʌktɪv/ *adj.* connected with reproducing babies, young animals or plants

regenerative /rɪˈdʒenərətɪv/ *adj.* growing again; making sth. grow again

angina /ænˈdʒaɪnə/ *n.* severe pain in the chest caused by a low supply of blood to the heart during exercise because the arteries are partly blocked

bypass /ˈbaɪpɑːs/ *n.* a medical operation on the heart in which blood is directed along a different route so that it does flow through a part that is damaged or blocked; the new route that the blood takes

angioplasty /ˈændʒɪəʊˌplæsti/ *n.* surgical operation of the blood vessels in which a balloon is inserted into a vessel and inflated in order to clear clogged arteries

supplement /ˈsʌplɪmənt/ *v.* to add sth. to sth. in order to improve it or make it more complete

supplant /səˈplɑːnt/ *v.* (written) to take place of sb./sth. (especially sb./sth. older or less modern)

innovative /ˈɪnəˌveɪtɪv/ *adj.* introducing or using new ideas, ways of doing sth., etc.

tissue /ˈtɪʃuː/ *n.* a mass of cells that form the different parts of humans, animals and plants

functionality /ˌfʌŋkʃəˈnælɪti/ *n.* performance

cardiac /ˈkɑːdiæk/ *adj.* connected with the heart or heart disease

chamber /ˈtʃeɪmbə/ *n.* an enclosed space in the body, in a plant or in machine

bioreactor /ˈbaɪəʊriˌæktə/ *n.* a device for growing organism such as bacteria or yeast that are used in the biotechnological production of substances

implant /ɪmˈplɑːnt/ *v.* to put sth. (usually sth. artificial) into a part of the body for medical purposes, usually by means of an operation

ments could focus on causing damaged tissues to repair themselves in the body. "Currently, chemically-based drugs serve mostly as temporary supports for the body's failing chemistry," says William A. Haseltine, chairman and CEO of Human Genome Sciences, Inc. "They usually do not repair what is wrong. If a patient with a tendency to depression stops taking medication, for example, the depression returns. Nor do chemically based drugs regenerate injured or worn tissues. Regenerative medicine, by contrast, has the potential to cure disease, because it can bring about long-lasting changes in the body."

3. Energy

It may seem counterintuitive to list energy among a list of reasons to be optimistic for the future. The conventional wisdom is that energy supplies are dwindling while demand is rising, creating a condition in which a serious social and economic dislocation is unavoidable, if not actually imminent. Nevertheless, as *The New American* has pointed out in the recent years, there is plenty of oil to go around. Estimates of oil in the world's proved reserves range from 1.025 trillion barrels (2002 U.S. estimate) to 1.15 trillion barrels (2003 British Petroleum estimate). This is enough oil to last as much as 40 years. And it does not include oil resources that could become available for development due to technological development and changing economics.

It is not just oil that is in abundance. Coal abounds in the United States and can be burned much more cleanly now than in the past, making it, once again, a very viable resource for the generation of electricity. U.S. coal reserves are large enough to meet current demand for coal for the next 200 years.

---

tendency /ˈtendənsi/ *n.* a new custom that is starting to develop
medication /ˌmedɪˈkeɪʃn/ *n.* a drug or another form of medicine that you can take to prevent or to treat an illness
counterintuitive /ˌkaʊntərɪnˈtjuːɪtɪv/ *adj.* contrary to what intuition or common sense would indicate
dwindle /ˈdwɪndl/ *v.* to become gradually less or smaller
dislocation /ˌdɪsləˈkeɪʃn/ *n.* stopping a system, plan etc. from working or continuing in the normal way
unavoidable /ˌʌnəˈvɔɪdəbl/ *adj.* impossible to avoid or prevent
imminent /ˈɪmɪnənt/ *adj.* likely to happen very soon
reserve /rɪˈzɜːv/ *n.* a supply of sth. that is available to be used in the future or when it is needed
barrel /ˈbærəl/ *n.* a large round container, usually made of wood or metal, with flat ends and usually, curved sides
petroleum /pɪˈtrəʊliəm/ *n.* mineral oil that is found under the ground or the sea and is used to produce petrol/gas, paraffin, diesel, oil, etc
abundance /əˈbʌndəns/ *n.* (formal) a large quantity that is more than enough
abound /əˈbaʊnd/ *v.* (written) to exist in great numbers or quantities
viable /ˈvaɪəbl/ *adj.* that can be done; that will be successful

Notes

1. Dennis Behreandt

Dennis Behreandt is a freelance writer and historian. He began his career in forestry, working in the forests of northern Wisconsin and Michigan's Upper Peninsula. As an undergraduate, Mr. Behreandt earned a degree in history with a minor in biology and has since studied at the graduate level in Catholic theology. He has been a long-time contributor to *The New American* magazine, writing hundreds of articles on subjects ranging from natural theology to history and from science and technology to philosophy. His work has also appeared at LewRockwell.com and elsewhere. As an editor, he has worked as Head Editor for a small book publishing firm and formerly served as managing editor for *The New American* magazine. At present, Behreandt serves as web editor for the John Birch Society. When not reading or writing, he spends his time with his wife Denise restoring an arts and crafts period bungalow home or, weather permitting, in his boat chasing a variety of game fish.

2. *Science Magazine*

International weekly science journal, published by the American Association for the Advancement of Science (AAAS).

3. National Geographic

A world leader in geography, cartography and exploration.

4. Health Day

is a daily consumer health news service. Its editorial staff has won many major journalism awards, including the Pulitzer Prize.

5. Human Genome Sciences, Inc.

Human Genome Sciences is a biopharmaceutical company with a pipeline of novel compounds in clinical development, including drugs to treat such diseases as hepatitis C, lupus, anthrax disease, cancer, rheumatoid arthritis and HIV/AIDS.

6. The New American

Magazine of the John Birch Society, providing in-depth reporting on US and worldwide issues and events, including weekly features, back issue archive, and links to articles from other news sources.

Comprehension Questions

Answer the following questions according to the text.

1. Describe two studies about life expectancy mentioned in the text.
2. What effect does the study of roundworms have?
3. Nowadays, how is the heart disease treated?
4. What progress have the scientists made on the research of heart "patches."
5. What is the most exciting part of the research into regenerative therapies?
6. What is the conventional thought about energy supplies?
7. What is the prospect future of oil and coal?
8. By far, what's the most important natural resource available?

Writing Practice

In this age of ultra-high technology, some people believe rapid technological advance will continue improving the way people live, while others show their bleak outlook about it. What's your opinion? Write a composition of about 200 words.

You are to write in three parts. In the first part, state clearly what your view is. In the second part, support your view with details. In the last part, bring what you have written to a natural conclusion with a summary or suggestion.

Further Study

1. The development of science and technology has been accompanied by a decline in traditional culture. Try to find some examples on that, and put forward some measures that can preserve our traditional culture.
2. Many far-sighted scholars and scientists have pointed out that our natural sources are very limited. Energy is one of the biggest problems that causes wide concern these days; Try to find some materials on energy shortage and measures to be taken in order to solve this problem.

Unit 15

Economy

Unit Goals

After completing the lessons in this unit, students will be able to:
- ☞ get some basic knowledge about economy and finance;
- ☞ develop the ability to make inferences and provide convincing evidence to support their inferences;
- ☞ extend vocabulary through recognition of adverbial suffixes.

Before Reading

Hands-on Activities

1. Yahoo began as a student hobby and evolved into a global brand that has changed the way people communicate with each other, find and access information. Try the website http://docs.yahoo.com/info/misc/history.html to get more ideas of the history of Yahoo.
2. The name "Google" derived from the word "googol" which was created by American mathematician Edward Kasner and his nephew Milton Sirrota. Try to get more information about the history of Google from the website http://www.wikicn.com/wiki/Google.
3. Euros are frequently referred to as the Euro zone or the Euro area, or more informally "Euro land" or the "Eurogroup". The euro is also legal currency in the Euro zone. You can get more ideas from the website http://www.en.wikipedia.org/wiki/Euro.

Brainstorming

Brainstorm the following questions. Work in pairs or groups to discuss these questions.

1. Nowadays, internet is being used widely all over the world; make a list of the uses of the internet in the society.
2. If you have a chance to build an internet company in the future, what kind of service do you think your company can offer to the people?
3. What's the development of European Union? Work in pairs and carry out a discussion about the current international free trade area.

A Glimpse at Words and Expressions

Please read the following sentences. Pay attention to the underlined part in each sentence and see how these expressions are used in the context, and then write down their meanings in the blanks provided.

1. He is trying to marshal various arguments to prove that his firm, the world's largest internet company by visitors to its website, has a coherent and winning strategy compared with Google.   (   )
2. Yahoo wants to launch a fully functional product, and therefore had to be cautious—and since the financial benefits will come next year, why should the stock market get into such a tizzy?   (   )
3. Quarterly earnings would be on the low side of his previous estimates.   (   )
4. At that time, it already wanted to become a portal, or a gateway to content on the web, but thought that search would be at most a feature, not a business in its own right.   (   )
5. Yahoo has fared less well with its social-networking site.   (   )
6. But none of these is a solid answer to Yahoo's woes.   (   )
7. It also wanted to buy AOL, a web portal owned by Time Warner, another media company, but Google swooped in.   (   )

Text A

Terry Semel's Long Pause; Yahoo

Anonymous
(Abridged and Edited)

While Google and small internet firms race ahead, Yahoo seems to be standing still.

"NOW let's just pause for a second." It is the fourth pause for thought that Terry Semel, chairman and chief executive of Yahoo, has requested in about ten minutes. He is trying to marshal various arguments to prove that his firm, the world's largest internet company by visitors to its website, has a coherent and winning strategy compared with Google, a phenomenally successful search engine. With only slightly bigger revenues, Google has three and a half times the market value of Yahoo. Twice in three months Wall Street has dumped the shares of Yahoo and widened the gap.

The first sell-off, in July, came after Mr. Semel announced that Panama, an ambitious project to improve Yahoo's technology so that it can make more money on each of its users' searches, would be delayed until the end of this year. Yes, agrees Mr. Semel, it was supposed to be released a quarter earlier, but this sort of market reaction was silly.

Unlike Google, which has a habit of releasing sloppy brainstorms in test versions called "beta," he says, Yahoo wants to launch a fully functional product, and therefore had to

---

executive /ɪɡˈzekjʊtɪv/ *n.* a person who has an important job as a manager of a company or an organization

marshal /ˈmɑːʃəl/ *v.* to gather together and organize the people, things, ideas, etc. that you need for a particular purpose

coherent /kəʊˈhɪərənt/ *adj.* (of ideas, thoughts, arguments, etc.) logical and well organized; easy to understand and clear

phenomenally /fɪˈnɒmənəli/ *adv.* in a very great or impressive way; extremely

revenue /ˈrevɪnjuː/ *n.* the money that a government receives from taxes or that an organization, etc. receives from its business

dump /dʌmp/ *v.* to get rid of sth. you do not want, especially in a place which is not suitable

gap /ɡæp/ *n.* a difference that separates people or other things

sell-off /ˈsel-ɔːf/ *n.* the sale of a large of stocks and shares, after which their value usually falls

ambitious /æmˈbɪʃəs/ *adj.* determined to be successful, rich, powerful, etc.

sloppy /ˈslɒpi/ *adj.* that shows a lack of care, thought or effort

brainstorm /ˈbreɪnˌstɔːm/ *n.* a sudden good idea

launch /lɔːntʃ/ *v.* to make a product available to the public for the first time

be cautious—and since the financial benefits will come next year, why should the stock market get into such a tizzy?

The second sell-off happened last week, when Mr. Semel warned investors at a conference hosted by Goldman Sachs that growth in online advertising was not quite what he had hoped. Quarterly earnings would be on the low side of his previous estimates. In particular, Mr. Semel noted slower growth in demand from carmakers and banks—Yahoo's biggest customers—for graphical advertisements, the category in which it outsells all its rivals. "Let's pause for a second," he says again. "We still expect to outgrow the segment in 2006. This is not about a tragedy or disaster; it's just pointing out something that we had seen."

Part of the problem for Yahoo, however, is that nobody else appears to be seeing a slowdown. This week the Interactive Advertising Bureau and PricewaterhouseCoopers, a consultancy, jointly released the latest industry numbers, which show that online advertising in America grew by 37% to $7.9 billion, a new record, in the first half of the year. Another firm that tracks online advertising, eMarketer, cut its forecasts, but that was in response to Mr. Semel's statement. Jim Lanzone, the boss of Ask.com, the fourth-largest search engine after Google, Yahoo and Microsoft's MSN, says that his firm is not seeing any similar easing of demand.

The deeper problem, says Henry Blodget, founder of Cherry Hill Research, a consultancy, is that Yahoo is still suffering from a "colossal error" it made in the late 1990s. At that time, it already wanted to become a portal, or a gateway to content on the web, but thought that search would be at most a feature, not a business in its own right. This allowed Google to dominate the category. "By the time Yahoo realized its mistake about three years ago it was too late," says Mr. Blodget. Google's share of search queries has been growing, and the enormous profits from this product allow Google to invest more than Yahoo does.

cautious /ˈkɔːʃəs/ *adj.* being careful about what you say or do, especially to avoid danger or mistakes; not taking any risks
tizzy /ˈtɪzi/ *n.* (informal) a state of nervous excitement or confusion
estimate /ˈestɪmɪt/ *n.* a judgment that you make without having the exact details or figures about the size, amount, cost, etc. of sth.
outsell /aʊtˈsel/ *v.* to sell more or to be sold in larger quantities that sb./sth.
segment /ˈsegmənt/ *n.* a part of sth. that is separate from the other parts or can be considered separately
colossal /kəˈlɒsəl/ *adj.* extremely large
portal /ˈpɔːtl/ *n.* (formal or literary) a large, impressive gate or entrance to a building
feature /ˈfiːtʃə/ *n.* something important, interesting or typical of a place or thing
query /ˈkwɪəri/ *n.* a question, especially one asking for information or expressing a doubt about sth.
enormous /ɪˈnɔːməs/ *adj.* very great in size, extent, number, or degree

Mr. Semel counters that Google's gains in search have not come at the expense of Yahoo, which has been a steady number two. MSN has been the primary loser. Panama will help. And there are differences between Yahoo and Google which favor his company. For advertisers, the difference is supposed to be that Yahoo is more of an all-round online media company, selling the full gamut of advertising, from pay-per-click text snippets on search pages to interactive banners, whereas Google sells almost exclusively pay-per-click advertisements. As such, Yahoo benefits from its huge leads in web-mail and finance and general news, where Google is a tiny, niche competitor.

For consumers, the difference is supposed to be that Yahoo is about human beings, whereas Google is about soulless machines and algorithms. So Yahoo has bought several young firms such as FlickR, a photo-sharing site, and Del.icio.us, a bookmark-sharing site, which both allow users to "tag" the pictures and web pages they encounter, and pass them on to each other. There is Yahoo Answers, where users can ask real questions and other users respond. Yahoo started the service nine months ago, and it now has more than 50m users in 20 countries. Yahoo has fared less well with its social-networking site, Yahoo 360, and is now negotiating to buy Facebook, a networking site used by many American college students.

But none of these is a solid answer to Yahoo's woes. The "tagging" that FlickR and Del.icio.us offer is still far from the mainstream, and are mostly used by hard-core technology geeks. Yahoo Answers is growing, but arguably full of rubbish. "What is the sexiest food?" is a typical recent question. Answers range from "bacon, mmmmm" to "a pickle" and "anything with a beautiful woman sitting across from it."

And Yahoo's efforts to buy Facebook may illustrate the older firm's shortcomings as much as its market

counter /ˈkaʊntə/ v. ~ (sb./sth.) (with sth.) to reply to sb. by trying to prove that what they said is not true
gamut /ˈgæmət/ n. the complete range of a particular kind of thing
snippet /ˈsnɪpɪt/ n. a small piece of information or news; a short piece of a conservation, piece of music, etc.
interactive /ˌɪntərˈæktɪv/ adj. acting or capable of acting on each other
banner /ˈbænə/ n. a line of words printed in large letters across the front page of a newspaper
niche /niːʃ/ n. (business) an opportunity to sell a particular product to a particular group of people
soulless /ˈsəʊlləs/ adj. (of things and places) lacking any attractive or interesting qualities that make people feel happy
algorithm /ˈælgərɪðəm/ n. (especially computing) a set of rules that must be followed when solving a particular problem
fare /feə/ v. ~ well, badly, better, etc. to be successful/unsuccessful in a particular situation
woe /wəʊ/ n. (old-fashioned or humorous) the troubles and problems that sb. has
mainstream /ˈmeɪnstriːm/ n. the ideas and opinions that are thought to be normal because they are shared by most people; the people whose ideas and opinions are most accepted
hard-core /ˌhɑːd-kɔː/ adj. intensely loyal
geek /giːk/ n. (slang, especially AmE) a person who is boring, who wears clothes that are not fashionable, etc.
arguably /ˈɑːɡjuəbəli/ adv. used, often before a comparative or superlative adjective, when you are stating an opinion which you believe you could give reasons to support
pickle /ˈpɪkəl/ n. a vegetable that has been preserved in vinegar or salt water and has a strong flavor, served cold with meat, salads, etc.

power. Yahoo was originally interested in MySpace, the biggest social network, but lost it to News Corporation, a media conglomerate. It also wanted to buy AOL, a web portal owned by Time Warner, another media company, but Google swooped in. Yahoo again lost to Google when the latter won a deal to supply the advertising on MySpace, and then to Microsoft when it struck a deal to deliver advertising on Facebook. Now Yahoo looks rather desperate, and will have to pay an enormous price for Facebook, a fast-growing company which many big firms have considered buying.

"Days go by and deals go away," says an outside adviser to Yahoo who has sat in on executive meetings. The firm has a "relatively constipated process of reviewing anything," he says. It is slow and cumbersome and "not an entrepreneurial culture" because Mr Semel is a "low-risk, non-confrontational guy", says this adviser. He recalls a meeting at which an engineer asked: how long do we take from idea to execution? Several people scrawled on the whiteboard and agreed on an answer of eight months.

None of this means that Yahoo is in dire trouble. If it turns out to be true that online advertising is growing more slowly as a whole, Google and all other internet firms will feel it sooner or later. Christopher Sherman, executive editor of SearchEngineWatch, an online newsletter, says he doesn't think that Yahoo has lost its way. But "we're past the days of radical innovation where somebody is really going to blow past a competitor." Yahoo will have to content itself with a position as the internet's number two, at best.

---

conglomerate /kən'glɒmərət/ *n.* (business) a large company formed by joining together different firms
swoop /swuːp/ *v.* (of a bird or plane) to fly quickly and suddenly downwards, especially in order to attack sth./sb.
constipated /'kɒnstɪpeɪtɪd/ *adj.* unable to get rid of waste material from the bowels easily
cumbersome /'kʌmbəsəm/ *adj.* large and heavy; difficult to carry; slow and complicated
entrepreneur /ˌɒntrəprə'nɜː/ *n.* a person who makes money by staring or running business, especially when this involves taking financial risks
confrontation /ˌkɒnfrən'teɪʃən/ *n.* the act of doing a piece of work, performing a duty, or putting a plan into action
scrawl /skrɔːl/ ~ (sth.) (across/in/on sth.) to write sth. in a careless untidy way, making it difficult to read
dire /'daɪə/ *adj.* very serious, very bad
newsletter /'njuːzˌletə(r)/ *n.* a printed report containing news of the activities of club or organization that is sent regularly to all its members
radical /'rædɪkəl/ *adj.* concerning the most basic and important parts of sth.; thorough and complete; new, different and likely to have a great effect

Better Know More

1. Sell-off

A sell-off may occur for many reasons. For example, if a company issues a disappointing earnings report, it can spark a sell-off of that company's stock. Sell-offs also can occur more broadly. For example, when oil prices surge, this often sparks a sell-off in the broad market (say, the S&P 500) due to increased fear about the energy costs companies will face.

2. Interactive Advertising Bureau (IAB)

The IAB is the only association dedicated to helping online, interactive broadcasting, email, wireless and interactive television media companies increase their revenues. The quality of the IAB leadership, membership and industry initiatives, such as standards, research, advocacy and education, benefit the membership as well as the industry as a whole.

3. PricewaterhouseCoopers

PricewaterhouseCoopers (or PwC) is the world's largest professional services firm. It was formed in 1998 from a merger between Price Waterhouse and Coopers & Lybrand. PwC is the largest of the Big Four auditors, whose other member firms include Deloitte Touche Tohmatsu, Ernst & Young and KPMG. PricewaterhouseCoopers earned aggregated worldwide revenues of $22 billion for fiscal 2006, and employed over 140,000 people in 149 countries. In the United States, where it is the fourth largest privately owned organization, it operates as PricewaterhouseCoopers.

4. eMarketer

eMarketer provides e-business research, statistics, demographics and Internet usage data for online marketers. Products and services include market research reports and online database subscriptions.

5. Cherry Hill Research

Cherry Hill Research is a business research firm focused on the Internet and eCommerce, it is not an investment advisory firm, and it does not offer stock ratings or investment advice.

6. Social networking

It refers to a category of Internet applications to help connect friends, business partners, or other individuals together using a variety of tools. These applications, known as online social networks are becoming increasingly popular.

7. Facebook

Facebook is a social utility that connects you with the people around you.

Facebook is made up of many networks, each based around a company, region, high school or college. You can use Facebook to: share information with people you know. See what's going on with your friends. Look up people around you.

Check Your Understanding

Answer the following questions based on the text you have just learned.

1. Is Google more successful than Yahoo?
2. When did the first sell-off of Yahoo's shares in the stock market? And in what condition?
3. What caused the second sell-off?
4. Is there easing of demand for online advertising?
5. What are the problems of Yahoo according to the author? Do you agree with the author?
6. What's the difference between Google and Yahoo?
7. To prove that Yahoo has a coherent and winning strategy compared with Google, what measures did Terry Semel take?
8. Will the project that Yahoo is carrying out be effective in enlarging the company's market share and increasing its revenues?
9. Do you think Yahoo teeters on the brink of catastrophe? And why?
10. What's the author's attitude towards Terry Semel and his capability of running Yahoo?

A Sip of Word Formation

Adjective Suffixes

-ly, *-ward(s)*, *-wise* and *-fold* are adverbial suffixes.

1. *-ly*: means "in the way mentioned," as in "happily, hardly and darkly."
2. *-ward*: means "towards a specified direction in time or space," as in "downward, leftward and eastward."
3. *-wise*: this suffix derives adverbs from nouns, with two distinguishable sub-groups: manner/dimension adverbs, and view-point adverbs. The former adverb type has the meaning "in the meaning of..., like..." as in "lengthwise." The smaller group of viewpoint adverbs is made up of adverbs whose meaning can be rendered as "with respect to, in regard to, concerning...," as in "They make no special demands food-wise" and "Statuswise, you're at a disadvantage."
4. *-fold*: means "multiplied; having the number of parts mentioned", as in "fivefold, fiftyfold."

Build Your Vocabulary

A. *Decide which form of the adverbial suffix to use to make each word an adverb or two adverbs with different suffixes. Add the suffix and write the whole word.*

stupid _____   clock _____   profit _____
short _____   other _____   ten _____
land _____   dark _____   cold _____
home _____   sky _____   up _____

B. *The word at the end of each of the following sentences can be used to form a word that fits suitably in the blank space. Fill each blank this way.*

Example: This magazine is published *fortnightly*. (fortnight)

1. You're probably thinking that David Berlind must have _____ lost his mind. (complete)
2. Very far off a tiny light twinkled a little way up the _____ shoulder of an invisible mountain. (sea)
3. This has not been a good year _____ (sales). _____ (tax), it is an unattractive arrangement.
4. Canada's oil sands production can grow _____ to 5 million barrels per day while still reducing greenhouse gas emissions by 60% in the coming 50 years. (five)
5. The children moved _____ round the room, then anticlockwise. (clock)
6. These advisers were always drawn from the literary class, and their duties appear to have been _____ administrative and diplomatic. (chief)
7. There it turned southward again and went zigzagging _____ through the forest. (down)
8. When their brethren had gone from Holland to America, they bethought themselves that they _____ might find refuge from persecution there. (like)

You'd Like to Be

A Skilled Text Weaver

Fill in each blank with an appropriate word from the text.

1. The American space agency, Nasa (the National Aeronautics and Space Administration), has drawn up a shortlist of ten research projects that will form the basis of an _____ program to explore Mars.
2. The _____ of the United States Environmental Protection Agency has announced her resignation.
3. The manager assistant came here to _____ a few small commissions for the manager.
4. They must all be considered together, in a _____ way.
5. Too much toxic waste is being _____ at sea.
6. The company _____ the new perfume with prime-time commercials on the major networks.
7. The schoolboys are more _____ not to make any mistakes in spelling than ever before.
8. This teacher believes in _____ teaching methods.
9. "While an author is yet living we _____ his powers by his worst performance." (Samuel Johnson)
10. She wants to avoid another _____ with her father.
11. The _____ among the two parties was blown up by the press.
12. Despite its immensity, it is both simple and elegant, fulfilling its designer's dream to create an _____ object drawn as faintly as possible.

A Sharp Interpreter

Paraphrase the following sentences, referring to the contexts in which the sentences are located.

1. While Google and small internet firms race ahead, Yahoo seems to be standing still.
2. The deeper problem, says Henry Blodget, founder of Cherry Hill Research, a consultancy, is that Yahoo is still suffering from a "colossal error" it made in the late 1990s.
3. Mr. Semel counters that Gooddgle's gains in search have not come at the expense of Yahoo.
4. But none of these is a solid answer to Yahoo's woes.
5. Yahoo's efforts to buy Facebook may illustrate the older firm's shortcomings as much as its market power.

6. If it turns out to be true that online advertising is growing more slowly as a whole, Google and all other internet firms will feel it sooner or later.

A Solid Sentence Constructor

Complete each sentences with one of the phrases listed below. Make changes where necessary.

sort of	on the low side	in response to	suffer from
in one's own right	at the expense of	lose one's way	content with
agree on	point out		

1. Those who resort to violence shall _____ from violence.
2. Cause sometimes when you _____, it's really just as well because you find yourself, yeah that's when you find yourself.
3. While this system would appear to reward those with faster connections with greater download speed, it does so _____ the entire group of connected users.
4. France, the United States and Britain have _____ a resolution to end the month—old conflict between Israel's and Hezbollah, and key Security Council members are hoping for a vote in hours at New York.
5. Mary _____ herself _____ a single glass of wine.
6. She's a rich woman _____ rather than by inheritance.
7. Harold March was the _____ man who knows everything about politics, and nothing about politicians.
8. Moore has generally refused to concede error _____ critics, in one case writing an angry email to Chicago.
9. For some people, an income of more than 2000 RMB a month is _____.
10. Let us first determine for whose sake a city is established; and _____ the different species of rule which man may submit to in social life.

A Careful Writer

Study the following synonyms and complete the sentences.

| chief | main | leading |

1. The library is the _____ building on the campus.

2. He is the _____ financial officer of the company.
3. She is one of the _____ physicians of the city.
4. A Big Nation having a quarrel with a Little Nation, resolved to terrify its antagonist by a grand naval demonstration in the latter's _____ port.

| estimate | evaluate | appraise |

5. It's difficult to _____ the possible results in advance.
6. It's necessary _____ the works of art before auctioning off them.
7. _____ a student's thesis for content and organization is the basis of score.

| enormous | colossal | huge |

8. The Wolf, with a lack of sense proportioned to his _____ size, thought that they gave him this name in earnest, and, leaving his own race, consorted exclusively with the lions.
9. "Why have you brought such excitement into my theater?" the _____ fellow asked Pinocchio with the voice of an ogre suffering with a cold.
10. There remained, then, only two possible solutions of the question, which created two distinct parties: on one side, those who were for a monster of _____ strength; on the other, those who were for a submarine vessel of enormous motive power.

A Superb Bilingualist

Translate the following sentences into English with the help of the words given in the brackets.

1. 为了满足病人的需要，我们开发了一种新药。(in response to)
2. 人们普遍认为，在发达国家人口增长的主要原因与其说是出生率的上升，还不如说是由于医疗保健的改善使死亡率下降了。(chief)
3. 很难估算出实行这个计划要花费多少金钱。(estimate)
4. 我们坚决要求要对欧盟的预算进行彻底的改革。(radical)
5. 石油巨头壳牌公司今天宣布公司在半年内的利润达到了58.4亿英镑，有关人士抨击壳牌公司所获得的利润是以人类和环境为代价的。(at the expense of)
6. 她试图向他指出抽烟的危害，但无济于事。(point out)
7. 公司总裁描绘出一个雄心勃勃的计划要将公司的收入在五年之内提高80亿美元。(ambitious)
8. 中国与俄罗斯经过四十年的对话终于就边界问题达成一致。(agree on)
9. 公司决定通过在主要广播媒体的黄金时段投放广告来推出这最新款的香水。(lauch)

290

10. 通过这份调查，我们能够明显地看出本届政府确实做到了维持政策的一致性。
(coherent)

Text B

Feeling Fitter? The Euro Area's Economy

Anonymous
(Abridged and Edited)

This year the euro area's economic strength has been a source of surprise. Its longer-term prospects may be brightening too.

A month ago Jean-Claude Trichet gave what markets see as his standard nod and wink: the European Central Bank (ECB), said its president, would continue to exercise "vigilance" against inflationary pressures. Stand by, in other words, for another increase in interest rates at the bank's next rate-setting meeting on October 5th. ECB-watchers were therefore well prepared when rates duly rose, by a quarter of a percentage point, to 3.25%.

A slide in consumer-price inflation to 1.8% last month, greased by weaker oil prices, raised no doubts, even though this is at last "below, but close to, 2%", the ECB's stated aim. Indeed, with real rates not much more than 1% even now, the ECB looks sure to put rates up again this year and is likely to carry on in 2007.

The euro area's economy has looked remarkably healthy this year, and keeps surprising forecasters. In The Economist's monthly poll, the average prediction for GDP growth in 2006 is now 2.5%, up by 0.2 percentage points since last month and by a full point since a year ago. Admittedly, the pace has probably slowed a little since the cracking second quarter, when GDP rose by 0.9%. But the third quarter, which has just ended, was probably more than decent—judging, for instance, by retail sales figures

---

prospect /ˈprɒspekt/ *n.* the chances of being successful
nod and wink *n.* used to say that a suggestion or a hint will be understood, without anything more being said
vigilant /ˈvɪdʒɪlənt/ *adj.* very careful to notice any sings of danger or trouble
inflationary /ɪnˈfleɪʃənəri/ *adj.* causing or connected with a general rise in the prices of services and goods
duly /ˈdjuːli/ *adv.* at the expected and correct time
slide /slaɪd/ *n.* a change to a lower or worse condition
inflation /ɪnˈfleɪʃn/ *n.* a general rise in the prices of services and goods in a particular country, resulting in a fall in the value of money; the rate ant which this happens
grease /griːs/ *v.* to facilitate the progress of stated
poll /pəʊl/ *n.* the process of questioning people who are representative of a larger group in order to get information about the general opinion
admittedly /ədˈmɪtədli/ *adv.* used, especially at the beginning of a sentence, when you are accepting that sth. is true
cracking /ˈkrækɪŋ/ *adj.* excellent
decent /ˈdiːsənt/ *adj.* of a good enough standard or quality

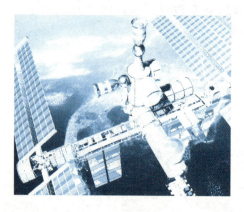

and purchasing managers' indices for both manufacturing and services published this week.

The question now is whether this year, set to be the best since 2000, heralds a pick-up in the zone's long-term growth rate—limited in recent years, by most estimates, to 2% or so—or merely marks the top of the cycle. Though it is too soon to tell, there are reasons to be cheerful. For a long time, the euro area has needed two things: first, that more of its people work; second, that their productivity (ie, output per hour) rises faster. On both counts, there are signs of improvement.

Take the labor market. At 7.9%, the euro zone's unemployment rate is roughly where it was at the peak of the last cycle, in late 2000. By now, on past form, wage pressures should be starting to burst through. But although wage costs have picked up a bit this year, their growth rate is still subdued—maybe 2.3% or 2.4% in the year to the second quarter, depending on your measure. The thought that jobs may go to central and eastern Europe, or to China, is having an effect.

It seems plain that the zone's NAIRU, the unemployment rate consistent with stable inflation, has fallen. Economists at the European Commission now put it at around 8%, one percentage point less than in 1997 (though well above America's 5%). By that estimate, the jobless rate is at its limit. But it may be too conservative, given that wage growth is not exactly resurgent. The NAIRU is virtually unknowable unless wages start to take off, something that a watchful ECB is unlikely to allow.

Better still, as the commission pointed out this week in its quarterly report on the euro area, the unemployment rate has fallen even though labor supply has been increasing—by about 1% a year since the late 1990s. Perhaps most encouraging is the increase in the proportion of people aged 55 to 64—a group that many European countries have been too eager to pension off—in work or seeking it, from 37.5% in 2000 to 43.7% last year.

On productivity, there are also encouraging early signs. Eric Chaney, an e-

---

indices /ˈɪndɪsiːz/ *n.* a plural of index, which is a system that shows the level of prices and wages, etc. so that they can be compared with those of a previous date

herald /ˈherəld/ *v.* to be a sign that sth. is going to happen

productivity /ˌprɒdʌkˈtɪvɪti/ *n.* the rate at which a worker, a company or a country produces goods, and the amount produced, compared with how much time, work and money is needed to produce them

peak /piːk/ *n.* the point of greatest development, value, or intensity

subdued /sʌbˈdjuːd/ *adj.* (of business activity) not very busy; with not much activity consistent with sth.; *adj.* in agreement with; not contradicting sth.

conservative /kənˈsɜːvətɪv/ *adj.* (of an estimate) lower than what is probably the real amount or number resurgent

conomist at Morgan Stanley, reckons that output per hour in the euro area grew at an annual rate of 2.6% in the first half of this year—twice the pace of 2000-05, the first six years of the single currency's life.

He has to make estimates, because not all the official numbers are out, but his reasoning squares with French data showing hourly output rising at an annual rate of 3%.

Start with GDP, which rose at an annual rate of 3.4%. For GDP per worker, deduct employment growth of 1.1%, from data for France, Germany and Spain, three of the top four economies in the club. Then adjust for hours per worker, which have been declining, largely because of the recent rise of part-time employment. Because firms are probably trying to get more hours out of the existing workforce before hiring new staff, Mr. Chaney supposes a slower decline than in recent years: 0.3%, against 0.9% in 2002 and 0.5% in 2004.

For the whole year, Mr Chaney forecasts that output per hour will grow by 2.1%. Is this purely cyclical, or will some of the extra growth endure? "You can't say for sure," he says, "but you get a feeling this is more than cyclical." Above all, he thinks, European firms are beginning to reap the benefits from investing in information technology, something that America has exploited to far greater effect than Europe has (see Economics focus).

Despite all this, euro-area optimists may face a testing few months. It is not hard to see demand growth being dragged down at the start of next year by a planned rise in value-added tax in Germany and budgetary tightening in Italy.

That said, some other possible sources of trouble may be less threatening than they now seem. America's slowdown, though hardly welcome, is one such: Europe's main source of pulling power these days is domestic demand. Oil prices may climb again, but the euro area weathered the recent spike fairly well and should get back a good slice of any extra it spends on energy imports. According to the commission's report, in 2000–05 oil exporters spent a bigger share of each extra dollar of export revenues on imports from the euro zone than they did in 1973–81. The euro area's exports to oil producers rose by 17% last year, adding 0.3% to GDP. The commission expects a further increase in 2006.

A healthier euro zone, of course, should be food for thought for the ECB. In the long run, theory suggests that higher growth, other things equal, should mean higher interest rates for a given rate of inflation. In the shorter term, increased capacity, especially if demand slows, may lean against higher rates—but it is hard to see the central bank relaxing its vigilance just yet.

---

reckon /ˈrekən/ *v.* to think sth. or have an opinion about sth. annual

deduct /dɪˈdʌkt/ *v.* to take away money, points, etc. from a total amount

decline /dɪˈklaɪn/ *v.* to become smaller, fewer, weaker, etc.

cyclical /ˈsaɪklɪk/ (also cyclic) *adj.* repeated many times and always happening in the same order endure

reap /riːp/ *v.* to obtain sth., especially sth. good, as a direct result of sth. that you have done budgetary

weather /ˈweðə/ *v.* to come safely through a difficult period or experience

spike /spaɪk/ *n.* a sharp rise

a slice of a portion or share

revenue /ˈrevɪnjuː/ *n.* the money that a government receives from taxes or that an organization, etc. receives from business

Notes

1. NAIRU

Non-accelerating-inflation rate of unemployment, which means that the rate of unemployment doesn't cause the inflation accelerate.

2. GDP

A region's gross domestic product, or GDP, is one of several measures of the size of its economy. This highlights the fact that GDP is intended to measure domestic production rather than total consumption or spending.

Comprehension Questions

1. A month ago, how did the ECB respond to the inflationary pressures?
2. Could you describe the general economic growth of euro area in 2006?
3. On what counts, we can see the signs of improvement of euro area?
4. Are the wage pressures starting to burst through? And give your reasons.
5. If the unemployment rate is over 8%, will that accelerate the inflation? And why?
6. Why did the jobless rate fall even though labor supply has been increasing by about 1% a year since 1990s?
7. How is about the productivity of euro area in 2006 compared with the past six years?
8. Is that output per hour purely cyclical, or will some of the extra growths endure?
9. Did America's slowdown threaten Europe's economic growth?
10. Why could the euro area weather the spike of the oil price fairly well?

Writing Practice

You are invited to join a debate concerning the operating of Yahoo. What do you hold about the running of Yahoo? Drawing on your debate, write an essay entitled *My Policy on Management of Yahoo*.

Further Study

In economics, business is the social science of managing people to organize and maintain collective productivity toward accomplishing particular creative and productive goals, usually to generate revenue.

The etymology of "business" refers to the state of being, in the context of the individual as well as the community or society. In other words, to be busy is to be doing commercially viable and profitable work.

There are four main types of business unit:

Single Proprietorship: a business owned by one person. The owner may operate on their own or may employ others.

Partnership: a partnership is a form of business in which two or more people operate for the common goal of making profit.

Private Limited Company (Ltd): a small to medium sized business that is often run by the family or the small group who own it.

Public Limited Company: a business with limited liability, a wide spread of shareholders and in the UK, a share capital of over £50,000.

The study of the efficient and effective operation of a business is called management. The main branches of management are financial management, marketing management, human resource management, strategic management, production management, service management, information technology management, and business intelligence.

From the brief introduction, we can see that business is complicated but very important to any countries. If you want to get more information about business, the following websites maybe useful: www.business.com; http://encyclopedia.thefreedictionary.com/Business; www.businessintroduction.com.

Vocabulary

生词总表

A

a slice of		Unit 15—B
abduction	n.	Unit 6—B
abode	n.	Unit 3—A
abominable	adj.	Unit 10—B
abortion	n.	Unit 5—B
abound	v.	Unit 14—B
absenteeism	n.	Unit 3—B
absurdity	n.	Unit 7—B
abundance	n.	Unit 14—B
access	n.	Unit 14—B
acclaim		Unit 7—A
acknowledge	v.	Unit 13—A
activate	v.	Unit 6—A
adage	n.	Unit 3—B
addiction	n.	Unit 6—B
administer	v.	Unit 6—A
admittedly	adv.	Unit 15—B
adolescent	adj.	Unit 5—A
adultery	n.	Unit 7—B
adverse	adj.	Unit 4—B
advocate	v.	Unit 4—A
advocate	v.	Unit 4—B
aerobic	adj.	Unit 13—B
affiliate	n.	Unit 4—B
affiliated	adj.	Unit 10—A
afflict	v.	Unit 5—A
affluence	n.	Unit 3—A
affluent	adj.	Unit 4—B
affordable	adj.	Unit 3—A
aforethought	n.	Unit 5—B
agency	n.	Unit 4—A
agenda	n.	Unit 6—A
aggressive	adj.	Unit 13—A
aggressive	adj.	Unit 5—A
agony	n.	Unit 10—A
air	n.	Unit 1—A
airstrip	n.	Unit 7—B
albeit	conj.	Unit 8—A
algebra	n.	Unit 4—B
algorithm	n.	Unit 15—A
alienate	v.	Unit 11—B
alimony	n.	Unit 5—B
allege	v.	Unit 12—B
allegory	n.	Unit 7—B
alliance	n.	Unit 12—A
aloof	adj.	Unit 2—B
aloof	adj.	Unit 8—B
alpha	n.	Unit 9—A
altar	n.	Unit 12—A
alter	v.	Unit 14—B
alternate	v.	Unit 3—B
alternative	adj.	Unit 14—A
alternative	n.	Unit 8—A
altitude	n.	Unit 14—A
ambitious	adj.	Unit 15—A
ambivalent	adj.	Unit 5—A
amble	v.	Unit 9—A
ambulance	n.	Unit 7—A
amendment	n.	Unit 4—B
amplify	v.	Unit 3—A
anathema	n.	Unit 11—B
anecdotal	adj.	Unit 4—B

Vocabulary

anemia	n.	Unit 5—A	beset	v.	Unit 4—A
angina	n.	Unit 14—B	bestir	v.	Unit 9—A
angioplasty	n.	Unit 14—B	bet	n.	Unit 12—A
animated	adj.	Unit 11—A	beta	n.	Unit 6—A
anonymous	adj.	Unit 2—B	bewilderment	n.	Unit 2—B
anthropologist	n.	Unit 9—A	bid	v.	Unit 1—A
anticipate	v.	Unit 3—A	binding	adj.	Unit 12—A
anticonvulsant	adj.	Unit 14—B	bioreactor	n.	Unit 14—B
appetite	n.	Unit 4—A	birch		Unit 2—B
appreciate	v.	Unit 3—B	blank	adj.	Unit 9—B
apprehension	n.	Unit 6—A	blasted	adj.	Unit 1—B
aptitude	n.	Unit 7—A	blatant	adj.	Unit 12—B
arguably	adv.	Unit 15—A	bleak	adj.	Unit 9—B
assent	v.	Unit 1—A	blissful	adj.	Unit 8—A
assert	v.	Unit 14—B	blogkumedia	n.	Unit 6—B
assets	n.	Unit 4—A	blogosphere	n.	Unit 6—B
assistance	n.	Unit 4—A	blossom	v.	Unit 7—A
assume	v.	Unit 5—B	blur	v.	Unit 12—B
astride	adv.	Unit 1—B	bluster	v.	Unit 12—A
			bombardier	n.	Unit 7—B
B			bonhomie	n.	Unit 2—B
			bonnet	n.	Unit 1—B
backflip	n.	Unit 11—A	boost	v.	Unit 4—A
bankroll	v.	Unit 12—A	borough	n.	Unit 11—B
banner	n.	Unit 15—A	boulevard	n.	Unit 10—B
bargain	n.	Unit 2—B	bracket	n.	Unit 10—A
barrel	n.	Unit 14—B	brainstorm	n.	Unit 15—A
bash	n.	Unit 8—B	breezy	adj.	Unit 11—B
bat	v.	Unit 1—B	brim	v.	Unit 3—A
batch	n.	Unit 6—A	brunt	n.	Unit 5—A
batter	n.	Unit 13—A	buckle down	v.	Unit 9—B
be puffed up with pride	v.	Unit 9—B	buddy	n.	Unit 8—A
			buffalo	n.	Unit 9—A
beckon	v.	Unit 2—B	buffer	v.	Unit 3—B
befit	v.	Unit 9—A	buggy	n.	Unit 5—B
behold	v.	Unit 1—A	bureaucratic	adj.	Unit 4—A
benefactor	n.	Unit 2—B	burlesque	n.	Unit 9—B
beseech	v.	Unit 1—A	butchery	n.	Unit 9—B

297

buzzword	n.	Unit 12—A	choreograph	v.	Unit 13—B
bypass	n.	Unit 14—B	choreograph	v.	Unit 11—A
			chromosome	n.	Unit 14—B
	C		chronological	adj.	Unit 7—B
			circuit	n.	Unit 11—A
callous	adj.	Unit 5—B	circuitry	n.	Unit 9—B
calves	n.	Unit 13—A	civic	adj.	Unit 3—A
camphoric	adj.	Unit 10—B	clairvoyant	adj.	Unit 2—A
capitalize	v.	Unit 6—A	claustrophobic	adj.	Unit 11—B
cappuccino	n.	Unit 10—B	clod	n.	Unit 9—B
cardiac	adj.	Unit 14—B	clumsy	adj.	Unit 7—B
cardiovascular	adj.	Unit 13—B	coalition	n.	Unit 4—B
carom	v.	Unit 11—B	coarse	adj.	Unit 9—B
cartwheel	n.	Unit 13—B	coast (into)		Unit 9—A
cast	n.	Unit 7—B	cognitive	adj.	Unit 5—A
catapult	v.	Unit 6—B	coherent	adj.	Unit 15—A
catastrophe	n.	Unit 9—A	cohort	n.	Unit 3—A
catcall	n.	Unit 1—B	collage	n.	Unit 11—A
cautious	adj.	Unit 15—A	collapse	v.	Unit 9—B
celebrity	n.	Unit 7—A	colossal	adj.	Unit 15—A
celebrity	n.	Unit 6—B	combat	n.	Unit 7—B
cement	n.	Unit 10—B	commandment	n.	Unit 5—B
census	n.	Unit 10—A	commission	n.	Unit 5—B
chalk sth. up to sth.		Unit 13—A	commit	v.	Unit 7—A
chalk up sth.		Unit 13—A	commotion	n.	Unit 12—B
chalk up		Unit 13—A	compelling	adj.	Unit 4—B
challenge	n.	Unit 7—A	competent	adj.	Unit 4—A
chamber	n.	Unit 14—B	complaisant	adj.	Unit 8—B
chance	v.	Unit 1—B	compliment	n.	Unit 1—A
changeup	n.	Unit 13—B	compromise	v.	Unit 6—A
charge	v.	Unit 5—B	concede	v.	Unit 9—B
charger	n.	Unit 1—B	condemn	v.	Unit 5—B
chart	v.	Unit 3—A	condemn	v.	Unit 1—A
cheerleading	n.	Unit 13—B	condemned	adj.	Unit 9—B
chirp	v.	Unit 1—B	condition	v.	Unit 3—A
chirp	v.	Unit 10—B	condom	n.	Unit 5—A
chlorine	n.	Unit 14—A	confer	v.	Unit 3—A
chop	v.	Unit 1—B	confess	v.	Unit 6—B

confidentiality	n.	Unit 6—A	correspondent	n.	Unit 7—A
confine	v.	Unit 6—B	corrupt	adj.	Unit 9—B
confinement	n.	Unit 10—B	cosmos	n.	Unit 14—A
confiscate	v.	Unit 4—A	count	n.	Unit 13—A
conform	v.	Unit 14—A	counter	v.	Unit 15—A
confrontation	n.	Unit 11—B	counterintuitive	adj.	Unit 14—B
confrontation	n.	Unit 15—A	crack	v.	Unit 2—B
conglomerate	n.	Unit 15—A	crackdown	n.	Unit 6—B
congregate	v.	Unit 2—B	cracking	adj.	Unit 15—B
conjure	v.	Unit 10—B	crap	n.	Unit 6—B
conman	n.	Unit 7—B	crave	v.	Unit 6—B
connectivity	n.	Unit 6—A	credibility	n.	Unit 12—A
consensus	n.	Unit 10—A	crisp	adj.	Unit 2—B
consequently	adv.	Unit 5—A	crooked	adj.	Unit 1—B
conservative	adj.	Unit 15—B	crumble	v.	Unit 11—A
conservative	n.	Unit 5—B	crystalline	adj.	Unit 14—A
consolation	n.	Unit 2—B	cue	n.	Unit 3—B
constantly	adv.	Unit 11—B	cultivate	v.	Unit 3—A
constipated	adj.	Unit 15—A	cumbersome	adj.	Unit 15—A
constituent	n.	Unit 14—A	cup	v.	Unit 11—A
constrain	v.	Unit 11—B	cushion	v.	Unit 8—A
constraint	n.	Unit 6—B	cusp	n.	Unit 9—A
contagious	adj.	Unit 8—A	cuss	v.	Unit 13—A
contemplate	v.	Unit 8—B	cyclical	adj.	Unit 15—B
contemplate	v.	Unit 8—A	cynically	adv.	Unit 7—B
contend	v.	Unit 4—A	cynicism	n.	Unit 12—A
contender	n.	Unit 12—A			
contentment	n.	Unit 2—B	**D**		
contentment	n.	Unit 3—B			
contraception	n.	Unit 5—A	daemon	n.	Unit 6—A
contraceptive	adj.	Unit 5—A	daring	adj.	Unit 8—B
contract	v.	Unit 5—A	dart	v.	Unit 13—A
convalescence	n.	Unit 7—A	dazzling	adj.	Unit 7—B
convert	v.	Unit 14—A	dazzlingly	adv.	Unit 11—B
convey	v.	Unit 9—B	dead	adv.	Unit 8—A
conviction	n.	Unit 10—B	debilitate	v.	Unit 3—A
coo	v.	Unit 11—A	decapitation	n.	Unit 7—B
copycat	v.	Unit 6—B	deceive	v.	Unit 9—B

Word	POS	Location	Word	POS	Location
decent	adj.	Unit 15—B	discern	v.	Unit 12—B
decent	adj.	Unit 3—A	discharge	n.	Unit 7—B
deceptive	adj.	Unit 13—A	discipline	n.	Unit 4—A
decline	v.	Unit 15—B	discrimination	n.	Unit 4—B
decline	v.	Unit 5—A	disillusioned	adj.	Unit 8—A
decoration	n.	Unit 7—A	dislocation	n.	Unit 14—B
decouple	v.	Unit 3—A	dispense	v.	Unit 2—B
decry	v.	Unit 7—A	disregard	n.	Unit 5—B
deduct	v.	Unit 15—B	disseminate	v.	Unit 6—A
defect	n.	Unit 9—B	dissidence	n.	Unit 6—B
deficiency	n.	Unit 14—B	dissipate	v.	Unit 9—A
deflate	v.	Unit 14—A	distort	v.	Unit 14—A
deformity	n.	Unit 1—A	distracted	adj.	Unit 2—B
delusion	n.	Unit 2—A	distressed	adj.	Unit 8—A
demeanor	n.	Unit 13—A	distribute	v.	Unit 4—A
dendrite	n.	Unit 14—A	distributor	n.	Unit 12—A
depart	v.	Unit 1—A	diverge	adj.	Unit 2—B
depart	v.	Unit 9—B	divorce	n.	Unit 5—A
dependency	n.	Unit 5—A	dizzy	adj.	Unit 2—B
depict	v.	Unit 7—B	dodecahedra	n.	Unit 14—A
depression	n.	Unit 3—A	dogma	n.	Unit 14—A
desert	v.	Unit 7—B	domain	n.	Unit 6—A
deserted	adj.	Unit 2—B	doom	v.	Unit 8—B
deserve	v.	Unit 11—B	dread	v.	Unit 2—B
destitute	adj.	Unit 3—A	dread	v.	Unit 1—A
desultory	adj.	Unit 9—A	dreadful	adj.	Unit 9—B
detached	adj.	Unit 2—B	drift	v.	Unit 4—A
deterrent	n.	Unit 6—A	driveway	n.	Unit 11—A
detrimental	adj.	Unit 12—B	drooping	adj.	Unit 10—A
devious	adj.	Unit 12—A	drumbeat	n.	Unit 9—B
devour	v.	Unit 1—A	dub	v.	Unit 6—B
devout	adj.	Unit 7—A	dubious	adj.	Unit 4—A
diabetes	n.	Unit 7—A	dugout	n.	Unit 13—A
dignity	n.	Unit 14—B	duly	adv.	Unit 15—B
dilemma	n.	Unit 12—A	dumbfounded	adj.	Unit 10—B
dip	n.	Unit 11—B	dump	v.	Unit 15—A
dire	adj.	Unit 15—A	duo	n.	Unit 6—B
disadvantaged	adj.	Unit 5—A	dwindle	v.	Unit 14—B

E

eccentricity	n.	Unit 9—A
ecstasy	n.	Unit 14—A
edict	n.	Unit 4—A
elapse	v.	Unit 6—A
elasticated	adj.	Unit 13—B
elevated	adj.	Unit 3—A
elusive	adj.	Unit 2—B
embolden	v.	Unit 2—B
emerge	v.	Unit 2—B
emulation		Unit 10—A
encompass	v.	Unit 14—A
encyclopedia	n.	Unit 6—B
endeavor	n.	Unit 14—B
endeavor	v.	Unit 1—A
endeavor	n.	Unit 2—B
endurance	n.	Unit 13—B
enforcement	n.	Unit 6—A
engage	v.	Unit 7—A
enhance	v.	Unit 5—A
enormous	adj.	Unit 15—A
entail	v.	Unit 8—A
enterprise	n.	Unit 4—A
entertain	v.	Unit 9—B
entitle	v.	Unit 4—A
entitlement	n.	Unit 10—B
entrepreneur	n.	Unit 15—A
entrepreneur	n.	Unit 12—A
ephemeral	adj.	Unit 3—B
epicure	n.	Unit 3—B
epigraph	n.	Unit 7—A
equalize	v.	Unit 4—A
equivalent	adj.	Unit 4—A
eradicate	v.	Unit 8—A
err	v.	Unit 5—B
escapade	n.	Unit 6—B
esteem	v.	Unit 1—A
estimate	n.	Unit 15—A
estimated	adj.	Unit 5—A
etch	v.	Unit 9—A
ethic	adj.	Unit 3—B
ethos	n.	Unit 9—A
etiquette	n.	Unit 11—B
euthanasia	n.	Unit 5—B
evict	v.	Unit 7—B
evocation	n.	Unit 7—B
evoke	v.	Unit 5—B
exaggeration	n.	Unit 12—A
exalt	v.	Unit 10—B
exalt	v.	Unit 9—B
exasperate	v.	Unit 11—A
exceed	v.	Unit 14—A
excel	v.	Unit 11—A
exception	n.	Unit 2—B
executive	n.	Unit 15—A
exhilaration	n.	Unit 14—A
expatriate	adj.	Unit 7—A
expatriate	adj.	Unit 10—B
expectancy	n.	Unit 14—B
expedient	adj.	Unit 12—A
expendability	n.	Unit 11—B
expertise	n.	Unit 6—A
explode	v.	Unit 8—A
exquisite	adj.	Unit 9—B
exterminate	v.	Unit 5—B
exterminator	n.	Unit 11—B
extravagant	adj.	Unit 12—A
eyeliner	n.	Unit 10—B

F

fabricate	v.	Unit 12—B
facility	n.	Unit 2—A
falter	v.	Unit 10—B

famine	n.	Unit 10—A	foyer	n.	Unit 7—B
fanatical	adj.	Unit 5—B	fragmented	adj.	Unit 7—B
fare	v.	Unit 15—A	fraternal	adj.	Unit 9—A
fascinating	adj.	Unit 7—A	fratricide	n.	Unit 7—B
fastball	n.	Unit 13—A	fraud	n.	Unit 12—A
fatigue	n.	Unit 1—A	fraud	n.	Unit 12—B
fatten	v.	Unit 4—A	freckle	n.	Unit 11—A
feature	n.	Unit 15—A	freebie	n.	Unit 9—A
federal	adj.	Unit 4—A	frenetic	adj.	Unit 13—B
feign	v.	Unit 2—B	frequent	v.	Unit 6—B
ferment	v.	Unit 14—A	fret	v.	Unit 8—A
ferocious	adj.	Unit 11—A	fret	v.	Unit 1—A
fertile	adj.	Unit 5—A	friction	n.	Unit 14—A
fervor	n.	Unit 10—B	frightful	adj.	Unit 1—A
fetus	n.	Unit 5—B	frustration	n.	Unit 3—A
fib	n.	Unit 12—B	fudge	v.	Unit 12—B
fiction	n.	Unit 9—B	functionality	n.	Unit 14—B
fictitious	adj.	Unit 7—B	functionary	n.	Unit 10—B
fiery	adj.	Unit 10—B	furious	adj.	Unit 10—A
flamboyant	adj.	Unit 7—A	furry	adj.	Unit 1—B
flamboyantly	adv.	Unit 10—B	furthermore	adv.	Unit 4—A
flap	v.	Unit 11—B	furtively	adv.	Unit 11—B
flatter	v.	Unit 1—A	fury	n.	Unit 9—B
flexible	adj.	Unit 4—B	fusion	n.	Unit 6—B
flick	n.	Unit 11—B	fuss	v.	Unit 12—A
fling	v.	Unit 11—B			
flip side		Unit 6—B		**G**	
flirt	v.	Unit 6—B			
fluff	n.	Unit 14—A	gait	n.	Unit 8—A
fluorescent	adj.	Unit 2—B	gallant	adj.	Unit 1—B
flush	v.	Unit 1—B	gallop	v.	Unit 1—B
folder	n.	Unit 7—B	gamut	n.	Unit 15—A
forebode	v.	Unit 9—B	gap	n.	Unit 15—A
foresee	v.	Unit 3—A	gape	v.	Unit 9—B
foreseeable	adj.	Unit 6—A	gaudy	adj.	Unit 9—B
forthcoming	adj.	Unit 5—B	geek	n.	Unit 15—A
foster	adj.	Unit 5—A	geek	n.	Unit 6—B
foster	v.	Unit 7—A	gender	n.	Unit 4—B

gene	n.	Unit 9—B
geneticist	n.	Unit 3—B
geneticist	n.	Unit 14—B
geriatric	n.	Unit 9—A
gin	n.	Unit 9—B
glamorous	adj.	Unit 9—A
glee	n.	Unit 1—B
gleefully	adv.	Unit 11—A
goody	n.	Unit 10—A
gourmet	n.	Unit 11—B
gown	n.	Unit 1—A
graciously	adv.	Unit 8—A
gratification	n.	Unit 9—B
gratitude	n.	Unit 2—B
grease	v.	Unit 15—B
grip	v.	Unit 13—A
groin	n.	Unit 13—B
groundout	n.	Unit 13—A
grunt	v.	Unit 1—B
guarantee	n.	Unit 8—B
guideline	n.	Unit 4—B
gulp	v.	Unit 1—B
gush	v.	Unit 13—A

H

hag	n.	Unit 1—B
hail	v.	Unit 7—B
hallucinogen	n.	Unit 14—A
hamstring	n.	Unit 13—B
handspring	n.	Unit 13—B
hangout	n.	Unit 2—B
harbinger	n.	Unit 3—B
hard-core	adj.	Unit 15—A
hardcore	adj.	Unit 6—B
hardwired	adj.	Unit 3—B
harness	v.	Unit 2—A
harness	v.	Unit 6—A

hassle	n.	Unit 6—B
hasten	v.	Unit 1—A
haul	v.	Unit 2—B
haven	n.	Unit 6—B
havoc	n.	Unit 10—A
hawk	v.	Unit 6—B
hearsay	n.	Unit 6—B
hegemony	n.	Unit 10—A
herald	v.	Unit 15—B
heretical	adj.	Unit 9—B
hideous	adj.	Unit 9—B
hilarious	adj.	Unit 6—B
hinder	v.	Unit 12—B
holocaust	n.	Unit 5—B
homicide	n.	Unit 5—B
hoodwink	v.	Unit 13—A
hoof	n.	Unit 1—B
hop	v.	Unit 13—B
hop	v.	Unit 1—B
horn	n.	Unit 10—B
horrible	adj.	Unit 8—B
hospitalize	v.	Unit 7—A
hostile	adj.	Unit 7—B
hostility	n.	Unit 5—B
hound	v.	Unit 9—B
hubris	n.	Unit 12—A
huddle	v.	Unit 11—A
hulk	n.	Unit 11—B
humanity	n.	Unit 5—B
humility	n.	Unit 13—A
hunch	v.	Unit 7—B
hurl	v.	Unit 2—B
hype	n.	Unit 12—A
hype	v.	Unit 6—B
hyperinflation	n.	Unit 10—A
hypertension	n.	Unit 10—A
hypertension	n.	Unit 5—A

I

identical	adj.	Unit 13—A
idiosyncrasy	n.	Unit 10—A
idiotic	adj.	Unit 9—B
illiteracy	n.	Unit 10—A
illusion	n.	Unit 2—A
imminent	adj.	Unit 14—B
immortalize	v.	Unit 7—A
immune	adj.	Unit 14—A
immune	adj.	Unit 3—B
immunization	n.	Unit 10—B
impart	v.	Unit 4—A
impeccable	adj.	Unit 13—A
impede	v.	Unit 4—A
impediment	n.	Unit 3—A
implant	v.	Unit 14—B
implant	v.	Unit 6—A
implication	n.	Unit 5—B
implore	v.	Unit 4—A
imponderable	n.	Unit 9—A
impose	v.	Unit 2—A
impoverish	v.	Unit 9—B
impoverished	adj.	Unit 5—A
impregnate	v.	Unit 5—A
improvise	v.	Unit 10—A
impulse	n.	Unit 9—A
inability	n.	Unit 4—A
inane	adj.	Unit 11—A
incentive	n.	Unit 4—A
incest	n.	Unit 7—B
incidence	n.	Unit 3—A
indices	n.	Unit 15—B
induce	v.	Unit 13—A
inescapable	adj.	Unit 2—A
inexhaustible	adj.	Unit 2—A
inexorable	adj.	Unit 2—A
infallible	adj.	Unit 14—A
infanticide	n.	Unit 7—B
infantry	n.	Unit 7—A
infidelity	n.	Unit 11—B
inflation	n.	Unit 15—B
inflation	n.	Unit 3—A
inflationary	adj.	Unit 15—B
inflict	v.	Unit 7—A
infrared	adj.	Unit 14—A
infrastructure	n.	Unit 6—A
inhabit	v.	Unit 7—A
inherent	adj.	Unit 4—A
inherit	v.	Unit 3—B
inhibition	n.	Unit 10—B
inhibition	n.	Unit 10—A
initiate	v.	Unit 3—B
initiative	n.	Unit 9—B
innovative	adj.	Unit 14—B
innumerable	adj.	Unit 4—A
inquisitive	adj.	Unit 10—A
insane	adj.	Unit 7—B
insomnia	n.	Unit 7—B
inspirational	adj.	Unit 2—B
inspire	v.	Unit 5—B
instigate	v.	Unit 11—A
instinct	n.	Unit 13—A
institutionalize	v.	Unit 9—B
integrity	n.	Unit 12—A
intellectual	adj.	Unit 4—A
intensify	v.	Unit 8—A
intentional	adj.	Unit 13—A
interactive	adj.	Unit 15—A
interloper	n.	Unit 11—B
internalize	v.	Unit 12—B
interweave	v.	Unit 1—A
(interwove, interwoven)		
intimidating	adj.	Unit 2—B
intrepid	adj.	Unit 14—A

intriguing	adj.	Unit 14—B
intriguing	adj.	Unit 3—B
intrinsic	adj.	Unit 12—B
intruder	n.	Unit 6—A
intuition	n.	Unit 14—A
invariably	adv.	Unit 2—A
invest	v.	Unit 5—A
invidious	adj.	Unit 11—B
invigorate	v.	Unit 10—B
invigorating	adj.	Unit 2—B
irradiate (literary)	v.	Unit 2—A
irrational	adj.	Unit 7—B

J

jangle	n.	Unit 3—A
jog	v.	Unit 5—B
jumble	n.	Unit 14—A

K

karmic	n.	Unit 10—B
kin	n.	Unit 9—B
kit	n.	Unit 4—B

L

lacy	adj.	Unit 10—B
languor	n.	Unit 14—A
lanky	adj.	Unit 11—A
lap up	v.	Unit 9—B
lattice	n.	Unit 14—A
launch	v.	Unit 15—A
lease	n.	Unit 5—B
legalistic	adj.	Unit 5—B
legendary	adj.	Unit 5—B
legitimate	adj.	Unit 6—B
legitimate	adj.	Unit 6—A

lengthy	adj.	Unit 4—A
lenient	adj.	Unit 12—B
libel	n.	Unit 5—B
licensed	adj.	Unit 3—A
lieutenant	n.	Unit 7—B
ligament	n.	Unit 13—B
limbo	n.	Unit 10—B
limousine	n.	Unit 10—B
linger	v.	Unit 2—B
lockstep	n.	Unit 3—A
log	n.	Unit 9—B
log on/in		Unit 6—B
longhand	n.	Unit 7—B
lore	n.	Unit 12—A
lot	n.	Unit 3—A
lotus	n.	Unit 14—A

M

magnolia	n.	Unit 10—B
mainstay	n.	Unit 13—B
mainstream	n.	Unit 15—A
make-or-break	adj.	Unit 12—A
malice	n.	Unit 5—B
malice	n.	Unit 2—A
malign	v.	Unit 14—A
maniacal	adj.	Unit 10—B
maniacal	adj.	Unit 9—A
manifest	v.	Unit 2—A
manipulate	v.	Unit 2—A
maple	n.	Unit 2—B
marsh	n.	Unit 2—B
marshal	v.	Unit 15—A
martini	n.	Unit 9—B
marvel	n.	Unit 14—B
masochist	n.	Unit 11—B
massacre	n.	Unit 5—B
massage	n.	Unit 10—B

305

materialistic	n.	Unit 7—A			
maternal	adj.	Unit 9—B		**N**	
maverick	n.	Unit 12—A			
maxim	n.	Unit 9—B	nag	adj.	Unit 2—B
median	adj.	Unit 3—A	narrative	n.	Unit 7—B
medication	n.	Unit 14—B	naysayer	n.	Unit 14—B
medieval	adj.	Unit 1—B	negativity	n.	Unit 8—A
mega	adj.	Unit 3—A	neural	adj.	Unit 3—B
melody	n.	Unit 9—A	neurobiology	n.	Unit 3—B
merchandise	n.	Unit 1—A	neurologist	n.	Unit 3—B
mercury	n.	Unit 2—B	neuroses	n.	Unit 11—B
mess	n.	Unit 7—B	newsletter	n.	Unit 15—A
migration	n.	Unit 10—A	niche	n.	Unit 15—A
militarism	n.	Unit 7—A	niche	n.	Unit 6—B
millennium	n.	Unit 3—B	nimble	adj.	Unit 10—B
minimize	v.	Unit 3—B	nod and wink	n.	Unit 15—B
misconfigure	v.	Unit 6—A	node	n.	Unit 6—A
mission	n.	Unit 7—B	notion	n.	Unit 5—B
mold	v.	Unit 10—A	nudge	v.	Unit 9—B
momentarily	adv.	Unit 10—B	nurture	v.	Unit 11—A
monitor	v.	Unit 6—A	nut	n.	Unit 1—B
monotonous	adj.	Unit 7—B			
monstrosity	n.	Unit 4—A		**O**	
monstrous	adj.	Unit 9—B			
moor	v.	Unit 9—A	oasis	n.	Unit 8—A
more often than not		Unit 8—B	obesity	n.	Unit 5—A
morph	v.	Unit 11—B	obesity	n.	Unit 10—A
mortality	n.	Unit 14—B	obligation	n.	Unit 8—A
mortgage	n.	Unit 8—A	obligatory	adj.	Unit 4—A
motivate	v.	Unit 11—A	oblige	v.	Unit 2—B
motto	n.	Unit 6—B	obsess	v.	Unit 13—A
mousetrap	n.	Unit 9—A	obsess	v.	Unit 6—B
muddled	adj.	Unit 14—A	octane	n.	Unit 9—A
musculature	n.	Unit 14—B	offset	v.	Unit 8—A
musk	n.	Unit 10—B	omission	n.	Unit 5—B
mutter	v.	Unit 13—A	ooze	v.	Unit 12—A
mutter	v.	Unit 10—B	opaque	adj.	Unit 10—B
mystify	v.	Unit 10—A	opportunistic	adj.	Unit 12—A

optical	adj.	Unit 12—A
optimal	adj.	Unit 5—A
organism	n.	Unit 14—A
out-of-wedlock	adj.	Unit 5—A
outrage	v.	Unit 7—B
outright	adj.	Unit 12—A
outright	adj.	Unit 12—B
outsell	v.	Unit 15—A
overarching	adj.	Unit 4—A
overpower	v.	Unit 13—A

P

pad	v.	Unit 11—B
pallbearer	n.	Unit 2—B
paradoxically	adv.	Unit 3—A
parlance	n.	Unit 2—B
parochial	adj.	Unit 4—B
partake	v.	Unit 12—B
participate	v.	Unit 5—B
particle	n.	Unit 14—A
pasture	n.	Unit 2—B
pat sb./yourself on the back	v.	Unit 9—B
patch	v.	Unit 9—B
pathetic	adj.	Unit 13—B
pathetic	adj.	Unit 4—A
patio	n.	Unit 8—A
patricide	n.	Unit 7—B
patriotism	n.	Unit 7—A
patron	n.	Unit 6—B
peak	n.	Unit 15—B
pedagogical	adj.	Unit 4—A
peek	n.	Unit 3—A
penalty	n.	Unit 4—A
penalty	n.	Unit 6—B
penetrate	v.	Unit 2—A
penetrate	v.	Unit 14—A

pep	n.	Unit 13—B
per capita	adj.	Unit 10—A
perceive	v.	Unit 3—B
perception	n.	Unit 14—A
perennial	adj.	Unit 13—B
perform	v.	Unit 5—B
performance	n.	Unit 5—A
peril	n.	Unit 14—A
peril	n.	Unit 12—A
perjury	n.	Unit 12—B
permanent	adj.	Unit 7—A
permissive	adj.	Unit 5—A
permit	v.	Unit 5—B
perpetuate	v.	Unit 4—B
persimmon	n.	Unit 3—B
persistent	adj.	Unit 5—A
petite	adj.	Unit 11—A
petroleum	n.	Unit 14—B
phenomenally	adv.	Unit 15—A
phenomenon	n.	Unit 3—A
phenomenon	n.	Unit 6—B
philanthropic	adj.	Unit 14—A
phlegmatic	adj.	Unit 9—A
physician	n.	Unit 7—A
pickle	n.	Unit 15—A
pine	n.	Unit 10—B
pine	v.	Unit 1—A
piranha-like	adj.	Unit 4—A
pitcher	n.	Unit 13—A
plain	adj.	Unit 1—B
plasticity	n.	Unit 3—B
plausible	adj.	Unit 5—B
plummet	v.	Unit 12—A
poll	n.	Unit 15—B
poll	n.	Unit 3—A
pom-pom	n.	Unit 13—B
ponder	v.	Unit 7—A
pornography	n.	Unit 6—B

307

portal	n.	Unit 15—A
portfolio	n.	Unit 9—A
pose	v.	Unit 14—A
posthumous	adj.	Unit 7—A
preach	v.	Unit 9—B
precious	adj.	Unit 5—B
predicament	n.	Unit 12—B
predictor	n.	Unit 3—A
preexisting	adj.	Unit 11—B
pregnancy	n.	Unit 5—A
preliminary	adj.	Unit 3—B
premarital	adj.	Unit 5—B
premature	adj.	Unit 5—B
prep	v.	Unit 12—A
preposterous	adj.	Unit 9—B
preservation	n.	Unit 5—B
prestige	n.	Unit 3—A
prestige	n.	Unit 9—A
presume	v.	Unit 13—B
primal	adj.	Unit 9—A
priority	n.	Unit 11—B
procession	n.	Unit 2—B
proctor	v.	Unit 12—B
productivity	n.	Unit 15—B
prognosis	n.	Unit 10—B
prohibit	v.	Unit 5—B
projection	n.	Unit 10—A
prolong	v.	Unit 8—A
prom	n.	Unit 11—A
promo	n.	Unit 6—B
promote	v.	Unit 4—B
promotion	n.	Unit 7—B
promptly	adv.	Unit 1—B
pronouncement	n.	Unit 14—A
prop	v.	Unit 4—A
propagation	n.	Unit 2—B
propel	v.	Unit 10—A
propel	v.	Unit 13—A

prophetic	adj.	Unit 7—B
prosecution	n.	Unit 6—A
prospect	n.	Unit 15—B
prosperous	adj.	Unit 4—A
protagonist	n.	Unit 7—A
provoke	v.	Unit 10—A
prune	v.	Unit 8—A
pseudonym	n.	Unit 7—B
psychopharmacological	adj.	Unit 3—B
psychotherapist	n.	Unit 3—B
puberty	n.	Unit 5—A
publicize	v.	Unit 6—A
pun	n.	Unit 7—B
punch out	v.	Unit 9—A
punctuate	v.	Unit 13—B
pup	n.	Unit 9—A
purebred	adj.	Unit 13—B
pursue	v.	Unit 14—B
pursue	v.	Unit 3—A

Q

quadruple	n.	Unit 1—B
quads	n.	Unit 13—B
quantum	n.	Unit 14—A
quench	v.	Unit 9—A
query	n.	Unit 15—A
quitter	n.	Unit 9—B
quote	n.	Unit 8—B

R

racquetball	n.	Unit 13—B
radiant	adj.	Unit 2—A
radical	adj.	Unit 15—A
rambunctious	adj.	Unit 11—A
random	adj.	Unit 5—A
rank-and-file	n.	Unit 12—A

Vocabulary

rat race	n.	Unit 9—B
rationalize	v.	Unit 12—B
rationalize	v.	Unit 10—A
rationally	adv.	Unit 1—A
raucous	adj.	Unit 2—B
razor-sharp	adj.	Unit 12—A
reap	v.	Unit 15—B
reassurance	n.	Unit 11—B
recipe	n.	Unit 4—A
reckon	v.	Unit 15—B
reclaim	v.	Unit 11—A
recommend	v.	Unit 3—B
recount	v.	Unit 7—B
recruit	v.	Unit 12—A
recuperation	n.	Unit 7—B
reflection	n.	Unit 1—B
regain	v.	Unit 7—B
regenerative	adj.	Unit 14—B
regicide	n.	Unit 7—B
regime	n.	Unit 4—A
regimen	n.	Unit 13—B
regulation	n.	Unit 7—B
reinforce	v.	Unit 3—B
reject	v.	Unit 7—A
release	v.	Unit 11—B
release	v.	Unit 12—A
relentless	adj.	Unit 3—A
relentless	adj.	Unit 12—A
relieve	v.	Unit 7—B
reluctantly	adv.	Unit 1—A
remarkable	adj.	Unit 14—B
remembrance	n.	Unit 11—A
render	v.	Unit 3—A
rental	n.	Unit 5—B
repertoire	n.	Unit 13—B
repetitious	adj.	Unit 7—B
replicate	v.	Unit 3—A
reproductive	adj.	Unit 14—B
requisite	adj.	Unit 5—B
rescind	v.	Unit 12—A
resemble	v.	Unit 1—A
reserve	n.	Unit 14—B
residential	adj.	Unit 5—A
resign oneself to	v.	Unit 9—B
resolution	n.	Unit 1—A
respite	n.	Unit 1—A
retention	n.	Unit 4—B
retrospect	n.	Unit 12—B
revenge	n.	Unit 5—B
revenge	n.	Unit 9—B
revenue	n.	Unit 5—A
revenue	n.	Unit 4—A
revenue	n.	Unit 15—A
revenue	n.	Unit 15—B
ritzy	adj.	Unit 4—A
rivet	v.	Unit 10—B
roundworm	n.	Unit 14—B
ruggedly	adv.	Unit 2—B
rumor	n.	Unit 6—B
ruse	n.	Unit 2—B
rustle	v.	Unit 2—B

S

sacrifice	v.	Unit 1—A
saddle	n.	Unit 1—B
safari	n.	Unit 7—A
sanctuary	n.	Unit 8—A
sanitation	n.	Unit 14—B
sanity	n.	Unit 7—B
savvy	adj.	Unit 6—B
scant	adj.	Unit 3—B
scar	v.	Unit 12—B
scarcity	n.	Unit 2—A
scary	adj.	Unit 6—B
scheme	n.	Unit 8—A

309

scheme	n.	Unit 3—A	slimy	adj.	Unit 6—B
scoff	v.	Unit 9—B	sloppy	adj.	Unit 15—A
scout	n.	Unit 13—A	smack	n.	Unit 1—B
scramble	n.	Unit 12—A	smock	n.	Unit 9—B
scramble	v.	Unit 1—B	snappy	adj.	Unit 13—B
scratch	n.	Unit 2—B	sneak	v.	Unit 12—B
scrawl	v.	Unit 15—A	sniffer	n.	Unit 6—A
screwball	n.	Unit 13—A	snippet	n.	Unit 15—A
scrutinize	v.	Unit 13—A	snitch	v.	Unit 12—B
sector	n.	Unit 12—A	snooty	adj.	Unit 2—B
segment	n.	Unit 15—A	snot	n.	Unit 13—A
self-indulgent	adj.	Unit 6—B	soar	v.	Unit 3—A
sell-off	n.	Unit 15—A	sobering	adj.	Unit 5—A
seminal	adj.	Unit 10—A	sodium	n.	Unit 14—A
sensitivity	adj.	Unit 4—A	sophisticated	adj.	Unit 6—A
sentiment	n.	Unit 2—A	sore	n.	Unit 1—B
sequel	adj.	Unit 7—B	soulless	adj.	Unit 15—A
sequential	adj.	Unit 6—A	span	n.	Unit 14—B
sermon	n.	Unit 1—B	spark	n.	Unit 8—A
shack	n.	Unit 1—B	spastic	adj.	Unit 10—B
shakeout	n.	Unit 12—A	spectacular	adj.	Unit 9—B
shoestring	adj.	Unit 4—A	spectrum	n.	Unit 11—B
shortstop	n.	Unit 13—A	speculation	n.	Unit 14—B
shrink	v.	Unit 14—A	spell	n.	Unit 1—B
shrink	n.	Unit 11—B	spell	v.	Unit 9—A
shrub	n.	Unit 8—A	spherical	adj.	Unit 14—A
shtick	n.	Unit 10—B	spike	n.	Unit 15—B
sift	v.	Unit 6—B	spin	v.	Unit 3—B
significant	adj.	Unit 3—A	spiral	n.	Unit 10—A
sinew	n.	Unit 14—A	splits	n.	Unit 13—B
sip	n.	Unit 8—A	spoof	n.	Unit 6—B
size sb. up	v.	Unit 9—B	spotter	n.	Unit 7—A
sketch	n.	Unit 7—A	spotter	n.	Unit 13—B
slanted	adj.	Unit 10—A	spouse	n.	Unit 11—B
slay	v.	Unit 1—A	sprawling	adj.	Unit 9—A
slick	adj.	Unit 13—A	sprawling	adj.	Unit 2—B
slide	n.	Unit 15—B	sprawling	adj.	Unit 10—B
slider	n.	Unit 13—A	spree	n.	Unit 12—A

sprint	v.	Unit 2—B	subdued	adj.	Unit 15—B
spun off		Unit 9—A	subdued	adj.	Unit 14—A
spur	n.	Unit 11—B	submarine	n.	Unit 7—A
squadron	n.	Unit 7—B	subscriber	n.	Unit 6—B
squash	n.	Unit 13—B	subset	n.	Unit 5—B
squeak	v.	Unit 10—B	substantial	adj.	Unit 3—A
squint	v.	Unit 2—B	substantial	adj.	Unit 14—B
squint	v.	Unit 11—A	substantially	adv.	Unit 5—A
stability	n.	Unit 3—A	substantiate	v.	Unit 14—A
staccato	adj.	Unit 10—B	subversive	adj.	Unit 6—B
stake	n.	Unit 12—A	suicidal	adj.	Unit 9—B
stamina	n.	Unit 13—B	superintendent	n.	Unit 4—B
standoffishness	n.	Unit 2—B	supervision	n.	Unit 5—A
standpoint	n.	Unit 8—A	supplant	v.	Unit 14—B
stardom	n.	Unit 6—B	supplant	v.	Unit 11—B
stark	adj.	Unit 10—A	supplement	v.	Unit 14—B
stark	adj.	Unit 3—A	surmise	v.	Unit 2—B
startup	n.	Unit 12—A	surreal	adj.	Unit 7—B
statistical	adj.	Unit 3—A	surround	v.	Unit 3—A
status quo	n.	Unit 9—B	survivability	n.	Unit 6—A
staunch	adj.	Unit 10—B	survive	v.	Unit 7—B
stead	n.	Unit 1—B	suspend	v.	Unit 10—B
steer	v.	Unit 9—B	suspicion	n.	Unit 9—B
stereotype	n.	Unit 4—B	sustain	v.	Unit 5—A
stimulating	adj.	Unit 2—A	sustain	v.	Unit 6—A
stimulation	n.	Unit 11—B	swamp	n.	Unit 4—A
stint	n.	Unit 7—A	swelter	v.	Unit 10—B
stoicism	n.	Unit 7—A	swingset	n.	Unit 11—A
straightforward	adj.	Unit 14—A	swoop	v.	Unit 12—A
strand	n.	Unit 2—B	swoop	v.	Unit 15—A
strikeout	n.	Unit 13—A	sympathize	v.	Unit 9—B
strive	v.	Unit 9—B	synchronize	adj.	Unit 13—B
strobe	n.	Unit 2—B	syndrome	n.	Unit 7—B
stroke	n.	Unit 3—B	synthetic	adj.	Unit 14—B
stunning	adj.	Unit 14—A			
stylishly	adv.	Unit 11—A	**T**		
subdivision	n.	Unit 11—A			
subdue	v.	Unit 12—A	taboo	n.	Unit 14—A

tackle	v.	Unit 9—B	tubercular	adj.	Unit 9—B
tap	v.	Unit 2—A	tuck	n.	Unit 13—B
teddy	n.	Unit 11—A	tuck	v.	Unit 2—B
teeter	v.	Unit 10—B	tuck	v.	Unit 11—A
telling	adj.	Unit 9—A	tuition	n.	Unit 8—A
temperamental	adj.	Unit 9—A	tumbling	n.	Unit 13—B
template	n.	Unit 9—A	turnover	n.	Unit 5—A
temptation	n.	Unit 11—B	twig	n.	Unit 14—A
tendency	n.	Unit 14—B	twinge	n.	Unit 12—B
tendency	n.	Unit 8—A	tyrannical	adj.	Unit 4—A
tenet	n.	Unit 7—A			
testimony	n.	Unit 14—A	**U**		
testosterone	n.	Unit 13—A			
testosterone	n.	Unit 5—A	ultimately	adv.	Unit 5—A
thence	adv.	Unit 14—A	umpire	n.	Unit 13—A
theologian	n.	Unit 14—A	unappealing	adj.	Unit 4—A
therapeutic	adj.	Unit 3—B	unavoidable	adj.	Unit 14—B
therapy	n.	Unit 10—B	uncertify	v.	Unit 4—A
throng	n.	Unit 2—B	undercurrent	n.	Unit 12—A
tile	n.	Unit 6—B	underexposed	adj.	Unit 6—B
tip	v.	Unit 1—B	undergrad	n.	Unit 13—B
tissue	n.	Unit 14—B	underlie	v.	Unit 5—A
tizzy	n.	Unit 15—A	undersell	v.	Unit 12—A
toll	n.	Unit 3—B	unequaled	adj.	Unit 14—B
torrent	n.	Unit 2—B	unfeeling	adj.	Unit 5—B
toss	v.	Unit 7—B	ungrateful	adj.	Unit 1—A
transgression	n.	Unit 12—B	unilateral	adj.	Unit 12—A
transportation	n.	Unit 14—B	unleash	v.	Unit 2—B
trap	n.	Unit 13—B	unlock	v.	Unit 2—A
traverse	v.	Unit 6—A	urn	n.	Unit 2—B
treacherous	adj.	Unit 1—A			
treadmill		Unit 13—B	**V**		
tremendous	adj.	Unit 5—B			
triceps	n.	Unit 13—B	vanquish	v.	Unit 12—A
trifle	n.	Unit 1—A	varsity	n.	Unit 13—B
trite	adj.	Unit 2—A	velocity	n.	Unit 14—A
trough	n.	Unit 4—A	vendor	n.	Unit 6—A
trusty	adj.	Unit 1—B	vengeance	n.	Unit 9—B

vengeance (formal)	n.	Unit 2—A
vent	v.	Unit 8—B
venture	n.	Unit 12—A
venture	v.	Unit 2—B
viable	adj.	Unit 14—B
vicious	adj.	Unit 13—A
vigilance	n.	Unit 12—B
vigilant	adj.	Unit 15—B
vindicate	v.	Unit 10—A
violate	v.	Unit 4—B
violate	v.	Unit 5—B
virtually	adv.	Unit 5—B
volatile	adj.	Unit 6—A
vow	n.	Unit 2—B
vulgar	adj.	Unit 9—B
vulnerability	n.	Unit 6—A
vulnerable	adj.	Unit 12—B

W

waiver	n.	Unit 13—B
wart	n.	Unit 1—B
wean	v.	Unit 9—A
weather	v.	Unit 15—B
weird	adj.	Unit 6—B
whack	v.	Unit 10—B
wham	n.	Unit 11—A
whip sb./sth. up		Unit 11—B
whir	v.	Unit 6—B
whirl	n.	Unit 11—B
whisk	v.	Unit 10—B
wield	v.	Unit 13—A
wiggle	v.	Unit 12—A
wire	v.	Unit 9—A
wisp	n.	Unit 2—B
withdraw	v.	Unit 1—A
wither	v.	Unit 14—A
woe	n.	Unit 15—A
woodchopper	n.	Unit 1—B
workaholism	n.	Unit 11—B

Y

yak	n.	Unit 1—B
yuan	n.	Unit 6—B

Z

zenith	n.	Unit 7—A
zero-sum game	n.	Unit 9—A